New Public Administration in Britain

Third edition

'Covers the whole spectrum of the subject . . . good, reliable, authoritative, sensible [and] balanced'

Richard Chapman, Emeritus Professor of Politics, *University of Durham*

First published in 1984, this book has established itself as the leading text in British public administration. The third edition builds on the previous editions' success to examine the considerable changes and very latest developments in the field.

This new edition:

- continues to provide an authoritative and incisive introduction to all the key elements of public administration in Britain;
- now covers the influence of Europe as well as regional and sub-national influences;
- focuses on new developments that have emerged in recent years such as managerialism, privatisation, consumerism, charters, contracting and regulation;
- offers boxed key facts, annotated guides to further reading and an extensive bibliography.

Written by three leading experts in the field, this text will be essential reading for those who want an authoritative and comprehensive introduction to public administration.

John Greenwood is Professor of Public Administration and Government, and a Director of the International Public Administration and Management Unit at De Montfort University. **Robert Pyper** is Professor of Government and Public Administration, Glasgow Caledonian University. **David Wilson** is Professor of Public Administration and Head of the Public Policy Department, De Montfort University.

New Public Administration in Britain

Third edition

John Greenwood, Robert Pyper
and David Wilson

London and New York

First published 1984 by Unwin Hyman Ltd
Second edition 1989
Second impression 1990
Reprinted by Routledge in 1993

Third edition published by Routledge 2002
11 New Fetter Lane, London EC4P 4EE

Simultaneously published in the USA and
Canada
by Routledge
29 West 35th Street, New York NY 10001

*Routledge is an imprint of the
Taylor & Francis Group*

© 2002 John Greenwood, Robert Pyper
and David Wilson

Typeset in Century Old Style by Keystroke,
Jacaranda Lodge, Wolverhampton
Printed and bound in Great Britain by
TJ International Ltd, Padstow, Cornwall

British Library Cataloguing in Publication Data
A catalogue record for this book is available
from the British Library

*Library of Congress Cataloging in Publication
Data*
Greenwood, John R.
New public administration in Britain.–3rd ed. /
John Greenwood, Robert Pyper & David
Wilson.
p. cm.
Rev. ed. of: Public administration in Britain
today/John Greenwood, David Wilson. 1989.
Includes bibliographical references and index.
1. Administration agencies–Great Britain.
2. Executive departments–Great Britain.
3. Great Britain–Politics and government.
4. Local government–Great Britain. I. Pyper,
Robert. II. Wilson, David J. (David Jack)
III. Greenwood, John R. Public administration
in Britain today. IV. Title.

JN318 .G73 2001
351.41–dc21   2001019933

ISBN 0–415–23679–7 (hbk)
ISBN 0–415–23680–0 (pbk)

Contents

Figures

Tables

Boxes

Preface

This text follows the publication in 1984 of *Public Administration in Britain* and in 1989 of *Public Administration in Britain Today*. While in one sense it updates those texts, in another it represents a completely new analysis. The theme of those earlier editions, the dynamic nature of British public administration, was borne out with a vengeance in the 1990s, so much so that it quickly became clear that simply writing a 'new edition' would not suffice. The British public sector changed so dramatically during the 1990s that a completely new text was required; hence the title, *New Public Administration in Britain*.

In all parts of the public sector, and all parts of the United Kingdom, substantial change has occurred since the end of the 1980s. In 1989, for example, the Next Steps initiative was still in its infancy; today it embraces over three-quarters of the civil service. In local government the community charge was still to be introduced in England, the tortuous structural reorganisation of the 1990s had not begun, and talk of elected mayors and 'cabinets' was not even on the horizon. In Scotland and Wales the prospect of devolution had considerably receded and devolved assemblies were little more than subjects for speculation. While the New Public Management revolution was already under way, we were still to witness developments such as the *Citizen's Charter* and Best Value.

The changes which have occurred in the public sector are readily apparent from even a cursory glance at this text and its predecessors. For example, the 1980s texts contained chapters on 'Co-ordinating central administration', 'The cabinet system' and 'Administering public ownership'; the present one covers instead 'The core executive' and 'Privatisation and the regulatory state'. In place of the former 'Regional administration' chapter there is now an entirely fresh one entitled 'Multi-level governance'. Even the vocabulary of discussion reflects change. Terms such as 'modernisation', 'fragmentation' and 'joined-up government', which figure prominently in this text, were barely mentioned in the earlier editions. Concepts such as 'governance', 'hollowing out' and 'post-Fordism', which inform current debate, were largely absent twelve years ago.

It is not simply that new developments have created new institutions, terms and concepts. In the years since the previous editions were published even the certainties of the past have come to be questioned. Whereas in the past we discussed whether local government or the civil service needed reforming, today we ask whether we have local government or local governance, and whether the civil service still exists. While in the 1980s we asked whether the discipline of public administration should be approached differently from the study of business, in the 1990s we asked with Rhodes (1991, p. 534) the 'troubling question: "What is Public Administration?"'

In trying to understand these changes, students and practitioners have been assisted by the new resources brought into play by the passage of time. For example, internet-based sources now offer a vast amount of readily accessible information, and we have not only utilised this in writing the text but identified it wherever possible as a learning resource. We have also sought to retain something of the structure and approach of earlier texts, presenting the subject wherever possible from the perspective of authoritative writings which provide a reference point for readers seeking more detail. Sections specifically identifying further reading have also been added and, where appropriate, exhibits provide fuller information.

This text is very much a collective effort. The bulk of it was written during 2000, although later material was added where this became available. One particular challenge was that much material issuing from the ESRC Whitehall Programme was actually being published while the text was being written, which meant that only part of this valuable material could be used. In other cases, developments such as implementation of the Wilson Report into the civil service were ongoing during the writing period, and this inevitably sometimes made analysis difficult.

We are conscious that we are indebted to numerous other people who kindly helped in various ways. Particular thanks are due to Dr David Richards (University of Liverpool) who read and commented most helpfully upon the initial draft of the first four chapters; and Professor Rob Baggott of De Montfort University who did likewise with the material covering the National Health Service. Professor Peter Barberis of Manchester Metropolitan University, Dr Michael Duggett (Secretary General of the International Institute of Administrative Sciences) and Professor Vivien Lowndes of De Montfort University also gave very helpful comments and advice. Thanks are also due to the librarians of De Montfort University's Scraptoft Campus and to the excellent secretarial staff within the University's Department of Public Policy for help in preparing the manuscript. Stephen Greenwood also provided assistance on innumerable occasions when his father's word-processing skills proved deficient. Mark Kavanagh of Routledge gave us much encouragement and spurred us on to meet deadlines which otherwise would have proved impossible. In the final analysis, of course, responsibility for any errors or omissions is ours and ours alone.

John Greenwood
Robert Pyper
David Wilson

March 2001

Chapter 1

The context of British public administration

Introduction

'The United Kingdom has undergone a large number of changes over the last twenty years', wrote Gray in 2000. As a result, he added, 'the state itself has been altered into new forms that allow for the management and administration of public goods and services to take place in new ways' (ibid., pp. 283, 299). He could have gone further. Their cumulative effect has arguably changed the 'very role of government in society' (Hughes, 1998, p. 1). Analysis of these 'new ways' of administering public services, and of the extent to which they have developed from and transformed institutions and procedures inherited from earlier periods, is the main focus of this text.

Initially, however, it is necessary to place that analysis into context. This chapter surveys the main developments to which Gray alludes, examines the scope and complexity of contemporary British public administration, and discusses the challenges which this presents to students. Firstly, however, it addresses the question 'What is public administration?'

What is public administration?

Defining 'public administration' has long presented difficulty. Waldo (1955, p. 2) observed, 'The immediate effect of all one-sentence or one-paragraph definitions of public administration is mental paralysis rather than enlightenment and stimulation.' The variegated nature of the subject's component parts and the complex linkages between them make analysis difficult. At one level misunderstandings occur because the term 'public administration' is used in different ways. Fletcher (1967, pp. 53–4) explains that it can denote:

1   the *activity* of public servants;
2   the *structure* of government: that is the institutions and relationships through which the activity of public servants is carried on;
3   the study of 1 and 2.

Slightly differently, Hughes (1998, p. 7) suggests that 'the term "public administration" always meant the *study* of the public sector, in addition to it being an activity and a profession'. More critically, Dunleavy (1982, p. 215) argues that public administration focuses pre-eminently on:

> institutions, organizational structures and decision/implementation processes of government. It is largely a 'formal' field, concerned with arrangements and procedures for making decisions, rather than with the substance or impacts of these decisions. . . . Finally, it is an area of study . . . largely 'applied' and closely linked with practical problems and practical solutions.

In 1991 Rhodes (p. 535), after an exhaustive analysis, concluded, 'There remains the troubling question: "What is Public Administration?"'

Because of definitional problems it is important to clarify the sense in which public administration is treated in this text. Our central concern is with analysing the first two of Fletcher's meanings, albeit as an aid to the third. However, the discipline is not fixed, but changes according to developments within the practice of public administration. This is something also discussed in this chapter.

The policy/administration dichotomy

A distinction is sometimes made between, on the one hand, 'policy' and 'politics' (perceived as the work of elected politicians) and, on the other, 'administration' (the work of officials or administrators). However, this distinction is problematic because the term 'administration' is not straightforward. Dunsire (1973) identified at least fifteen meanings, ranging from implementing decisions to initiating policy. Moreover, the distinction between policy and administration breaks down because of the so-called *policy/administration dichotomy*. This has two main aspects:

1   Policy and administration are largely indistinguishable because policy decisions are to some extent predicated upon considerations about implementation. No government, for example, could realistically decide to mount a moon landing until means of implementation were available. Moreover, administrative decisions – about how to implement a policy – themselves require implementation, and often themselves become policy decisions. For example, a decision to reduce inflation might be implemented in various ways: controlling prices and incomes, making tax changes, imposing monetary controls, etc. Assuming that the first of these is chosen, this will become a policy – a prices and incomes policy – which will itself require decisions regarding implementation. Should, for example, all wages and prices be controlled? Should machinery be established to monitor price and income movements? Should penalties be imposed upon companies breaking the law? There is a 'seamless web' of policy and administration. Precisely where 'policy' ends and 'administration' begins is impossible to determine.

2   Administrative considerations bulk large in policy-making, and much policy-making requires specialist advice. Consequently, politicians rely heavily on officials when formulating policy. Recently, moreover, efficiency considerations have become increasingly important as factors in policy-making. The distinction between policy determined by politicians and administration performed by officials has little credibility in practice.

Despite these observations, changes in recent years have led to a redefinition of political and managerial roles in a manner seemingly reminiscent of the distinction between policy and administration (Stewart, 2000a). We shall discuss this theme later.

The changing context of public administration

Public bodies do not exist in a vacuum. They are closely related to the environment which they inhabit, and they influence, and are influenced by, that environment.

Environmental influences upon organisations

A number of external influences assist and constrain public administrators. Particularly important are the following:

The political environment

Public administration is heavily influenced by the political environment, changes in which have had a profound impact in recent years. Isaac-Henry (1997, pp. 3–6) notes in particular:

1   The ideas of the New Right and Thatcherism which, while supporting a 'strong state' on issues such as law and order, emphasise individualism, personal freedom, choice and the primacy of markets rather than politics as a vehicle for efficient distribution of goods and services. While the state necessarily provides goods and services which individuals cannot provide (e.g. defence) or which are socially desirable (e.g. education), the New Right generally sees a reduced role for government. Under Thatcher and Major these ideas were reflected in economic policy – where collectivist Keynesian policies were replaced by a free-market, monetarist approach – and in a reduced public sector.

2   The end of consensus: It is generally held (although contested by some) that the post-war period in Britain witnessed a political consensus which emphasised welfarism and collectivism, and resulted in rises in both the size of government and public spending. However, the tax burden necessary to support these policies, as well as a growing realisation that government could not solve all society's problems, caused political disillusionment. Thatcher significantly broke from post-war consensus policies, a position seemingly endorsed by electors who returned Conservative governments to power at four successive general elections between 1979 and 1992.

The social and cultural environment

This also impacts upon public administration. For example, late twentieth-century demographic changes saw a rapidly ageing population place increasing strain on public services such as social security and health. A better-educated and informed electorate demanded better public services, while multiculturalism necessitated attention to the needs of a more diverse society.

Nationalism and Europeanisation

British public administration has been affected by the contradictory pulls of nationalism and European integration. Nationalism led to dramatic changes in the United Kingdom's political and administrative systems in the 1990s, while membership of the European Union (EU) has given a European dimension to policy and administration in many fields (see Chapter 10).

Globalisation

This has had profound influences upon most national governments. Held *et al.* (1999, p. 20) define globalisation as 'the widening, deepening and speeding up of world-wide interconnectedness in all aspects of life'. While globalisation takes a number of forms (political, ecnomic, etc.), to which individual governments have responded in different ways, one manifestation has been widespread adoption of new patterns of public management. Generally known as new public management (NPM), this, as seen below, has transformed British public administration in recent decades.

Information and communications technologies

ICTs have influenced public administration in many countries. In British public administration ICTs emerged initially in

> a piecemeal, bottom-up way, within such data-heavy sectors as tax admin-
> istration, social security, the health service and the criminal justice system.
> The main stimuli . . . were . . . severe difficulties associated with attempting
> to shed costs and enhance these politically sensitive services in the context of
> an inflexible and fragmented government machine.
>
> (Bellamy, 1999, p. 134)

Subsequently, with the development of the 'information superhighway' the British along with many other governments developed a more strategic and coordinated approach. In 1995 the government created the Central IT Unit (CITU) with responsibility for developing ICTs across government, and in 1996 published a Green Paper (Cabinet Office, 1996) outlining proposals for electronic forms of service delivery. These proposals were subsequently adopted by Blair's government within a wider programme of 're-engineering government services in the information age' (COI, 1997). The vision is of re-engineering government through ICTs leading to an age of 'Electronic Government' (Bellamy, 1999, p. 141).

Even without such visions ICTs have already influenced the way that bureaucracies function, replacing largely paper-driven administrative systems with electronic means of collating, storing and retrieving information, and also enhancing the research, planning, intelligence and management capacity of governments. Networks now permit data linkages between different parts of government: for example, the Department of Social Security (DSS) matches social security data against information in other departments to detect fraud. ICTs have also reduced staffing requirements, as well as impacting on organisational roles – for example, in local government there has been a diffusion of computer usage from specialist IT departments to front-line professional and administrative staff and even councillors; and also upon structures – for example, in the 1990s the DSS developed proposals for 'one-stop' benefits shops as a way of breaking down functional groupings. More recent developments such as email and the internet have revolutionised the ability of not just officials and politicians but all sectors of society to communicate information through global networks. Of course, ICTs also present problems of data protection, privacy and civil liberties. There is also concern that, while information may become more accessible to many, minority and disadvantaged groups without access or the ability to use the necessary technology may not benefit.

While the importance of environmental factors upon public administration is profound, relationships between organisations and their environment are never purely mechanistic; the importance of choice within organisations must always be recognised.

Organisational influences upon the environment

Public authorities are not simply passive systems; they themselves can affect the environment. Civil servants, for example, can manipulate their environment by selecting the pressure groups which are admitted into departmental policy-making processes. Likewise, ministers manipulate public opinion by 'leaking' information to the media, or through speeches which mould public debate.

Organisational interdependence

Organisational interdependence is an important element of contemporary public administration. Rhodes (1981, p. 7) illustrates this with central/local government relationships:

> Local authorities are not 'mere agents' of central government. They are political systems in their own right with the capacity to resist central demands. Moreover, central government is dependent upon local authorities for information, for expertise and for the implementation of policy.

Similar reciprocity is replicated at all levels of public administration. Indeed, in recent years tendencies towards fragmentation within the public sector have heightened the significance of organisational interdependence, leading to increasing emphasis on joined-up government and inter-organisational networks drawn from the public, voluntary and even the private sectors (see p. 15).

Public administration or public management?

A further problem in defining public administration stems from its relationship to 'private management'. Farnham and Horton (1999, p. 26) explain that tradition-ally '"management" described the way private businesses were run, whilst "administration" was a description of the approach to running public bodies.' Whereas 'management' occurs within voluntary bodies, partnerships and businesses, 'public administration' relates to state activities usually within a political setting. Private sector management also generally has more restricted aims than public admin-istration, usually being motivated by profit. Public administration not only has wider

---

Box 1.1 Key principles in public administration

Public accountability

Public bodies have to account for their activities to other people and provide a justification for what has been done in a way that private bodies do not. In other words, public bodies are subject to external checks and supervision (e.g. ministers are accountable to Parliament for conduct of their departments by the convention of ministerial responsibility) from which private companies are relatively immune. The nearest private sector analogy is the accountability of company boards to shareholders, although this rarely involves the same degree of external supervision as in the public sector.

Equity

Administrators are expected to treat members of the public fairly, without showing partiality to one at the expense of another. While there is often ambiguity about precisely what this means, at some levels it is relatively easy to determine. With income tax, for example, taxpayers in identical circumstances should receive identical treatment – even though they may be dealing with different local offices. In the private sector, by contrast, favouritism may be shown towards special customers, for example with discounts; or customers may be treated differently in different market situations, e.g. sales.

Legality

Decisions and actions of officials must never be *ultra vires* (or beyond their legal powers). Whereas private individuals and companies are generally free to perform any act not prohibited in law, public authorities can only do those things which they are specifically empowered by law to perform.

Source: Adapted from Greenwood and Wilson (1989, pp. 9–10)

---

goals than private management, but its practitioners were traditionally required to have special regard to principles such as *public accountability, equity* and *legality* (Box 1.1).

The relevance of these principles has been complicated in recent years by the widespread adoption within the public sector of management tools and techniques originally designed for private sector analysis. Part of the NPM, their use has reflected a concern to make the public sector more efficient. Other influences included suspicions of bureaucratic inefficiency, an environment of scarce resources, and the Thatcher and Major governments' belief in the superior efficiency of private sector techniques. Consequently, the last decades of the twentieth century witnessed a concerted effort to improve public sector efficiency by introducing practices from the 'more efficient' private sector.

A further problem of distinguishing between public administration and private management is that when comparisons are made the impression is frequently given that each is opposed to the other and occupies a distinct field. In practice, much public administration is conducted with the collaboration of private groups and individuals; indeed, even before the advent of NPM, 'the line between "private" and "public" [had] . . . become so blurred that it [was] difficult to tell where government leaves off and private business begins' (Nigro and Nigro, 1973, p. 17). Public and private enterprises, while legally distinguishable, are less clearly disentangled in practice. Did, for example, the privatisation of British Airways turn public administrators overnight into private 'managers'?

Private organisations such as political parties and pressure groups are also involved with public administration, setting the 'political agenda' within which public policy is formulated. Public bodies use private companies to build houses, hospitals, etc., as well, increasingly, as to deliver 'public' services through contracting. Hybrid organisations such as public/private partnerships and charities are also much in evidence in contemporary public administration. These spend vast amounts of public money and employ workers who, while not government employees, are in many respects a real part of its workforce. Equally, private business depends heavily upon public authorities to supply services essential for economic performance (e.g. roads) and an effective workforce (e.g. health, education). Increasingly in recent times the private sector has been involved, in arrangements such as public/private partnerships. The interdependence of the two sectors quickly becomes apparent.

Nevertheless, the late twentieth-century demand for value for money (VFM) raised the issue of whether private sector techniques, tools and structures could produce a more efficient public sector, and whether such instruments were easily transferable to public organisations. In the 1980s, Gunn (1988, p. 21) argued, 'the idea that public administration has everything to learn from the private sector [was] dominant'. Although Gunn rejected this view as 'simplistic', its implications are clear. Managing is a generic activity and private sector managerial practices can readily be transferred to the public sector.

Contributing to this debate, Peters and Waterman (1982) argue the case for excellence as a managerial philosophy, stressing that in 'excellent' companies certain features are prevalent, such as the belief that customers come first. Similarly, Osborne and Gaebler (1992) argue for 'reinvention' of government and offer a ten-point programme, based upon principles such as competition, citizen empowerment, measured outcomes, missions, customers, earning money, decentralising authority and 'catalysing all sectors'. While conceding that government cannot operate 'just like a business', they argued that it could 'become more entrepreneurial' and 'shift its position on that spectrum'. The proper role of government, they claimed, was 'steering not rowing'. Government should make policies and take decisions, but need not deliver services itself. The policy/administration dichotomy might become entrenched – for example, through contracting out service delivery – in developing their entrepreneurial model of government.

These ideas rest on two main assumptions. Firstly, that public services will be more effective the more they are organised along market principles. Secondly, that public services management will be more efficient the more it resembles private sector management. These views, of course, have been challenged. Jordan (1994,

p. 92) criticises the 'excellence' school as 'more successful as a piece of marketing than as a source of practical advice'. Pollitt and Harrison (1992, p. 2) argue that 'many of the prescriptions of generic management will require considerable adaptation before they will fit in [the] distinctive [public sector] context'. Some aspects of managerialism also fit uneasily alongside equity and accountability. While this debate cannot be pursued here, what can be emphasised is the impact of such views on public services worldwide. In the next section we discuss some key features to which they have given rise in British public administration.

The managerialisation of British public administration

'Recent years have seen wider-ranging reforms than any other period of the twentieth century . . . represent[ing] a paradigm shift from the traditional model of public administration . . . to "managerialism" or new public management' (Hughes, 1998, p. vi). This NPM, Rhodes (1991, p. 548) claims, contains several central doctrines:

> a focus on management, not policy, and on performance appraisal and efficiency; . . . the dis-aggregation of public bureaucracies into agencies . . . ; the use of quasi-markets and contracting-out to foster competition; . . . cost-cutting; . . . a style of management which emphasizes *inter alia* output targets, limited-term contracts, monetary incentives, and freedom to manage.

The application of many of these 'doctrines' to different parts of the British public sector are examined elsewhere in this text. Here, however, it is possible to summarise briefly some of the main developments.

The decline of bureaucracy

Public bodies have been traditionally organised according to bureaucratic principles posited by Weber. Fundamentally, bureaucratically organised bodies exhibit a hierarchical structure. Each official has clearly defined duties within specified limits, and operates under supervision of a higher officer within a 'line' command structure. While some private companies also organise around bureaucratic principles, this pattern has traditionally been regarded as particularly appropriate for public agencies given their typically multifunctional nature and size, and the principles of account-ability and equity under which they operate. For example, bureaucratic organisation, by allowing detailed control of subordinates within a hierarchic command structure – and usually with elected politicians at the apex – allows functions to be divided consistent with the principles of public accountability. Again, the enforcement of rules through line management extending from the highest departmental levels, through local controllers of field offices, down to officials in contact with the public bureaucratic structures, helped to ensure equity.

    Of course, there are disadvantages to bureaucratic organisation (hence the pejorative use of the term 'bureaucratic'). Characterised by rules, regulations, routine and a large and expanding career staff, bureaucracy was increasingly seen as unresponsive, costly and inefficient. Towards the end of the twentieth century, however, criticisms of bureaucratic organisation intertwined with arguments supporting a new approach to public management. Osborne and Gaebler (1992, pp. 12–15), for example, complained of 'the bankruptcy of bureaucracy. . . . For a long time . . . it solved the basic problems people wanted solved . . . and provided the basic, no-frills, one-size-fits-all services people needed and expected during the industrial era'. Today, however, 'in a global market place . . . in which customers have become accustomed to high quality and extensive choice', bureaucratic models are outdated.

In recent years, in response to perceived inadequacies of bureaucracy, new models have appeared which, despite the policy/administration dichotomy, are mainly developed around a distinction between policy and management. Politicians make policy, but implementation is increasingly left to 'managers' who have much more managerial freedom than bureaucratic models ever envisaged. Indeed, arguably we have now entered a new historical epoch of public administration. Weberian bureaucracy which characterised modern public administration has been replaced by *new postmodern* forms characterised by features such as differentiation, choice, flexibility, networks and markets (Clegg, 1990).

Such analyses, however, are not universally accepted. Not only does bureaucracy still have apologists (Goodsell, 1994; du Gay, 2000), it is, claims Rhodes (1997a, p. 182), 'still with us' and arguably still has a place alongside new forms such as markets and networks. As he observes (pp. 187–8), while 'post-modernism . . . has arrived both in mainstream Public Administration and the study of organizations . . . it is possible to take post-modern arguments too seriously'.

Public choice and marketisation

Bureaucracy also came under attack from *public choice* theorists (see, for example, Mueller, 1989; and Niskanen, 1971) who argue that public bureaucrats pursuing their own interests and promoting expansion of public services lead to government 'overload'. Their solution is to extend the market place, allowing citizens to buy services they want (e.g. through instruments such as education vouchers), or public sector 'clients' to buy them on citizens' behalf (e.g. through internal markets), rather than have governments supply services that individuals would not choose themselves. Bureaucracies should be slimmed down, activities wherever possible returned to the private sector, and accountability provided through market mechanisms (e.g. contracts and charging) rather than through political accountability which left bureaucrats effectively accountable to no one. In Britain public choice theory fitted well with New Right ideas, with their stress on market forces and a reduced role for the state.

One effect of these ideas is that 'the rigid, hierarchical, bureaucratic form of public administration, which has predominated for most of the twentieth century, is changing to a flexible, market-based form of public management' (Hughes, 1998, p. 1). For example, within many public bodies, internal markets have been established with different elements buying and selling services to each other. In local authorities compulsory competitive tendering introduced in the 1980s required many services to be contracted-out (see pp. 142–3). Where contracts were won by private sector companies the local authority ceased to be the 'direct provider of the service'. Even where the council's own workforce won the contract new internal relationships – between clients and contractors (or purchasers and providers) – developed. In central government, following publication of *Competing for Quality* (HM Treasury, 1991), contracting-out and market testing became central concerns.

By such measures the market has increasingly determined who supplies public goods and at what cost. In many cases public bodies are no longer the 'direct provider'. This has led to the concept of 'enabling', which sees public bodies facilitating private companies and other bodies to provide services on their behalf (see Ridley, 1988). While contested as a concept – Clarke and Stewart (1988), for example, see enabling in more expansive terms, empowering councils to meet communities' needs in the most effective way – it underlies approaches which support minimalist and residual models in which government at every level *directly* provides less and less.

Privatisation

The ultimate solution for those believing that the private sector allocates goods and services more efficiently than the public sector is privatisation. While this takes various forms (see Chapter 11), including contracting, its most dramatic manifestation in Britain has been asset sales. Many nationalised industries have been turned into public limited companies with shares sold to the public, a practice generating some £64 billion pounds between 1979 and 1996 (Horton and Farnham, 1999a, p. 6). Elsewhere functions once directly provided by public bodies – ranging from council houses to prisons – have been placed in the hands of private or voluntary bodies. Devices such as the Private Finance Initiative (PFI), used to secure private finance for government projects which are leased back to the state, represent a further form of privatisation. Compared with the pre-Thatcher years, by the 1990s over 50 per cent of the public sector had been placed in private hands, with over 650,000 workers transferring directly to the private sector (Isaac-Henry, 1993, p. 6). Blair's government, with its commitment to continued privatisation (e.g. air traffic control) and to public/private financing of projects such as the modernisation of London Underground, suggests little will change.

Consumerism and choice

Traditionally, citizens had little opportunity to choose between services offered by public bodies, many of which were monopoly suppliers. Indeed, as many services were funded by taxpayers and were free at the point of delivery, analogies with private 'customers' appeared false. Nevertheless, a key theme of NPM has been 'an emphasis on the public as customer and on customer choice' (Ranson and Stewart, 1994, p. 15). Choice, for example, has been enabled by opportunities to purchase gas, electricity and telecommunications – once supplied by monopoly nationalised industries – from competing private suppliers; and by different forms of school management (e.g. grant maintained, technology college, city technology college, etc.). Consumerism was symbolised by the Major government's *Citizen's Charter* which sought to increase competition and choice for consumers (see Chapter 12). It has been further developed by Blair, whose White Paper *Modernising Government* (Prime Minister and Minister for the Cabinet Office, 1999, p. 25) declared, 'We will deliver public services to meet the need of citizens, not the convenience of service providers.' Specific innovations include the People's Panel – a 5,000-strong nationally representative group to advise about 'what people really think about their public services' – and initiatives 'such as citizens' juries, community fora and focus groups' (ibid., pp. 13, 25).

There are, of course, limits to consumerism and choice within the public sector. Some 'public services', Rouse (1999, p. 79) suggests, 'are different from private ones in that, for example, they involve coercive relationships (policing), dependency (social security), and are non-rejectable (arrest)'. With police, for example, the public (consumers?) have no choice about being policed. Those arrested are unlikely to see themselves as consumers, although crime victims – as well as neighbourhoods receiving policing – may see themselves as such. Consumerist analogies are arguably also inappropriate with inspection, regulation and control. In some cases (e.g. contracting) public bodies act on behalf of consumers; in others (e.g. prisons) it is difficult even to identify 'customers' (prisoners, courts, taxpayers?). Often, too, choice lies simply between provision by different arms of the state, or within rules determined by the state. It is also debatable whether consumerism and choice empower citizens or simply redefine them as consumers.

Some analyses explain such developments in terms of a public sector shift towards *post-Fordist* service delivery patterns (Hoggett, 1987; Stoker and Mossberger, 1995). Previously, mass production, exemplified by early Ford cars, resulted in largely similar products offering little customer choice. By analogy, *Fordist* approaches in public administration relied heavily on bureaucratic structures and offered little or no choice. Today, however, different groups demand customised products, including public sector goods and services. 'Flexible specialisation', rather than mass production, provides the means of serving specialised niche markets.

Performance measurement

Within the private sector profit and loss are generally used to indicate efficiency. In the public sector, however, profitability as an efficiency measure is generally not possible. Nevertheless, increased emphasis has been placed upon measuring performance in public sector bodies, drawing especially upon the essentially private sector concept of *management accounting* (Pendlebury, 1989). Unlike conventional accounting, geared to inputs or subjects of expenditure (e.g. wages), management accounting relates to 'outputs' or objects of expenditure, enabling specific programmes or services to be costed, costs to be analysed against benefits, and some assessment of VFM to be obtained. Thus, *outputs* (e.g. value of tax collected) might be measured against *inputs* (e.g. staff, consumables), leading to the construction of *performance indicators* or *measures* (e.g. tax collected per employee).

Public sector performance measurement is important 'both for the accountability of organizations and individuals and for managers to produce better services' (Flynn, 1997, p. 170). It replaces (reinforces?) traditional political accountability with a managerial accountability whereby managers in public service organisations demonstrate their ability to meet performance targets. It enables measurement particularly of VFM and the *'three Es'* – *efficiency, effectiveness* and *economy*. Unfortunately, there is no universally accepted definition of these terms, and they are often incorrectly used interchangeably. *Economy* – using fewer resources (input reduction) – is perhaps the most easily understood. *Efficiency* and *effectiveness*, by contrast, often give rise to confusion. According to the Treasury and Civil Service Select Committee (1982, HC 236, Appendix 1; see also HM Treasury, 1986, Annex B), *effectiveness* is essentially concerned with objectives, and is measurable by the extent to which objectives are achieved. *Efficiency*, however, concerns relationships between inputs (resources) into a particular activity and outputs (goods/services) produced by it. Consequently, an effective manager, meeting desired objectives, might be regarded as inefficient if more resources were used than necessary. Of course, for either term to be used meaningfully, organisations must be clear about not only their inputs and outputs but also their objectives. In the private sector, where profit is usually the main objective, this is *relatively* straightforward. In the public sector, however, defining objectives is usually more difficult. Not only is there a problem in defining the objectives of, say, the Prime Minister's Office, but political considerations – difficult to quantify or assess objectively – often influence policy decisions and outcomes.

Of course, it is possible to measure not only the 'three Es' but other factors such as accuracy, timeliness, customer satisfaction, etc. In particular parts of the public sector specific measures might be used – e.g. hospital waiting lists. These measures can then be used to construct 'league tables' (e.g. of schools' performance) enabling both managers and the public to measure performance of different organisations. Published targets can also be set and performance audits conducted against these. This approach has been widely adopted to drive improvements in *quality* – another important theme of contemporary public administration – as part of the *Citizen's Charter* and, more recently, *Best Value* in local government (see pp. 143–5). For example, performance reviews of all local government services are now required over a five-year period, commencing with the worst performing.

Public sector performance measurement is not unproblematic. In addition to problems of identifying relevant outputs – not just those easily counted – performance measurement is sometimes used for different purposes.

> Measures . . . appropriate for external accountability may not be the right ones for improving management. Measures which are used to expose publicly poor performers may not be the best ones for helping management to bring about improvements. In any case managers will necessarily become defensive if the systems are used to punish the weak.
>
> (Flynn, 1997, pp. 184–5)

There is also a danger of what Rouse (1997, p. 99) calls 'targetology'. (For example, a target of reduced hospital waiting lists might adversely affect health if it leads to reduced post-operative hospital care.) Nevertheless, performance measurement has developed apace, and 'if anything . . . has become even more pronounced' under Blair (Rouse, 1999, p. 89).

Regulation and inspection

Regulation – using laws or government powers to affect private operators – has long featured within British public administration; as also has inspection, the process whereby the state supervises and monitors service provision. Pyper (1996, p. 165), however, notes increasing use of regulation and inspection during the twentieth century as the scope of public administration widened. Part of this increase in recent times has been due to a 'crisis of self-regulation' as 'state control' was strengthened over institutions such as the City and universities which previously enjoyed 'significant latitude' (Moran, 1995, p. 176). No less important has been the regulatory framework developed around privatised utilities. Usually independent of government, such regulators ensure that accountability is not just to private shareholders (although questions can be asked about the accountability of regulators themselves). (For discussion see Chapter 11.)

Fragmentation

One effect of the developments outlined above is fragmentation within British public administration. In central government, for example, over 100 Next Steps Agencies (NSAs) have appeared alongside government departments for delivering services. Privatisation also often produces fragmentation as competing suppliers emerge. One extreme case is the privatisation of British Rail into about 100 components including twenty-five train operating companies, five freight operators, three rolling stock leasing companies and nineteen maintenance suppliers, as well as Railtrack which owns the lines and the Railways Inspectorate. Throughout the public sector contracting has led to a client/purchaser contractor/provider split, while the PFI has resulted in public projects being leased from, and financed and operated by, the private sector. Fragmentation, moreover, has occurred even where services have not been privatised or contracted-out. Internal markets and budgetary decentral-isation, for example, have led to the establishment of cost centres, budget-holders and business units. In particular sectors, too, fragmentation can be discerned, for example self-governing hospital trusts within the NHS. The resulting 'fragmentation', Rhodes (1997b, p. 24) claims, 'is plain for all to see'. In addition to Next Steps Agencies, he identified 5,521 'special-purpose bodies involving 70,000 government appointments and £52 billion of public spending'. 'Add in privatization, services contracted-out to the private and voluntary sector and functions run by the [EU] and the extent of service fragmentation is still understated.'

One conceptualisation of fragmentation, the *'hollowing-out of the State'*, emphasises 'the loss of functions by central and local government departments to alternative delivery systems (such as agencies)' and by the 'British government to European Union institutions', and the 'limits set to the discretion of public servants

... through a sharper distinction between politics and management'. According to Rhodes (1996, pp. 661–2), the state is not only fragmenting and 'becoming smaller', it is 'hollowing out'. (See also Rhodes, 1994.)

Joined-up government

By the 1990s, as fragmentation became increasingly visible, a demand developed for *'joined-up government'* – coordination between the various government agencies and private and voluntary organisations involved in service delivery. This is a major theme of the Blair government's White Paper, *Modernising Government* (Prime Minister and Minister for the Cabinet Office, 1999, p. 32) which emphasises the need 'for more joined up and responsive services'. Massey (1999, p. 22) explains: '[T]he Government wants to look at how services can be provided in a way that puts the individual first by addressing issues that extend across departmental boundaries'. ICTs also have a role through information-sharing partnerships between service delivery agencies, providing the vision of an 'apparently seamless public service' (Bellamy, 1999, p. 141).

Particularly helpful here is the concept of *governance*, which distinguishes between formal institutions – such as government departments – and governing structures outside formal institutions. Although somewhat imprecise – Rhodes (1997a, Chapter 3) identifies seven different usages – *governance* refers essentially to 'self-organising, inter-organisational networks' (Rhodes, 2000e, p. 8) drawn from the public, private and voluntary sectors (see also pp.187–8). In many fields, *policy communities* and *networks* (Richardson and Jordan 1979; Rhodes, 1992), comprising not only public administrators but businesses, voluntary groups, academics, spokespersons of various interests, professional groups and the like, are involved in policy formulation and implementation. Rhodes (1996) exemplifies 'care of the elderly' which 'can involve upwards of a dozen people drawn from more than six agencies   covering every sector'. Most such organisations and networks largely control themselves. Administrative action is not imposed by central government, but emerges, often through negotiation, from arrangements adopted in the field. Governance results from interactive socio-political forms of governing which can pose a challenge to central government in so far as networks may develop distinctive management styles and near monopolies of expertise enabling them to 'resist central guidance'.

According to Taylor and Williams (1991, p. 174), the 1970s represented the 'last decade of established order for public administration'. Since then developments such as those above have profoundly altered the size and shape of British public administration. While concepts such as postmodernism, post-Fordism, governance and hollowing out sometimes lack precision, they offer useful perspectives for analysing a fundamental shift which has occurred, perhaps for ever, in the way the public sector is structured and managed.

The scope of British public administration

During the first three-quarters of the twentieth century Britain's public sector increased enormously. Government intervention in economic and social fields produced steady expansion. By 1979 social provision – health, social security, education and, to a large extent, housing – was largely a public sector concern. Nationalised industries – dominating such fields as transport, energy and aerospace – were valued at £123.5 billion. Their share of national capital stock stood at 17.7 per cent (Gretton *et al.*, 1987, p. 23). Reflecting this expansion, the public sector workforce in 1978 represented 28 per cent of the working population (compared with 3.6 per cent in 1891). Altogether, by 1979 about 'seven million officials [were] employed in public organisations and many millions of private-sector workers were dependent . . . on governmental contracts and state subsidies' (Horton and Farnham, 1999a, p. 5). The civil service alone expanded from 16,000 in 1868 to 748,000 in 1976. By 1979 there was a 'feeling that the State was too big, was getting bigger and ought to be smaller' (Gretton *et al.*, 1987, p. 17), an attitude manifested in Thatcher's commitment to 'rolling back the frontiers of the state'.

From the mid-1970s the public sector began to contract, reinforced after 1979 by Thatcherite policies reflecting not only privatisation and contracting-out, but also increasing private and voluntary provision. Although precise figures are difficult to quantify, public sector employment diminished. Between 1988 and 1998 it fell from around 6.3 million to 5 million, compared with a private sector increase from 20 million to 22.5 million (Cabinet Office, 2000a). In 1999 (a year in which jobs in the public sector increased for the first time since 1979) the public sector employed approximately 18 per cent of UK workers. *Economic Trends* (Office of National Statistics, June 2000) records some 4,967,000 public sector workers in 1999, reducible for statistical purposes to 4,048,000 full-time equivalents. Table 1.1 gives corresponding figures for 1979.

As Table 1.1 shows, public sector employment fell by approximately 2.5 million between 1979 and 1998. The biggest fall was in nationalised industries (over 1.5 million). However, not all sectors declined; for example, police and social services manpower increased. Yet, official statistics reflect numerous reclassifications and other factors which make it difficult to obtain a clear picture. For example, health statistics are confusing because NHS Trusts created after 1991 were 'reclassified' as public corporations. Again, in 1979 local government figures included polytechnics and further education colleges. But 1999 figures exclude them because, following their removal from local authority control (and the redesignation of polytechnics as universities), their employees are now officially in private sector employment. Again, some publicly owned institutions (e.g. the Bank of England) are not officially included within public sector employment; neither are private company employees engaged on public sector contracts. Obviously, too, not all employees listed in Table 1.1 are engaged strictly in public administration; for example, police, health workers and the armed forces.

Despite the loss of public sector jobs, the state's 'rolling back' since 1979 is somewhat less than government rhetoric might suggest. Cutting public expenditure, for example, has proved elusive. The proportion of gross domestic product (GDP) absorbed by the public sector (around 40 per cent) when the Conservatives left office

Table 1.1 UK public sector employment, 1979–99*

	1979	1999
Central government		
HM Forces	314,000	208,000
NHS	977,000	64,000
Other central government* (including government departments, agencies and quangos)	897,000	550,000
Total	2,188,000	822,000
Local government		
Education	1,110,000	836,000
Social services	235,000	270,000
Police (including civilians)	172,000	201,000
Construction	150,000	58,000
Other	701,000	606,000
Total	2,368,000	1,971,000
Nationalised industries	1,818,000	223,000
NHS Trusts	–	912,000
Other public corporations	216,000	120,000
Total public sector	6,590,000	4,048,000

Source: Office of National Statistics (June 2000, Table D)
Note: * Full-time equivalents mid-year.

in 1997 'was almost the same' as when they entered office in 1979 (Horton and Farnham, 1999a, p. 6). While the Blair government remains committed to reducing public expenditure as a proportion of GDP, previous experience would suggest that the public sector seems destined to remain an activity of considerable extent. Most obvious candidates for privatisation have been sold already and much of the remaining public sector is unattractive to private companies. There is also among many public sector professionals a service ethos which fits uneasily with profit motives, while among the public there remains widespread support – particularly in welfare – to 'free' public provision.

The complexity of British public administration

As should be clear, boundaries of the public sector are difficult to define. Indeed, misunderstanding was rife even before the managerialist developments of recent decades. In 1976 Stanyer and Smith (p. 21) observed:

> Many past studies have made the mistake of confusing public administration with the civil service and central departmental administration. Several books whose titles would lead one to expect a discussion of the whole system of public administration are found to have omitted local government, public corporations, field administration and bodies with uncertain or unusual status.

Limiting public administration to central government excludes much of the public sector, although today precisely what else should be included remains problematic. As Isaac-Henry (1997, p. 6) notes, 'the physical landscape of the public sector has changed significantly since 1979', and now includes a complex array of bodies. One analysis (Times Books, 1995) identifies seven main elements:

- *the core of the state*, which includes government departments and the Cabinet system staffed by the Senior Civil Service working directly to ministers;
- *the inner ring*, which is part of central government consisting mainly of Next Steps Agencies and 'what's left' following initiatives such as market testing;
- *the peripheral state*, comprising non-departmental public bodies (quangos) and public corporations (e.g. the BBC);
- *the new state*, including local governance (which includes elected local government and education and training bodies as well as local quangos) and the NHS;
- *the European state*, comprising mainly European institutions such as the Commission and Council of Ministers;
- *the regional state*, which today would include devolved administrations in Northern Ireland, Scotland and Wales and Regional Development Agencies in England;
- *the miscellaneous state*, which includes various bodies (e.g. Bank of England, Metropolitan Police).

Even the above is neither exhaustive nor definitive; for example, should one include employees of private firms undertaking public sector contract work and government taskforce members (see p. 78) as public employees? Diversity and fragmentation make it difficult to define the contemporary public sector with precision.

One feature which the post-1979 retreat from state provision cannot reverse is the *complexity* of British public administration. Many institutions evolved over long periods and although the terms describing them have been retained the institutions themselves have changed markedly. Thus the Cabinet, the civil service and local authorities – all originally created to perform functions in the pre-twentieth-century state – have had to adapt to new and more exacting circumstances. Other institutions such as public corporations have been added and removed piecemeal as state functions have changed.

Such developments increased sharply in intensity and significance after 1979, fuelled by the New Right agenda and the NPM. The privatisation of many former nationalised industries spawned a new breed of regulatory agencies. Contracting-out resulted in public services increasingly being delivered by private and voluntary organisations. The enabling state brought a plethora of quangos, public/private partnerships and networks at both local and national levels. The 1980s saw 'opting out' legislation, notably in education and health. In central government, executive functions have been largely 'hived off' from central departments to Next Steps Agencies. Following publication in 1991 of the *Citizen's Charter* (Prime Minister's Office, 1991) and the White Paper, *Competing for Quality* (HM Treasury, 1991), performance standards, contracting out and market testing all became central concerns. The creation in the 1990s of assemblies and executives in Scotland, Wales and Northern Ireland, and closer European integration, have further complicated the public sector's 'physical landscape'.

Another aspect of complexity is that public administrators today are frequently required to adopt a technical orientation unimaginable in the nineteenth century. A century ago any reasonably intelligent, literate person could make a competent administrator. Today, however, public administrators perform functions (e.g. economic planning) and use techniques (e.g. cost–benefit analysis) unheard of then. Today's civil service has 'a greater diversity of function than any other organisation in the country, performing tasks from weather forecasting to economic forecasting, from the management of conference facilities to the administration of social security benefits' (Treasury and Civil Service Committee, 1993–4, p. xiv). Changes in political environment have also increased complexity. The rise of the mass media, and expanded pressure group activity, for example, have introduced new constraints to which public administrators must respond. Recent governments have found that policy presentation is often no less important than policy formulation itself, leading to the rise of 'spin doctors', some of whom are now employed as special advisers or temporary civil servants (see pp. 77–8). Complexity is compounded, moreover, by tremendous diversity within parts of the public sector. Within local government, for example, Birmingham City Council (with over one million inhabitants) is worlds apart from Walton-on-the-Wolds, a rural parish council with an electorate of some 200. Statutorily, both are 'local authorities' but in practice they are very different. Similarly, central government departments vary enormously in terms of size, structures and operating styles (see Chapter 2). The 'typical' government department does not exist, which makes the core of central government particularly complex. With quasi-government one finds similar diversity. Wilson (1995, p. 5) observes, 'Ambiguity . . . characterises the diversity of "quangos". . . in terms of finance, organisation, objectives and accountability'.

Further ambiguity and confusion stem from blurred terminology. For example, the designation 'government department' is now almost incapable of precise definition (see Chapter 2). Similar confusion surrounds the term 'civil service'. The unified, permanent, politically neutral and anonymous career civil service of yesteryear has now been fragmented into over 100 different agencies, and joined by special advisers, taskforces and outsiders recruited in mid-career or on secondment (see Chapter 4). Greer (1994, p. 103) sees the term 'civil servant' becoming 'increasingly meaningless'. Chapman (1992, p. 4) even suggests that the British civil service 'no longer exists'. Apparently simple terms are far from straightforward.

For students such developments present particular problems. One is that, in reality, nothing is simple about the practice of British administration. Organisation charts invariably present a neat, ordered universe, but nothing could be further removed from reality. Another problem is that British public administration must be seen within the context of adaptation to changing circumstances. Indeed, as the subject is continually changing, models are liable to prove misleading within even a short time frame. Generalisations must also be used with caution. There is no universally applicable pattern of public administration. One approach, perhaps, is to think not of one but of several 'public sectors' with different administrative practices.

The discipline of public administration

Until the 1970s 'public administration was relatively clearly defined both as an activity and as a subject of academic study' (Elcock, 1991, p. 2). Its 'historic home' was political science (Rhodes, 1991, p. 534) and for many years it was taught in British universities mainly as a component in Politics and Government degrees. From the late 1960s, however, degree courses in Public Administration appeared in what were then polytechnics. 'The subject was largely approached from a social science perspective' and Public Administration programmes were located mainly in social science departments (Greenwood and Eggins, 1995, p. 143). The last two decades of the twentieth century, however,

> witnessed a paradigm shift in the approach to public administration both as a field of study and an area of practice. . . . Students of Public Administration . . . interpreted what has been taking place in practice and developed critiques of the theories and concepts that have informed that practice.
>
> (Davies, 2000, p. 192)

The main curricular effect of these developments was a shift after the 1970s away from the social sciences and towards management, a development which reflected the changing structure and operations of public bureaucracies – in both Britain and much of the Western world. The discipline also sought to concern itself with new technologies and with emerging areas such as the environment, Europe and globalisation. One consequence, as new areas of interest within the discipline were added to the old, was that the curriculum became unstable and overloaded. Many Public Administration courses were replaced by others focusing on aspects such as Public Policy or Public Management. This, in turn, stimulated debate about the fundamental nature of the discipline and even its location within the academic spectrum.

There was also increased emphasis from the 1980s upon *skills* within the Public Administration curriculum. This was part of a drive for more vocational education led by a government-appointed body, the Business and Technology Education Council (BTEC) (formerly Business and Technician Educational Council), which validated sub-degree-level programmes. BTEC's emphasis on vocationally relevant skills, as opposed (in addition?) to knowledge, impacted on both the curriculum and teaching methodology. The emphasis on skills (e.g. problem-solving, numeracy) within the curriculum, it was argued, required a shift away from traditional teaching towards more student-centred, participative, action-learning approaches which simulated work experience and developed skills. BTEC teachers found that their role changed from 'academic expert' to 'facilitator'. And as teachers on BTEC courses often also often taught on undergraduate programmes, the 'BTEC philosophy' increasingly impacted on degree teaching as well (Greenwood and Robins, 1998a). There was increasing debate about the appropriate balance between knowledge and skills within the curriculum, and about whether the purpose of Public Administration education was the study *of* government structures and processes or training *for* a career within public administration (or both?). While these debates are still unresolved, during the 1990s most Public Administration teachers accepted that study cannot be confined to a narrow emphasis on skills. Contextual knowledge is crucial. Future administrators need contextual knowledge about the administrative world which they will inhabit and in which their joint mastery of skills and knowledge will help them perform (Greenwood and Robins, 1998b).

BTEC's approach coincided, significantly, with wider concerns about whether public administration could be subsumed within a generic management concept. Notable advocates of the latter view, Perry and Kramer (1983, p. ix), claim that 'knowledge, techniques and skills necessary for administration are similar for organizations in a variety of sectors'. 'The field of administration', they add (ibid., p. 9), 'is a field of business . . . removed from the hurry and strife of politics'. This view conflicts with the more traditional concept that 'public administration is more than private management writ public . . . [having] a political environment, theoretical foundations, an ethos, a culture, and a sheer diversity which makes it distinctive from the private sector' (Greenwood, 1988, p. 225). While this debate cannot be pursued here, it is clear that the managerialisation of public administration has increased significantly the contribution of business and management concepts to the study of Public Administration.

Conclusion

The complexity of contemporary public administration, plus differing approaches to its study, present considerable challenges to students. The theme of earlier editions – that the 'ambiguity, confusion and complexity' characterising central/local government relations (Rhodes, 1981, p. 28) typify British public administration generally – will probably be even more true of the twenty-first century than it was of the twentieth. Inevitably this book is divided into constituent parts for material to be manageable. While there are sections on government departments, the civil service, local government, etc., these should not be regarded as neat, self-contained compartments operating in isolation. Extensive interrelationships occur both formally and informally. Actual working relationships are invariably much more ambiguous than organisational charts would indicate. Public administration responds to many values – efficiency, rationality, equity and so forth – thus defying neat labels.

Further reading

NPM receives comprehensive coverage in Hughes (1998). A discussion of recent developments in specific parts of the UK public sector is found in Horton and Farnham (1999b). Material about the British public sector is spread across a wide range of sources but a concise and up-to-date summary is Massey (1999). Pyper and Robins (2000) also summarises recent developments and contains a useful chapter which discusses the 'hollow state'. The UK government web site (www.open.gov.uk) gives access to web sites for numerous public sector bodies.

Rhodes (1997a) contains authoritative discussion of policy networks, accountability and governance, as well as concepts such as hollowing out, post-Fordism and postmodernism. For discussion about Public Administration as an academic discipline see Rhodes (1991); Greenwood and Eggins (1995). Davies *et al.* (1998, 2000) offer global perspectives on public administration education and training, including a chapter on Britain.

Chapter 2

The Whitehall universe

Departments and agencies

Introduction

This chapter examines 'Whitehall', the collective name for central administration. Although many public services are provided by subordinate agencies (such as devolved assemblies and local authorities), Britain's political system has traditionally been highly centralised, and fundamental decisions are usually taken at the centre. It is to central administration, therefore, that we turn, focusing on government departments and the executive agencies, popularly known as Next Steps Agencies (NSAs), which represent the main organisational units in Whitehall.

What is a government department?

'Whitehall', Wright (2000, p. 241) observes, 'is organised through a series of separate departments'. In government, however, the word 'department' is ambiguous, sometimes being used synonymously with other terms such as 'ministry' or 'office', at other times describing divisions within government departments themselves.

Attempting to define a 'government department' is 'elusive and difficult', not least because official definitions produce different listings (McLean *et al.*, 2000, especially Appendix 8.2). Smith *et al.* (1995, p. 39) identified sixty-one departments listed in the *Civil Service Year Book*. Of these, nineteen were headed by Cabinet ministers and two others, the Law Officers' Department and the Lord Advocate's Department, were defined as departments of state. Dunleavy (1989, p. 273), however, recognising that many departments had agencies or similar bodies attached to them, identified forty-four 'ministerial departments (and elements of)' and a further thirty-eight 'non-ministerial departments, departmental agencies, and other semi-detached agencies etc.' Defining 'ministries' as 'organizations headed by a member of Cabinet or in the sole charge of a minister of Cabinet rank', Rose (1987, pp. 22–3), by contrast, identified about twenty bodies. Hood and Dunsire (1981, pp. 41–51, 157–69), however, in an earlier study identified sixty-nine departments accounting 'for a vote in the budget estimates in . . . 1976–77'. Defining a government department, they observed (ibid., p. 40), was 'a deep seated legal (indeed philosophical)' problem. In fact, Hogwood (1995) offers 'families' as a unit for analysis, a concept including other organisational forms – such as NSAs and quangos – focused around the main ministerial departments.

Ambiguity surrounding the term 'government department' is not simply a philosophical point but indicates the difficulty of delineating the boundaries of central administration. Whether, for example, the Royal Mint should be included within central administration depends largely upon criteria used for defining government departments. Indeed, the position has become complicated through the proliferation from the late 1980s of NSAs. Thus, *Civil Service Statistics 1999* (Cabinet Office, 2000a, Table A) identifies 150 'departments and agencies': 107 executive agencies in the Home Civil Service; seventeen departments headed by Cabinet ministers; and numerous other bodies described variously as Trading Funds, departments operating fully on Next Steps lines, executive units of Customs and Excise and Inland Revenue, the Crown Prosecution Service, Serious Fraud Office; and the Valuation Office 'which is a free-standing agency'. About these bodies only two generalisations can be made:

(1) most have links, however tenuous, with ministers; (2) the most politically salient are usually ministerial departments.

Problems exist also with classifying government departments. Jordan (1994), however, offers a useful three-fold classification.

1 Five-star departments

Jordan describes these (ibid., p. 15) as 'mainstream departments headed by a Cabinet Minister'. Usually, one minister – carrying the title Secretary of State – represents 'five-star' departments in Cabinet, although there are exceptions. The Treasury, for example, is nominally headed by the Prime Minister (as 'First Lord of the Treasury'), although the Chancellor of the Exchequer and Chief Secretary to the Treasury usually also sit in Cabinet. Occasionally, other departments may have more than one Cabinet representative, for example the Foreign Office for a period under Thatcher. Sometimes the position is more complicated. In 2000 the Minister of Transport (a second-tier minister in the Department of the Environment, Transport and the Regions) attended Cabinet meetings but was not a Cabinet minister. Again, Cabinet ministers sometimes head quite minor departments – such as the Chancellor of the Duchy of Lancaster who administers the Duchy of Lancaster Office. Sometimes such 'sinecure' posts 'camouflage pivotal governmental and parliamentary roles' such as chairing Cabinet committees or long-term planning (Lee *et al.*, 1998, p. 206). Some Cabinet ministers may not head a department, and departments enjoying Cabinet representation in one government may not enjoy it in another. Nevertheless, major areas of government are usually represented by 'five-star' departments. Those identifiable in 2000 are shown in Table 2.1.

2 Second division or non-Cabinet-headed departments

Jordan (1994, p. 20) explains, 'there is no clear explanation of why these are not headed by a Cabinet Minister but there is perhaps the implication that these activities are thought to be less politically contentious'. The Attorney General, for example, has responsibility for several departments including the Treasury Solicitor's Department, Crown Prosecution Service and Legal Secretariat.

3 Bureaucratic-led departments

These are also called 'non-ministerial' departments and may be headed by a civil servant (e.g. National Debt Office), board (e.g. Inland Revenue), commission (e.g. Charity Commission), regulator (Office of the Rail Regulator) or some combination of these. The *List of Ministerial Responsibilities* (Cabinet Office, November 1999) identified twenty-five such bodies in 1999, ranging from such significant departments as Inland Revenue (with over 66,000 employees) to the obscure Registrar of Friendly Societies with only fifty. Bureaucratic-led departments, Jordan (1994, p. 21) suggests, are so constituted 'because there seems merit in having them at some

Table 2.1 Major departments and staff in post, April 2000[a]

Ministry of Agriculture, Fisheries and Food (MAFF)	9,590[b]
Cabinet Office	1,980[c]
Ministry of Defence (MOD)	100,330
Department of Culture, Media and Sport	620
Department of Education and Employment (DfEE)	36,060[d]
Department of the Environment, Transport and the Regions (DETR)	17,070[e]
Department of Health	5,160[f]
Department for International Development	1,210
Department of Social Security	83,530
Department of Trade and Industry	8,840[g]
Foreign and Commonwealth Office (FCO)	5,470
HM Treasury	830[h]
Home Office	12,540[i]
Lord Chancellor's Department	10,640[j]
Northern Ireland Office	190
Scotland Office	40[k]
Wales (Office of the Secretary of State for Wales)	30[l]

Source: Cabinet Office (November 2000)

Notes

a   Full-time equivalents including industrial civil service and agency staff.

b   Excludes Intervention Board.

c   Excludes Central Office of Information, Security and Intelligence Services.

d   Includes Employment Service. Excludes Office for Standards in Education (OFSTED).

e   Excludes Health and Safety Executive/Commission, Shadow Strategic Rail Authority, Office of the Rail Regulator, Office of Water Service, Ordnance Survey.

f   Excludes Food Standards Agency, Meat Hygiene Service.

g   Excludes Advisory and Conciliation Service, Export Credit Guarantee Department, OFGEM, Office of Fair Trading, Office of Telecommunications.

h   Excludes Customs and Excise (21,910 staff), Inland Revenue (66,330 staff), Office of Government Commerce, Debt Management Office, Government Actuary, Department of National Savings, National Investment and Loans Office, Office for National Statistics, Registrar of Friendly Societies, Royal Mint.

i   Excludes Charity Commission, HM Prison Service (40,560 staff).

j   Excludes HM Land Registry, Public Record Office and departments for which the Attorney General has responsibility (Crown Prosecution Service, Legal Secretariat, Serious Fraud Office, Treasury Solicitor's Department).

k   Excludes Scottish Executive (10,850 staff), Crown Office and Procurator Fiscal, General Register Office-Scotland, National Archive for Scotland, Registers of Scotland.

l   Excludes National Assembly for Wales (2,570 staff), Office of the Chief Inspector of Schools in Wales (Estyn).

distance from Government' – for example, where they have regulatory functions. Nevertheless, while they usually operate independently of ministers unless major issues are involved, questions about administration and policy are usually answered by ministers.

While the organisations categorised above might all be thought of as departments through being staffed by civil servants, being in receipt of budgetary estimates, or being classified as a Crown body, Jordan's classification is nevertheless problematic.

For example, the Office of HM Paymaster General could at different times in recent decades arguably have been located in each of the three categories. It is also unclear where the boundary lies between Jordan's 'government departments' and other bodies. For example, some 'bureaucratic-led departments' share many features with quangos (see Chapter 8) and NSAs (see below). Defining and classifying departments, and distinguishing them from other public sector bodies, is not easy.

Departmental organisation

Although internal organisation varies widely, three important features can be identified: size; decentralisation; bureaucratic organisation.

Size

Departments vary in size. In 2000 the three smallest (Legal Secretariat, Privy Council Office, and Debt Management Office) had thirty staff or less, while the four largest (Defence, Social Security, Inland Revenue and Education and Employment) together employed 60 per cent of civil servants.

Size is relevant to how departments operate. 'Size increases the complexity of organizations. . . . This requires the development of rules and procedures as an alternative to personal control by superiors of their subordinates' (Pitt and Smith, 1981, p. 63). In short, bureaucratic characteristics of departments – written rules, hierarchical structures – partly result from size, and are usually most marked in larger departments. Also in larger departments effective ministerial control is usually more difficult, and problems with coordination and planning more prevalent. Since the 1980s, however, with executive functions increasingly delegated to NSAs, the effect has been to produce smaller Whitehall units. Thus of 100,330 civil servants in the MOD in 2000, 62 per cent worked in forty-three different agencies, and only 38 per cent in the 'parent' department.

Size does not, however, indicate influence. The Treasury, for example, is a small department. Essentially, size reflects the nature of departmental work: departments concerned mainly with policy formulation or supervisory functions are usually smaller than those directly providing public services. The Department of Health (DoH), with 5,160 staff (including agencies) in 2000, is relatively small. It does not provide medical care direct to the public, its main responsibility being to plan, finance and advise hospitals and other health providers which do. The DSS, by contrast, employed 83,530 staff, most of whom (69,230) worked in the Benefits Agency through local offices dealing with the public.

Decentralisation

Most departments administer services over large areas. Some (Northern Ireland, Scotland, and Wales Offices) cover constituent parts of the United Kingdom; others operate on a United Kingdom (Customs and Excise) or world (Foreign and

Commonwealth Office, FCO) basis. To discharge functions over such wide areas departments may work closely with local or regionally based bodies such as local authorities, NHS Trusts or police authorities. In other cases departments may operate through local or regional 'field offices'. This process, *territorial decentralisation*, is a familiar feature of government departments, although there is little standardisation of field office functions. Some have executive functions, others are concerned with inspection, regulation, planning or a mixture of functions. The amount of authority delegated has invariably been limited.

Traditionally each department developed its own local pattern; indeed, individual departments sometimes had different field networks (Draper, 1977, especially pp. 51–2). In 1994, however, regional offices of four departments – Trade and Industry, Employment (in 1995 Education and Employment), Environment and Transport – came together. In 2000 there were nine 'government offices for the regions' (GORs) for England: located in the North East, North West, Yorkshire and Humber, West Midlands, East Midlands, East of England, South West, South East and London. Each office is headed by a Senior Regional Director responsible for staff and expenditure routed through it, and has close links with departments without regional offices, with regional businesses and local authorities, with Regional Development Agencies (RDAs) and chambers (see p. 203) (Mawson and Spencer, 1997; Mawson, 1998; Spencer and Mawson, 1998, 2000; Wood, 1998; see also Chapter 10).

Decentralisation should not be confused with the location in Belfast, Edinburgh and Cardiff of headquarters divisions of the Northern Ireland, Scotland and Wales Offices; nor with deconcentration from London of headquarters units of departments and agencies (e.g. the Social Security Benefit Inspectorate headquarters in Harrogate). Over two-thirds of civil servants work outside London and the south-east.

Bureaucratic organisation

Traditionally departments were organised largely on bureaucratic lines. This facilitated both accountability and equity, allowing detailed control of subordinates, and enforcement of rules, through a hierarchic structure extending from top departmental levels, through field offices, down to officials dealing with the public. Indeed, elements of bureaucratic organisation are evident from even a brief glance inside government departments. While arrangements vary, in most departments large blocks of work are brought together into groups or directorates, which, in turn, allocate work between divisions and branches. Thus in 2000 the Department for Culture, Media and Sport had a Strategy and Communications Directorate, and five main groups (Education, Training, Arts and Sports; Museums, Galleries, Libraries and Heritage; Creative Industries, Media and Broadcasting; Regions, Tourism, Millennium and International; and Corporate Services). The first of these groups was, in turn, divided into three divisions: an Arts Division; a Sports and Recreation Division; and an Education Unit. The Arts Division, in its turn, had branches for Arts Support, Arts Education and Arts Funding (Stationery Office, 2000). Built into departmental structures are the private offices of ministers which deal with ministerial correspondence and engagements. Typically these include a private secretary (often a young 'high flier'), diary secretary and any special advisers (see Chapter 4).

Since the 1980s, in line with NPM (see Chapter 1), bureaucratic structures have been partly replaced in departments by cost centres, responsibility centres, etc., alongside NSAs delivering services. While this may make departments more efficient, it also makes them more complex. Rose (1987, p. 234) calculated that Cabinet ministers had beneath them 526 departmental divisions, plus seventy-five or so in the defence field. In 2000 the position was even more complicated with, for example, 78 per cent of civil servants housed in around 140 NSAs, forty-three attached to the MOD alone. (All the above figures, unless otherwise stated, are from Cabinet Office, November 2000.)

Departmental organisation and civil servants

Departmental organisation was traditionally linked with civil service grades. Until recently senior ranks were organised around a seven-grade structure. Policy sections were typically headed by an officer at principal level (Grade 7), branches by an assistant secretary (Grade 5), divisions by an under secretary (Grade 3), and a group of divisions by a deputy secretary (Grade 2) (or in larger departments by a second permanent secretary). Finally the permanent secretary (Grade 1) – or designated permanent secretary if more than one – was the senior departmental manager, adviser and confidant of ministers, and the department's accounting officer (Barberis, 1996a; Theakston, 2000b, p. 144).

This congruence of departmental and civil service hierarchies exacerbated the problems inherent within bureaucratic organisations. Because civil service career patterns were involved, gradings sometimes determined task allocation rather than vice versa. This could cause delay and inefficiency: for example, if the grades through which communications passed were unnecessarily extended.

Of course, many departments require specialist skills and employ appropriate staff (scientists, engineers, doctors, etc.). Such *specialists* traditionally had separate career and grading structures, and their own specialist branch and divisional hierarchies. Under this system of *parallel hierarchies*, a generalist policy formulator requiring technical advice would typically refer to specialists of similar rank. This arrangement, a legacy from periods when government required less technical information, not only placed specialists in subordinate positions (as technical advisers to generalists who formulated policy and briefed ministers) but required continual cross-referencing between specialist and generalist hierarchies.

Some of these difficulties were reduced in 1996 when the Senior Civil Service (SCS), comprising the most senior staff (roughly equivalent to former grades 1 to 5) on a nine-point scale, was created in all departments and agencies. This produced a leaner, flatter structure – a whole tier of Whitehall equivalent to the old Grade 3 was removed – and flexibility to assess jobs according to responsibilities. Management structures could be related more to departmental work, and individuals could be appointed to a specific job on merit, irrespective of hierarchical position. The SCS also includes specialists, although the majority of its members, about 40 per cent, are in policy and operational roles. Nevertheless, while departmental structures are more flexible than previously, elements of the bureaucratic pattern remain. Although departmental arrangements vary, typically a permanent secretary has overall departmental responsibility, with other senior SCS members (broadly equivalent to old Grade 2) being responsible for groups or directorates. These often have specific departmental titles such as director, director-general or, if running an NSA, chief executive. Less senior SCS members (broadly equivalent to old Grades 5 and 7) manage divisions or branches.

Reforming departmental organisation: 'from MINIS to FMI'

Before the 1980s the most authoritative demand for reforming departmental organisation was the Fulton Report (1968) which included two particularly important recommendations: (1) the establishment of *departmental agencies* within departments; and (2) 'hiving off' departmental functions to non-departmental agencies. Progress with introducing these arrangements was limited in the 1970s but the underlying idea was to re-emerge in the 1980s. Three measures introduced by the Thatcher government were also of long-term significance.

Rayner scrutinies

In 1979 Sir Derek (later Lord) Rayner, of Marks & Spencer, was appointed as an adviser on administrative efficiency. Supported by an Efficiency Unit – composed of civil servants and outsiders – he began a series of efficiency scrutinies of departmental activities. The main objective was to uncover waste and improve efficiency, although critics argued that the real aim was cost-cutting. By the 1990s claimed savings totalled £1.5 billion (Theakston, 1995, pp. 127–8).

Two scrutinies were particularly important: the first, in 1979, led to a management information system for ministers (MINIS) in the Department of the Environment (DoE). The second, in 1981 (the Joubert study), divided the DoE into cost centres as a basis for a financial management system.

Management Information System for Ministers (MINIS)

MINIS, introduced into the DoE in 1980, represented 'an . . . attempt to collect information about a Department's activities and to place responsibility for using this information with the Department's top management, Ministerial and official' (Richards, 1987, p. 26). It enabled departmental 'top management' to ascertain who does what, why and at what cost. Theakston (1995, p. 128) suggests it was 'designed to provide ministers with . . . a menu . . . for . . . where to cut staff numbers'. The DoE shed 15,000 jobs by 1983.

Following the Joubert study 120 cost centres were established in the DoE, each controlled by a manager with budgetary responsibility (Fry, 1984, p. 332; *Financial Management in Government Departments*, 1983, pp. 50–2). Subsequently all departments were required to introduce 'management systems like MINIS' (*Efficiency and Effectiveness in the Civil Service*, 1982, para. 29 and Annex C).

Financial Management Initiative (FMI)

The FMI, launched in 1982, was 'a general approach' rather than a single strategy (Gray and Jenkins, 1986, p. 173; 1985, p. 124), although four distinctive features can be identified.

1 Top management systems

By 1984 all departments had taken steps to introduce MINIS-like systems enabling ministers and managers 'to review regularly the department's aims, examine its "businesses" and the "customers" they serve, set objectives, and establish priorities' (*Progress in Financial Management in Government Departments*, 1984, p. 3). Such language, Theakston (1995, p. 129) suggests, illustrates 'the "business methods" approach' underlying FMI.

2 Statement of objectives

All departments were obliged to specify objectives as a basis for determining priorities and measuring achievement. In reality, however, many statements of objectives were vague and generalised, describing functions or responsibilities rather than objectives. This partly reflects problems of goal-setting in the (generally) non-profit-oriented public sector. Goal identification, moreover, is often inseparable in Whitehall from policy questions. Consequently, the FMI experienced 'difficulties created by imprecise, broad, policy objectives' (National Audit Office, 1986, para. 13).

3 Decentralisation and delegation

The FMI required each department to 'examine the scope for breaking its structure down into cost-centres or responsibility-centres' (*Efficiency and Effectiveness in the Civil Service*, 1982, Appendix 3). Cost centre managers were to become budget-holders responsible for costs and results, in contrast to traditional departmental practice whereby finance and staffing were centrally controlled. By 1984, for example, the Department of Health and Social Security (DHSS) had developed 800 cost centres, with managers having 'to bid for their requirements' (*Progress in Financial Management in Government Departments*, 1984, pp. 62–3). While progress varied between departments, '"decentralized budgetary control" saw middle- and lower-level managers . . . being made accountable for their budgets and performance' (Theakston, 1995, p. 129).

4 Performance measurement

The FMI aimed to give all managers 'means to assess, and wherever possible measure, outputs or performance' (Carter, 1994, p. 209). Initially emphasis was placed upon measuring administrative functions, although subsequently this switched to programme measurement (which – as costs may be spread among numerous departmental sections as well as outside agencies – is usually more difficult).

These measures undoubtedly had an impact. Rayner scrutinies produced substantial savings; every department adopted MINIS-type systems, and the FMI led to widespread objective-setting, departmental decentralisation and performance measurement. Nevertheless, it is debatable whether real change occurred. The FMI was implemented over time, and at different paces in different departments. In 1987, the Public Accounts Committee (1986–7, paras 20, 44) claimed that 'a major effort' was needed to speed up implementation of the FMI; for 'some' departments, 'full implementation [was] still many years away'.

The Next Steps report

One response to the slow progress achieved through the initiatives outlined above was the 1988 Efficiency Unit report *Improving Management in Government: the Next Steps* (sometimes called the Ibbs Report after the Efficiency Unit's head, Sir Robin Ibbs). This report (Efficiency Unit, 1988) highlighted seven main findings (see Box 2.1).

Box 2.1 The Next Steps report: key findings

- Of all civil servants, 95 per cent are 'concerned with the delivery of government services';
- Senior civil servants lack skill in service delivery; 'senior management is dominated by people whose skills are in policy formulation';
- There is insufficient emphasis on improving performance, mainly because 'senior civil servants inevitably and rightly respond to [ministerial] priorities . . . which tend to be dominated by the demands of Parliament and communicating government policies';
- Ministers are overloaded; 'the greater diversity and complexity of work in many departments, together with demands from Parliament, the media and the public for more information . . . has added to ministerial overload';
- There is too little emphasis on 'the results to be achieved with the resources', mainly because of pressure on departments relating to 'expenditure and activities';
- There are 'relatively few external pressures demanding improvement in performance';
- The Civil Service is too big and too diverse to manage as a single service.

Source: Efficiency Unit (1988: paras 3–10)

Underlying this analysis was the realisation that departmental functions overwhelmingly concerned service delivery, not policy; and that the almost uniform design of departments – with largely common systems of organisation, grading and pay – was not appropriate for all government activities. Each department, it was therefore recommended (ibid., p. 7), 'must be organised in a way which focuses on the job to be done'. Policy work should be separated from service delivery, with the latter becoming the responsibility of 'agencies'. Headed by chief executives with substantial managerial autonomy, agencies would become largely responsible for operational matters within ministerially imposed policy objectives, budgets and performance targets. Departments would remain but their role and size would diminish. Agency relationships with departments would vary according to the job being done: thus some agencies might remain within departments, others might become non-departmental bodies, while others still might 'no longer [be] inside the Civil Service' (ibid., p. 10).

Thatcher's government responded by establishing a Next Steps project team within the Cabinet Office, and anticipating that within ten years three-quarters of civil servants would work in agencies (Hansard, VI, vol. 138, cols 21–4, 25 July 1988). When Thatcher resigned in 1990 twenty-five NSAs existed, and numerous other activities had been identified for agency status.

Under Major, Next Steps accelerated. By 1997 130 agencies containing 387,000 civil servants (approximately 74 per cent) had been established (Cabinet Office, March 1997, p. 2). Lee *et al.* (1998, p. 244) suggest several reasons for such rapid development: Next Steps promised ministers 'freedom from operational detail', 'top officials' more freedom to act as ministerial advisers, 'and middle-level officials [freedom] to manage'. It also had prime ministerial backing. Under Major a five-yearly review, *Prior Options*, was introduced, requiring each agency to examine whether agency status was still appropriate or whether privatisation, contractorisation or some other arrangement was preferred. By 1998 eleven agencies had been privatised, seven merged and one demerged, three had had all their functions contracted-out, two had been disbanded, and one changed in status to a Non Departmental Public Body. It also became normal for chief executives to be appointed by open competition: by 1997 23 per cent had been recruited from outside and 67 per cent appointed by open competition (Cabinet Office, 1998a, Annexes E and F.)

Under Blair NSAs were accepted as 'an integral part of the government machine' (Butcher, 1998, p. 1). While some new agencies were formed, in 1998 the government announced that agency creation was largely complete and that emphasis would switch to performance improvement. However, *Prior Options* was reaffirmed, as was recruitment of chief executives through open competition. In 2000 78 per cent of civil servants were working within Next Steps arrangements (Cabinet Office, November 2000) and agencies numbered 133. Four departments (Crown Prosecution Service, Customs and Excise, Inland Revenue, and Serious Fraud Office) were operating fully on Next Steps lines (Stationery Office, 2000, p. 539).

Evaluating Next Steps

NSA functions vary enormously. They include: inspecting public service vehicles; running conference centres and prisons; providing IT services; issuing driving licences, passports and social security benefits. In 2000 the largest NSA, the Social Security Benefits Agency, employed 69,230 people, and the smallest, the Debt Management Office, just thirty. Box 2.2 outlines their main characteristics.

The impact of Next Steps is debatable. Foster and Plowden (1996, p. 166), for example, speculate whether the FMI 'was at least as instrumental in bringing about change as the subsequent creation of agencies', while Hogwood *et al.* (2000a, pp. 197–8) observe that even before 1988 departments were not entirely monolithic; many 'had distinct organisational units within them'. Nevertheless, according to Massey (1999, p. 20), NSAs represent 'a reform both . . . of structure and account-ability'. Agencies, claim Foster and Plowden (1996, p. 166), 'have begun to transform the operations they are responsible for. There is . . . greater clarity of purpose, commitment to the organization and real changes in management systems.' Departmental roles have also been refocused: they are now responsible for policy-making, ministerial support, legislation, finance and personnel, plus performance-monitoring and target-setting for agencies. Major also required departments to undertake fundamental expenditure reviews and senior management reviews, identifying objectives and better ways of meeting goals, leading to staffing and core budget reductions in most departments.

The relationship between each NSA and its parent department is contained in a framework document which typically has 'five main ingredients': aims and objectives; relations with Parliament, ministers, parent department, other depart-ments and other agencies; financial responsibilities; performance measures; and delegated responsibilities for personnel and training. While precise relationships,

---

Box 2.2   Next Steps Agencies: main characteristics

- They operate within a rigorous framework with clear targets set by Ministers for the task to be done, the results to be achieved and the resources to be provided.
- The day-to-day responsibility for running the organisation is delegated to a chief executive.
- They have the management tools and freedoms they need to do the job.
- [A] framework document is created. This is a published document, tailored to the needs of the agency, and includes the terms and objectives of the agency, its financial and accounting arrangements and its approach to pay and personnel issues. Framework documents are reviewed and revised at least every five years. Each agency publishes an annual report and statement of accounts, . . . which sets out their achievements . . . against the published targets.

Source: Massey (1999, Figure 5)

---

and divisions of responsibility between departments and NSAs, vary quite widely, the underlying principle is a repositioning of central government executive operations 'at arm's length' from departments, allowing 'more managerial autonomy within a quasi-contractual framework' (Foster and Plowden, 1996, p. 154). Managerial freedom for chief executives, in fact, is central to Next Steps. Initially the Treasury feared losing control of departmental budgets. Gradually, however, Treasury controls were relaxed. In 1996 all departments and agencies received delegated responsibility for the pay and grading of all staff except the SCS. Thus while strengthening the culture of management in Whitehall, Next Steps has 'destroyed the near-uniform pay and grading structure' which 'had done much to unify the service' (Lee *et al.*, 1998, p. 245).

From 1998, with the switch of emphasis to performance improvement, activity was increasingly focused on target-setting and benchmarking. Linked to wider emphasis on Whitehall performance, the Next Steps team was given responsibility for the Public Sector Benchmarking Project which encourages public sector organisations to conduct self-assessments of performance against the Business Excellence Model and to share best practice (HM Treasury, 1998; Samuels, 1998).

Despite their rapid development agencies have not been unproblematic. Two aspects are particularly controversial.

1   The *separation of policy-making and administration* which underlies the division of responsibility between departments and agencies raises issues inherent in the policy/administration dichotomy (see p. 3). Because policy and implementation cannot be easily differentiated, the relative responsibility of ministers and chief executives is not always clear, which sometimes leads chief executives 'to feel that departments are intervening too much in their work' (Smith, 1999, p. 196). Moreover, some agencies have policy roles. The UK Passport Agency, for example, 'services policy and management questions' (Stationery Office, 2000, p. 192). Invariably, too, ministers and departments consult agencies before making policy. Indeed, in some cases the very creation of agencies has left too few advisers in core departments (Foster and Plowden, 1996, p. 178). As O'Toole and Chapman (1995, p. 135) observe, 'At the very heart of . . . Next Steps . . . is . . . the dichotomy between policy and administration. . . . That concept has been recognised by most commentators to be bankrupt.'

2   There are also implications for *accountability*. While ministers remain accountable to Parliament for policy, if agencies have a policy role then ministerial accountability is partially eroded. Delegating executive functions to chief executives also erodes ministerial responsibility. While officially Next Steps does not 'change the fundamental principles of parliamentary accountability' (Greer, 1994, p. 82), some observers see ministerial responsibility as 'incompatible with the managerialist philosophy of Next Steps' (O'Toole, 1995, p. 670).

An alternative view sees NSAs strengthening accountability. While ministerial responsibility holds ministers – rather than civil servants – responsible for departmental work, under Next Steps chief executives are accountable for the operational performance of agencies. Targets reinforce this accountability; indeed if targets are not met chief executives' contracts may be terminated or their pay reduced. Chief executives, moreover, answer MPs' letters and written Parliamentary questions about operational matters. (With questions for oral answer, ministers normally reply that they will be dealt with by the relevant chief executive.) Agency officials also appear before Parliamentary select committees. In this sense Next Steps clarifies accountability – making ministers answer for policy and chief executives for operational matters. William Waldegrave, the minister responsible for Next Steps, claimed: 'There is now a clear distinction between "responsibility", which can be delegated, and "accountability", which remains firmly with the minister' (Treasury and Civil Service Select Committee, 1992–3). Agencies also have 'other constituencies of accountability' such as 'customers' and specialist media (Hogwood *et al.*, 2000a). Nevertheless, the potential for blurring accountability undoubtedly remains. The Treasury and Civil Service Select Committee (1990–1), for example, has complained that ministers refer to chief executives questions which they should have answered themselves.

Two cases illustrate 'the ambiguities' which can arise:

1   *Social Security Child Support Agency.* This agency was responsible for assessing, collecting and enforcing child support maintenance from absent fathers. However, it appeared to be more concerned with cost-saving; it failed to meet targets; and it was criticised for delays and alleged insensitivity in handling cases. Although ministers were inevitably drawn into the controversy surrounding the agency, and the Chief Executive, Ros Hepplewhite, a civil servant, complained that ministerially imposed constraints had created difficulties, she, rather than the 'responsible' minister, resigned. 'The change to [agency] status seemed to have undermined the anonymity of a civil servant, and . . . responsibility for a policy shifted away from the minister' (Smith, 1999, p. 197).

2   *HM Prison Service Agency.* This agency provides prison services in England and Wales. Following prison escapes, the Chief Executive, Derek Lewis, was sacked in 1995 by the Home Secretary, Michael Howard. Despite evidence of ministerial interference in operational management, Howard claimed that failure was due to operational factors and that Lewis was, therefore, blameworthy (Barker, 1998; Learmont, 1995).

Significantly, these cases involved politically salient agencies. With many agencies, most of the time 'most MPs are not interested', and 'direct contact with ministers or Parliament is limited' (Hogwood *et al.*, 2000a, pp. 221–2). Nevertheless, such cases illustrate the difficulty of dividing responsibility between ministers (for policy) and chief executives (for administration or service delivery). Policy and operations overlap, ministerially set targets may be unrealistic, and operational failures can arise from departmentally imposed constraints. With Lewis it was also unclear precisely what was policy and what was operational. The Home Secretary – by claiming failures were operational – effectively denied responsibility other than for answering Parliamentary questions. Subsequently Blair attempted to dispel confusion by announcing that Home Office ministers, rather than Prison Service staff, would in future answer parliamentary questions (Butcher, 2000, pp. 74–5).

It must, of course, be acknowledged that ministerial responsibility rests on a fiction as ministers in practice have little or no involvement in most departmental actions. Nevertheless, while Next Steps has changed the constitutional tradition that ministers accept responsibility for *all* the actions of *all* their officials, the result may have been to blur accountability. Today ministers can avoid accepting blame by blaming chief executives for operational failures, even though these may be affected by ministerial intervention and policy.

Market testing

Market testing was introduced following publication of the 1991 White Paper *Competing for Quality* (HM Treasury, 1991). This set out three broad aims for departments: to concentrate on core activities; to introduce more competition and choice into service provision; and to improve service standards. From 1992 all departments and agencies had to set targets for market testing, a process involving competition with outside suppliers. By 1996 £3.6 billion of activities had been reviewed, resulting in gross annual savings of £720 million (Cabinet Office, March 1997, p. 11), a claim suggestive of the view 'that the civil service could be radically downsized without reducing outputs' (Foster and Plowden, 1996, p. 112).

While market testing arguably increases efficiency, preparing tenders and associated work possibly make it more difficult for agencies to focus on service delivery, and the *requirement* to market test agency services contradicted Next Steps principles of managerial autonomy. There are also important structural considerations. While departments can focus more on core activities, they are also more difficult to manage: in addition to relationships with agencies and outside contractors, for example, there are internal contractual arrangements where market testing applies. In 1994 it was announced that decisions to market test would be left to departments and agencies, not imposed from the centre, one interpretation of which was as an 'acknowledgement of the limitations of market testing' (Lee *et al.*, 1998, p. 246).

Market testing also has implications for accountability. Just as agency framework documents define ministerial/chief executive responsibilities, so contractorisation demarcates contractor and client departmental (or agency) roles. While this arguably clarifies accountability, in practice – particularly when applied to NSAs – confusion can occur. Group 4's contract with HM Prison Service Agency, for example, aroused controversy following several highly publicised prison escapes. Should responsibility lie with the Home Secretary (who determined the framework document), with the agency (for negotiating Group 4's contract) or with the contractor (for poor performance)? In such situations accountability disappears into a 'black hole' with no one accepting full responsibility. Accountability through ministers to Parliament is replaced by a system of accountability by contractors (O'Toole, 1995, p. 67).

Nevertheless, these developments have brought significant changes. Service delivery has passed from ministers and departmental civil servants to agency chief executives and contractors. The result has been a shift from line bureaucracy to fragmented patterns of service delivery. The structure of Whitehall has undergone a 'quiet revolution'.

Advisory machinery

Also important is the advisory machinery which assists departmental policy-making, notably advisory non-departmental public bodies which form part of the quango universe (see Chapter 8). These are generally formed at ministerial discretion, are serviced by civil servants, and consist of outside 'experts' and pressure group representatives as well as departmental officials. Their existence is largely a response to two developments: (1) as government work has become more technical, departments have increasingly needed advice from outside experts; (2) departments have recognised the need to consult affected interests, both because these have a 'right' to consultation and because cooperation is often essential to policy implementation. Most departments are keen to establish close relations with client groups – e.g. the Department of Health with the British Medical Association – while 'outside interests' welcome access to departmental policy-making.

Much of the value of advisory bodies lies in enabling departmental officials and client groups to achieve consensus privately before submitting 'agreed policy' to ministers. They rarely 'hit the headlines', mainly because they advise on highly technical areas. However, there are exceptions, for example the Spongiform Encephalopathy Advisory Committee which provided scientific advice to the Ministry of Agriculture, Fisheries and Food (MAFF) during the BSE scare. In many policy fields new forms of advisory machinery have appeared, for example fora (such as the Transport Forum) and reference groups. Examples of the latter are the Reference Groups on National Health Service Frameworks (such as the Mental Health National Service Framework Group established to set up a framework for the development of mental health services in England and including among its members key stakeholders such as patients' organisations and professional groups). These formal channels are often supplemented by informal consultations and negotiations, a result of the fact that in Britain most influential groups have traditionally concentrated pressure upon departmental civil servants (Eckstein, 1960), and such officials play a crucial policy-making role. Widely known as 'clientelism', negotiation and consultation between departments and groups is a marked feature of British central administration and crucially important in policy formulation.

Blair further extended advisory machinery by developing 'taskforces' consisting of civil servants as well as outside experts (see Chapter 4), together with initiatives such as the People's Panel, a 5,000-strong nationally representative group. This supplements views represented through devices such as local citizens' juries, community fora and focus groups. Today departmental policy-making involves 'developing new relationships' within and 'between Whitehall, the devolved administrations, local government and the voluntary and private sectors; consulting outside experts, those who implement policy and those affected by it' (Prime Minister and Minister for the Cabinet Office, 1999, pp. 16, 25).

The departmental pattern

While efficient work allocation is important in all organisations, in Whitehall it is especially so. Ministerial responsibility (see pp. 228–32) requires a minister to be answerable for every aspect of government work; consequently, any confusion about work distribution between departments blurs ministerial responsibility. Partly because of this, ultimate decisions about the number and jurisdiction of departments – the departmental pattern – rest with the Prime Minister. Nevertheless the departmental pattern tends to reflect three main influences: (1) the role of the state; (2) political factors; (3) administrative considerations.

Role of the state

The mid-nineteenth-century state had a minimalist role and the departmental pattern reflected this. In 1851, for example, the main departments were: the Treasury, Customs and Excise, Inland Revenue, Board of Trade, Post Office, Home Office, Irish Office, Lord Chancellor's Office, Privy Council Office, Admiralty, War Office Ordnance Board, Foreign Office and Colonial Office. By 1951 social and economic intervention, plus technological and industrial developments, had transformed the departmental pattern. While some of the 1851 departments had disappeared, nineteen 'new' ones had been added, including: Defence, Civil Aviation, Labour, Transport, Health, National Insurance, Education, and Fuel and Power.

After 1951, new governmental concerns were reflected in the departmental pattern, for example decline of empire (the Colonial and Commonwealth Relations Offices merged with the Foreign Office), the environment (creation of the Department of the Environment), and national minorities (creation of the Welsh and Northern Ireland Offices). Nevertheless, the gradualness of Britain's historical development has sustained considerable continuity. Several current departments (e.g. Home Office, Treasury), for example, predate modern government, while others (e.g. Education) originated in Victorian times.

Political factors

The departmental pattern reflects political considerations. A new department, for example, may reflect policy changes (e.g. the Northern Ireland Office, created in 1972, after 'direct rule' was introduced); new problems (e.g. the Energy Department, created in 1974, following fuel crises); reassurance that 'something is being done' about pressing issues (re-creation of the Department of Health, 1988); or an attempt to appeal to important electoral or client groups (e.g. the Welsh Office, created in 1964). Short-term political factors (e.g. the need to accommodate a particular politician) often take precedence over administrative considerations. Because of such influences, the departmental pattern may become untidy, but most prime ministers apparently feel that political image is more important than administrative considerations. Consequently, while long-overdue administrative reforms might be ignored, political changes may produce sudden and frequent alterations to the departmental pattern.

Administrative considerations

The departmental pattern has developed largely haphazardly. Generally, new functions have been allocated either to existing departments or, where existing departments were overloaded or political considerations dictated otherwise, to newly created ones. However, the Haldane Report (1918) identified two main principles for allocating functions between departments: 'distribution according to the persons or classes to be dealt with, and distribution according to the services to be performed'. The former, the clientele principle, was rejected. Although clientele-based agencies are not unknown, as a principle for allocating government functions the outcome would be massive duplication (e.g. different hospitals for students, for the elderly and for the unemployed), an arrangement Haldane described as 'Lilliputian administration'.

The alternative, Haldane recommended, was 'distribution according to . . . services . . . performed' for the whole community. Usually known as the 'functional' principle, this, Haldane argued, would produce 'the minimum amount of confusion and overlapping'. Ten services were identified, each of which could be placed 'under separate administration': finance, national defence, external affairs, research and information, production, employment, supplies, education, health and justice.

Haldane's recommendations can be questioned on three main grounds.

1   Haldane ignored other principles such as *purpose*, *process* and *area* (Gulick, 1937; Hogwood, 1992). The omission of *area* is surprising, for departments with territorial responsibilities existed in Haldane's time (e.g. the Irish and India Offices) as well as today (e.g. the Scotland Office). Nevertheless, the areal principle is unsuitable for allocating all central functions, for some (e.g. defence, economic affairs) have national dimensions not easily divisible by area.

2   The report can be criticised for oversimplification. Haldane acknowledged that the functional/clientele distinction is not always clear: a department administering the 'function' of education, for example, serves a specific clientele (students). Equally, research and information, and supplies, from Haldane's list, could both be regarded as processes.

3   The functional principle does not always indicate clearly 'how policy responsibilities are in fact allocated' (Hogwood, 1992, p. 166). Thus aviation, just emerging in Haldane's day, could be placed with research and information, with production or even with defence.

Giant departments

While never consciously implemented, Haldane's functional principle has, nevertheless, provided the main basis for departmental arrangements, and in 1970 was reaffirmed in the White Paper *Reorganisation of Central Government* (Prime Minister and Minister for the Civil Service, 1970). This endorsed (paras 8 and 11) 'the functional principle as the basis for the allocation of responsibilities', an approach which foreshadowed creation of two 'giant' departments, Trade and Industry (DTI) and the Environment (DoE). A major objective was to try and counteract the departmentalism which was believed to have previously characterised policy-making (Smith, 1999, p. 166).

Merging departments with related functions is not new. The process started in the 1950s, and gathered pace in the 1960s when three major mergers occurred (creating the Department of Health and Social Security, the Foreign and Commonwealth Office, and the Ministry of Defence). Although 'giant' departments were supposedly unitary departments in their own right, in practice they sometimes failed to develop cohesion (Painter, 1980, p. 142). They were, moreover, difficult to manage. The DoE had nine ministers at one stage and extensive formal machinery was often necessary for internal coordination.

From the mid-1970s the tendency towards 'giantism' was reversed, allowing departments to 'correspond more closely to the major public expenditure functions' (Hogwood, 1992, p. 175). The DTI was broken up in the 1970s into four separate departments (Energy, Trade, Industry, Prices and Consumer Protection) and Transport detached from the DoE. In 1988 the DHSS split into two separate departments: Social Security and Health. However, this trend has not been altogether consistent. In 1983 Trade and Industry merged into a Department of Trade and Industry. In 1997 Blair created a 'giant' Department of the Environment, Transport and the Regions, and merged the Education and Employment departments into a new Department for Education and Employment.

The contemporary departmental pattern

The departmental pattern changes quite frequently, and given the scale, complexity and political environment of contemporary public administration, searching for one universal principle for allocating functions is doomed to failure. Nevertheless, several of Haldane's functions are recognisable today. Finance (Treasury), defence (Ministry of Defence), external affairs (Foreign and Commonwealth Office), employment/education (Department for Education and Employment) and health (Department of Health) were all main functions of particular departments in 2000. While Haldane foreshadowed later developments quite well – reflecting a general preference for the fewest possible combinations of functionally coherent departments – political and administrative exigencies have continued to intrude.

The dynamics of departmental work

Departments are not simply responsible for administration, they also perform a policy-making role. Smith *et al.* (1995, pp. 38, 40) observe, 'Except on particular issues of interest to the Prime Minister, or of central strategic policy, or a high level of controversy, the majority of policy making occurs within departments.'

Constitutionally, policy-making is a ministerial preserve. In reality the position is *much* more complex. Departments are not monolithic: they contain a myriad personnel hierarchies, organisational units, client groups, advisory bodies and so forth, each with its own distinctive perspectives and influence. One important division lies between ministers and civil servants (see Chapter 4) and debate exists about the relative influence of these two groups. Most policy decisions, however, do not involve ministers, and civil servants may attempt to shape decisions to serve their own perceived interests. Dunleavy (1989), for example, using a bureau-shaping model, argues that bureaucrats try to insulate their departments or sections from adverse spending restrictions in their policy area. Differences, however, can appear between civil servants: for example, between headquarters and field offices, or between specialist and generalists.

Departments, moreover, are dynamic, living organisms: officials have their own perspectives, values and experiences, all of which can influence decisions. Smith *et al.* (2000) show how different cultures are found both between and within departments and, since Next Steps, 'distinct cultures [even] within agencies'. Consequently, most departments exhibit enormous heterogeneity leading to differences over resources, structure, and policy, and the creation of internal relationships which are highly political and infinitely variable. Differences within departments sometimes relate to the departmental pattern. If a department's scope is too wide, divisions may develop (for instance between agricultural and food 'interests' in MAFF during the BSE crisis); if it is too narrow, the department may be 'captured' by a client group (MAFF by the National Farmers' Union is a possible example). Again, departmental size may affect the balance of ministerial/civil service influence: for example, transport was detached from the DoE in 1976 partly owing to the belief that transport policy was insufficiently under ministerial control.

Differences may also occur between advisory committees, between departmental client groups and between policy communities and networks (see Chapter 1). Rhodes (1986) depicts a spectrum ranging from highly integrated and stable policy communities to loosely integrated issue networks. The latter take various forms: professional networks, intergovernmental networks, producer networks and issue networks. James (1997, p. 12) gives the example of 'the policy community surrounding the Home Office' which includes prison governors, police, local authorities, civil liberties groups, etc.; and the 'much narrower circle of contacts' including the parole board, prison governors and prison reform groups comprising the issue network relating to the parole system.

Networks differ widely in form, influence and membership (Marsh and Rhodes, 1992). Relationships between members also vary considerably. Many networks are informal with interests crossing organisational boundaries, which leads to conflict between and within departments. Others have overlapping membership, which helps develop shared values across different issue areas. Again, networks are rarely stable – 'the majority . . . are temporary, flexible and fast moving' (Smith *et al.*, 2000, p. 159). Consequently, 'departmental' policy-making is conducted through a complex and often bewildering process, much of which is informal and unrelated to organisational structures.

Just as sections within departments develop distinctive viewpoints, so might departments themselves. Theakston (1995, p. 18) notes the importance of '"departmental views" which shape the advice ministers receive'. The Treasury, for example, during much of the late twentieth century, was identified with negative views about government spending (Smith *et al.*, 1995, p. 52). The 'departmental view', often developed over time, may close off competing policies and become a source of interdepartmental conflict. Often this results in 'departmentalitis', the condition whereby civil servants and ministers perceive policy purely from their department's perspective, which prevents the development of coherent and collective government-wide policies. Civil servants may try to persuade ministers to adopt the 'departmental view' and, if they fail, pursue it anyway or impose it on successors. Foster and Plowden (1996, p. 174) observe, 'Departments . . . may have their own agenda (of little direct interest to ministers) or . . . [pursue] long-term objectives (or prejudices) independent of ministers.'

Inevitably, departments compete with one another. Spending departments compete with one another, as well as with the Treasury, for finance. Departments also fight over 'territory' (see Box 2.3). Sometimes territorial battles last for years. The Civil Service Department, established in 1968, was never popular with the Treasury. In 1981, four governments later, it was abolished. Many of its functions returned to the Treasury, with others following in 1987. The victory was short-lived, however, for a new Office of Public Service (OPS) subsequently took responsibility for civil service management. In 1999, however, the OPS was itself integrated with the Cabinet Office following a further review. New departments often experience difficulty establishing themselves. The Department of Economic Affairs, created in 1964, for example, survived only five years. Its minister explained: 'Our success meant a tremendous threat to half a dozen old-established departments' (Brown, 1972, p. 112).

Departments sometimes disagree over policy. This may sometimes become apparent through 'leaks' to MPs, pressure groups, journalists, etc. Smith (1999, p. 34) reveals how the Heritage Ministry leaked information that the Treasury was attempting to replace government spending with lottery money to force the Treasury

---

Box 2.3 Whitehall pair fight to head job agency

Two Whitehall civil servants are at loggerheads over who will take charge of the new super-agency to cover job centres and benefits.

Rachel Lomax, Permanent Secretary at the Department of Social Security, is fighting hard to ensure that the new Working Age agency that will merge 400 benefits offices with 1,000 job centres is part of her empire.

Sir Michael Bichard, her counterpart at the Department for Education and Employment, is equally determined that he will be responsible for the new agency with its 90,000 civil servants.

The stakes are high as the loser will forfeit a substantial part of his or her territory. Ms Lomax, 55, risks losing more than 60,000 benefit staff to her rival, while Sir Michael, 53, would have to hand over more than 30,000 employment staff. 'There hasn't been such a Whitehall battle for years', one official said.

Tony Blair announced the merger last March but did not say which minister would take charge.

Source: Adapted from *The Times*, 4 September 2000

---

into denying any such intention. One very public conflict, which led to ministerial resignations, was the Westland affair (Jordan and Richardson, 1987, p. 166). Another was the arms to Iraq affair, where the MOD, FCO and DTI had competing perspectives (Scott Report, 1996). Usually, however, departments recognise mutual interest in not publicising disagreement. One former mandarin also suggests that safeguards exist which prevent departmental philosophies hardening into conflict: 'frequent staff changes within and between departments, the need for departments to co-operate, and Whitehall's collegiate approach to decision making' (Chapman, 1988, pp. 286–90). Also, departments may ally on one issue, but disagree or remain neutral on others. Frequent ministerial turnover may also make ministers less likely to adopt the 'departmental view' (Alderman, 1995).

Conclusion

'It is important to take departments seriously. They are where concentrations of political and bureaucratic resources are located. . . . Both ministers and prime ministers are highly dependent on departments' (Smith *et al.*, 2000, p. 163). At the same time departments vary considerably, they have different cultures and policy perspectives, both of which may change over time. Nor does the Whitehall structure remain static: Next Steps, particularly, has introduced radical changes into it. Central government has fragmented around a distinction between policy-making and execution which both confronts the policy/administration dichotomy and increasingly invites the concept of governance (see Chapter 1) as the most effective way of viewing the work of central government.

This chapter, however, has examined only part of Whitehall. Despite their crucial importance, departmental influences are not always decisive. Indeed, because many programmes involve several departments, and 'departmentalitis' may impede coherent policy development, various supra-departmental bodies exist within Whitehall which not only resolve departmental disputes but forge a collective view. These are examined in the following chapter.

Further reading

All major departments have web sites accessible through www.open.gov.uk. The *Civil Service Yearbook*, published annually, provides information about personnel and internal structures within departments. However, there are relatively few detailed up-to-date studies of internal structures and processes of government departments. A three-volume historical survey by Clifford *et al.* (1997) is complemented by a chapter from the same authors (Maclean *et al.*, 2000) in Rhodes (2000a). Hennessy's highly readable, if now dated, study *Whitehall* (1990) contains much interesting information. Smith *et al.* (1995) examine departmental roles in the policy process and give a summary of departmental studies existing at that time. This has now been superseded by analysis of the role of departments within the core executive by Smith (1999). Smith *et al.* (2000) bring the role of departments up to date in an essay informed by the Economic and Social Research Council (ESRC) Whitehall study.

There is a considerable literature on Next Steps. Greer (1994) and O'Toole and Jordan (1995) both offer useful analyses. Hogwood *et al.* (2000a) examine agencies and accountability, while chapters in Foster and Plowden (1996) offer insights into department/agency relationships. Butcher (2000) gives an up-to-date summary of developments affecting both Next Steps and market testing. Jordan (1994) contains a contemporary discussion of the Haldane principles plus an analysis of Next Steps.

The core executive

Introduction

This chapter examines coordination within Whitehall, an important subject given the tendency towards departmentalism and agencification discussed in Chapter 2. It is also of crucial importance given the emphasis upon the voguish concept *joined-up government* (see p. 15), often now deployed in place of coordination. Its significance within contemporary central government is emphasised by Rhodes (2000c, p. 157), who cites one former-mandarin's concern that Whitehall should 'not reach the point where individual Departments and their Agencies become simply different unconnected elements . . . *with no real working mechanisms for policy coordination*' (Rhodes's emphasis).

Coordination is fundamental to public administration; without it, policy-making and administration would be conducted without reference to different governmental components or overall goals. In British central government, however, it is especially important. Each minister has *individual responsibility* for all aspects of departmental work. Consequently, without effective coordination within departments, ministers may have to defend incompatible actions. *Collective responsibility* also requires consistency between departments, while equity demands coordination in order to facilitate equitable treatment of clients by different parts of government.

Davis (1997, p. 133) identifies three distinct coordination tasks confronting executives:

- '*political* – the need for government to appear in control with common objectives and agreed procedures . . .
- *policy* – the need to achieve objectives, and to prevent contradictory policies . . .
- *administrative* – . . . working efficiently and effectively towards goals set by cabinet'.

Coordination also concerns both conflict *avoidance* and *resolution*, and has both *preventive* and *strategic aspects*. Preventive coordination primarily involves preventing (or resolving) conflict; strategic coordination is more concerned with relating particular policies to overall goals.

According to Rhodes (1995, p. 12) coordination within central government occurs mainly within '*the core executive*'. This term describes

> organisations and procedures which coordinate central government policies, and act as final arbiters of conflict between different parts of the government machine. . . . [t]he 'core executive' . . . cover[s] the complex web of institutions, networks and practices surrounding the prime minister, cabinet, cabinet committees and their official counterparts, less formalised ministerial 'clubs', bilateral negotiations and inter-departmental committees. It also includes coordinating departments, chiefly the Cabinet Office, Treasury, the Foreign Office, the law officers, and security and intelligence services.

Despite this extensive definition, the core executive's precise boundaries are not entirely clear; indeed, Rhodes himself suggests (ibid., p. 26) that 'there is no one executive but multiple executives'. Moreover, not all observers accept his definition – Smith (1999, p. 5), for example, includes government departments; coordination within these, therefore, requires discussion.

Coordination within departments

While much intra-departmental coordination occurs informally (e.g. by email, telephone), departments also need formal mechanisms. Normally at least three such mechanisms are found:

- common service divisions (e.g. finance) with horizontal links throughout the department;
- hierarchic structure enforcing common rules and guidelines;
- the functional principle of work allocation (see p. 40): applied widely inside departments, this locates similar functions within related sections.

Despite these features intra-departmental coordination is often problematic and from the 1960s several initiatives occurred designed to bring improvements. These included: *planning units*, responsible for coordinating departmental policy, and *programme analysis and review* (PAR), established in 1970 to provide regular review and coordination of departmental programmes. These developments, however, had limited impact. Most planning units were as much concerned with short-term problems as long-term policy coordination, while in 1979 PAR was wound up.

After 1979 further developments such as agencification and contracting affected intra-departmental coordination. Rhodes (2000d, p. 5) explains how departmental policy networks 'became broader, incorporating the private and voluntary sectors', and questions (1995, p. 33) whether departments can now 'develop a strategic management ability to steer their agencies'. Intra-departmental coordination is now a function which ministers and civil servants share with other actors. While some officials play a particular important role – for example, the Principal Establishments Officer (or similar) in each department usually has some responsibility for ensuring cross-departmental connectedness – coordination today is more about building networks and negotiation, and requires increasing focus on *joined-up government*.

Coordination between departments

Coordination *between* departments generally poses greater problems than coordination *within* them: there are more functions and more personnel, and coordinated departments are often strongly placed to challenge 'unsympathetic' coordinators. Every department, moreover, has its own distinct culture (Smith *et al.*, 2000, p. 148). Also, because no department is officially 'superior' to any other, interdepartmental coordination is largely conducted through horizontal channels between theoretically equal departments. At a formal level coordination can be facilitated where different departments utilise common machinery (e.g. government offices for the regions; see p. 28). Obviously, however, such alignments are not always possible.

Much Whitehall coordination occurs in 'bilateral discussions between departments, at both official and ministerial level' (James, 1999, pp. 49–56). This involves both *administrative coordination* (e.g. a lead department clearing lines with other departments) and *policy coordination*. Since much policy crosses departmental boundaries, and departments often rely on each other for expertise, interdepartmental coordination is crucial for efficient government. Several characteristics, James suggests, apply to such discussions including: (1) settling issues at the lowest level; and (2) sensitivity to the importance of issues necessitating reference upwards to higher officials or ministers.

Much, perhaps most, interdepartmental coordination is resolved informally (e.g. by letter or telephone). In fact, several aspects of British central administration facilitate informal coordination. Traditionally senior civil servants have come from similar social backgrounds, have shared common grading systems, and still represent 'a rather closed society with its own character, thought processes and professional values'. Ministers, similarly, have usually worked together for many years in political circles and share similar political attitudes. Consequently, negotiations often tend towards 'compromise and flexibility' (ibid., p. 26).

Strauss *et al.*s' (1971) negotiated order model is helpful here. Coordination within and between groups involves multiple linkages. Governed by formal rules, as well as by informal understandings, each linkage is uniquely built around individual perceptions and interests. As circumstances change, actors bargain and negotiate. Consequently, coordination within large organisations occurs, not between monolithic blocs, but through ever-changing patterns of negotiation and compromise at many levels and contact points. Applied to Whitehall, this model emphasises diffusion of power rather than the master/subordinate relationships often portrayed in organisation charts. As Smith *et al.* (1995, p. 59) observe, relationships between departments need to be seen in terms of power-dependence 'rather than as a zero-sum game'.

In some fields networks are significant. James (1999, p. 50) exemplifies the local government finance 'network of officials . . . co-ordinated by the Department of the Environment, Transport and the Regions but involving all the other departments whose work local government funds'. When a department initiates a proposal 'the existing network will be used to sound out reactions'. If problems occur, 'a new network will spring up impromptu across departments, initially by telephone, to co-ordinate the response'. Such networks may operate informally, offering flexible means of negotiation across departmental boundaries.

While informal coordination is important, central administration's size and complexity – and inability sometimes to reach agreement informally – necessitate formal interdepartmental coordinating mechanisms. Particularly important are *interdepartmental committees*. Some of these, being serviced by the Cabinet Office, are technically Cabinet committees although they usually contain only civil servants. Numbers of interdepartmental committees fluctuate with circumstances. Some are *ad hoc*. Others are permanent, for example the weekly meeting of permanent secretaries and the 'official' committees which 'shadow' ministerial Cabinet committees. Such committees usually meet prior to ministerial committees, which led Crossman (1975, p. 198) to claim that they 'pre-cook[ed]' ministerial decisions. However, James (1999, pp. 51–2) observes, 'the world has moved on . . . since Crossman'. Today, with emails and faxes these committees often do not meet formally, and when they do they usually filter the last stages of departmental consultation, providing ministers with clear facts and choices. Some, however, do wield considerable influence. The Scott Report (1996) reveals how an interdepartmental committee – representing the Foreign Office, Trade and Industry, and the Ministry of Defence – had responsibility for reviewing arms export licences. Many decisions were made without reference to ministers, partly in order to accelerate decision-making, despite ministerial instructions to the contrary,

James (1999, p. 49) suggests that much Whitehall decision-making is dominated by civil servants and characterised by 'give and take', partly because disagreement might mean issues have to be passed to higher levels where officials have less autonomy: to ministers, and to machinery surrounding the Prime Minister and Cabinet where the most complex, politically sensitive, and irreconcilable differences are resolved.

Coordinating ministers

Where major interdepartmental coordination is required, special coordinating ministers are sometimes appointed. In 1936, for example, a Minister for the Coordination of Defence was appointed to integrate the service ministries. Churchill experimented along similar lines in 1951, appointing coordinating ministers (or 'overlords') to coordinate related departments (e.g. Food and Agriculture). These arrangements, however, effectively ceased in 1953, mainly because they were felt to blur accountability. Consequently, subsequent prime ministers have used coordinating ministers more sparingly. Unlike 'overlords', such ministers have rarely had powers of direction, and have usually been appointed:

- to coordinate policies or activities across several departments: for example, Baroness Jay, Minister for Women in Blair's first government, was responsible for presenting women's issues across government, sitting on relevant Cabinet committees and chairing the Cabinet Sub-Committee on Women's Issues (Cabinet Office, November 1999, p. 34);
- to chair Cabinet committees covering several departments' work.

In the 1990s, however, coordinating ministers enjoyed a resurgence. David Hunt, Chancellor of the Duchy of Lancaster, served as coordinating minister within the Cabinet Office under Major. Subsequently, in 1995, Major appointed Michael Heseltine as Deputy Prime Minister. Whereas previous deputy prime ministers usually only substituted for the Prime Minister in the Cabinet or the House Commons, Heseltine could attend any Cabinet committee, sat on fourteen Cabinet committees, and chaired more important Cabinet committees than the Prime Minister (including a committee on coordination and presentation which met daily). He also had responsibility for the Office of Public Service and specific policy areas, and was powerfully placed 'to coordinate government policy and oversee its presentation' (Burch and Holliday, 1996, p. 105). However, Blair abandoned this arrangement in his first government. His Deputy, John Prescott, headed a large, new Department of Transport, Environment and the Regions and had few coordination responsibilities. These mainly fell to Peter Mandelson, Minister without Portfolio. Although not a Cabinet minister, he sat on all important committees and had key responsibilities for policy coordination and presentation. In 1998, however, this arrangement ceased and policy coordination responsibility was given to a new Minister for the Cabinet Office.

Coordinating departments

Theoretically, coordinating departments have effective capability, there usually being clearly defined divisions of responsibility between the coordinating and coordinated departments. However, most coordinating departments have been barely more effective than 'overlords', often being dependent upon the coordinated departments to implement decisions. The MOD, for example, which between 1947 and 1964 coordinated aspects of the service departments, often failed to develop coherent policies (Clarke, 1975, pp. 70, 75). Significantly, in this case, the coordinating and coordinated departments were subsequently amalgamated, forming an integrated MOD which still survives.

Formal coordination is also facilitated by common service organisations and departments with 'horizontal' linkages across Whitehall. These, Rhodes (1995, p. 12) suggests, include the Cabinet Office, Treasury, FCO, the law offices, and security and intelligence services. Some of these are discussed below. Of others the law offices provide legal advice throughout Whitehall, while the security and intelligence services – which include MI5 (security services) and MI6 (secret intelligence service) – process security and intelligence information. The FCO's coordinating role stems from its 'monopoly of dealing with "abroad"' (Hennessy, 1990, p. 405). It operates within 'the overseas policy network'; and the European policy 'network' which also includes the Cabinet Office European Secretariat which coordinates EU policy across Whitehall (see Chapter 10).

The *Office of Public Service* (previously Office of Public Service and Science), established by Major, also performed coordinating functions. Growing out of the earlier Civil Service Department and Management and Personnel Office, the OPS was responsible for civil service policy and management functions, public service reform, Next Steps and civil service management and efficiency. It provided an important vehicle for Heseltine's coordinating role as Deputy Prime Minister, and for Mandelson early in Blair's first government. However, it disappeared with the Cabinet Office reforms of the late 1990s (see p. 62).

Arguably the most important coordinating department is the *Treasury* which is both a financial and an economic department. Smith (2000, p. 40) explains, 'The Treasury controls and plans the expenditure of all departments, and before recent reforms it controlled the manpower, pay and gradings of all civil servants.' Financial responsibilities include vetting departmental estimates before presentation to Parliament and ensuring that departments spend to agreed policies. This inevitably involves policy coordination as departments initiating new policies (requiring expenditure) must first bargain with the Treasury. Indeed, as many departments also provide funds for local authorities and other public bodies, the Treasury's coordinating capability extends to the wider public sector.

To perform these functions the Treasury has extensively 'colonised' Whitehall. It employs expenditure controllers who work with principal finance officers in departments examining estimates and checking expenditure. A Treasury minister usually sits on all cabinet committees, and a Treasury official on shadowing inter-departmental committees. Also, many senior officials in other departments are former Treasury civil servants. While Treasury relationships with other departments are characterised by interdependence, 'from its central position . . . [it] is uniquely placed to see "the bigger picture" . . . and make connections between policy issues and expenditure items which have arisen separately in different programmes' (Thain and Wright, 1995, p. 104).

Inevitably, Treasury influence varies with circumstances. Its coordinating role has probably diminished since the interwar years when the Cabinet Office and Prime Minister's Office were less developed. Until 1968, moreover, its permanent secretary was 'head of the Home Civil Service', a title regained in 1981 and held jointly with the Cabinet secretary but since 1983 held by the latter alone. Initiatives like Next Steps have also tended to reduce Treasury control over civil service manpower and pay.

Nevertheless the Treasury still occupies a central coordinating role. At the time of writing this is further enhanced by the political influence of the Chancellor, Gordon Brown, who chairs key Cabinet economic committees including the Committee on Public Service and Public Spending (PSX) which plans spending over a three-year period. Departments are also now required to sign Public Service Agreements which link departmental spending increases to VFM and policy improvements monitored by PSX. Consequently, the Treasury now plays an unprecedented 'role in shaping departmental spending plans and priorities' (Holliday, 2000, p. 97).

The Cabinet

The core executive includes 'the complex web of institutions, networks and practices surrounding the prime minister, cabinet, [and] cabinet committees'. In 1867 Bagehot (1963, pp. 6–9) wrote that Britain enjoyed 'Cabinet government'. Developments since then have greatly increased the Cabinet's significance. Modern Cabinets normally consist of leading members of the majority party and, so long as party discipline is maintained, they can control both the legislative and executive branches of government.

Cabinet functions

The Cabinet is conventionally seen 'as the formal locus of power' (Burch and Holliday, 1996, p. 42). While technically the Cabinet determines its own functions, administrative and political demands necessitate performance of three main tasks:

1 Policy-making

Officially, 'the Cabinet . . . is the ultimate arbiter of all Government policy' (www. cabinet-office.gov.uk). Containing ministers from all main departments, it allows collegial decision-making reflective of the diversity of departmental interests. However, meeting for only a few hours per week, it cannot determine all policies. Where several departments are involved, or conflict exists, decisions may be taken by interdepartmental or Cabinet committees. Urgent decisions may be taken by the Prime Minister alone or in consultation with key ministers, or by an inner or partial Cabinet (see below). Even when Cabinet discussion does occur, however, decisions often merely ratify conclusions reached elsewhere. The main participants in discussions, for example, are frequently departmental ministers who speak to civil service-prepared briefs.

Several developments illustrate the Cabinet's decline as a policy-making body. For example, Cabinet meetings fell from around sixty in 1974 (and a post-war record of 108 in 1952) to about forty per annum in the mid-1990s (Burch and Holliday, 1996, p. 44). In the thirty years to the mid-1980s papers submitted to Cabinet for decision also fell by around 80 per cent. Today it receives almost none (James, 1999, p. 84). Meetings have also decreased in length. Blair's cabinets in 1997 'rarely lasted for more than an hour', and much discussion was about policy presentation. Also, Blair reportedly does not use formal agendas (Hennessy, *The Times*, 25 September 2000).

Despite these limitations the Cabinet does still have a policy-making role. Although the Cabinet agenda is drawn up by the Cabinet Secretary in consultation with the Prime Minister, it 'includes regular items on Parliamentary, Current Events (encompassing both Home and European Affairs) and Foreign Affairs' (www.cabinet-office.gov.uk/cabsec/2000/guide/brief.htm). During the budget process general economic strategy is discussed, although final details are only revealed to Cabinet shortly before presentation to Parliament when it is 'too late to make changes' (Burch and Holliday, 1996, p. 125).

The Cabinet also takes decisions not resolved at lower levels, and provides a court of appeal in cases of ministerial disagreement. Consequently, most important issues come before the Cabinet, at some point. For example, decisions concerning all, or nearly all, departments – such as a public expenditure 'package' – usually go direct to the Cabinet, as do those too difficult to be resolved elsewhere. Usually departmental ministers, committee chairs or the Prime Minister decide which issues enter this category, although some come before the Cabinet as urgent or important items. For example, an 'emergency Cabinet meeting' was summoned following the 1982 Falklands invasion. Nevertheless, prime ministers have sometimes prevented important issues from reaching the Cabinet. James (1999, p. 81) suggests Thatcher 'often' kept 'major issues . . . away from it'. During the Westland affair, for example, Thatcher reportedly 'refused to allow a discussion' requested by her Defence Secretary (Hennessy, 1986a, p. 108).

The Cabinet's policy-making role, of course, varies with circumstances and personalities. Thatcher, for example, transferred much business to informal groups outside the formal system. Major's cabinets were more 'relaxed . . . [and] discussed the great issues of the day', although committees still made many key decisions

(James, 1999, pp. 59–61, 85). Roles also change over time. Nevertheless, the Cabinet retains four major functions:

> It provides ministers with information. It decides issues which have proved impossible to settle at a lower level. . . . It takes final (and often no more than ratifying) decisions on some major policy issues. . . . It is a forum for discussion of difficult political matters, and a sounding board for the leadership group.
>
> (Burch and Holliday, 1996, p. 45)

These functions are not performed in isolation. The Cabinet responds to issues emanating not only from within central government, but also from the wider political system. This might include other parts of the administrative system, Parliament, pressure groups, parties (especially the 'governing party'), the media, foreign governments, the EU and international agencies. The Cabinet is also influenced by events, election commitments, opinion polls and public opinion.

2 Administrative control

The Cabinet is ultimately responsible for administrative efficiency. Although most policy decisions are implemented by departments, occasionally the Cabinet's role is more positive. It would, for example, discuss a serious breakdown in administration. In such circumstances the Cabinet may decide to authorise a Cabinet committee to maintain supervision or establish new procedures. In recent years concern with managerial efficiency has heightened the significance of 'administrative' issues. For example, the 1988 Next Steps report was approved, initially by a Cabinet committee, and then formally by the Cabinet (Burch and Holliday, 1996, p. 229).

3 Coordination

'Formally, the core executive is coordinated by the cabinet' (Smith, 1999, p. 143). Composed of ministerial heads of all major departments, its primacy in policy determination, and as a court of appeal, gives it final responsibility for both preventive and strategic policy coordination. It also has an important role in administrative coordination. Nevertheless, the limited time devoted to cabinet meetings suggests that coordination has now 'shifted elsewhere' (Smith *et al.*, 1995, p. 56).

Cabinet composition and size

Although normally all Cabinet members are leading politicians of the same party, the Cabinet's composition reflects diversity. Cabinet ministers are usually ambitious politicians drawn from different party factions. Most, moreover, are departmental ministers whose perspectives invariably reflect departmental attitudes. Because of its coordinating role, all major departments – and any coordinating ministers – usually have representation. Indeed, while Cabinet composition is theoretically a matter of prime ministerial discretion, in practice administrative and political factors greatly restrict choice. Departments and their client groups, for example, are likely to feel loss of influence without Cabinet representation. Patronage and party considerations also intrude: prime ministers use Cabinet posts to reward supporters, 'neutralise' rivals, and represent different viewpoints.

Surprisingly, perhaps, the Cabinet was barely larger in 2000 (twenty-two) than in 1900 (nineteen). Other than in wartime – when small 'war cabinets' were formed – most twentieth-century Cabinets have contained about twenty members. Since the war, for example, size has fluctuated between sixteen and twenty-four. Prime ministers have balanced the need for Cabinets large enough to allow effective coordination, and adequate patronage, with the need to keep them below the level – around twenty – beyond which they become too unwieldy for effective decision-making.

Even with Cabinets of around twenty, *inner Cabinets* may exist. Sometimes, these are 'properly established and recognised, with some degree of authority for taking decisions on behalf of other ministers . . . Only two, possibly three, inner Cabinets' (James, 1999, pp. 133–5) have existed since the war. Between 1968 and 1970, for example, Wilson established a Cabinet 'Parliamentary Committee' comprising senior ministers and serviced by the Cabinet Secretariat. Sometimes, however, 'inner Cabinet' denotes merely an informal grouping of prime ministerial friends or Cabinet confidants which, James suggests, should more accurately be termed an 'inner circle'.

Some writers also refer to '*partial Cabinets*'. Here 'Ministers who constitute part only of the Cabinet . . . act for a time as if they were the Cabinet . . . and . . . take decisions without prior consultation with the Cabinet'. Gordon Walker (1972, pp. 87–90) suggests partial Cabinets decided to manufacture the atom bomb in Attlee's government, and drafted plans to invade Suez in 1956. Similar arrangements existed during the Falklands dispute when an inner group of Cabinet ministers, chosen by the Prime Minister, was entrusted with day-to-day handling of the crisis (Seymour-Ure, 1984). By utilising inner and partial Cabinets prime ministers are able to discuss issues more thoroughly, swiftly and urgently than would otherwise be possible.

Cabinet committees

Technically, these comprise all committees serviced by the Cabinet Office, but as composition varies widely – and numbers may be considerable – this definition has little value. Some committees, for example, consist of ministers, others of civil servants, and others still of both; some are permanent and others temporary or *ad hoc*. Again, the distinction between interdepartmental committees and Cabinet committees is not always clear.

Despite occasional prior use of committees, a Cabinet committee *system* did not come into being until the First World War. Under war pressures, work was delegated to numerous newly created Cabinet committees. Between the wars these were largely dismantled. However, similar arrangements were reintroduced during the Second World War, after which subsequent governments retained them as a permanent feature.

Box 3.1 The Blair Cabinet (February 2001)

Prime Minister, First Lord of the Treasury and Minister for the Civil Service	*The Rt Hon. Tony Blair MP*
Deputy Prime Minister and Secretary of State for Environment, Transport and Regions	*The Rt Hon. John Prescott MP*
Chancellor of the Exchequer	*The Rt Hon. Gordon Brown MP*
Secretary of State for Foreign and Commonwealth Affairs	*The Rt Hon. Robin Cook MP*
Lord Chancellor	*The Rt Hon. The Lord Irvine of Lairg*
Secretary of State for the Home Department	*The Rt Hon. Jack Straw MP*
Secretary of State for Education and Employment	*The Rt Hon. David Blunkett MP*
President of the Council and Leader of the House of Commons	*The Rt Hon. Margaret Beckett MP*
Chief Whip and Parliamentary Secretary to the Treasury	*The Rt Hon. Ann Taylor MP*
Secretary of State for Culture, Media and Sport	*The Rt Hon. Chris Smith MP*
Minister for the Cabinet Office*	*The Rt Hon. Dr Marjorie Mowlam MP*
Secretary of State for International Development	*The Rt Hon. Clare Short MP*
Secretary of State for Social Security	*The Rt Hon. Alistair Darling MP*
Minister for Agriculture, Fisheries and Food	*The Rt Hon. Nick Brown MP*
Leader of the House of Lords and Minister for Women†	*The Rt Hon. The Baroness Jay of Paddington*
Secretary of State for Trade and Industry	*The Rt Hon. Stephen Byers MP*
Secretary of State for Health	*The Rt Hon. Alan Milburn MP*
Secretary of State for Scotland	*The Rt Hon. Helen Liddell MP*
Secretary of State for Wales	*The Rt Hon. Paul Murphy MP*
Secretary of State for Northern Ireland	*The Rt Hon. Dr John Reid MP*
Secretary of State for Defence	*The Rt Hon. Geoffrey Hoon MP*
Chief Secretary to the Treasury	*The Rt Hon. Andrew Smith MP*
Minister of State (Minister for Transport)‡	*The Rt Hon. The Lord MacDonald of Tradeston*
Captain of the Gentlemen-at-Arms (Government Chief Whip, House of Lords)‡	*The Rt Hon. The Lord Carter*

Source: www.cabinet-office.gov.uk/central/2000/minister.htm#cab
Notes
* *Appointed as Chancellor of the Duchy of Lancaster.*
† *Appointed as Lord Privy Seal.*
‡ *Not members of the Cabinet but attend meetings.*

Two main types of ministerial Cabinet committee are identifiable: *standing committees* and *ad hoc committees*. Most recent governments have contained a core of five main *standing committees*: Economic Affairs; Home and Social Affairs; Defence and Overseas Policy; Legislation (vets government Bills before introduction to Parliament); and Legislative Programme (discusses the government's future legislative programme and the Queen's Speech). These are usually supplemented by others dealing with pressing problems (e.g. Blair's Ministerial Committee on Constitutional Reform Policy). Consisting essentially of Cabinet ministers (Cabinet Office officials also attend), chaired by senior Cabinet ministers (including the Prime Minister), standing committees are now a permanent feature, and often the main vehicle for taking critical decisions. The main standing committees in 2000 are shown in Box 3.2.

Standing committees may form *sub-committees*. (Those in Box 3.2 spawned twelve.) Sub-committees may consist wholly or mainly of Cabinet ministers or mainly of junior ministers. Occasionally they take final policy decisions, but more usually allow collective discussion of issues ranging across different departments. Since 1997 Cabinet committees and sub-committees have been supplemented by the Ministerial Consultative Committee with the Liberal Democratic Party – which includes senior Liberal Democratic Party members and discusses constitutional issues; and since 1999 by the Joint Ministerial Committee which includes members of devolved administrations. Unusually, these contain members from outside the UK government and have an essentially consultative role.

Ad hoc committees are usually temporary and deal with particular issues. They are normally numbered and prefixed 'MISC' or 'GEN' (the prefix changing from one Prime Minister to another). Some wield considerable influence. Under Thatcher, for example, MISC 7 was effectively responsible for deciding to replace Polaris with the Trident missile system (Hennessy, 1986a, p. 29). Under Major GEN 27 made decisions regarding sanctions against Yugoslavia (Burch and Holliday, 1996, p. 43). Box 3.2 shows eight 'ministerial groups' dealing with issues varying from Food Safety (MISC 1) to the Millennium Date Change (MISC 4).

Box 3.2 Cabinet committee structure

Economic and Domestic

Economic issues

Ministerial Committee on <u>Economic Affairs</u> (EA)
Ministerial Sub-Committee on <u>Welfare to Work</u> (EA(WW))
Ministerial Sub-Committee on <u>Energy Policy</u> (EA(N))
Ministerial Sub-Committee on <u>Productivity and Competitiveness</u> (EA(PC))
Ministerial Committee on <u>Public Services and Public Expenditure</u> (PSX)
Ministerial Committee on the <u>Environment</u> (ENV)
Ministerial Committee on <u>Local Government</u> (GL)
Ministerial Sub-Committee on <u>London</u> (GL(L))
Ministerial Group on <u>Utility Regulation</u> (MISC3)

continued . . .

Ministerial Group on Biotechnology and Genetic Modification (MISC6)
Ministerial Group on Better Government (MISC7)

Domestic issues

Ministerial Committee on Home and Social Affairs (HS)
Ministerial Sub-Committee on Health Strategy (HS(H))
Ministerial Sub-Committee on Drug Misuse (HS(D))
Ministerial Sub-Committee on Women's Issues (HS(W))
Ministerial Committee on Legislative Programme (LP)
Ministerial Group on Food Safety (MISC1)
Ministerial Group on Crime Reduction and Youth Justice (MISC2)
Ministerial Group on Millennium Date Change (MISC4)
Ministerial Group on Rural Areas (MISC8)
Health Performance and Expenditure (PHX)
Civil Contingencies Committee (CCC)

Constitution

Ministerial Committee on Constitutional Reform Policy (CRP)
Ministerial Sub-Committee on Incorporation of the European Convention of Human
    Rights (CRP(EC))
Ministerial Sub-Committee on Freedom of Information (CRP(FOI))
Ministerial Sub-Committee on House of Lords Reform (CRP(HL))
Ministerial Committee on Devolution Policy (DP)
Ministerial Consultative Committee with the Liberal Democratic Party (JCC)

Overseas and Defence

Ministerial Committee on Defence and Overseas Policy (DOP)
Ministerial Committee on Northern Ireland (IN)
Ministerial Committee on Intelligence Services (CSI)
Ministerial Group on the Restructuring of the European Aerospace and Defence
    Industry (MISC5)

European

(Note: European issues also covered by DOP)
Ministerial Sub-Committee on European Issues ((E)DOP))
Ministerial Committee on Defence and Overseas Policy – Sub-Committee on
    European Trade Issues ((E)DOP(T))

Source: www.cabinet-office.gov.uk/cabsec/index/cabcom/index.htm (January 2001)

Mirroring many ministerial committees are civil service *official committees*. Designated by the prefixes 'GEN (O)' or 'MISC (O)', these may have decision-making authority, but usually investigate issues, assemble material and present options for ministers. For example, MISC (O) 4, which oversees biotechnology developments, reports to MISC 6 (www.cabinet-office.gov.uk/cabsec/2000/ guide /cabcom/index. htm). Official committees themselves may be mirrored by *ad hoc working parties* of officials (Burch and Holliday, 1996, p. 44). Occasionally, too, mixed ministerial/civil service committees are established, although these generally do not work well as officials are 'reluctant to contradict' ministers (Hennessy, 1986a, p. 31).

Cabinet committee *composition*, as well as structure, is determined by the Prime Minister, although usually representatives from all 'interested' departments are included. Most Cabinet ministers serve on several committees; in 1992, the Prime Minister served on nine (chairing them all) and thirteen Cabinet colleagues served on six or more. Some also served on sub-committees: nine on three or more (Dunleavy, 1995, Table 13.2). While frequency and meeting length vary – committees usually meet as and when business requires – most Cabinet ministers spend more time in committee than in Cabinet. Partly to ease their load, junior ministers often represent departments, particularly on sub-committees.

Cabinet committee *functions* are also technically determined by the Prime Minister, although they perform two main roles:

- they enable problems to be delegated for detailed consideration, allowing issues to be clarified and/or matters to be resolved on the Cabinet's behalf;
- they allow less important items to be resolved before reaching Cabinet, saving Cabinet time and allowing business to be settled at lower levels. Normally a policy initiative from a department is sent by the Cabinet Office to the appropriate standing or sub-committee for decision. (Usually, it will also be discussed beforehand by the shadowing official committee or, if the Cabinet Office feels more work is required, an *ad hoc* official committee may be formed.)

In 1967 it was ruled that appeals to Cabinet against committee decisions would be disallowed without approval from committee chairs. Theoretically, ministers may still appeal but this is rare. Thatcher further strengthened committees by not reporting their decisions to Cabinet. Effectively, therefore, committee decisions 'have the same' status 'as decisions by the full Cabinet' (www.cabinet-office.gov.uk/ cabsec/2000/guide/cabcom.htm). Often their deliberations are preceded by informal activity, with departmental ministers and officials checking likely reaction to departmental proposals with the Treasury and Number 10.

While Cabinet committees provide a vehicle for collective decision-making, reconciling the interests of different departments into coherent policy, they have altered decision-making processes in ways arguably strengthening the Prime Minister. Structure, composition and chairs of committees, for example, are determined by the Prime Minister, providing scope to engineer preferred outcomes. 'Attlee's decision to manufacture the atomic bomb and Eden's to invade Suez were both taken in small and highly secret committees' (Thomas, 1998, pp. 211–15). James (1999, p. 68) suggests that Thatcher arranged membership to secure support for her economic policy, while during the Westland affair she allegedly cancelled one sub-committee meeting to prevent Heseltine from reporting to sympathetic colleagues (Hennessy, 1986b, especially pp. 426–7). Similar manipulation can occur with *ad hoc meetings* consisting of prime ministerial meetings with one colleague (*bilaterals*) or several colleagues (*multilaterals*). Under Thatcher such meetings sometimes took important decisions. Blair also uses them. A particular innovation is his 'bimonthly stocktaking bilaterals' with secretaries of state and top officials in key areas such as education, crime and health, an illustration, claim Kavanagh and Seldon (2000, p. 77), of 'his determination to exercise strong control from No. 10'.

Not all observers accept these analyses. Some writers (Gordon Walker, 1972, pp. 85–91; Hennessy, 1986a, p. 131; Seymour-Ure, 1984, p. 184) reject 'prime ministerial' interpretations of decisions such as manufacturing the atom bomb and Suez. Cabinet committees, and even 'inner cabinets' and 'inner circles', include ministers whose support the Prime Minister must retain. *Ad hoc meetings*, moreover, are sometimes initiated by departmental ministers themselves to clear policies with the Prime Minister. Nevertheless, Cabinet committee usage has clearly declined in recent governments. During the 1980s such meetings' frequency fell by about half. Under Major, standing ministerial committees were reduced, ministerial and official Cabinet committee meetings fell, and few *ad hoc* committees were created. Under Blair, Cabinet committee meetings are relatively 'little used', with increasing use instead of 'taskforces' to tackle interdepartmental issues (Smith, 1999, p. 171).

Nevertheless, committees are still crucially important. Catterall and Brady (2000, p. 159) see their development as reflecting the 'long search for a more effective device than full Cabinet to co-ordinate . . . departments'. Thomas (1998, p. 215) believes they are 'essential' to avoid the 'system . . . being overloaded'. One conclusion, however, is clear. Today, in addition to Cabinet, there are committees, bilateral and multilateral *ad hoc* meetings and 'taskforces'. James (1999, p. 177) claims to perceive a 'fragmentation of the Cabinet system', and Smith (1999, p. 171) 'a hole in the centre of government'. To avoid this, effective machinery is required in those core executive structures supporting the Cabinet system.

The Cabinet Office

Cabinet business is coordinated by the Cabinet Office. A small department, in 2000 it comprised 1,980 staff. Many are senior civil servants seconded from other departments. Its head, the Cabinet Secretary, is the head of the Home Civil Service. The Office has two main functions; 'servicing Cabinet and its committees and co-ordinating policy across government; and managing the civil service and the machinery of government' (Burch and Holliday, 1999, p. 17; see also Lee *et al.*, 1998, especially Chapters 9 and 10).

Formed in 1916, the Cabinet Office was initially 'little more than an aggregation of committee secretariats' (Lee *et al.*, 1998, p. 154). Subsequently, however, its functions increased, reflecting twentieth-century government expansion and the increase in potential points of interdepartmental conflict. In the interests of coordination the 'centre' has been strengthened against the departments. Significantly, the Treasury – the original coordinating department – long sought to absorb the Cabinet Office (Peden, 1983). It failed partly because the Treasury was not neutral in interdepartmental battles; and partly because prime ministers had more control by having important functions performed in the Cabinet Office.

In 1998 a restructuring (Hansard, 28 July 1998, cols 132–4) followed a review by the Cabinet secretary, Sir Richard Wilson. Part of Blair's emphasis on *joined-up government*, key elements were the integration of the Cabinet Office with the former OPS. While remaining accountable to the Prime Minister, the Cabinet Office was brought under the day-to-day direction of a Minister for the Cabinet Office (popularly known as the 'Cabinet Enforcer') and a junior ministerial team. The Enforcer was given responsibility for interdepartmental coordination in specific policy areas, plus coherent policy formulation and implementation across government.

In 2000 the Cabinet Office included the following components (www.cabinet-office.gov.uk/2000/organisation/index.htm):

1 The Cabinet Secretariat

The original component, its basic task is servicing the Cabinet and its committees. It provides an 'impartial' (non-departmental) service to the Cabinet, committees and sub-committees, arranging meetings, setting agendas, circulating papers, briefing the Prime Minister and committee chairs, taking minutes, transmitting decisions to departments and monitoring implementation. It also has an important coordinating role, tracking interdepartmental issues, advising when they require consideration, and taking the lead in coordinating work affecting several departments. Its work is conducted through six individual secretariats: Economic and Domestic Affairs; Defence and Overseas Affairs; European (coordinates departments' responses to the EU); Constitution (coordinates administrative aspects of constitutional reform, including devolution and freedom of information); Central (which assists the Cabinet secretary in matters affecting the machinery of government, propriety and relations with Parliament); and Intelligence (the Central Intelligence machinery which comprises Intelligence Assessments Staff and the Intelligence Support Secretariat). Each Secretariat works closely with ministerial private offices and handles paperwork for Cabinet committees. In this way the Secretariat coordinates views of different departments helping Cabinet and committees to reach collective decisions (www.cabinet-office.gov.uk.cabsec/2000/guide/cabsec.htm).

2 Cross-cutting units

In 2000 these included:

1   *Social Exclusion Unit.* This was established in 1997 'to help improve Government action to reduce social exclusion by producing "joined up" solutions to "joined up" problems'. Part of the Economic and Domestic Affairs Secretariat, it comprises both civil servants and outsiders. Its work has an interdepartmental focus, including projects chosen by the Prime Minister. Its associated 'ministerial network' involves members from nine Whitehall

departments, the Scottish Executive and the Welsh Assembly (www.cabinet-office.gov.uk/seu/ index/.htm).

2   *Performance and Innovation Unit*. Launched in 1998 this 'focuses on selected issues that cross departmental boundaries and propos[es] policy innovations to improve the delivery of government objectives' (James, 1999, p. 247). The emphasis is on promoting 'joined-up government' in Whitehall. Staffed by civil servants it assembles teams from inside and outside the service to conduct reviews (Burch and Holliday, 1999, p. 39).

3   *Women's Unit*. This was transferred from the Department of Social Security, and aims to coordinate work across departments to promote women's interests.

4   *UK Anti-Drugs Co-ordination Unit*. This drives implementation of the government's strategy to tackle drugs misuse. It works under the direction of the UK Anti-Drugs Co-ordinator (popularly known as the 'Drugs Czar').

3 Public service delivery units

The Cabinet Office has a lead role in delivering reforms envisioned in the White Paper *Modernising Government* (Prime Minister and Minister for the Cabinet Office, 1999). Units include the Central IT Unit (which promotes e-commerce and information age government); the Modernising Public Services Group (responsible for public service quality and standards); and the Regulatory Impact Group (responsible for improving the way new policies and regulations are drawn up and enforced). These work closely with Cabinet committees (e.g. the Modernising Public Services Group with MISC 7) and taskforces (e.g. the Regulatory Impact Group with the Better Regulation Task Force) (Holliday, 2000, p. 103).

4 Civil Service Corporate Management Command

This is responsible for corporate management of civil servants and lead responsibility for civil service reform proposed in the Wilson Report (1999) (see Chapter 4).

5 Centre for Management and Policy Studies

Formed in 1999, the CMPS has responsibility for corporate civil service training, and for ensuring departments have access to best practice and research. It incorporates the Civil Service College.

6 Parliamentary Counsel Office

This is responsible for drafting government bills and advising departments on parliamentary procedure.

7 Corporate Resources and Services Group

This is responsible for development of Cabinet Office staff and systems.

8 The Government's Chief Scientific Adviser

This officer is housed in the Cabinet Office.

Although not part of the Cabinet Office, the *Central Office of Information*, which procures and advises on publicity services for departments, reports to Cabinet Office ministers.

The Cabinet Office's role and resources can be overstated. Dynes and Walker (1995, p. 21) see it more as a 'post office' than a 'nerve centre'. It lacks the resources to effectively oversee, let alone coordinate, the departments which alone are capable of formulating and implementing policy. Its influence may also have diminished through decisions being taken increasingly in *ad hoc* ministerial and other groups and with the increasing delegation of 'policy making and implementation . . . to agencies, regions and the EU' (Smith, 2000, p. 41). Even the Cabinet Secretary's influence depends largely on the individual office-holder's relationship with the Prime Minister. Nevertheless, the Cabinet Office still plays a crucial policy coordination role. Normally a department wishing to raise an item in Cabinet (or committee) produces a paper. Other 'interested' departments may also produce papers, the Cabinet Office's minimum role being to circulate these and consult appropriate departments. Its maximum role is to try to remove any defects in proposals, and resolve interdepartmental differences. Where conflict exists, it may suggest a compromise. It may also produce a 'neutral' brief for committee chairs. Vast areas of work are coordinated in this way. To perform these roles the Cabinet Office possesses considerable resources. Its prestige usually enables it to obtain advice and cooperation from departments and most Secretariat officials specialise in specific fields.

Blair's reforms significantly strengthened the Cabinet Office. Reports (see *The Times, Guardian, Daily Telegraph*, 29 July 1998) suggest a major objective was for the Cabinet Office to become an alternative coordinating power base to the Treasury. Thus creation of the Central and Constitution Secretariats allows the Cabinet Office to oversee the machinery of government and constitutional reform initiatives, and the cross-cutting units to oversee specific issues crossing organisational boundaries. Prime ministerial authority over the Cabinet Office has also been strengthened. One example is the Enforcer, whose role is 'to ensure that the Prime Minister's objectives . . . [are] running right across Whitehall' (James, 1999, p. 247). Another is the position of the Social Exclusion and Performance and Innovation Units which, though within the Cabinet Office, 'belonged to Blair, who laid down the tasks and to whom they reported' (Hennessy, *The Times*, 25 September 2000). More significant still is the 'effective fusion' of the Cabinet Office and the Prime Minister's Office, making them 'a single executive office in all but name' (Holliday, 2000, p. 92). The implications of this are discussed below.

The Prime Minister's Office

The Prime Minister is the Cabinet's focal point, summoning and chairing meetings, determining its agenda, appointing its members, summing up discussion, and controlling the Cabinet Office. Thus, while subject like other ministers to Cabinet authority, the Prime Minister exercises considerable influence over it. He/she is heavily involved in the policy-making, administrative and coordinating work of government. Major policy initiatives usually come to the Prime Minister's notice before reaching Cabinet, while most important subjects usually receive his/her personal attention. Prime ministerial involvement is selective but, when it occurs, is often decisive.

Prime ministers also become involved in major administrative issues. While departmental ministers are primarily responsible for implementation, prime ministers usually react to 'danger signals' suggesting that departmental administration is suspect. The Prime Minister, moreover, exercises substantial control over the government machine: he/she largely controls the departmental pattern (see Chapter 2), while the most senior civil service appointments usually require personal approval. He/she also plays a crucial coordinating role, having access to all ministers and communications with all departments.

Despite these responsibilities, however, prime ministers have limited resources. For example, the Cabinet Office, although its development has increased the Prime Minister's administrative support, serves the Cabinet collectively. Indeed, lacking a department, the Prime Minister is under-resourced relative to chief executives in most other countries. Such resources as the Prime Minister does have are mainly located in the *Prime Minister's Office* which in the 1990s contained over 100 full-time staff (Lee *et al.*, 1998, Tables 3.1 and 3.2). In 2000 it comprised five main sections:

1   *The Private Office* keeps the Prime Minister's diary, deals with correspondence, and provides briefing. Headed by the Prime Minister's Principal Private Secretary, it contains a small civil service team – normally 'high fliers' seconded from departments, each covering broad policy areas. It also contains parliamentary clerks, support staff and – under Blair – a special assistant for presentation and planning. It provides the main link between the Prime Minister, the rest of Whitehall and beyond (Lee *et al.*, 1998, especially Chapter 4).
2   *The Political Office* usually consists of political appointees chosen by the Prime Minister. Its essential function is 'serving the prime minister as party leader' (Lee *et al.*, 1998, p. 99), and providing political advice, help with constituency and party duties, and liaison with party headquarters and backbenchers.
3   *The Press Office* provides a link between the Prime Minister and 'the media of mass communications, the press and broadcasting organizations' (Lee *et al.*, 1998, p. 69). Although consisting mostly of civil servants it may be headed by either civil servants or journalists sympathetic to the Prime Minister. Several such Press Officers have been controversial; for example Bernard Ingham, a civil servant and former journalist, whose vigorous lobby briefings on behalf of Thatcher occasioned comment (Cockerell *et al.*, 1984). Blair's

Press Secretary, Alistair Campbell, formerly political editor of the *Daily Mirror*, occupied a particularly powerful position in Blair's first government. All ministerial interviews, media appearances and major speeches must have Press Office clearance (Box 3.3).

4   *The Policy Unit*, created in 1974, is capable of providing policy advice independently of departments (Lee *et al.*, 1998, Chapter 7). Usually headed by a political sympathiser of the Prime Minister, it consists of 'special advisers' (see Chapter 4), although civil servants on secondment are sometimes employed. Additionally, most recent prime ministers have had 'free standing' special advisers to advise on specific policy areas. Under Blair special advisers in the Prime Minister's Office trebled to twenty-four by 2000.

5   *The Strategic Communications Unit*, created in 1998, coordinates departmental policy announcements.

Some recent prime ministers have also employed a Chief of Staff (under Blair, at the time of writing, Jonathan Powell). Responsible to the Prime Minister for the work of the Prime Minister's Office, and for coordinating activities with the Cabinet Office, he occupies a strategic position within the core executive. Arguably, Powell's role has 'changed if not undermined the position' of the Prime Minister's Principal Private Secretary and other Private Office officials (Barberis, 2000, p. 29).

Collectively these resources are meagre, leaving prime ministers with limited ability to impose policies or 'prevent . . . departmental policy initiatives' (Smith, 1999, p. 176). Significantly, some prime ministers have sought to strengthen their bureaucratic support. In 1971, for example, Heath established a Central Policy Review Staff to strengthen policy coordination and 'support the Prime Minister' (Thomas, 1998, p. 172). Although Thatcher abolished it, she simultaneously expanded the Policy Unit. The Policy Unit, in fact, has expanded steadily in recent governments. Members now routinely monitor areas of departmental responsibility, receive policy papers, and, according to some accounts, participate in committee proceedings and ministerial meetings. Whereas previously prime ministers depended 'on colleagues and departments for advice and information, [they] . . . now increasingly [rely] on advisers within the PM's Office' (Smith, 1999, p. 173). Thatcher

---

Box 3.3 Coordination of government policy

In order to ensure the effective presentation of government policy, all major interviews and media appearances, both print and broadcast, should be agreed with the No 10 Press Office before any commitments are entered into. The policy content of all major speeches, press releases and new policy initiatives should be cleared in good time with the No 10 Private Office; the timing and form of announcements should be cleared with the No 10 Press Office.

Source: Cabinet Office (July 1997, para. 88)

---

also appointed specialist advisers independent of the Policy Unit and drew advice from people without positions in Downing Street (e.g. from the Centre for Policy Studies, a right-wing 'ginger group'), a practice continued by Blair (whose office has close links with DEMOS, a 'post-modern think tank') (Denham and Garnett, 1999). Of course, while well-informed prime ministers are possibly better able to arbitrate between colleagues there is a danger of exacerbating relations with departments by 'seeking to give a personal slant to policy programmes' (Lee *et al.*, 1998, pp. 129–30).

Such developments inevitably arouse speculation about establishing a Prime Minister's Department, plans for which were made – but not implemented – in 1970 and 1982. The case *for* a Prime Minister's Department rests on three main arguments.

1   Prime Ministers require briefing and policy options other than those presented by departments. While the Policy Unit and special advisers can provide this, a Prime Minister's Department would have more resources, present more options, and produce more thoroughgoing analysis.
2   Increasing responsibilities have not been matched by growth in bureaucratic support. 'A prime minister has a tiny budget, a small staff and few formal powers' (Kavanagh and Seldon, 2000, p. 75), yet is expected to answer for almost every government action and have increasing international and media exposure. Prime ministers also operate in most key policy networks. Consequently, they need 'a support system' capable of working 'in some depth across the whole range of government activities' (Thomas, 1998, p. 183).
3   The need is perceived to strengthen the Prime Minister's coordinating role (Hoskyns, 1983; Berrill, 1985). Given the fragmentation that exists within the core executive, 'coherence is provided not by structure but by political direction. That, ultimately, has to come from the prime minister' (Catterall and Brady, 2000, p. 173). While premiers and their staff are strategically placed to detect departmental failings or inconsistencies with overall goals, a Prime Minister's Department would enable them more effectively to shape strategic policy.

There are, however, arguments *against* establishing such a department.

1   Present arrangements are adequate, 'flexible and adaptable' (Lee *et al.*, 1998, p. 260). They link 'the prime minister effectively to Cabinet, Parliament, party and the media . . . [without] the appearance of an over-mighty prime minister'. A central department could also create serious administrative burdens diverting the Prime Minister from strategic issues and 'put institutional obstacles in the way of evolution' (Burnham and Jones, 2000, p. 191).
2   A Prime Minister's Department might inexpertly challenge expert departments. It might also urge its own attitudes upon the Prime Minister, undermining his/her status as a 'neutral' Cabinet chairman and the ability to help Cabinet colleagues reach unified decisions.
3   Such a department 'might set No. 10 apart from the Cabinet or increase strife with a department'. It would undermine 'the sense of collegial decision-making' (Kavanagh and Seldon, 2000, p. 76) and be inappropriate 'for a non-presidential premiership' (Hennessy, 2000, p. 538).

These arguments link with a wider debate, namely that *Cabinet government*, described by Bagehot, has now been replaced by *prime ministerial government* (Crossman, 1963; Benn, 1982; Foley, 1993). While some observers (Jones, 1985; Hennessy, 1986a; James, 1999) reject this view – emphasising the reality of Cabinet government – others argue that a *Cabinet system* has replaced *Cabinet government*, the implication being that central government institutional structures 'need to be analysed as a totality in themselves and as part of a wider totality' (Barberis, 2000, p. 28). Rhodes (1995, pp. 23–6) also rejects claims that either Prime Minister or Cabinet 'co-ordinate[s] government policy or resolve[s] conflicts', arguing that the core executive contains '*multiple actors* whose *relative power* shifts over *time* and between *policy areas*'. Smith *et al.* (1995, p. 41) also remind us that power within the core executive is based on resource dependencies and that 'the prime minister needs departmental ministers in order to exercise power'. Nevertheless, a Prime Minister's Department would undoubtedly reinforce fears of prime ministerial government.

Conclusion

'While the core executive is institutionally strong at departmental level, it is institutionally weak at the centre . . . consequently there is a problem of co-ordination', according to Smith (2000, p. 40). Many of the developments discussed in this chapter represent attempts to address this problem: 'to promote co-ordination to curb the centrifugal effects of departmentalism' (Kavanagh and Seldon, 2000, p. 71). Traditionally Whitehall had three main coordinating centres, the Treasury, the Cabinet Office and the Prime Minister's Office, which posed the question 'whether three co-ordinators can co-ordinate'. It also fuelled demands for the Cabinet Office to play a greater role in strategic planning, as well as arguments about a Prime Minister's Department.

Blair has not created a Prime Minister's Department. As part of a longer-term trend, and in line with his emphasis on *joined-up government*, he has, however, strengthened the centre's strategic capacity. Control is now more sharply focused at the heart of the core executive. The Cabinet Office has been shaped to function as 'more of a policy-oriented and . . . pro-active co-ordinating body' (Kavanagh and Seldon, 2000, p. 70), while the Prime Minister's Office has been effectively transformed into 'an unavowed Prime Minister's Department' (Hennessy, *The Times*, 25 September 2000). Power has shifted away from the Treasury to a new nexus . . . focused around No 10' (Smith, 2000, p. 41). The Prime Minister's and Cabinet Offices now 'operate in a more unified way than ever before' (Burch and Holliday, 1999, pp. 41–3). Calls for a Prime Minister's Department thus arguably miss the point; 'an executive office in all but name already exists'.

Further reading

Numerous sources discuss Prime Minister and Cabinet, but Burch and Holliday (1996), Thomas (1998) and James (1999) are relatively up to date. Lee *et al.* (1998) discuss the Prime Minister's and Cabinet Offices, while Burch and Holliday (1999) examine Blair's reforms.

Rhodes and Dunleavy (1995) contains essays around the theme of Prime Minister, Cabinet and core executive. However, the core executive has since been comprehensively examined by Smith (1999). Rhodes (2000a, 2000b) contain useful essays informed by the ESRC Whitehall Programme. Hennessy (2000) was published after this chapter had largely been written but contains an exhaustive and authoritative account of the office of Prime Minister and its holders since 1945.

The Cabinet Office web site (www.cabinet-office.gov.uk/) contains much useful, up-to-date information.

Ministers and civil servants

Introduction

In this chapter we examine personnel working within the core executive. These comprise two main groups: elected politicians (*ministers*) and the permanent officials who serve them (*civil servants*). Both groups have experienced considerable change in recent years. Ministers, who collectively form the government, have 'multiple roles' which have changed in recent decades (Marsh *et al.*, 2000, p. 305). The civil service has also undergone radical change through developments such as Next Steps and market testing and the appearance of alternative sources of policy advice such as special advisers and taskforces.

After explaining the work of ministers and civil servants this chapter will examine minister/civil service relationships, analyse the civil service reform agenda and discuss the extent to which the service today reflects the competing tensions of tradition and change.

Ministers

Ministers provide political leadership. Normally drawn from the majority party in the House of Commons, most are MPs, although a minority – about 25 per cent – may be peers. During the twentieth century, as central administration expanded, so too did numbers of ministers, from sixty in 1900 to 109 in 2000 (eighty-eight MPs and twenty-one peers).

While ministerial posts vary between departments, the average is about four or five. They comprise a small team, one of whom – usually entitled *Secretary of State* or equivalent (e.g. Chancellor of the Exchequer) – represents the department in Cabinet and has overall control.

Below Cabinet rank are two subordinate tiers. First, full ministers not in the Cabinet: sometimes these head small departments (e.g. Paymaster General) but more usually they are second-rank ministers – known as *ministers of state* – in large departments. Below these are *parliamentary under-secretaries of state*, often colloquially called junior ministers (not to be confused with *parliamentary private secretaries*, backbench MPs who act as unsalaried ministerial aides). Although the Secretary of State remains constitutionally responsible to Parliament for the work of junior ministers, in practice departmental business is usually allocated among the ministerial team. Junior ministers often take 'final' ministerial decisions, leaving the Secretary of State free to concentrate on the most important matters.

Because most policy-making takes place in departments, and departments enjoy considerable autonomy, UK ministers enjoy more policy influence than counterparts in many other countries. Nevertheless, their role extends well beyond policy. James (1999, pp. 12–17) identifies seven *ministerial roles*:

- *policy innovation*: initiating new, and altering existing, policies;
- *policy management*: implementing departmental policies, most of which require ministerial decisions;
- *executive work*: e.g. writing letters, issuing regulations;
- *parliamentary duties*: e.g. parliamentary questions, legislation;

- *departmental ambassador*: e.g. meeting deputations, attending receptions;
- *departmental advocate*: e.g. promoting departmental interests in Cabinet, committees, bilateral meetings, etc.;
- *public presentation of policy*: e.g. television interviews.

Marsh *et al.* (2000), by contrast, identify four generic roles: policy, political, managerial or executive, and public relations. However, the balance between them, they suggest, is not static. The policy role, for example, has become more pronounced as ministers have become less dependent on civil service advice, and more likely – especially under Thatcher and Major – to adopt ideological positions. The public relations role has also become more important, and political roles more complex. Although most ministers devote attention to all these roles, workloads are usually too demanding to allow sufficient time to pursue all simultaneously with any effect. Individual ministers, moreover, approach their job differently. Thus Norton (2000a, pp. 109–10) distinguishes between five main ministerial 'types': commanders, managers, ideologues, agents and team players. The first two represent the predominant types. These pursue goals derived from personal experience (commanders) or through a pragmatic approach designed 'to ensure the smooth administration of the department' (managers).

Before taking office Cabinet ministers often serve long 'apprenticeships' in different departments. However, usually 'they do not arrive in their department technically expert' (Alderman, 1995, p. 498) (which can inhibit their role of policy innovation), or have prior experience of running large organisations (which inhibits the 'executive' role). British ministers, in fact, differ from those in many other countries: for example, Dutch ministers are often specialists in the work of their departments. In the USA they are often experienced business executives.

Civil servants

Working under ministerial direction are 'civil servants'. However, defining a 'civil servant' is far from easy (Chapman, 1997), involving ambiguities which, while sometimes convenient for ministers claiming manpower savings, make interpreting civil service statistics extremely difficult.

As a working definition, civil servants can be regarded as comprising overwhelmingly the salaried employees working in government departments (both ministerial and non-ministerial) and Next Steps Agencies (NSAs). They also include civil servants working for devolved executives in Scotland and Wales. A separate Northern Ireland Civil Service has long existed (although this excludes officials working for the Northern Ireland Office, a 'Whitehall' department employing civil servants from the home, British, civil service). One authoritative definition, used in *Civil Service Statistics* defines a civil servant as:

> A servant of the Crown working in a civil capacity who is not: the holder of a political (or judicial) office; the holder of certain other offices in respect of whose tenure of office special provision has been made; a servant of the Crown in a personal capacity paid from the Civil List.
>
> (*Cabinet Office*, 2000a)

This definition, while leaving ambiguity as to whom precisely it includes, nevertheless excludes ministers, judges, the armed forces and employees of nationalised industries, local government, the NHS and quangos. It also allows government machinery changes to change civil service numbers overnight. For example, in 1999 4,000 civil servants disappeared from official statistics when much of the Department of National Savings was privatised. However, officially some 475,420 (full-time equivalent) civil servants were employed at April 2000, comprising 445,980 non-industrials ('white collar') and 29,440 industrials ('blue collar'). Of these 11,300 were casuals (Cabinet Office, November, 2000).

Features of the civil service

Four main features have traditionally characterised the civil service.

1   *Permanence.* Britain does not have a 'spoils system', where administrative posts in the gift of politicians change with governments. Neither does it have French-type 'ministerial cabinets' whereby a small private staff chosen by the minister provide advice. British civil servants traditionally are permanent career officials working with governments of all political complexions.

2   *Unity.* 'The most important characteristic of the British civil service . . . was its sense of unity' (Chapman, 1992, p. 2), maintained by centralised recruitment; common pay, grading and conditions; and service-wide promotion opportunities.

3   *Anonymity.* Civil servants have traditionally enjoyed anonymity. Their advice to ministers is confidential; and the convention of individual responsibility (pp. 228–32) normally ensures that ministers answer for their actions publicly and in Parliament.

4   *Neutrality.* Because civil servants serve ministers with differing views, they must observe political neutrality. For example, they must avoid partisan political activity, and not express views contrary to ministers.

Despite their importance, it is debatable how far these features still apply. Managerial reforms, particularly, have eroded their force under modern conditions. Permanence, for example, has been eroded by fixed-term appointments of Next Steps Agency chief executives; and unity by the fragmentation of the service into NSAs. Heightened media interest, and appearance before Parliamentary select committees, for example, have given civil servants higher public profiles compromising their anonymity; indeed it is arguable that the concept of anonymity was given too much emphasis even in the past. The themes of this chapter include the extent to which the service's traditional characteristics have become weakened and whether they still exist.

A neutral civil service?

Particular controversy surrounds civil service *neutrality* which, Ridley (1986, p. 23) observes, is capable of different interpretations:

- civil servants should provide objective and impartial advice to ministers: i.e. they should give honest advice, however unpalatable ministers might find it;
- civil servants should give advice in the spirit of government policy: i.e. they should 'tailor' their advice to ministers' political requirements.

If neutrality is an ambiguous concept, in practice it can be difficult to apply. Greenwood (2000, p. 73) identifies four factors which have placed increased strains on political neutrality.

1 *Breakdown of the post-war political consensus.* A former Prime Minister, Lord Callaghan (1996, p. 74), states, 'When you have a government like the government . . . in the 1980s, which emanates a very strong flavour, the civil service picks up the scent. Some are repelled . . . some are attracted . . . [consequently] the civil service . . . become[s] more politicised.'
2 *Massive increase in media influence.* Today ministers are concerned not just with policy making but with policy presentation. 'Neutral' officials are not best placed to do this.
3 The drive towards *greater managerial efficiency.* Performance-related pay, fixed-term contracts, etc. may make officials reluctant to give advice prejudicial to future pay or reappointment.
4 *Greater complexity of policy-making.* Ministers may legitimately require advisers with alternative expertise.

Notions of neutrality caused particular strain under Thatcher. The Willmore, Tisdall and Ponting cases, for example, saw civil servants leaking information to third parties (Drewry and Butcher, 1991, pp. 2–4, 176–7). Ponting (1986) leaked information to an Opposition MP and was prosecuted but, claiming a 'public interest' defence, was acquitted. Shortly afterwards, the Cabinet Secretary issued *A Note of Guidance on the Duties and Responsibilities of Civil Servants in Relation to Ministers.* Known as the *Armstrong Memorandum* (1985), this asserted that civil servants were servants of the Crown, which meant the government of the day. It emphasised their duty to implement ministerial decisions irrespective of their own views. In conscience cases they could approach their permanent secretary who, in turn, could consult the head of the Home Civil Service.

Difficulties arose again during the Westland affair (Drewry and Butcher, 1991, pp. 4–7) when a civil servant, unable to contact her permanent secretary, leaked ministerial correspondence allegedly on her minister's instructions. The outcome was a revised memorandum (Hansard, VI, vol. 123, cols 572–5, 2 December 1987) which also largely reaffirmed traditional views. Subsequently, this was incorporated into the *Civil Service Management Code* which identifies conduct and standards required of civil servants. Arguably, Armstrong's own neutrality, and certainly his anonymity, were compromised when he defended government attempts to suppress publication of *Spycatcher*, written by a former MI5 official, in Australian courts.

Thatcher's premiership also brought allegations about *politicisation*. In 1981, following industrial unrest, Thatcher abolished the Civil Service Department. Its permanent secretary (and head of the Home Civil Service) 'was despatched into early retirement' (Hennessy, 1990, p. 309). There were also allegations that Thatcher intervened to secure the advancement of preferred candidates, arousing accusations of politicisation and favouritism (Hennessy, 1990, pp. 633–4; Richards, 1997). While a Royal Institute of Public Administration investigation (1987) effectively cleared her, Kavanagh (1990, p. 252) suggests that Thatcher helped promote 'managerial can-do' types. Richards (1997) also claims that, while Thatcher did not support appointments on the basis of Conservative sympathies, officials who impressed her may have improved their promotional prospects – which possibly encouraged them to tailor their advice to ministerial preferences.

Thatcher's lengthy premiership may also have produced a 'mind set' among civil servants which resulted in alternative policy options not being explored, and this probably continued under Major. According to Barberis (1996a, p. 217), 'Thatcherism . . . coloured the roles of permanent secretaries and their relationships with ministers under the Major governments'. Although Major intervened less in promotions, several civil service 'departures', not only of NSA chief executives but also of permanent secretaries, aroused controversy. Notable was Sir Peter Kemp, Second Permanent Secretary at the Office of Public Service and Science (OPSS) and Next Steps Project Manager, who was not only sacked but – contrary to previous practice – was not found another post (Richards, 1997, pp. 229–32). Theakston (2000a, p. 49) also reports two early retirements after conflicts with ministers, and one engineered 'retirement' after a departmental merger. Richards (1997, p. 232) sees such developments creating precedents. 'If this were the case', he argues, 'two . . . fundamental . . . principles . . . permanence and impartiality, would have been dismantled.'

In 1992 Major published *Questions of Procedure for Ministers* (Cabinet Office, 1992) which stated that civil servants 'should not be asked to engage in activities likely to call in question their political impartiality' (para. 55). Despite this civil servants were controversially used to cost Labour's expenditure plans before the 1997 general election (Pilkington, 1999, pp. 56–7). The Scott Report (1996) also named and blamed civil servants for allegedly colluding with ministers in concealing policy from Parliament, and for insufficient frankness in assisting the inquiry. Anxieties were also expressed that developments such as performance-linked pay should not compromise neutrality (see, for example, Nolan Committee, 1995, para. 48).

Reflecting such concerns the Treasury and Civil Service Committee (TCSC) (1993–4, paras 103–12) called in 1994 for a *Civil Service Code* to clarify duties and responsibilities, and a right of appeal to independent civil service commissioners. The first Nolan Report (1995) recommended an even tougher code. Although Major subsequently adopted a code it, again, reaffirmed civil service 'loyalty to the duly constituted government' (Prime Minister, 1995, Annex). The government also ignored calls for the code to have a statutory basis.

Blair's government was also criticised for politicisation. One permanent secretary who had previously worked on privatisation accepted retirement shortly after the election, and there were reports that Ed Balls, the Chancellor's special adviser, had marginalised the influence of the Treasury permanent secretary, who subsequently retired. The Government Information Service was also reorganised and several departmental heads of information removed. The Select Committee on Public Administration subsequently divided on party lines when investigating the

---

Box 4.1 Ministerial code

Ministers and civil servants

Ministers have a duty to give fair consideration and due weight to informed and impartial advice from civil servants, as well as to other considerations and advice, in reaching policy decisions; a duty to uphold the political impartiality of the Civil Service, and not to ask civil servants to act in any way which would conflict with the Civil Service Code; a duty to ensure that influence over appointments is not abused for partisan purposes; and the duty to observe the obligations of a good employer with regard to terms and conditions of those who serve them. Civil servants should not be asked to engage in activities likely to call in question their political impartiality, or to give rise to the criticism that people paid from public funds are being used for Party political purposes.

Source: Cabinet Office (July 1997, para. 56)

---

issue (Theakston, 2000a, pp. 54–5). Nevertheless, when Blair took office, most senior officials adapted easily. Blair himself acknowledged the 'smooth, almost seamless handover . . . in the best traditions of a . . . non-partisan service' (www. cabinetoffice. gov.uk/civilservice/1999/mcg/conference/pmxscript.htm). He also issued a revised *Questions of Procedure* entitled *Ministerial Code* (Box 4.1). However, the government failed to accept a Nolan Committee recommendation that the code should give the Prime Minister responsibility for its enforcement (Wright, 2000, p. 256), although it did promise statutory backing.

Special advisers and taskforces

One response to problems of neutrality has been the appointment, since 1964, of *special advisers*. Appointed initially on a small scale, their numbers subsequently increased. When Major left office thirty-eight were in post. Blair by 2000 had increased their numbers to above seventy. Although enjoying status as temporary civil servants, special advisers are neither neutral (being appointed for political sympathies as well as expertise), nor permanent (usually retiring when 'their' minister leaves office), nor always anonymous. In Blair's government, several are high profile. These include Alistair Campbell, the Prime Minister's Press Secretary; Jonathan Powell, the Prime Minister's Chief of Staff; and Ed Balls, economic adviser to the Chancellor of the Exchequer. Some, like Campbell, occupy a role which requires media exposure; others (like Charlie Whelan who controversially resigned from the Treasury in 1999) have been employed not as policy 'experts' but as 'spin doctors'.

Views about special advisers vary. Policy-making today is so complex that ministers may legitimately require alternative expertise. (During the 1980s, for example, Conservative governments also made use of consultancy agencies as an alternative source of policy advice.) The influence of special advisers, however, is arguably limited because they are few in number and influence depends on 'convinc[ing] their minister' (James, 1999, p. 224). Relations with civil servants also vary. While some meet obstruction, Hennessy *et al.* (1997, p. 10) believe they are 'warmly welcomed'. While more overtly partisan activities arguably compromise neutrality, much of their work – liaising with party officials, briefing ministers about political sensitivities – could not properly be undertaken by civil servants. Indeed, Blair suggests that using special advisers for political work actually protects civil service neutrality (*The Times*, 2 June 1997).

Blair has also massively increased the use of *taskforces*. With Major's 'deregulation taskforce' used as a model, about 300 new taskforces, involving some 2,500 outsiders, had been formed by 2000. Typically, taskforces 'are given a specific brief, a clear deadline and a set of outsiders to work alongside civil servants. Key aspects . . . are . . . use of outsiders and a willingness to ignore traditional departmental boundaries in the search for policy solutions' (Holliday, 2000, p. 103). Falling outside the embrace of formal departmental structures they are intended to make the participants think holistically. They therefore contribute to both joined-up government and 'inclusive' policy-making. They bring experts, often unpaid, into policy-making and they can work flexibly alongside civil servants (and sometimes ministers). Examples include those dealing with important policy areas (Better Regulation Task Force), high-profile ones (David Mellor's Football Task Force) and obscure ones (Thaumasite Expert Group which advises on damage to concrete). (See also Box 8.1) They also include the four 'cross-cutting units' established by Blair within the Cabinet Office (See pp. 62–3).

Despite their recent arrival, taskforces arouse concerns. Their appointment by departments gives rise to concerns about patronage and accountability. Appointments also fall outside the Nolan rules for quango appointments (see Chapter 8). Membership is also biased towards business (35 per cent of members are businessmen) and producers (66 per cent) as opposed to consumers (15 per cent) and trade unionists (2 per cent) (Barker *et al.*, 2000, Table 2). Some members also have strong Labour links. Lord Haskins (Box 4.2), a veteran Labour supporter, received a Labour peerage, and reportedly donated £40,000 to Labour (Barker, 2000, p. 18; *Sunday Times*, 21 November 1999). Moreover, there are doubts about taskforces' contributions to policy. Ministers establish them, agree membership, and define their remit, arguably producing 'ministerially managed' outside advice. Barker (2000, pp. 34–5), however, sees them as 'a welcome innovation; good for the interests involved; good for the civil service; and for ministers'. Their use goes some way towards recognising arguments for politicisation without abandoning neutrality which still overwhelmingly applies.

Civil servants and ministers: working relationships

Each minister/civil service relationship is unique, varying with time, circumstance and personality as well as policy. Nevertheless, much debate seeks to analyse where power lies. Theakston (1991–2) outlines four models:

Box 4.2 Labour's taskforce king: Lord Haskins of Skidby

Task Force Chair:
Better Regulation Task Force (based in the Cabinet Office, where Lord Haskins spends about two days per week. About fifty staff work indirectly for him).

Task Force membership:
Interchange Steering Council (provides strategic direction for interchange between civil service and other occupations). New Deal Task Force (DfEE: ensures New Deal takes full account of needs of employers and wider community).

Quango member:
UK Round Table on Sustainable Development (advises DETR; helps build consensus on ways of making development more sustainable).

Sources: Barker *et al.* (2000); 'Labour's Task Force Kings', *Sunday Times,* 21 November 1999

---

1   *The formal-constitutional model* emphasises the constitutional position that ministers make policy and civil servants provide advice and implement the decisions for which ministers are responsible.
2   *The adversarial model* sees the relationship as conflictual with a constant struggle for power.
3   *Village life in the Whitehall community*, a model originating in writings by Heclo and Wildavsky (1981), argues that divisions invariably exist not *between* politicians and civil servants but *within* them, as alliances of ministers *and* officials compete with each other. Ministers and mandarins frequently work together and are mutually dependent on each other.
4   *The public choice model* focuses less on civil service power than on the consequences of that power, namely an expanding bureaucracy, serving its own rather than the public's interests.

While other models exist, and it is important always to remember the power-dependency relationships which are present within the core executive, Theakston's four models nevertheless summarise varying analyses quite well. The six variables explored below allow assessment of their usefulness.

Tenure

Service officials acquire lengthy Whitehall experience. Of twenty-one permanent secretaries in 1993, eighteen had had conventional careers with an average of twenty-seven years' prior service. Only three of the eighteen had more than one year's outside experience (Plowden, 1994, pp. 42–3). While many senior officials frequently change jobs, between 1979 and 1994 most permanent secretaries had spent entire careers in three departments or fewer, enabling them to develop contacts useful for 'stitch[ing] up' ministers (Barberis, 1996a, p. 172, Table 2, pp. 204–5).

Civil service permanence contrasts with the transitory nature of ministers. While some ministers hold office for long periods, they usually change ministerial posts frequently. Between 1964 and 1991 tenure of Cabinet posts averaged under two and a half years (Rose, 1991). While frequent ministerial turnover has some advantages, for example making ministers less likely to identify with departments' traditional interests (Alderman, 1995), it allows little time to master complex subjects.

Expertise

Ministers move between departments, often for political reasons, at prime ministerial discretion. Few have worked as civil servants themselves or have experience in departmental policy areas. While this offers some advantages – expert ministers may become 'too close' to their department's subject area – it leaves most ministers ill-equipped to challenge departmental views. John Major's career (Box 4.3) exemplifies this. Excluding service as a Whip, in six years Major held five posts in three departments before becoming Prime Minister. He was Foreign Secretary for barely three months. He himself complained that 'moving ministers around too quickly is not conducive to good government' (Alderman, 1995, p. 497). Such problems may become severe when wholesale changes occur. Of Blair's first Cabinet, only four had previous ministerial experience, none at Cabinet level. Blair had never served in government before becoming Prime Minister.

Some ministers, of course, stay in departments for several years. In Blair's first government the Foreign Secretary, Home Secretary and Chancellor of the Exchequer had all occupied the same post for nearly four years at the time of writing. Some departments are less technical than others, so ministers 'pick things up' quickly. Chandler (1988, pp. 57–8) also suggests that most ministers 'have no small measure of faith in their own ideas'. Nevertheless, in many areas ministers 'are disadvantaged ... because they do not have the knowledge ... to make policy' (Smith, 1999, pp. 115–16).

Box 4.3 John Major's career development?

1983–4	Assistant Government Whip
1984–5	Government Whip
1985–6	Under-Secretary for Social Security
1986–7	Minister for Social Security and the Disabled
1987–9	Chief Secretary to the Treasury
1989 (July to October)	Foreign Secretary
1989–90	Chancellor of the Exchequer
1990–7	Prime Minister

Departmental size

In 2000 109 ministers were nominally responsible for some 475,000 civil servants. A massive department like Social Security, with 83,530 civil servants in 2000, cannot be effectively managed by a single Secretary of State, one Minister of State, and three under secretaries. In large departments, moreover, officials generally have more discretion 'to decide what issues' can and cannot 'be resolved without ministerial intervention' (Pitt and Smith, 1981, p. 53).

Of course, some departments are relatively small (see Table 2.1). Also, Next Steps has devolved much operational management to agencies, although it has also given ministers new responsibilities – such as communicating with chief executives. Nevertheless, civil servants always outnumber ministers.

Workload

Workload prevents ministers from dealing with more than a limited number of issues. Ministers not only have departmental responsibilities. They also have duties *outside* their departments: in Cabinet, committees, Parliament and their constituency, to name but some. Increasing 'internationalisation' of policy-making has also increased workloads, requiring wider consultation and increased travel. Consequently, ministers can easily become diverted from policy-making.

Of course civil servants also have heavy workloads. Managerialsm has obliged civil servants to pursue management as well as policy work, while developments such as the EU have also impacted on officials in many departments. The policy-making function has also been pushed further down the Whitehall hierarchy in the last ten years. Nevertheless workload constrains ministers. Not only are ministers' diaries organised by civil servants but sheer practicality requires all but the most important departmental decisions to be taken by officials.

Information

Ministers rely heavily on civil servants for information and advice. Issues working their way up the hierarchy are documented at every level in reports and minutes drafted by officials. Consequently, ministers frequently take 'their' decisions on the basis of civil service briefs containing sifted information and official recommendations. Even if ministers disagree, civil servants 'may resubmit the papers, plead with the minister, bombard him with ingenious explanations' (James, 1999, p. 41).

The way information is presented may also shape decisions. Benn (1982, p. 56) cites a draft defence White Paper presented to Cabinet:

> In calculating the [West's] military strength . . . the Ministry of Defence had left out the French armed forces. When questioned the reason given was that NATO did not exercise the same operational control over the French forces as applied to the rest of the alliance. . . . [This] crude misinformation was designed to win public support for a bigger defence budget by suggesting a more serious imbalance than existed.

Implementation

Once policy has been decided, implementation is left largely to officials. Occasionally ministerial instructions will be unwittingly overlooked, but there are tactics civil servants may deliberately employ to thwart implementation of disliked policies: procrastination, discovering obstacles, effecting unworkable solutions, even 'losing things'.

Numerous examples exist of bureaucratic inertia frustrating ministers' intentions. One is the 'implementation' of Fulton's proposed civil service reforms (see pp. 83–5 below). Even where bureaucratic obstruction does not occur, however, ministers may find implementation difficult to control. Major's pensions policy, for example, required fifteen years for implementation.

A ruling class?

Senior civil servants can sometimes thwart ministers. In the 1970s and early 1980s political memoirs (Crossman, 1975; Castle, 1980; Benn, 1982) suggested that officials sometimes did precisely that, particularly under Wilson and Callaghan. However, criticisms were not solely from the Left: Thatcher, for example, reportedly criticised civil service influence 'over both ministers and the choice of . . . expenditure cuts' (Norton, 1982, p. 83). The period to 1979 also witnessed substantial growth of the state, leading 'New Right' analysts to develop 'public choice' models of civil service self-interest as explanations for governmental failure to reduce public spending. Adversarial and public choice models clearly had supporters.

However, not all ministers agreed. Heath, for example, believed 'civil servants were . . . clearly and definitely . . . under Ministerial control' (Expenditure Committee, 1977, 11.2, para. 1877). Sometimes, moreover, bureaucratic obstruction may be used as a scapegoat for ministerial failure. Benn, for example, allegedly achieved so little because, lacking prime ministerial support, departmental officials could obstruct his policies (Young and Sloman, 1982, p. 29).

After 1979, however, the formal-constitutional model enjoyed a resurgence. Public expenditure cuts and privatisation were not easily reconciled with public choice models, while Thatcher's ideological policies, coupled with the Conservatives' long period in office, led to reassertions of ministerial authority. 'Thatcherites scorned Whitehall's consensus outlook and the departmental orthodoxies' (Theakston, 2000a, pp. 47–8). The political climate also changed. As the two main parties shared office during the 1960s and 1970s civil servants were a force for continuity. After 1979 ministers themselves provided continuity and direction. They also became more proactive in policy-making. By the mid-1990s 'few' observers still believed 'that permanent secretaries or other senior officials really run the country' (Barberis, 1996a, pp. 215–19). Under Blair, early signs are that 'the machine will be subject to effective ministerial control and direction' (Theakston, 2000a, p. 58).

As the above suggests, minister/civil service relationships do not remain constant; they are dynamic and interactive. Different ministers have different goals, and operate in differing political circumstances. Nevertheless ministers 'are important. Civil servants cannot act alone; they lack the legitimacy to do anything without ministerial authority' (Marsh *et al.*, 2000, p. 324). Norton (2000a) in fact characterises ministers as 'territorial barons' whose resources make them 'particularly powerful', especially within their ministerial territory. Thus a new minister can bring 'considerable change in both policy and the way the department is actually run'. Ministers, however, are not 'all-powerful. . . . They have to form alliances and cultivate support . . . in an increasingly crowded political environment.' In fact analyses depicting dominance by *either* ministers *or* civil servants are too simplistic. 'The two need one another. Civil servants provide information and advice, ministers provide political judgment and political skills' (Marsh *et al.*, 2000, p. 311). Shades of the *Village life in the Whitehall community* model?

Reforming the civil service

Despite massive changes during the twentieth century, today's civil service still displays many features of its past. Indeed, until the nineteenth century there was no clear distinction between civil service and ministerial roles. 'Civil servants' were appointed largely by patronage, and promotion was by seniority. However, the emergence of a 'constitutional bureaucracy' (Parris, 1969) can be traced to the late eighteenth century, when it became normal for ministers to resign *en bloc* and enter opposition.

Demands for reform have been a feature of the civil service throughout much of the last two centuries. In the early nineteenth century they gathered momentum as the state acquired new functions and administrative costs began to rise. One consequence was the Northcote–Trevelyan Report which laid the foundations of the civil service.

Northcote–Trevelyan Report (1854)

This made four main recommendations: (1) recruitment by open competitive examination; (2) promotion by merit; (3) unification of the service; (4) a division between intellectual work performed by graduates and mechanical work allocated to those of lesser ability. These proposals were implemented only slowly. However, their influence was considerable, heralding the creation of hierarchical class divisions and the dominance of *generalist* administrators.

Fulton Report (1968)

The Fulton Report was published in 1968 after a major inquiry into the service. Its central finding (1968, vol. 1, para. 6) was that, more than a century on, 'the basic principles and philosophy of the Northcote–Trevelyan Report [still] prevailed'. The report identified four main defects.

1   *Generalist dominance.* The service was still essentially based on the philosophy of the amateur (or 'generalist' or 'all-rounder'), especially within the adminis-trative class whose members largely monopolised top posts. Specialists,

traditionally organised in separate hierarchies, held subordinate positions advising generalists who made final policy recommendations to ministers.

2   *The 'class system'.* Northcote–Trevelyan's 'mechanicals' and 'intellectuals' division had developed by the 1960s into a complex network of over 1,400 classes. Most officials found it difficult to move from the class to which they were appointed.

3   *Poor management.* Mainly a Treasury responsibility, its Pay and Management Group was ill-equipped to manage the service. Training was also deficient. The generalist ethos emphasised 'on the job learning'; consequently, formal training usually involved only short induction courses.

4   *Isolation and exclusivity.* The highest levels – overwhelmingly recruited direct from university – were mostly arts graduates, from fee-paying schools and from Oxbridge.

Some of Fulton's recommendations concerned departmental organisation (see Chapter 2). Others specifically concerned civil servants:

- *classes should be abolished* and replaced by a single unified grading structure covering the service from top to bottom;
- *a Civil Service Department* responsible for management should be established under prime ministerial control. Its permanent secretary should be head of the Home Civil Service;
- *preference for relevance*: graduate recruitment should give more consideration to relevance of university courses;
- *a Civil Service College* should be formed to provide training.

Although Fulton's main recommendations were accepted, many never materialised. A *single unified grading structure*, for example, never appeared. Many specialist grades were retained and only at the top, in the *open structure* established in 1972, did unified grading appear. Although technically open to all staff, generalists continued to dominate the senior open structure.

Other recommendations also had limited effect. In 1968 a Civil Service Department (CSD) was established under prime ministerial control, and its permanent secretary designated head of the Home Civil Service. However, in 1981 it was abolished, and its permanent secretary 'retired' (see pp. 75–6). Its functions were initially divided between the Treasury and other departments, but under Major the Office of Public Service and Science (Office of Public Service after 1995), and under Blair the Civil Service Corporate Command within the Cabinet Office (see Chapter 3), were made responsible for civil service management. Prime ministers, however, retained the designation 'Minister for the Civil Service'. Since CSD abolition, therefore, civil service management has effectively shifted from the Prime Minister and Treasury to the Prime Minister and Cabinet Office, ending pre-Fulton patterns of Treasury control.

With *recruitment*, preference for relevance was rejected and a new Administration Trainee (AT) scheme did not significantly widen entry. The AT scheme underwent various changes and by 2000 functioned as a *Fast Stream Development Programme* recruiting specialists and generalists in five different strands. However, some pre-Fulton trends remain. In 1999 40 per cent of recruits to the General Fast Stream (concerned with the Home Civil Service, Diplomatic Service and European Fast Stream) were from Oxbridge, and 74 per cent had arts-related degrees (Cabinet Office, 2000b).

The *Civil Service College* (CSC), established in 1970, also had limited impact. In 1989 it became an NSA running courses on a repayment basis and throughout the 1990s provided AT training, and some senior staff retraining (Duggett, 1996). However, its overall contribution was 'peripheral', reflecting 'traditional mandarin [preference for] practical experience' (Theakston, 1995, p. 103). In 2000 it lost NSA status and was integrated with the Centre for Management and Policy Studies within the Cabinet Office, which was given responsibility for 'corporate civil service training and development'. Blair also proposed a Central National Training Organisation to develop corporate training and development strategy (Prime Minister and Minister for the Cabinet Office, 1999, p. 57).

Although Fulton arguably 'set the agenda' for subsequent debate, and its 'central philosophy' presaged later reforms such as Next Steps (Drewry and Butcher, 1991, p. 54), its significance can be exaggerated. Some recommendations never materialised, lower levels were largely ignored and reforms might have occurred anyway. Moreover, from the 1970s Fulton gradually faded from view as civil service reform became increasingly intertwined with the Conservatives' managerialist agenda.

Thatcher and Major's 'civil service revolution'

Thatcher's premiership coincided with paradigm changes in public administration, as outlined in Chapter 1. At the forefront of Thatcher's approach was the application of managerial techniques intended to deliver 'Value for Money' (VFM) for taxpayers, the main implications of which for departments were discussed in Chapter 2. However, here it can be noted that with Next Steps the move towards greater unification of the service went into reverse. Indeed the Next Steps Report (Efficiency Unit, 1988, p. 5) specifically acknowledged that 'the advantages which a unified Civil Service are intended to bring are seen as outweighed by the practical disadvantages'.

Interestingly, this view both endorsed and contradicted Fulton's earlier recommendations. While it rejected conventional wisdom – which Fulton attempted to reinforce – that the service should be unified, and managed as such, it built also upon Fulton's earlier vision of accountable management and 'hiving off' (see p. 30). The effect, however, was to reduce unity within the service, with most civil servants (74 per cent when Major resigned in 1997) increasingly fragmented within NSAs. In less tangible ways, also, NSAs reduced unity. As managerial autonomy was extended to conditions, pay and grading, and staff were encouraged to identify with particular departments or agencies, the common ethos and culture began to erode. As Chapman (1992, p. 3) observed, 'there [was] now no real sense of unity in the civil service'.

Major continued with further initiatives. Some, such as *market testing* and the *Citizen's Charter*, are discussed elsewhere (see Chapters 2 and 12). However, their implications for civil servants were considerable. A key *Citizen's Charter* theme, for example, was explaining 'to the public just how well or how badly civil servants . . .

are performing' (Pilkington, 1999, p. 117). Most departments subsequently produced charters with performance targets. With market testing only 68 per cent of market-tested activities remained in-house at the cost of 27,000 civil service jobs (Pilkington, 1999, pp. 79, 80). One reason is that in-house bids were often precluded. In 1996 the government abandoned market testing targets, instead requiring departments and agencies to produce annual efficiency plans explaining 'how they proposed to achieve their efficiency targets and . . . to demonstrate their use of market testing and other management techniques' (Horton, 1999, p. 149). These 'other' techniques included the *Private Finance Initiative* (PFI) launched in 1992 as a means of using private money to finance public project (see pp. 218–20); and the *Benchmarking Exercise* (relaunched as the *Benchmarking Project* under Blair) which requires agencies to adopt best management practice 'benchmarked' against a business excellence model (see Cabinet Office, October 1997; Horton, 1999, p. 15).

The new efficiency agenda

In 1994 and 1995 Major issued two White Papers: *The Civil Service: Continuity and Change* (Prime Minister, 1994); and *The Civil Service: Taking Forward Continuity and Change* (Prime Minister, 1995). In between the two White Papers the Treasury and Civil Service Committee issued its own report (TCSC, 1993–4).

The two White Papers anticipated a fall in civil service numbers to below 500,000 by 1998. An underlying aim was to break away from Whitehall's traditional hierarchical (Weberian) working patterns and to this end they contained proposals concerning structure, pay and grading, recruitment and promotion.

Structure

The 1994 White Paper proposed a new Senior Civil Service (SCS). Broader than the senior open structure, it would comprise about 3,500 civil servants at Grade 5 or above including NSA chief executives. Formed in 1996, a major objective was strengthening 'cohesion not only of the senior management of departments but of the wider Senior Civil Service' (Prime Minister, 1994). As other changes were increasingly fragmenting the service, SCS was intended to provide a unifying element at the top.

Pay and grading

Traditionally most civil servants were employed on centralised pay scales. However, as Next Steps developed, pay bargaining was gradually decentralised and the 1994 White Paper announced further delegation. As a result, SCS pay is now based on individual contracts linked to performance and job weighting. Below SCS level the pay systems of all grades are now delegated to individual departments. *Continuity and Change* also urged the removal of unnecessary layers. Apart from permanent

Table 4.1 Civil service numbers by responsibility levels (1999)*

Senior Civil Service	3,570
Grades 6 and 7	21,690
Senior/Higher Executive Officer	73,010
Executive Officer	103,110
Administrative Officer/Assistant	227,540
Unknown	380
Total	429,300

Source: *Cabinet Office* (2000a, Table E)
Note: * Full-time equivalent, non-industrial staff, 1 April 1999.

secretary, all grades were discarded in SCS and staff brought within a framework of nine overlapping pay bands. *Taking Forward Continuity and Change* further required departments to conduct senior management reviews of grading arrangements. The result in most departments was a combination of 'delayering' and staff cuts.

One side-effect of these changes is that it is difficult to count civil servants by grade or category. Recent versions of *Civil Service Statistics*, therefore, now use the concept of 'responsibility levels' (Table 4.1).

Recruitment

Traditionally only limited recruitment and secondment to the top posts from outside had occurred. However, with Next Steps outside recruitment increased significantly. Between 1990 and 1992 about 14 per cent senior open structure vacancies – mostly agency chief executives – were filled by open competition (TCSC, 1993–4, para. 277). *Continuity and Change* gave further impetus to this process. Although, partly to mollify mandarins who preferred internal promotion (Theakston, 1995, p. 186), it merely recommended that with senior appointments agencies/departments should *consider* full open competition. Following publication, recruitment by open competition increased steadily, particularly to specialist, technical posts or NSA chief executive positions. (By March 1997 ninety chief executive appointments, 68 per cent, had been made by open competition – Cabinet Office, March 1997.) Open competition was also extended to permanent secretary level when in 1995 Michael Bichard was appointed permanent secretary at the Department of Employment. Subsequently, when the Employment and Education Departments merged, Bichard was again appointed permanent secretary following open competition. (For discussion, see Richards, 1997, especially Chapter 10.) Thus, open competition was 'no longer restricted to a few posts, but cover[ed] all the civil service' (Rhodes, 1997a, p. 99).

These changes ended the Northcote–Trevelyan–inspired pattern of centralised recruitment through a Civil Service Commission. In 1991 recruitment below Grade 7 was delegated to departments and agencies, and the Civil Service Commission abolished. Above Grade 7 recruitment functions were transferred to a new NSA, the Recruitment and Assessment Services Agency (RAS). A new Office of the Civil

Service Commissioners was also created with responsibility mainly for monitoring recruitment functions (Chapman, 1997, p. 29). (The Office was also given responsibility for fast-stream recruitment, although it contracted this to the RAS. In 1996 the RAS was privatised.) Independent of ministers and civil servants the 1995 White Paper gave the Commissioners responsibility for approving outside appointments to the SCS and for issuing a Recruitment Code governing departmental/agency recruitment (Prime Minister, 1995, para. 2.13).

The effect of these arrangements is that civil service recruitment is today fragmented among different departments and agencies. Some services found in more than one department or agency (e.g. the Government Statistical Service) still recruit through centralised management units, and departments and agencies may choose to recruit specialists through these units. Again, however, unity has been eroded. Chapman (1997, p. 29) also detects wider concerns: 'confusion in recruitment [for] ... candidates ... inefficiencies in commercial agencies ... [administering] the arrangements, and ... dilution of the high standards [of] the former Civil Service Commission'.

Promotion

In conformity with Northcote–Trevelyan principles civil service promotion has traditionally been by merit. At permanent and deputy secretary levels appointments were made by the Prime Minister on advice from the head of the Home Civil Service, following recommendation by the Senior Appointments Selection Committee (SASC). Prime ministerial involvement was largely nominal, although Thatcher, as we have seen, did intervene more actively (see p. 76). In 1993–4 following TCSC investigation (paras 274–6), *Taking Forward Continuity and Change* proposed that the First Civil Service Commissioner should attend all SASC meetings, and have powers to comment directly to ministers 'on the choice between open competition and internal appointment' (Prime Minister, 1995, para. 2.13). It also proposed that the first Civil Service Commissioner should be appointed by open competition and not be a serving civil servant (ibid., para. 2.14).

Collectively these developments seem likely to have considerable impact. How much, however, remains a matter of doubt. Rhodes (2000c, p. 162), for example, notes that 'departments and agencies need only "consider" open competition', and that real change will take time to work through. Chapman (2000, p. 12), however, claims to detect radical change, in ethos as well as structure.

> [The Civil Service Commission] had an important role to play in the ethos of the civil service. That ethos had as its basic features a unified system for recruitment ... common standards including pay and conditions and service, service-wide opportunities for promotion and transfer, and attitudes and ... attitudes developed from these features. .... Most of these features no longer apply, and in that sense there is now no unified civil service.

The Blair government and the civil service

'The public management revolution has continued under the Blair government' (Butcher 2000, p. 77). As observed in Chapter 2, Next Steps was accepted by Labour, as were market testing, contracting-out and PFI. Unsurprisingly, civil service numbers have remained at levels similar to those inherited in 1997 (around 475,000 in 2000), with a slight increase (from 77 to 78 per cent) in those working on Next Steps lines (Cabinet Office, November 2000).

Recruitment by open competition, however, has increased sharply, at senior levels from 96 posts in 1996–7 to 158 in 1999–2000. In the latter year 65.2 per cent of open competition appointees were from outside the service, 27.8 per cent from the private sector. As part of Blair's Cabinet Office reorganisation the Office of the Civil Service Commissioners has been relocated within the Cabinet Office Constitution Secretariat alongside the offices of the Commissioner for Public Appointments and the Business Appointments Advisory Committee (*Civil Service Commissioners Annual Reports, 1997, 2000*). In 1998 it was announced that selection stages of fast-stream recruitment would return 'to direct Civil Service management' when the RAS's contract expired in 2001, although the private sector would continue to deliver support services such as advertising (Cabinet Office, 2000b, and Chapman, 2000). The SCS has also been retained and the corporate nature of the service reaffirmed by the decision that staff serving the new devolved administrations in Scotland and Wales will continue to be part of a unified civil service (see p. 195). In such ways Blair has consolidated his predecessors' civil service reforms.

Modernising government

In 1999 the government signalled further reform in the White Paper *Modernising Government* (Prime Minister and Minister for the Cabinet Office, 1999). While dealing with public services generally, it proposed 'a change of course for the Civil Service for the next 10 years as important as Next Steps 10 years previously' (www.cabinet-office.gov.uk/1999/senior/rw_speech.htm). It outlined 'seven challenges for the civil service' (Box 4.4.)

These 'challenges' both advance the efficiency agenda of previous governments and address other important issues. For example, reference to a 'unified civil service' reflects heightened concern at fragmentation occasioned by the devolved administrations. The reception was mixed. Chapman (1999, p. 8) acknowledged that 'in ten or twenty years', its significance may be 'comparable to that of . . . Next Steps', but questioned the consequences of developing a less 'risk-averse culture'. Rhodes (2000c, pp. 154, 163) noted the absence of 'proposals for evaluating policy advice and the work of top civil servants', and the 'tensions' likely to arise with UK civil servants working for administrations in Scotland and Wales.

Box 4.4 Seven challenges for the civil service

- Implementing constitutional reform in a way that preserves a unified civil service and ensures close working between the UK government and the devolved administrations
- Getting staff in all Departments to integrate the EU dimension into policy thinking
- Focusing work on public services so as to improve their quality, make them more innovative and responsive to users and ensure that they are delivered in an efficient and joined up way
- Creating a more innovative and less risk-averse culture in the civil service
- Improving collaborative working across organisational boundaries
- Managing the civil service to help it to meet these challenges
- Thinking ahead strategically to future priorities.

Source: Prime Minister and Minister for the Cabinet Office (1999, p. 56)

The Wilson Report

Subsequently, the Cabinet Secretary was invited to respond. That response, produced after consultation within senior ranks, constituted the Wilson Report (1999). This contained six key themes (Box 4.5)

Responsibility for implementing these proposals was given to the Cabinet Office Corporate Management Command section. Departments were to prepare departmental action plans linked to targets. Some of the most far-reaching targets included: an annual 10 per cent increase in open competition for five years, 65 per cent of the SCS to have outside experience by 2005, 100 key tasks to attract high-quality inward secondees during 2000; and diversity targets (women and ethnic minorities to constitute 35 and 3.2 per cent respectively of the SCS by 2005). There were also commitments to recruit more mid-career outsiders; to broaden fast-stream entry; to

---

Box 4.5 The Wilson Report: six 'key themes'

- Stronger **leadership** with a clear sense of purpose
- Better **business planning** from top to bottom
- Sharper **performance management**
- A dramatic improvement in **diversity**
- A Service **more open** to people and ideas, which brings on talent
- A better **deal for staff**

Source: Wilson Report (1999, para. 2; emphasis in original)

---

expand interdepartmental mobility; and to introduce a new scheme to develop 100 non-fast-stream managers. It was also anticipated that targeted 'early retirement' would 'create more space at the top'.

Initial reactions, again, were mixed. Some perceived Wilson's proposals as largely extending earlier initiatives such as Next Steps; others as 'a smokescreen' concealing 'substantial "politicisation"' (*The Times*, 16 December 1999). Still others (Sherman, *The Times*, 16 December 1999; Hutton, *The Observer*, 19 December 1999) claimed to detect 'sweeping reforms to shake up Whitehall' which could potentially 'transform' the service. This view rests on the belief that more staff mobility, private sector experience, fast-track promotions, etc. will 'transform' the service 'along the lines of a thriving private enterprise'. It would also, however, further erode permanence and unity, and dilute its public service ethos.

Conclusion: the end of the civil service?

Since the 1960s much appears to have changed. Traditional features such as permanence, unity, anonymity and neutrality are less firmly rooted than before. Special advisers, for example, are neither permanent nor neutral and some are far from anonymous. Unity has been eroded by dismantling common pay, grading and centralised recruitment, and by fragmentation into NSAs. Hennessy (1995, p. 125) quotes one mandarin: the civil service has been 'balkanized' into 'a lot of civil services . . . clustered around a small, almost nineteenth-century-style core' of departments. Chapman (1992, 1997) goes further. Many traditional features have gone. Arguably, we have witnessed 'the end of the civil service'.

Recent change, however, must be kept in perspective. As Barberis (1997, pp. 1, 2) notes, while recent decades have been 'an era of change', even before Fulton 'things never stood still'. Moreover, the civil service is still a significant and substantial organisation. Civil servants are overwhelmingly still permanent, neutral and anonymous. Arguably, too, the civil service has retained its unity. One recent mandarin, for example, described today's civil service as 'unified but not uniform' (Chapman, 1997, p. 29). Also, for many officials little has changed. At lower levels administrative work, and at higher levels policy work, go on much as before. As Graham Wilson (1993, p. 43) comments, 'Even after the radical Thatcher governments, ministers remain[ed] extraordinarily dependent by international standards on permanent civil servants. While this situation endures, one may query how much has changed fundamentally.' Indeed in many respects fundamental change has clearly not occurred. Rhodes (2000c, p. 162) observes, 'In 2000 a permanent secretary is white and over 50, with an Oxbridge degree in the humanities, has worked in the Civil Service for twenty-five years. . . . And, of course, he is male'.

Within Whitehall itself there are fairly open tensions between managerial modernisers on the one hand and 'the old guard' on the other. The Wilson Report probably occupies a middle position. In any event Wilson's proposals may in time prove less radical than they appear today. Whereas previous reforms were largely formulated by outsiders – Fulton, Rayner, Ibbs – Wilson's proposals represent reform 'devised by the Civil Service for the Civil Service and led by the Civil Service'. It is, therefore, very possible that 'only incremental change will . . . follow' (*The Times*,

16 December 1999). The Wilson Report may be seen in the future like the Fulton Report, 'as a document which promised much change, but led to little' (Rathbone, 2000, p. 29).

Further reading

For developments before the 1990s Drewry and Butcher (1991) offers comprehensive treatment, while Hennessy (1990) is also highly readable. More recent analysis is contained in R. Pyper, *The British Civil Service* (Prentice Hall, 1995); K. Dowding, *The Civil Service* (London: Routledge, 1995), as well as Theakston (1995) and Pilkington (1999). Barberis (1996b) contains useful readings. Butcher (2000) and Theakston (2000a) offer short up-to-date summaries of civil service structure and management and minister/civil servant relations respectively. Greenwood (2000) brings discussion of civil service neutrality up to date.

Foster and Plowden (1996) offer specialised analysis of central government changes including chapters on 'Ministers and agencies' and 'The role of ministers'. Rhodes (2000a, 2000b) contains authoritative up-to-date material on ministers and civil servants in the core executive, and the roles of ministers and permanent secretaries.

Whitehall itself produces useful information. Much of this, including civil service statistics, the Civil Service Code and the Wilson Report, is available at www.cabinet-office.gov.uk. *The Civil Service Year Book*, produced annually by the Stationery Office, contains detailed information about government departments and agencies plus statistical information.

Local government in context

Introduction

Until the advent of devolved assemblies (see Chapter 10) the only layer of elected government below the centre was local government. Traditionally this has been responsible for a wide range of services – including at various times gas, electricity, further and higher education, and water. Today, however, things are very different. Elected local government has seen a loss of powers and responsibilities. It now 'shares the turf' with a wide variety of agencies (e.g. health authorities, police authorities, primary care groups, action zones, partnerships), none of which is directly elected. Elected local government is now but one part of a complex mosaic of organisations delivering services at the local level; the term 'local governance' (see Chapter 1) is used increasingly to describe public administrative activity at the local level. As Loughlin (1996, p. 56) observes, 'Local councils have been stripped of governmental responsibility for certain services which continue to be public services but which are now provided by agencies which are directly funded from the centre.' The once dominant position of elected local government in service provision has been challenged both by the rise of local quangos (see Chapter 8) and by the increased involvement of private sector organisations, voluntary bodies and other governmental agencies.

Local governance brings together governmental and non-governmental agencies in flexible partnerships to deal with problems (e.g. urban redevelopment, crime and disorder) by using different strategies. It is not based on a single structure or a new set of structures, but on a fusion of different styles and working relationships. Flexibility of approach is of fundamental importance. The Blair government has attempted to find ways of working which cross organisational boundaries. There is no likelihood that local authorities will go back to being near monopolistic service providers; provision will be shared with a range of partners. Elected local government is but one part of the complex world of local governance, albeit a uniquely important one because of its directly elected status.

The advent of 'governance', however, should not obscure the continuing importance of elected local authorities in their own right. Their responsibilities are still central to building the environment in which we live and work. Overall, councils in the United Kingdom spent (in the year 2000) some £75 billion from taxes, around a quarter of all public expenditure. Local government remains big business.

Development and structure

As Stewart notes (2000b, p. 15), the nature of local government has been shaped by its history. 'Shared understandings that have been developed over time have become part of the assumptive world of local government.' Each local authority, partly as the result of history, remains a unique miniature political system. The following discussion about the development of local government on a national scale should not obscure the continued significance of local context.

In January 2000 local government in Britain consisted of 441 principal local authorities: 387 in England, thirty-two in Scotland and twenty-two in Wales. Later in 2000 the newly established Greater London Authority was added to this list. What is the genesis of the contemporary pattern? The early nineteenth century provides an appropriate starting point. The pressures brought about by the Industrial Revolution – urban poverty, unemployment, poor sanitation, disease, etc. – showed the need for a robust system of local government. The 'tangle' of local agencies that existed (see Hollis, 1987, pp. 2–3) was unable to cope with ever-increasing demands. The response of government took contrasting forms, reflected in the two major reform Acts of the 1830s. On the one hand, the Poor Law Amendment Act, 1834, which created Boards of Guardians responsible for local administration of the Poor Law, heralded the creation of more single-purpose *ad hoc* authorities (e.g. local health boards, highway boards, elementary school boards). On the other hand, the Municipal Corporations Act, 1835, created a network of seventy-eight multipurpose elected local authorities in urban areas providing a range of services; despite a limited franchise, the principle of elected local self-government had been established.

There nevertheless still remained a tangle of appointed and elected bodies. Further rationalisation came in legislation enacted towards the end of the nineteenth century. The Local Government Act, 1888, created sixty-two county councils (including one for London, the LCC), and sixty-one (all-purpose) county boroughs, all directly elected. The Local Government Act, 1894, completed the reform of English and Welsh local government outside London by creating, as a second tier in county areas, elected urban district councils (UDCs) and rural district councils (RDCs). The London Government Act, 1899, established twenty-eight metropolitan borough councils to provide the capital with a second tier of local government under the LCC. The unique 700-year-old City of London Corporation remained unscathed throughout the reform process. With some modifications – notably the creation of the Greater London Council and thirty-two London boroughs in 1965 – this structure lasted until the 1972 Local Government Act ushered in a new pattern of elected local government for England and Wales (see Figure 5.1).

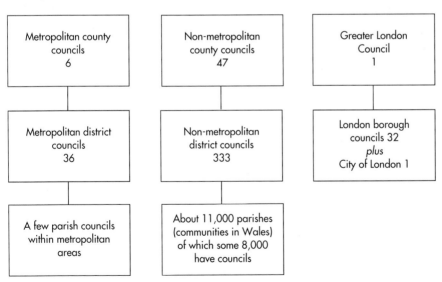

Figure 5.1 Elected local government in England and Wales, 1974–86

This new pattern became operative from April 1974. It abolished all county boroughs and reduced the fifty-eight county councils in England and Wales to forty-seven. Within these counties 1,250 municipal boroughs, and urban and rural districts were replaced by 333 district councils. In the major conurbations six metropolitan county councils were established incorporating thirty-six metropolitan districts with populations ranging from 172,000 (South Tyneside) to almost 1.1 million (Birmingham). The two-tier structure remained although the Redcliffe–Maud Royal Commission (1996–9) favoured a pattern based predominantly on all-purpose unitary authorities embracing both town and country. While the Labour government substantially accepted these proposals, it was voted out of office in June 1970 and the new Conservative government retained the two-tier system. In Scotland the Wheatley Royal Commission saw its proposals for a two-tier system largely adopted by the Conservative government and what emerged was a pattern in which 431 authorities were reduced to nine regions, fifty-three districts and three 'most purpose' island authorities – Orkney, Shetland and the Western Isles (see Figure 5.2).

By the mid-1970s the dual town/country structure of local government, set up at the end of the nineteenth century, had been comprehensively reorganised. But there were still more changes to come with Margaret Thatcher's election in 1979. First to go was the Greater London Council (GLC) and the six metropolitan county councils, all of which had fallen under Labour control in 1981. The Local Government Act, 1985, allocated their responsibilities partly to the London boroughs and metropolitan district councils, but also partly to a range of joint boards, joint commit-tees, *ad hoc* agencies and central government departments. The 'administrative tangle' of the early nineteenth century was raising its head again. The party political dimension behind this particular structural reform (i.e. reducing the influence of Labour at local level) was overt. Next to go was the separate Inner London Education Authority (ILEA). Its almost inevitable Labour majority, along with its high expenditure levels, led to its abolition by the Education Reform Act, 1988, under

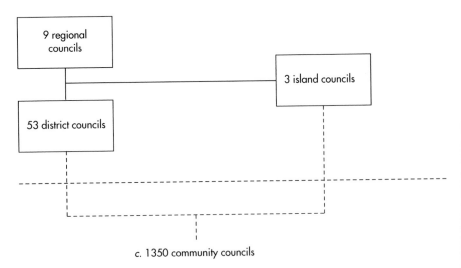

Figure 5.2 Elected local government in Scotland, 1975–96

which responsibility for education services passed to the individual London boroughs with effect from 1 April 1990.

There was a further structural reform in England, Scotland and Wales during the 1990s which centred on Michael Heseltine, whose enthusiasm, initially when Environment Secretary, drove the reform process forward even when other members of the government (and, indeed, his own successors at the Department of the Environment) seemed lukewarm. One-tier systems are often felt to be more efficient than two tiers, and the Conservative government in its quest for efficiency had wanted to see a substantial increase in the number of single-tier unitary authorities as a result of the findings of the commission it had established under Sir John Banham. At one point it looked as though almost 100 new unitary authorities embracing more than two-thirds of the population of the English non-metropolitan counties would emerge but, faced with a public sceptical about the likely benefit of such fundamental change, the commission adapted many of its draft recommendations to 'hybrid' solutions: the occasional unitary authority in otherwise unchanged two-tier counties.

The reform saga was tortuous. Few people regarded the upheaval and turmoil as worthwhile. In the end a total of forty-six new unitary authorities were created in England. In Scotland and Wales there was no commission to oversee the reform process. Here the respective secretaries of state effectively determined the outcomes. In April 1996, twenty-two new Welsh single-tier unitary authorities replaced the existing forty-five councils and in Scotland thirty-two single tier authorities replaced the existing sixty-five authorities. The more complex situation in England is high-lighted in Figure 5.3. There was no change in Northern Ireland where the twenty-six

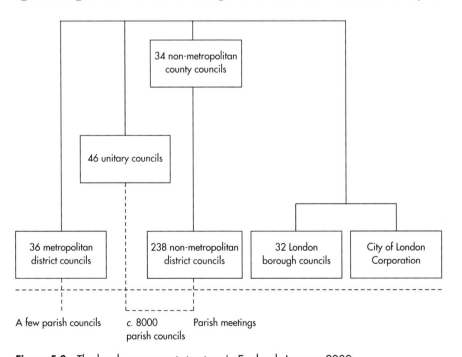

Figure 5.3 The local government structure in England, January 2000

district councils remained, albeit with substantially fewer functions than their counterparts in mainland Britain.

In addition to the above, in many parts of the country there is also a third tier of local government. In England, outside the major cities, the parish has been retained. Of the more than 10,000 parishes, about 8,000 have elected councils, some of which are known as town councils. Small parishes with under 200 electors can instead hold parish meetings which all electors can attend. Parish councils have very limited powers connected with street level administration but also act as a pressure group in dealing with other levels of government. In Wales, parishes were replaced in 1974 by 'communities', which have either elected councils, or community meetings on a similar basis to English parishes, while in Scotland some 1,350 localities have set up their own optional community councils as a kind of their tier, though these have no statutory powers.

The number of local authories has fallen substantially since the 1970s. In the early 1970s there were 1,855 principal local authorities in Britain. By the mid-1970s this was cut back to 521. By 2001 there were only 442 (This figure includes the Greater London Authority – see p. 203). One consequence of this reduction is that, compared with much of Europe, Britain now has significantly bigger authorities and far more inhabitants per elected member (see Table 5.1).

The rationale for this strategy has invariably had financial and managerial origins (albeit against a strong political backdrop) and has focused on economies of scale. From the standpoint of ordinary citizens, however, the massive reduction in the numbers of both local authorities and elected councillors is frequently said to represent a 'democratic deficit' in that larger authorities and fewer councillors can serve to further increase remoteness from local decision-making. Linked with this is the erosion of services *directly* provided by elected local authorities. It is to this topic that we now turn.

Table 5.1 Britain's large-scale local government

	Inhabitants per elected member	Average population per council
France	116	1,580
Iceland	194	1,330
Germany	250	4,925
Italy	397	7,130
Norway	515	9,000
Spain	597	4,930
Sweden	667	30,040
Belgium	783	16,960
Denmark	1,084	18,760
Portugal	1,125	32,300
UK	2,605	118,400

Source: Council of Europe, *Local and Regional Authorities in Europe*, 56 (1996)

Local authority functions

Local authorities can only do what the law allows; all council powers derive from Acts of Parliament. Indeed local government itself exists only by courtesy of Parliament, which frequently alters its powers and functions. Should a local authority provide a service, or spend money, for which there is no statutory authority, it would be acting *ultra vires* (see Box 1.1) and may be declared unlawful by the courts. Local authorities which fail to carry out statutory duties required by law can, like other public bodies, be compelled by the courts to perform them.

Stewart (2000b, p. 80) argues that the range of local authority functions 'seems more dependent on historical accident than on any worked-out approach to the government of local communities'. Different services are allocated to different organisational tiers. Although with the rise of local governance there are now a number of alternative service delivery systems – including voluntary sector and private sector provision – service provision remains a major role for local authorities. As we have seen, elected local government is still big business. Midwinter (1995, p. 131) reminds us of the continuing importance of service provision: 'Despite the welter of rhetoric, the image of radical reform, the language of the new public management, the glitz of marketing and public relations, the central role of a local authority remains – municipal provision of services.' As Box 5.1 shows, Leach and Stewart (1992) include this as one of the four primary roles for elected local government.

Despite the considerable restraining legislation of recent years, especially in the financial sphere, elected local government remains very important. If individual local authorities were listed in terms of their expenditure levels, almost 100 would rank alongside the top 500 British companies. To take just one example, Kent County Council in the early 1990s served a population larger than that of forty member states

---

Box 5.1 The primary functions of elected local government

1   *Service provision*: the planning, resourcing and provision, directly or indirectly, of individual local services.

2   *Regulation*: the regulation of the economic behaviour of individuals or other agencies in the public interest by insisting on their compliance with standards, rules and procedures of various kinds for exchange or provision of goods and services. This is where licensing, inspection, monitoring, registration and certification come in.

3   *Strategic planning*: the provision of a longer-term planning framework to influence the activities of internal departments and external organisations in relation to individual service areas or authority-wide issues.

4   *Promotion and advocacy*: the persuasion of one or more other organisations (e.g. private industry, voluntary bodies) to carry out activities which are likely to benefit the local community (e.g. by loans to small businesses, by grants to voluntary organisations).

Source: Leach and Stewart (1992)

---

of the United Nations. With an annual turnover in excess of £1 billion, 50,000 employees and 1,400 service points, it was not only the biggest single employer in Kent, but larger than many national and international companies such as the Beecham Group, Unigate and Burmah Oil (Wilson and Game, 1998, p. 84).

County councils like Kent, along with the unitary authorities such as Birmingham, plus the metropolitan districts (e.g. Stockport) and the London boroughs (e.g. Wandsworth), are responsible either for most of the council-provided services in their areas or at least for the most labour-intensive and biggest-spending ones, notably education and social services. The Scottish, Welsh and English unitary authorities have responsibility for all those services that in the two-tier areas of England are split between the counties and districts. The division of responsibilities between English county and district councils is presented in Table 5.2.

The range of services provided by local authorities is massive, but provision is not uniform throughout the country. Slum clearance, for example, is only a major problem in some areas. Again, standards of service vary; beyond the minimum standards which are usually laid down by law there is, in practice, often a wide area of discretion. Not all functions, moreover, are mandatory upon local authorities; some, like the provision of leisure centres, art galleries and playing fields, are permissive (which means the authority has a choice about whether or not to provide them). It is, moreover, open to any authority to promote a private Bill in order to extend its powers. Although this is a complex and costly procedure, over the years many authorities have acquired powers by this means to perform particular functions in their localities: for example, to maintain the external decoration of listed buildings (Kensington and Chelsea), and to operate a municipal bank (Birmingham).

As we noted earlier, the relative simplicity of government by large locally elected authorities has been supplemented by networks of public, semi-public and private organisations involved in local governance. John (1997, p. 256) provides a list of such bodies:

- hospital trusts and a large complex network of health providers such as primary care groups;
- new central government agencies administering new or former local government functions, particularly in urban economic development, such as training and enterprise councils (TECs), urban development corporations and housing action trusts;
- partnership organisations such as Business Links, Single Regeneration Budget steering groups and business marketing bodies;
- micro agencies formerly under the umbrella of the local authority, e.g. further education colleges;
- existing public agencies which have been given an enhanced new role, such as housing associations;
- the regional offices of central government departments including the government offices for the regions (GORs), established in 1995 (see p. 28);
- new or rejuvenated regional organisations such as the Regional Development Agencies (RDAs) (see p. 202), regional organisations of local authorities, and the regional CBIs and TUCs;
- dynamic voluntary associations, such as community organisations.

Table 5.2 English county and district councils: who does what?

Activity	County councils	District councils
County farms	All services	
Education	All services	
Highways and transportation	Transportation planning Constructing new county roads Maintenance of county roads* Public transport Infrastructure and co-ordination Highways and street lighting Public rights of way	Street cleansing Street lighting
Housing		All services

Leisure and amenities	Libraries
	Archaeology
	Archives
	County parks and picnic sites
	Grants to village halls, sports,
	  arts, countryside and
	  community projects
		Allotments
		Museums/art galleries
		County parks, local parks and
		  open spaces
		Playing fields, other than schools
		Swimming pools and sports
		  centres

Planning	Structure plans Minerals control Environment and conservation Economic and tourism development Waste disposal control	Local plans Development control Local land charges Environment and conservation Economic development

Public protection	Waste regulation and disposal,
	  waste recycling centres
	Trading standards
	Registration of births, deaths
	  and marriages
	Coroners' courts
	Fire and rescue
		Refuse collection
		Food safety and hygiene
		Markets
		Control of pollution
		Cemeteries/crematoria

Social services	All services	
Council tax		Collection of own tax, plus precepts for county and parishes

Note: * Some highways functions are undertaken by district councils on an agency basis.

The transition from local government to local governance has increased complexity. This complexity is illustrated by Figure 5.4 which shows the large number of organisations which are involved in the governance of one city, Liverpool. While the advent of such a complex governance network has serious implications for local accountability and democratic control, elected local government nevertheless remains centrally important. As Wilson and Game (1998, p. 88) note:

Tourism & Conference Bureau	English Partnership (National)
Merseyside Probation Committee	NWDA
MCVS	North West Arts
National Museums and Galleries on Merseyside	North West Council for Sports and Recreation
Mersey Partnership	North West Regional Assembly
Merseyside Racial Equality Council	CBI (NW)
MTEC/Business Link	North West Tourist Board
Health Action Zone	Government Office North West
Other Merseyside LA's	Funding Agency for Schools
Joint Boards (Fire, Police, Passenger Transport,	Employment Service
Waste Disposal)	NHS Executive North West
MDHC	Environment Agency
Liverpool & Sefton Employment Zone	Inward
Merseyside Co-ordinating Committee	Benefits Agency
Objective One Monitoring Communication	North West Partnership
Safer Merseyside Partnership	English Heritage
	National Lottery (NW)

MERSEYSIDE NATIONAL/REGIONAL

LIVERPOOL CITY COUNCIL

LOCAL CITY

City of Learning	Leap SRBS
ICVS	11 Local Partnerships
Liverpool Health Authority	Dingle SRB
Community Health Councils	North Liverpool SRB
Chamber of Commerce	Primary Step SRB
Liverpool Airport PLC	Neth/Val SRB
Liverpool Hat	Speke/Garston
JMU	SRB/Development Company
Liverpool University	Voluntary Bodies
Lipa	LCVS
Liverpool Community College	Speke/Garston Housing Co.
Liverpool Hope University College	NHS Trust
City Safe	Kensington NDC
Health Improvement Programme	City Centre Partnership
	Granby Toxteth Dev. Trust
	Liverpool Partnership Group/Forum
	Ropewalks
	Primary Care Groups

Figure 5.4 The complexity of local governance: Liverpool
Source: Liverpool Democracy Commission (1999)

Local authorities may nowadays be just part of a complex mosaic of agencies operating at the local level, but they remain a uniquely large, pivotal, multifunctional, locally knowledgeable and experienced, and, above all, directly elected part of that mosaic, not easily sidelined by even an antipathetic central government.

Although local authorities require statutory authority for the functions they perform, since the Local Government Act, 1972 (section 137), they have had a general power to spend up to the product of a 2p rate on purposes not specifically authorised by statute. This has given local councils power to initiate a limited number of developments, a capability reinforced by the Local Government Act, 2000, which extended the horizon by including a power (but not a duty) for councils to promote the social, economic and environmental well-being of their area. This can be exercised on behalf of all/some residents and all or part of the council's area. It can even be used to benefit people, or areas, outside the council's boundary. There are limitations: there must be regard paid to guidance; the power does not include a power to charge and does not override existing legal constraints – though the Secretary of State can remove such constraints. But at least local government has a new legal framework and the enactment of this legislation offers real possibilities for local authorities to exercise a leadership role within the local community. Indeed, this goes some way towards giving British local authorities an equivalent of the 'power of general competence' possessed by their counterparts in most other European countries. French *communes*, German *Gemeinden*, Norwegian and Swedish *Kommuner* – though mostly much smaller than our district councils – all have the constitutional right to take any action that they believe to be in the interests of their residents that is not statutorily prohibited to them. This new power of 'well-being', included in the Local Government Act, 2000, promises to reduce the shackles of *ultra vires*, which has hitherto restricted the ability of local authorities to take major initiatives on behalf of their communities. For this to be meaningful, however, local authorities require appropriate financial resources.

Local government finance

Local government finance is important both economically and politically: economically because councils in the United Kingdom currently spend around a quarter of all public expenditure; politically because the finance available to local authorities largely determines the level of services which they can provide. While it is theoretically true that local authorities, through the council tax, have a source of finance independent of central government, finance which can be spent on any object within their statutory jurisdiction, this is not the whole story. The reality is far more complex.

Understanding local government finance is not easy. As a starting point, however, it is helpful to make a distinction (although the two do interconnect) between *current* (or *revenue*) finance and *capital* finance.

Current (or revenue) finance

Councils need money to finance services on an ongoing basis: staff wages and salaries, books for schools, office equipment, petrol for refuse collection vehicles, heating bills in children's homes, etc. Education and housing are the biggest expenditure items in authorities that have responsibility for these services. The *income* to finance this expenditure is raised from four major sources: (1) council tax; (2) government grants; (3) uniform business rate; (4) charges.

Council tax

The first source of local authorities' current income is their own taxation – traditionally the rates, then the community charge (poll tax) and since 1993 the council tax. Whereas the rates were a tax on property and the community charge/poll tax was a tax on the individual, the council tax is a combination of the two. It is a domestic property tax, but with the size of the bill depending in part on the number of residents in a property as well as on its value, since taxpayers living alone get at least a 25 per cent reduction, regardless of their income. Homes are assigned to one of eight property bands with the assumption that a two-adult household is the norm. No account is taken of any adults above the two-person norm, but the scale of discounts reflects the banding (see McConnell, 1999). The local council tax raised only 24 per cent of money spent in 1998–9 and this was forecast by the government to drop to 22 per cent in 2000–1.

Government grants

The vast majority of local government income is provided by the centre, mainly through grants. These have long been an integral part of local government finance. Hitherto the bulk of such grants has been either *specific* or *general*. *Specific* grants must be spent on a specified project or service, e.g. social services training grant. These grants account for almost 30 per cent of central government support for local authorities. *General* grants can be spent at the discretion of the local councils themselves and account for nearly 40 per cent of total central government support. The main such grant is the Revenue Support Grant, which each local authority receives annually. This is calculated on the basis of a Standard Spending Assessment (SSA) – the government calculation of what each council needs to spend to achieve a standard level of service – which takes into account the different context and nature of each local authority. Councils frequently plead that the formula used by central government does not take account of their own special needs. In 1999–2000 the amount of spending supported by central government grants was £25.86 billion, almost twice as much as raised by the council tax (£13.27 billion). Interestingly, the uniform business rate (see below) at £13.6 billion exceeded the amount raised by the council tax (see DETR, 1999a).

The uniform business rate

Sometimes called the non-domestic rate, the UBR came into operation at the same time as the community charge though it did not produce a similar public outcry. Previously each local authority had been free to set rate levels for local business properties itself. Now central government each year sets a standard or uniform rate poundage for all non-domestic properties in England and Wales – though not in Scotland where existing rate poundages were retained (Wilson and Game, 1998, p. 167). Local councils send out the bills and collect the UBR, but the money is now paid into a national fund and redistributed back to the councils in proportion to their populations. In effect the UBR has become part of the central government grant. Former local ratepayers have become national taxpayers, and there is no longer any direct financial link between businesses and local authorities. The White Paper *Modern Local Government: in Touch with the People* (DETR, 1998a, para. 10.8) made it clear that central government intended to retain a UBR and that 'the revenue from the rate will be paid into a non-domestic rating pool and redistributed to councils'. Local authorities with large numbers of businesses remain particularly aggrieved about 'pooling' this revenue rather than being permitted to spend it locally.

Charges

Local authorities have always set fees and charges for the use of some of their services – car parks, tolls, passenger transport, school meals, swimming baths and other leisure facilities, rents, etc. Obviously the amounts received by individual authorities vary widely, according to the type and range of chargeable services provided and the levels at which charges are set. Levels vary enormously from authority to authority. For example, Derbyshire County Council charges 35p per meal for their meals on wheels service, while Kent charges £1.50. Lambeth charges £300 per adult internment compared with only £27 in neighbouring Brent. Local authorities can encourage services by subsidising them, or they can effectively limit use by charging a great deal. The variety of charges levied is a reminder that local authorities retain considerable discretion in this particular sphere of revenue income. Table 5.3 presents details of the funding of revenue expenditure from the inception of the council tax system.

The revenue regime is also subject to *expenditure* controls; indeed, local authorities can only spend money as allowed by statute. Since the Rates Act, 1984, moreover, expenditure controls have tightened through what is known as 'capping', which means that the Secretary of State has the power to cap, or impose a ceiling on, the planned budget of any local authority which is viewed as excessive. Capping is based on spending criteria determined by central government. As Stewart (2000b, p. 184) observed:

> The capping of local authority expenditure was achieved in a way that minimised political costs. By announcing the criteria in advance the government ensured that nearly all authorities capped themselves, rather than set budgets above the cap and have a cap imposed, with the uncertainties and costs involved.

Table 5.3 Funding of revenue expenditure in England

Year	Revenue expenditure £bn	Government grant £bn	%	Uniform business rate £bn	%	Council tax £bn	%
1993–4	41,506	21,685	52	11,584	28	8,912	21
1994–5	43,602	23,679	54	10,692	25	9,239	21
1995–6	44,827	23,335	52	11,361	25	9,777	22
1996–7	46,532	23,003	49	12,743	27	10,461	22
1997–8	47,256	23,840	50	12,034	25	11,241	24
1998–9	50,990	25,179	49	12,531	25	12,332	24
1999–2000*	53,761	25,862	48	13,619	25	13,278	25
2000–1†	53,617	26,416	49	15,407	29	11,801	22

Source: *Local Government Finance Statistics Key Facts: England* (DETR, March 2000)
Notes:
* Budget estimates.
† Provisional settlement.

By the 1999 Local Government Act the Blair government claimed to have abolished 'crude and universal capping', although it has retained reserve powers, should it deem intervention necessary. In 1999 no council actually had its budget capped – for what was the first time since capping was introduced in 1985. But the Secretary of State chose to look 'particularly closely' at those authorities that increased their council tax rates by more than 9 per cent. As a result, the twelve councils in this group with the biggest increases were given a 'yellow card' or put on warning, and told that they would be looked at again in 2000 when a judgement would be made as to whether their budget increase over the two years had been 'excessive'.

While Labour has kept its manifesto promise to end 'crude and universal capping' it has not ended capping *per se*. It is now selective capping, with a set of reserve powers that enable ministers to decide what are 'excessive' council tax increases. An authority whose budget is judged, by the minister's criteria, to be 'excessive' can be designated for what is now termed 'limitation' and set a revised maximum budget requirement to be achieved within a specified time period. Universal capping has become selective and subjective, and what is the most centrally controlled local finance system in Western Europe remains essentially unchanged. The 'capping holiday' announced in 1999 cannot obscure the continued domination of the centre via the standard spending assessments, a nationalised business rate and tightly controlled capital finance. As Lowndes (1999, p. 130) has observed:

> For central government, there is no way in which a 'trusting' relationship with local government can be equated with significant increases in financial autonomy. For many local government leaders, the retention of reserve capping powers and the tightly restricted discretion over business rates provide further evidence of the government's refusal to turn the rhetoric of trust into reality.

Local authorities are likely to keep pressing for some restoration of financial discretion. Central government for its part is only likely to countenance increased discretion for those authorities which take seriously its modernisation agenda and which are committed to move restrictions that stand in the way of better performance.

Capital finance

Councils need money to spend on longer-term items such as the purchase, construction or improvement of land, property or equipment. (In 1999–2000 capital expenditure by local authorities in England amounted to £7.1 billion.) Central government has kept a very firm grip on capital finance for many years through a system of credit control. As Wilson and Game show (1998, pp. 155–7), there are currently four major sources of capital finance, three of which are directly subject to central government control.

Credit

Each year individual local authorities are given a Basic Credit Approval (BCA) which specifies the maximum sum they can borrow to finance capital projects in education, housing, social services and other specific areas (although credit not used by one authority can be transferred to another). In addition, individual authorities might be given a Supplementary Credit Approval (SCA) for particular government-approved projects such as policies to address homelessness. Taken together, these credit approvals (known as net capital allocation in Scotland) account for well over half of all local authority capital investment.

Capital receipts

Councils are able to supplement their BCAs and SCAs by using money they raise through selling assets such as land, buildings and housing. Tight controls are once again in force. Through most of the 1990s councils were permitted to spend only 25 per cent of receipts from housing sales and 50 per cent of receipts from the disposal of other assets; the remainder had to be used to pay off outstanding debts. One of the first acts of the Blair government was to permit greater flexibility by allowing local authorities to reinvest up to £5 billion of their accumulated receipts from council house sales in building new houses and renovating old ones.

Capital grants

Central government, chiefly through its various urban programmes, and the European Union, through vehicles such as the European Regional Development Fund, provide grants towards the financing of specific projects. Here, too, however, there are likely to be conditions. Indeed, receipt of certain grants might simply lead to the government reducing a council's credit approval by the same amount.

Current (revenue) income

The only source of capital finance not subject to direct government control is a local authority's own revenue income – from local taxes, rents and other charges. But in a period of financial constraint most current revenue is required for current expenditure; there is little or nothing left over for capital projects. In other words, this is far more of a theoretical than an actual source of capital expenditure. Table 5.4 provides a breakdown of the financing of local authority capital expenditure in England.

In addition to controls over local government income and expenditure, local authorities' financial affairs are subject to rigorous scrutiny. This is overseen by the Audit Commission in England and Wales and the Accounts Commission in Scotland, which appoint external auditors either from their own staff (district auditors) or from private accountancy firms. Auditors are concerned not only with the detection of fraud and wilful misconduct, but with the legality of expenditure, its reasonableness, and with whether it provides Value for Money (VFM). The Audit Commission also produces 'league tables' of Performance Indicators which allow authorities to compare their expenditure and efficiency with those of other councils.

Traditionally councillors (or officers) could be surcharged (held personally liable) for illegal expenditure or wilful misconduct and, in the case of councillors, expelled from office. This latter fate befell councillors from Clay Cross who refused to operate provisions in the 1972 Housing Finance Act, and in 1985–6 in Lambeth and Liverpool where councillors were adjudged guilty of wilful misconduct by delaying the fixing of their council's rates. However, under the Local Government Act 2000 surcharge has disappeared as a delineated sanction against individual erring councillors, although their conduct can be reported to their council's standards committee and then sent to an external standards officer who has the task of operating the National Code of Conduct for councillors. Sanctions for inappropriate conduct by councillors can include removal from office.

Table 5.4 Local authority capital expenditure in England (£bn)

	1996–7	1997–8	1998–9*	1999–2000†
Credit approvals	2.1	2.1	2.3	2.3
Central government grants	1.4	1.3	1.2	1.1
Capital receipts	1.2	1.2	1.2	1.5
Revenue finance	1.4	1.4	1.2	1.3
Other resources	0.5	0.5	0.7	0.9
Total	6.6	6.5	6.6	7.1

Source: *Local Government Finance Statistics Key Facts: England* (DETR, March 2000)
Notes:
*Provisional.
† Forecast.

Local democracy: theoretical perspectives

Local government is not only concerned with providing services, it is also widely perceived as an instrument of democratic self-government. Indeed, a central plank of the Blair government's modernisation agenda is the theme of democratic renewal. Pratchett (1999, p. 1) has observed that 'democratic renewal' is an ingenious title for the Labour government's modernisation programme:

> As a phrase it captures both the perceived problems with the existing institutions of local government and the ambitions of the current reform process. It suggests that local democracy is failing and that new proposals will address these failings in order to revitalise democratic practice.

At a practical level democratic renewal is about addressing clearly identifiable problems such as low electoral turnout, service delivery failures, and decision-making structures that have outlived their usefulness. At a more macro level, it focuses on systemic failings in the practice of local democracy and attempts to instigate broader political, cultural and constitutional change. At the heart of this is the nature of contemporary democracy. This section examines the theoretical perspectives underpinning this debate.

Democratic government does not necessarily entail locally elected councils. Indeed, one strand of continental thinking argues that democracy is essentially concerned with the nation-state and with majority rule, equality and uniformity. From such a perspective local government is seen as parochial and concerned with inequalities and differences between localities. This stance, however, contrasts with the traditional British view that local government enhances democracy, both by providing a vehicle of political education and as a means of increasing the liberty of the citizen by breaking down the power of the centralised state. This view emphasises that democracy is not simply concerned with national majority rule, social and political equality, and uniformity of standards but is, rather, an essential means of enabling individuals and local communities to voice their needs. (For discussion, see King and Stoker 1996; Pratchett and Wilson 1996.)

The accountability of decision-makers to those who elect them is widely perceived to be at the heart of local democracy. Councillors are elected for four-year periods of office, but in practice turnout in local elections is often low (29 per cent in 1998; 32 per cent in 1999; 29 per cent in 2000) and compares unfavourably with most other European countries. As Bulpitt (1993) has shown, too idealistic a model of accountability via elected local government can all too easily emerge, particularly given the fragmentation of service delivery which now characterises local governance. While local quangos compare unfavouably with local authorities through not being elected, they frequently circulate annual reports and accounts through local newspapers. Nevertheless, as King (1996, p. 216) observes, 'the lines of accountability between voters and quangos are murky', and the lack of interest and involvement in the representative system hardly makes it an ideal role model of accountability at its best.

It is frequently argued that local councillors are *representative* of the local population as a whole. This is not so. A census by the Local Government Management Board (LGMB 1998) showed that 76 per cent of councillors in England and Wales

Box 5.2 How representative are councillors?

England		All councillors (England and Wales)	
Male	72.1%	Retired	34.9%
Female	27.8%	Employed full-time	29.6%
Average age	55.4	Employed part-time	8.2%
		Self-employed	15.2%
		Not working	11.9%
Wales			
Male	79.6%	White	96.9%
Female	20.4%	Indian	0.7%
Average age	57.8	Black Caribbean	0.5%
		Pakistani	0.5%
		Other	2.4%

Source: LGMB (1998)

were male and that almost 97 per cent were white; the average age was 56. Box 5.2 emphasises the lack of social representativeness among democratically elected councillors. Such aggregate data do, of course, mask significant differences between specific localities. In some cities ethnic minority representation does mirror their overall position in the population. The representation of ideas and ideals (as well as socio-economic factors) also needs to be built into discussions about representativeness.

Participation is frequently espoused as a virtue of elected local government. Largely because of the perceived deficiencies of representative democracy, this received particular attention under the Blair government. Given poor turnouts in local elections, public participation is seen as crucial to the health of local democracy. A new raft of consultative mechanisms has emerged – such as citizens' juries, citizens' panels, visioning exercises – to work alongside more traditional devices such as public meetings. Participatory schemes abound, but it is important to remember that more participation is not the same thing as more democracy. More participation can often simply reinforce the existing power base within a community. Beetham (1996, p. 33) reminds us that the most 'participatory' political regimes in the twentieth century 'were communist systems, so-called people's democracies; yet that participation delivered little popular control over the personnel or policies of government'. While public participation has an educative role, it is important not to exaggerate its contribution to policy-making. As Parry and Moyser (1990, p. 169) emphasise: 'A participatory democrat will not look merely to maximising participation but to equalising it' (for further discussion see Wilson, 1999).

The most frequently cited theoretical justification for local government is pluralism. As the Layfield Committee (1976) observed: 'By providing a large number of points where decisions are taken by people of different political persuasion . . . it acts as a counterweight to the uniformity inherent in government decisions. It spreads political power.' While at one level this is clearly true, it needs to be emphasised that local authorities are established – and can be abolished – by Parliament, and in normal political circumstances the sovereignty of Parliament invariably equates with the sovereignty of government. Nor do smaller communities necessarily automatically behave in a more democratic manner than national political institutions: 'They can be stifling or disabling in reinforcing relationships of subordination and narrow parochialism' (Stoker, 1996, p. 24). On the other hand, being on the spot, councils are frequently able to identify faster and better than central government the most appropriate response to local situations. A centralised system of administration would be unlikely to foster the innovation and experimentation that frequently take place locally. The increased use by local authorities in recent years of opinion polls, referenda, customer satisfaction surveys and the like has enhanced responsivenes. The crucial challenge nevertheless remains to reconcile local choice needs with concerns about equal treatment for all.

Political parties

Party politics is now an established part of contemporary local government. In 1972 only 53 per cent of local authorities were run on party lines. Following the reorganisation in the 1970s which brought larger, more urban authorities, independent councillors have steadily declined in number as local parties have come to dominate. In 2000 Independents controlled only eighteen British local authorities (4.1 per cent), although they occasionally exercised influence in those authorities which had no overall control. Today, the overwhelming majority of councillors are elected under the labels of national or nationalist political parties and, once elected, they organise themselves into separate party groups, debating council policy – and determining the party 'line' – in advance of formal meetings. Of the 22,000 councillors in post following the May 2000 local elections less than 10 per cent (2,071) had an Independent/Other designation.

The party political dimension is rarely included in diagrammatic representations of local authorities because it complicates organisation charts. It is, however, central to a realistic understanding of local decision-making. The respective sizes of party groups on a council are the direct outcome of the elections. The elected leader of the majority or largest group generally becomes leader of the council. The majority group's manifesto becomes the council's agenda, to be translated into practical policy proposals by the relevant departments. The majority group will dominate committee membership. Before each council meeting and major committee meeting there will be private meetings of each party group (sometimes known as caucuses) at which they will determine tactics: which issues to focus on, who will speak on them, how to vote. A proper understanding of how most councils work requires a recognition of the 'unofficial' organisation of the political parties as well as the 'official' structure of committees, departments and full council.

The above discussion makes the assumption that local party groups are homogeneous. In practice, however, there are frequently factions or divisions within groups. Sir Peter Soulsby, Leader of Leicester City Council for many years until 1999, delineated four factions in the ruling Labour group in the late 1980s:

- the 'left', numbering nine or ten (thirteen at their height), who regularly met in a local pub, with formal agendas, in advance of Labour group meetings;
- the 'black' caucus (about eight members, including one white Muslim councillor) which again had formal pre-meetings;
- the 'right', a group known by this name (although it gave itself no name), which had about eight members, operated relatively informally and came largely from Leicester West constituency;
- the 'non-aligned' group (NAG), as they called themselves, whose membership varied between six and eight.

In addition, there were three or four members (including Soulsby) who did not belong to any of the factions (see Leach and Wilson, 2000, pp. 128, 129).

Party politics are firmly entrenched in local government. Dunsire (1956, p. 87) saw political parties as the 'indispensable element in the conversion of local councils into responsible governments'. Compared with shifting coalitions of Independent councillors, party groupings, with their strict discipline, can make for coherent policy planning and administration. The existence of electorally endorsed party policies and programmes can also help to reduce the potential policy influence of unelected local government officers.

On the other hand, the dominance of party politics makes it increasingly difficult for Independents to get elected. It also means that clashes of party rhetoric are all too frequent in the council chamber – often at the expense of rational discussion. Additionally, the 'caucus' system effectively means that policy decisions are made behind closed doors by party groups, usually without the benefit of professionally trained, experienced officers in attendance. The fact is, however, that the comprehensive party politicisation of most of local government is not only here to stay but has recently received a significant boost with the reorganisation in the 1990s and the spread of geographically larger unitary authorities.

Pressure groups

Like political parties, pressure group activity is an important part of local politics. Newton (1976) in a study of Birmingham in the late 1960s and early 1970s identified no fewer than 4,264 voluntary organisations in the city. Maloney *et al.* (2000) carried out a similar mapping exercise in 1998 and discovered 5,781 voluntary associations – an increase of nearly a third in two decades. Even in small district councils Bishop and Hoggett (1986) found extensive group networks. Parry *et al.* (1992) found that groups were a major source of local protest, and although many voluntary organisations do not carry out a pressure group function, at a basic level local groups serve to increase levels of participation.

In practice there is a wide variety of pressure groups operating at the local level. Stoker (1991) identifies four main types: producer or economic groups (which may represent local economic interests such as the Chamber of Commerce and important elements within the local government workforce – e.g. UNISON); community groups (e.g. tenants' associations); cause groups (e.g. local branches of the Campaign for Nuclear Disarmament); and voluntary groups (e.g. Barnardos).

The relationships between such groups and local authorities are infinitely variable. As Stoker and Wilson (1991, p. 20) note, 'the pattern of local pressure group activity' will 'vary depending on the composition of the local political system'. Clearly, political culture, as defined by the nature of local political parties, the ideological disposition within the ruling group and the fear of electoral rejection are important. Such factors play a crucial role in shaping a local authority's predisposition towards local groups, particularly those with a potential for electoral embarrassment.

Since the late 1980s there has been government pressure on local authorities to make use of voluntary organisations, for example through contracting, to deliver services. The local voluntary sector is both massive and diverse. Leach and Wilson (1998) identify three different perspectives delineating relationships between local authorities and voluntary groups:

1   *Instrumentalist/value for money.* Local authorities see voluntary groups primarily as external agencies with the potential for providing services for which the authority has statutory responsibility; they are valued partners in so far as they can provide better value-for-money alternatives to service provision.
2   *Participative democratic ethos.* Voluntary groups are seen as an essential element in the kind of participative ethos the council is trying to encourage; the capacity to provide services is likely to be a secondary consideration.
3   *Traditional/incremental.* Authorities support a limited range of local groups through tradition and precedent rather than as an expression of a more explicit view of their value, typically allocating sums for their support with incremental adjustment.

The increased emphasis in recent years on contracting-out local services, often to voluntary groups, does not always sit happily with the traditional group roles of advocacy, research and campaigning. If an organisation is operating 'under contract' to a council it becomes increasingly likely to recognise the dangers of publicly criticising the authority. This constrains the nature of democratic debate in a way which could be considered unhealthy.

Maloney *et al.* (2000) argue that in Birmingham some areas of the city appear to be 'overloaded' with voluntary and community organisations, while others have very little coverage. Increasing financial restraint has seen smaller, community-level groups suffer disproportionately: survival has often been related to patronage. In other words, mainly those groups survive which the local authority supports financially.

Legislative changes have increased the dependence of local authorities on the voluntary sector to implement its programmes and deliver its services. Community care is one obvious illustration. Cochrane (1993, p. 14) has highlighted the dilemma:

Those voluntary organisations which look and operate most like businesses are likely to benefit most from these arrangements. Other smaller community-based organisations, often run by women who are the main users of the services involved, are in danger of being so dependent on financial support from councils that they find it hard to retain their autonomy.

There are no signs that such dilemmas will go away. Indeed, the increasing number of service-level contracts offered to groups by local authorities promises to focus the issue even more sharply.

Conclusion

This chapter has shown that elected local government is but one part of what has become known as community governance. It nevertheless remains centrally important in delivering major services such as education, housing and social services. Local government also remains unique in that it is the only element in the world of local governance which is directly elected.

The complexity of local government finance, notably the heavy dependence upon central government financing, remains a problem. Unless a means can be found whereby local authorities can have greater financial independence, there will remain questions about their political viability and their ability to respond to local needs and priorities. Nevertheless, local authorities are not simply the unthinking agents of central government policy. There is frequently a vitality at local level which means that policy outputs do differ significantly from one authority to another. Political parties and pressure groups are of particular importance in this context.

According to Stoker (1999b, p. 18), the value of local government is not to be judged by the services it delivers (the dominant paradigm of the 1970s)

> but by its capacity to lead a process of social, economic and political development in our communities. The vision and virtue of this community governance role is widely accepted. What is far from clear is whether central government – under the new Labour leadership – is prepared to will the means for local authorities to take on that role.

There have been numerous initiatives by the Labour government to attempt to 'modernise' local authorities which later chapters will examine (e.g. Best Value, Beacon Councils, executive leadership); all have been carefully orchestrated by the centre, but local distinctiveness still remains important.

Further reading

A good starting point is Stewart (2000b) which contains the accumulated wisdom of one of the leading academics on local government. Stoker's two edited volumes (1999a, 2000) bring together research findings from the ESRC Local Governance Programme and contain some excellent essays. The White Paper *Modern Local Government: in Touch with the People* (DETR, 1998a) is an essential read in the context of the Labour government's modernisation agenda. There is a good summary of the urban dimensions of local government in Hill (2000), while McConnell (1999) is an excellent read on the council tax and related issues. A useful general text is that by Wilson and Game (1998).

Inside local government

Introduction

This chapter moves debate on from external structures, local politics and democracy to an analysis of the internal workings of local authorities. Traditionally, local authorities have been divided into a series of professionally focused departments (e.g. education, housing, social services) which were invariably mirrored by committees, consisting of elected councillors, each of which oversaw the work of the 'parent' department. Committees proliferated and compartmentalism was rife, with little integration between related service areas (e.g. social services and housing). As this chapter shows, there have been attempts in the past decade to develop greater integration between departments. While this has been successful in many authorities, the continued dominance of professional interests should not be underestimated. New structures are much easier to create than cultural change, yet without the latter strategic organisational change remains vulnerable. Deeply entrenched departmental 'silos' are rarely easy to displace.

The world inside local government is dominated by two sets of actors: *elected* councillors and *appointed* officers. Formal power resides with elected councillors but in practice officers, by virtue of their knowledge and expertise, frequently exert considerable influence in shaping policy. Not all councillors and officers are equal; senior officers and senior councillors together frequently exert particular influence, comprising what is often known as a 'joint elite'. As this chapter shows, the crude divide between elected councillors (who make policy) and appointed officers (who advise and implement) is not helpful; the realities are far more complex. Nor is it helpful to see a joint elite of senior officers and senior councillors as totally dominant in policy-making terms. On a number of issues, influences from, for example, junior officers or councillors or party backbenchers can be important in shaping policy. The joint elite model needs to be broadened out.

At the heart of the Blair government's modernisation agenda is the desire to establish executive leadership in local authorities and to abolish the traditional departmentally based committee structures. As this chapter shows, the government has proposed a number of alternative models, the most radical of which is a directly elected mayor, to streamline decision-making processes. The danger with executive models of leadership, however, is that the bulk of councillors can very easily become marginalised as a small elite group assumes increased prominence. While there remains an important scrutiny and representative function for non-executive councillors, many are resentful that their policy-making role has been reduced in importance. This increasingly elitist orientation contrasts sharply with the more participative ethos which the same government is propounding. This elitist/ participative tension is explored later in this chapter.

The traditional pattern: committees and departments

Local government is rooted in a traditional service-based committee system. While the administrative style of local authorities varied enormously, all conducted their work through: a) meetings of the council, consisting of elected members; and b) committees and sub-committees, consisting of small groups of members (and occasionally, in some cases, also of non-members). Chaired by councillors and serviced and advised by officers, some committees focused on individual services (e.g. Housing); others with a single aspect of all services (e.g. Personnel). At the apex of the system would be a Policy and Resources (or similar) committee, usually chaired by the leader of the council and consisting of the more experienced councillors, which provided the council with strategic policy leadership. The committee system generally ensured detailed coverage of council business. Membership represented the balance of party strength within the council, meetings were generally held in public, and the relative informality of proceedings encouraged frank discussion by councillors and officers alike. There was often also a close working relationship between a committee (e.g. Housing Committee) and its corresponding service department (e.g. Housing Department). Committees also enabled councillors to acquire specialist knowledge in specific policy areas and hence contribute meaningfully to decision-making. At the same time the committee system had a number of disadvantages. Members could sometimes become blinkered and fail to appreciate the work of the council as a whole. Committee rivalries were not uncommon. Moreover, the committee system was often criticised for lengthening the decision-making process, and for the proliferation of sub-committees and working groups. Even before the Blair Government's push towards reform many councils had drastically reduced the number of committees, in an attempt to better integrate policy-making and reduce bureaucracy.

The 1998 White Paper *Modern Local Government: in Touch with the People* was particularly critical of the committee system (DETR, 1998a, para. 1.15):

> At the heart of council decision taking and leadership is the committee system. It is an inefficient and opaque structure for this purpose. It results in councillors spending too many hours on often fruitless meetings. . . . Above all, the committee system leads to real decisions being taken elsewhere, behind closed doors, with little open, democratic scrutiny and where many councillors feel unable to influence events.

By 2002, in all but some of the smallest shire districts, the committee system is likely to have largely been replaced, at government insistence, by some form of executive leadership, held to account through the work of scrutiny committees. However, the traditional committee system, existing alongside professionally oriented departments, is deeply ingrained and many local authorities are reluctant to change in line with government proposals. In January 2000, for example, Camden London Borough Council (LBC) overwhelmingly voted against the November 1999 Local Government Bill's proposal for a new system of executive leadership. Camden's motion rejected the government's proposals on the grounds that they would 'reduce democracy, lessen effective decision-making and seriously weaken accountability'. It was passed with no opposition and three abstentions. This evoked a strong response from Local Government Minister Hilary Armstrong:

> Let us be clear; no change is not an option. We cannot afford to hold on to an outdated committee culture that ties councils up in red tape in the town hall

when the demands of modern society require us to be better advocates, working in and with the community.

(*Local Government Chronicle*, 11 February 2000)

Despite the minister's enthusiasm for the 'new world' of executive government, the traditional structures still enjoy support, especially among backbench councillors. Indeed, the way in which local authorities have organised themselves since the inception of elected local government has been through committees of councillors and professionally based departments. While precise structures vary from authority to authority, Table 6.1 outlines a traditional committee structure, one which was operating in Nottinghamshire County Council in January 2000.

Local authorities divide up their workforce between departments, which often have a professional focus. Each department is headed by a chief officer or director, usually a qualified specialist in the functional area concerned, and will also employ both specialist and generalist staff at more junior levels. Service departments such as Education, Social Services, Housing and Leisure provide services direct to the public, while central departments such as the Chief Executive's, the Treasurer's and Personnel have more of a servicing role for other departments.

As with committees, departmental patterns vary enormously from authority to authority. Most local authorities have a chief executive who is the chief officer in charge of the council and its departments – or 'head of the paid service', as it is sometimes known. Professionalism and hierarchy have traditionally characterised the internal organisation of local authorities. Departments can easily become self-contained 'silos' with little integration between related areas – hence the move in many authorities towards flatter, cross-cutting departmental structures which help to facilitate authority-wide strategic planning (see Leach and Collinge, 1998).

There have been numerous reviews of internal management, notably the Maud Report (1967), the Bains Committee (1972), the Paterson Report (1973), and the Widdicombe Report (1986). Each has played a role in modernising elements of internal management, but none has been as radical as the 1998 White Paper which ushered in executive forms of political management and scrutiny committees. Under the Local Government Act, 2000, this new pattern will become obligatory for all but the smallest shire district local authorities. The traditional committee system is on the verge of extinction in most local authorities with backbench councillors becoming marginalised as executive elites become increasingly dominant.

Executive leadership

The three models of local executive leadership advocated by the government in the 1998 White Paper (DETR, 1998a) (and incorporated into the Local Government Act, 2000) are presented in Box 6.1.

In July 2000 the government accepted a number of amendments to the Local Government Bill in order to get the legislation through the House of Lords. One concession it made was that small shire districts with a population of 85,000 or less are to be given a fourth option, namely a 'revamped' committee system which could

Table 6.1 Nottinghamshire County Council's committee structure, January 2000

Committees								
Community Services	Economic Development	Education	Environment	Finance	Leisure Services	Policy and General	Resources	Social Services
Sub-Committees								
Public Protection	Tourism	Monitoring & Evaluation	Development Operations	Land & Buildings	Partnerships & Grants	Fund for Disabled	Corporate Services	Registration & Inspection
Planning Applications		Special Needs Joint Advisory Committee (Primary & Secondary)	Environment Review Panel	Charitable Grants Fund		Shortlisting/ Selection	Energy & Building Services	Sheltered Employment Management Board
Community Legal Service Partnership		Grievance		Capital Programmes		Early Years & Childcare	Trading Services	Partnership Committee
		Appeals				Rail Initiatives	Suggestion Scheme	
		Appointments				Best Value Appeals	Appeals	
		Discipline				Standards Committee		
		Local Education Authority Governance				Investment Board		

Box 6.1 New models of political management

Option 1   *A directly elected mayor with a cabinet.* The mayor will be directly elected by the whole electorate and will appoint a cabinet drawn from councillors.

Option 2   *A cabinet with a leader.* The leader will be elected by the council, and the cabinet will be made up of councillors either appointed by the leader or elected by the council.

Option 3   *A directly elected mayor with a council manager.* The mayor will be directly elected by local people, with a full-time manager appointed by the council to whom both strategic policy and day-to-day decision-making could be delegated.

Source: DETR (1998a: Chapter 3)

---

can into force *if* councils can demonstrate that they have the backing of the full community. Hence some eighty-six councils (21 per cent of local authorities) were free to begin consulting in autumn 2000 if they wanted to reject the three options presented in the White Paper. Consultation could be through meetings, a questionnaire, a citizens' panel or even a referendum. Despite this tactical concession, a government spokesperson emphasised: 'This is not about the status quo – it's about an alternative option.'

The Local Government Act, 2000, therefore ushers in executive leadership for all but the smallest shire district authorities. Indeed, the government has retained a reserve power to deal with councils that fail to develop any reform plans or neglect to implement their reform proposals. Where a directly elected mayor is proposed by either the council, or 5 per cent of the electorate, or the Secretary of State, there has to be a referendum. Elected mayors remain the government's favoured option but only a few authorities (e.g. Watford Borough Council and Lewisham LBC) are enthusiastic about this model.

In every local authority, therefore, executive leadership is set to become the norm from June 2002. The vast majority of councils seem set to operate option 2, namely a leader elected by the council and a cabinet of not more than ten senior councillors. These new executives can be composed of a single party, but the scrutiny committees designed to keep a check on the executive must reflect proportionately the overall composition of the council. The 2000 Local Government Act requires at least one scrutiny committee per authority but in practice there are likely to be several. This prospect has produced a major tension between backbenchers who invariably see the move towards executive government as elitist, and party leaders, who, surveys show, generally favour change. Backbench councillors are particularly fearful of being pushed to the margins and having only scrutiny and representative roles left. Miller and Dickson (2000, p. 142) show that while 78 per cent of the public believed that the council leader should be directly elected, only 18 per cent of councillors held this opinion. Under executive government marginalisation of backbench councillors could easily become the order of the day.

Advocates of elected mayors argue that executive leadership works well in other countries. But all political systems have their own particular and distinctive values, cultures and legal arrangements; what works well in one country is not necessarily appropriate elsewhere. Labour's proposals for local political leadership are sometimes seen as elitist. Internally this argument has some credence, but they are less elitist in relation to the public where, especially in the context of the mayoral model, the public are able to vote *directly* for one individual. Critics who emphasise the elitism associated with executive leadership invariably focus on internal government arrangements, not on the broader relationship between local government and the public.

There nevertheless remains a tension between the 'enhancing public participation' strand and the elected mayor/cabinet government strand of the Labour government's modernisation agenda. Public participation relies heavily on the openness of committee agendas and the ability of the media to spot issues. If more issues disappear into a mayor/cabinet office for decisions, it will become much harder to extract details about policies, and levels of meaningful participation would be likely to decline.

Here again, however, the government made a number of concessions following a campaign by the Campaign for Freedom of Information, the Society of Editors and others. Such groups were concerned that the move from the committee to a cabinet system would lead to decisions being taken behind closed doors. In July 2000 the government finally ruled that council executives must meet in public when making 'key decisions'. This applies to key decisions taken by mayors, executive members or officers, and will prevent politicians exploiting a possible loophole to avoid open meetings by delegating decisions to a single member. Despite concerns about the definition of 'key decisions', Lord Whitty (Local Government Minister in the House of Lords) maintained in a Lords debate, that 'where a decision will have any significant impact on the community, the electorate involved should be able to influence that decision. That means that it must be made openly and in public.'

It is notable that one of the claimed strengths of the directly elected mayor model – the provision of a single clear 'voice' for the area – was recognised by 60 per cent in a survey by Rao and Young (1999). Certainly, the increased complexity of local governance demands creative leadership, something discussed at length in Leach and Wilson (2000). One irony is that the new patterns of political leadership have largely been centrally inspired by way of 'top-down' initiatives. Gray and Jenkins (1999, p. 42) argue that there is a tendency for new administrations, wishing to flex their legislative muscles, to rely on governance by command: 'Gradually they learn that legislation may provide a framework but cannot resolve problems without a set of values shared with policy implementers.' More than legislation is required if democratic renewal is to be more than simply a veneer. Structural change is relatively easy; embedding a new political culture is far less straightforward.

Councillors

As shown in Chapter 5, while councillors are elected representatives, they are not socially representative. In 1998 some 76 per cent of English and Welsh councillors were male; about 97 per cent were white; and the average age was 56. While this represents aggregate data, and despite the fact that there are marked variations between authorities, the councillor population fails to mirror broader socio-economic patterns. The Labour government is keen to try and redress this balance. In this context the 1998 White Paper emphasised the need for a greater mirroring of the whole population, arguing that, 'In particular, there is a need for more talented, vigorous young people in local government able and willing to make a difference to the world around them' (DETR, 1998a, p. 36).

Councillors spend many hours on council duties. Bloch's research (1992) showed that eighty-two hours per month was the norm; Rao's (1994) non-random sample survey put the figure at ninety-seven hours a month, two-thirds of this being meeting-related. About one-fifth of their time is spent on dealing with electors' problems. Not only is 'overload' apparent, but councillors have traditionally received relatively little by way of financial compensation. Basic allowances for all councillors in London, for example (1998–9), varied between £175 in Merton and £7,500 in Hammersmith and Fulham. Attendance allowances and Special Responsibility Allowances (SRAs) increased the total received but financial remuneration has traditionally not been a major factor in attracting councillors. Indeed, many lose out in career terms and in pension contributions by becoming councillors. In Scotland, the basic allowance for councillors was set by the government following local government reorganisation in 1995. The scheme has three bands, according to population, as follows:

Population	Allowance
Not exceeding 100,000	£5,000
Between 100,000 and 150,000	£5,500
Exceeding 150,000	£6,000

The advent of executive government in local authorities has seen formal recognition of the role of the leader and other cabinet members. The allowances scheme in Nottingham City Council, for example, operating from April 2000, awarded a basic allowance of £4,285 to all councillors but, in addition, allocated the leader of the council £35,000, the deputy leader £26,000, and cabinet members £17,500. The grand total of allowances for that authority under the new political management structure was £458,500 per year. There was a clear recognition that not all councillors have equal responsibilities and that executive leadership requires able, well-paid, full-time councillors. Each local authority is developing its own scheme of allowances; these have recognised the increased importance of local political leadership and have rewarded councillors accordingly. The Scottish Local Authority Association (COSLA) recommended an allowance for leaders which would, when combined with their basic allowance, produce a figure for a median council (in population terms) of £19,500. Differential financial rewards (based upon designated responsibilities) have become increasingly commonplace throughout the world of local government, although detail varies considerably from authority to authority, the highest paid being Ken Livingstone, the newly elected Mayor of the Greater London Authority, who receives some £85,000 per year.

As the 'graded' pattern of remuneration implies, councillors have a range of roles. Most backbenchers are not policy-makers; indeed, about 75 per cent of them are mainly concerned with representing local 'patch' interests. The government's 1998 White Paper argued that, far from marginalising backbenchers, new patterns of executive leadership will actually enhance their position (DETR, 1998a, para 3.40) – a view not widely shared:

> The separation of the executive role will give all councillors a new enhanced and more rewarding role. Currently, councillors can in practice be excluded from the real decision taking and yet have no power to challenge or scrutinise those decisions.

As we have already seen, scrutiny committees, dominated by backbenchers, with an explicit duty to review and question the decisions and performance of the executive are being created. In addition, it is anticipated that backbench councillors will spend less time in council meetings and more in the local community at residents' meetings or surgeries. They will, in effect, become champions for their local community. The 1998 White Paper (ibid., para 3.44) outlined five backbench (i.e. non-executive) responsibilities in the new world of local political leadership:

- reviewing and questioning decisions taken by the executive;
- advising the executive on decisions and policy on local issues;
- reviewing policy, formulating policy proposals and submitting proposals to the executive;
- considering the budget proposed by the executive, proposing amendments and voting on the final budget; and
- taking responsibility, either with or without members of the executive, for those quasi-judicial functions, such as planning, licensing and appeals, which it would not normally be appropriate to delegate to an individual member of the executive.

The government sees political modernisation offering new opportunities to backbench councillors. Sceptics argue strongly that their policy-making influence is subsiding and that scrutiny and representative roles are all that remain. Executive leadership invariably allocates specific powers to a small number of elected councillors; in the context of policy-making, the remainder inevitably have a secondary role. Indeed, in one-party authorities there is likely to be pressure on backbenchers to avoid critical public discussion in scrutiny committees.

The local government workforce

Alongside *elected* councillors there exists a wide range of local authority *employees*. Numbers are massive. In December 1998, there were 2,091,963 staff (1,107,801 full-time and 984,162 part-time) working in local authorities in England and Wales. Of these, female part-time workers make up the largest proportion of employees (42.1 per cent). Table 6.2 provides the detail.

Education and social services are the biggest employers of labour, with teachers prominent in the education category. Local authorities are highly labour

Table 6.2 Local authority (England and Wales) employment levels by authority type as at December 1998

	Male		Female		Total	
	Full-time (%)	Part-time (%)	Full-time (%)	Part-time (%)		
Non-metropolitan counties	15.0	5.5	27.0	52.5	683,873	(32.7%)
Non-metropolitan districts	44.9	5.6	28.7	20.8	139,617	(6.7%)
Metropolitan areas Of which:						
Metropolitan districts	25.3	4.4	29.8	40.4	513,504	(24.5%)
Other met. authorities	87.1	0.2	7.7	5.1	11,841	(0.6%)
Unitary authorities	24.8	5.1	29.1	41.0	488,307	(23.3%)
Greater London Of which:						
Inner London boroughs	29.8	5.3	35.9	29.1	103,471	(4.9%)
Outer London boroughs	22.7	3.7	36.8	36.8	143,129	(6.8)
Other London authorities	80.4	4.2	6.5	8.9	8,221	(0.4%)
Total	496,393 (23.7%)	104,217 (5.0%)	611,408 (29.2%)	879,945 (42.1%)	2,091,963	(100%)

Source: DETR (2000, p. 29)

intensive; up to half their total expenditure goes on staff costs. To the aggregate figures for England and Wales should be added about 235,000 full-time equivalents (FTEs) for Scotland, essentially similarly distributed. Table 6.3 provides details of the differential levels of staffing between services in England in December 1998.

The spectrum of employees is huge, comprising professionals such as social workers and teachers, administrative and clerical staff, skilled manual and non-manual staff, and a large number of semi-skilled and unskilled manual employees such as cleaners, gardeners and caretakers. At the top of the local authority employment ladder is a cadre of senior managers and professionals, frequently collectively referred to as 'officers', the senior employee within an authority invariably designated as chief executive.

Women are poorly represented in these senior posts. While women comprise over 70 per cent of the total local government workforce, this is not reflected at the top managerial levels. A survey of English and Welsh councils published by the Local Government Employers' Organisation in October 2000 showed that only 11.3 per cent of chief executives (7.5 per cent in 1996) were women. Only 1.6 per cent of chief executives were black, Asian or from another ethnic minority, while nationally black people alone made up 7 per cent of the population. Table 6.4 provides details of the percentages of female and ethnic minority senior officers.

In brief, white male domination of senior positions in local authorities remains intact. The pattern among paid employees and elected councillors has remarkable similarities despite virtually all local authorities signing up enthusiastically to equal opportunities policies. There are battalions of employees who actually provide local

Table 6.3 English local authority staff employment levels as at December 1998

	Male		Female		Total
	Full-time	Part-time	Full-time	Part-time	
Education					
Teachers	101,551	24,121	228,600	103,650	457,922
Others	36,684	33,870	85,012	444,297	602,863
Construction	49,098	332	2,603	581	52,614
Social services	38,357	12,301	106,191	157,311	314,160
Libraries	6,920	2,630	12,442	20,254	42,246
Recreation	28,666	11,869	12,056	26,722	76,313
Environmental health	10,277	432	5,667	1,717	18,093
Refuse	21,135	556	1,288	1,493	24,472
Housing	26,059	1,439	31,567	12,570	71,635
Planning	14,852	532	9,782	3,518	28,684
Engineering	33,050	1,500	10,025	4,368	48,943
Finance & computing	22,288	466	24,626	7,451	54,831
Corp. services	24,950	2,786	28,324	18,014	74,074
Fire service	34,513	199	3,399	1,700	39,811
Other services	9,833	4,409	4,758	15,815	34,815
Total	458,233	97,442	556,340	819,461	1,941,476
Magistrates' courts	2,545	468	4,972	1,825	9,810

Source: DETR (2000)

Table 6.4 Senior posts in local government: gender and ethnicity

		% women	
	1998	1999	2000
Chief executives	10.3	11.5	11.3
First-tier officers	10.5	12.4	12.8
Second-tier officers	16.1	19.2	19.0
	% black, Asian and Irish		
Chief executives	0.8	1.9	1.6
First-tier officers	1.4	1.8	2.1
Second-tier officers	2.0	2.5	2.5

Women chief executives % by council type

9.8	9.7	17.2	9.8	16.7
counties	mets	unitaries	shires	London boroughs

Source: Local Government Employers' Association Survey, October 2000

services; these people are managed by senior officers at the top of the organisation. These senior officers have a major role in supporting, advising and monitoring politicians (this is explored later in this chapter). They are also involved in representing the authority's interests externally, via partnerships, networks and the like. The third role of senior officers is the management of the authority's staff and resources against the backdrop of Best Value and performance indicators (see pp. 143–7). The modernisation agenda has made their job even more challenging as executive cabinet members assume formal responsibility for specific spheres of activity. Innovation and change have become integral parts of the world of local governance.

Councillor/officer relations

As Stewart (2000b, p. 225) observes, 'In the interactions between councillors and officers two worlds meet. Councillors and officers are cast for different roles and are drawn from different backgrounds.' Box 6.2 emphasises the contrasts. The interaction between these two worlds (i.e. the officer world and the councillor world) is of central importance in the determination of policy. Often informal rather than formal relationships are crucial. Three analytical models have been widely used to explain the distribution of power and influence inside authorities.

The formal model

This takes as its frame of reference the 'legal-institutional' approach which dominated the study of local government until the 1970s. It sees power relationships in purely formal terms and focuses on formal structures within local authorities. In a nutshell, this model asserts that councillors make policy while officers advise and implement. As such, the model perhaps tells us more about what should happen than about what actually happens. Yet though frequently dismissed out of hand as naive, the formal

---

Box 6.2 The separate worlds of councillors and officers

Councillors	*Officers*
Political	Non-political
Lay	Professional
Often part-time	Full-time
Recruited outside the organisation	Recruited by the organisation
Elected	Appointed
Representative	Non-representative
Allowances	Salaried

Source: Stewart (2000b, p. 225)

---

model had some credence during the Thatcher years when assertive councillors of both the New Urban Left and Radical Right set out to run authorities themselves and thereby minimise the role of officers.

The technocratic model

This model developed as a rival to the formal model and views officers as the dominant force in local politics. Their influence, it is asserted, centres upon their control of professional and technical knowledge, something foreign to the world of councillors. Yet in the same way that the formal model exaggerates the actual role of councillors, so this model exaggerates the power of officers and the ineptitude of councillors. In practice, many leading councillors have political skills, local knowledge and, on occasion, professional knowledge too. Nevertheless, officers, by virtue of their expertise, can be powerful policy-makers in the absence of any positive lead from their members. Their influence is particularly strong in small rural authorities dominated by independent councillors. Professional officers are invariably ready and willing to fill any policy vacuum.

The joint elite model

In the light of deficiencies in the two models outlined above the joint elite model has been developed. This argues that policy-making is dominated by a small group of senior councillors *and* senior officers, with non-executive councillors and junior officers only marginally involved. This model has plenty of supporters. It distinguishes helpfully between senior councillors and officers and their more junior colleagues. But it focuses almost exclusively on the elite. In practice, both junior officers and councillors can, on occasion, exert considerable influence in shaping policy. In a similar vein, the model assumes that senior officers and councillors are a coherent group; in practice there are often a number of cross-cutting tensions. While the importance of senior personnel clearly requires recognition, the joint elite model needs supplementing if the ambiguities and complexities of internal power relationships are to emerge.

Additional influences

In order to obtain a realistic picture of internal power relationships the joint elite model needs to incorporate several additional elements (see Stoker and Wilson, 1986).

1   *Intra-party influences.* Relations *within* (especially) ruling party groups, and between groups and the wider party. There are occasions on which the whole ruling party group, not only its leading members, can have a significant influence on policy-making. Indeed, sometimes leaders can even be voted out of office by their own party group. For example, in May 1999 Theresa Stewart

was ousted as leader of the ruling Labour group on Birmingham City Council by forty votes to thirty-six at the party's annual leadership election. Links with the wider party organisation outside the council can also be influential. Liverpool in the 1980s is a reminder that it is even possible for the power of the local party to become absolute. Parkinson (1985, p. 27) observed that the Labour group on the council 'does what the district Labour party tells it to do'.

2 *Backbench councillors.* In their capacity as ward representatives backbench (or non-executive) councillors can sometimes enter the policy arena in a very influential way. For example, in Leicester in the mid-1980s two Asian councillors initiated a campaign which overthrew the majority Labour group's housing policy by blocking a demolition plan in their ward (see Stoker and Brindley, 1985). By developing alliances and lobbying, backbench councillors can, especially on local 'patch' issues, be critically important. The government's consultation paper, *Local Leadership, Local Choice* (DETR, 1999b) argued that under executive government the majority of backbenchers 'will have greater freedom and a greater impact on the direction of the council and the services it provides to local people than is currently often the case' (p. 6).

3 *Interdepartmental tensions.* Tensions between local authority departments can be intense, especially at times of limited resources. There are also professional rivalries within policy areas between, for example, the technical departments involved in land development. 'Planners, architects, housing managers, valuation officers and engineers all claim an involvement and there is a long history of rivalry between these professions' (Stoker, 1991, p. 102). The extent of professionalisation within local government means that tensions occasionally spill over into the policy sphere. While the advent of strategic, cross-departmental management plus an increase in the numbers of partnerships with outside organisations has blurred departmental edges somewhat, the significance of professional rivalries should never be underplayed in developing a realistic model of policy influence within the town hall.

4 *Divisions inside departments.* Tensions inside departments can be important in the policy-making equation. Many departments are massive, comprising numerous, relatively self-contained sections. The span of control chief officers can exercise is limited, thereby providing junior officers, who often have greater technical knowledge by virtue of their more recent training, with considerable scope for influence. Relatively junior officers working in decentralised area offices can also frequently exercise influence in the context of that particular locality.

5 *Hung councils.* In 2000 there were 147 hung (or balanced) local authorities in which no one party enjoyed an overall majority, some 34.1 per cent of all authorities. In such councils party groups have to take account of each other's policies. There is extensive inter-party contact and negotiation, and officers frequently perform a brokerage role between the different parties. In hung situations backbench councillors can find their position strengthened. No elite of members from a single party can be sure of delivering a policy programme without help. Bargaining becomes a dominant ethos in such authorities; this involves more than simply a joint elite of senior councillors and officers. If

coalition arrangements are to stick there has to be support throughout each party; this can strengthen the role of ordinary group members since their support is necessary to keep the administration afloat (see Leach and Pratchett, 1996).

The joint elite model emphasises joint activity between senior officers and councillors. Yet in many respects officers and councillors inhabit separate worlds. Stewart (2000b, p. 225) develops this point:

> The councillor is the outsider drawn from beyond the organisation, yet formally within. The officer is the insider and a part of the organisation, appointed to it, and carrying out its business. Councillors can become insiders, almost a part of the organisation – although then they may begin to lose their distinctive contribution. Against this background, conflict or tension is often found. Councillors and officers can have difficulty understanding each other; finding a common language; appreciating each other's point of view.

Essentially, councillors are political beings who need to get elected in order to survive. The world of the full-time permanent officer is very different. The most crucial relationship inside an authority is that between the leader and the chief executive. The nature of this relationship deeply affects the workings of an authority, most notably its strategic direction.

Councillor/officer relationships are infinitely variable. Models such as those outlined earlier help to provide a framework for analysis but none provides a complete set of insights. The realities are invariably ambiguous rather than clear-cut. There are a variety of settings; a variety of managerial styles; different patterns of acceptable behaviour; different local political cultures. Stewart (2000b, p. 252) argues that no pattern of relationship can be regarded as fixed: 'Rather it is a dynamic whose impact varies depending on the mix of history, experience, politics and personality that drives it.'

Customers, clients and citizens

During the 1980s the impact of the new public management (NPM) (see pp. 9–16) introduced by successive Conservative governments became increasingly pervasive. This was the context out of which the focus by local authorities upon *customers* and *clients* emerged. By contrast, the role of individuals as actively participating *citizens* barely featured. The Labour government addressed this issue by encouraging the development of new vehicles for enhancing public participation at local level. 'Bringing the citizen back in' or 'rehabilitating citizens' is useful shorthand for this strategy. However, as we saw in the last chapter, more citizen participation is not necessarily the same thing as more democracy.

Conservative administrations focused on promoting public participation in relation to service use, in terms both of assessing service quality (e.g. through *Citizen's Charter* initiatives or satisfaction surveys) and of contributing to service management (e.g. through more powerful school governing bodies or tenant management). The consumer of local services (i.e. the customer) was sovereign; local authorities developed techniques such as market research in order to become more customer-sensitive. Developments like compulsory competitive tendering (CCT), which required local authorities to put specific services out to tender, focused attention upon the need for local authorities to have regard to service standards, customer needs and efficient service delivery. The Conservatives attempted to recast local government in terms of 'customers' and 'value for money' (see Wilson, 1999).

While the Labour government has not jettisoned the above emphasis on service quality, enhanced public participation has become part of an explicitly political agenda incorporating broader issues of democratic renewal. This message came over clearly in the 1998 consultation paper *Modernising Local Government: Local Democracy and Community Leadership:* 'Increasingly, the degree to which an authority is engaged with its stakeholders may become a touchstone for the authority's general effectiveness' (DETR, 1998b, para 4.4). Given the intermittent nature of local elections and the poor turnout levels, greater public participation is regarded as 'crucial to the health of local democracy'.

Public participation is seen by Labour as having a central role in the modernisation of local government. Research by Lowndes *et al.* (1998a, 1998b) shows that traditional forms of participation concerned with seeking citizens' views are well established in local authorities: in 1997, 86 per cent of local authorities held public meetings; 86 per cent issued consultation documents; service satisfaction surveys were used by 89 per cent; complaints/suggestion schemes by 92 per cent. But more innovative methods which involve citizens directly in decision-making are rapidly developing: 50 per cent had focus groups; 25 per cent visioning exercises; 5 per cent citizens' juries, with numbers of such new forms of consultation increasing annually. In terms of the application of new communication technologies, 24 per cent had interactive web sites in 1997, and 33 per cent were planning to use them in 1998.

The use of referenda at local level has also increased. In February 1999 Milton Keynes Borough Council conducted a referendum on its 1999–2000 budget levels. In the same year Brighton and Hove Council held a referendum on whether the local football league team (then playing its home games at Gillingham) should be resited locally. There will have to be referenda if local authorities are to move in the direction of directly elected mayors. This reflects the increased emphasis on engaging with the community under New Labour. A wide variety of participation methods exist but these do not necessarily broaden the base of decision-making.

Public participation initiatives struggle to make an impact with both the socially excluded and the young. Patterns of social exclusion can be reproduced *within* participation initiatives. Long-term community development initiatives are one important way of developing the confidence and trust of traditionally excluded groups. Citizen education – from school onwards – could assist in challenging the attitudes of those who dominate. (Robins and Robins, 2000). Indeed Pateman (1970, p. 42) argues that the 'major function of participation in the theory of participatory democracy is an educative one, educative in the very widest sense, including both the psychological aspect and the gaining of practice in democratic skills and procedures'. While the importance of citizen education requires recognition the question still remains: is the focus upon process (i.e. citizen education) being emphasised because of the unlikelihood of direct influence upon policy outcomes? In other words, are citizens (particularly the socially excluded) being bought off with something that, in policy terms, is very much second best?

The Labour government's commitment to increasing levels of public participation is, then, certainly not problem-free. A number of issues require addressing:

1   The new language of participatory democracy fails to take on board the role of political parties; parties are central to democratic renewal.
2   There is a danger of consulting with people on local government issues about which they know very little. Ideally, citizen knowledge needs increasing if participation is to maximise its potential.
3   Is participation always necessarily a good thing? What about the costs of consulting? Are the results being used? What are its negative effects (for example, people perceiving it as a waste of money; disillusionment when change fails to materialise; initiative overload)? What happens if the consultation process gives results that are completely unreasonable or simply wrong, or local authorities lack the resources or powers to respond to legitimate local demands?
4   There are evaluation problems. More research is needed on how to evaluate innovations. There is currently very little guidance on methods of assessing the wide range of techniques and approaches that are being developed.

In contrast to other aspects of its modernisation agenda (e.g. political leadership structures) the Labour government has not pursued an overly prescriptive stance on public participation. The 1998 White Paper (DETR, 1998a, para 4.7) states that:

> Every council will have to decide which methods are the most appropriate in their own particular circumstances. . . . The way in which a council conducts consultation will be one of the issues taken into account in assessing how far an authority is meeting its duty of best value or is fit to become a beacon council.

There is, however, a deeply held view among many backbench councillors that local democracy means representative democracy – hence their desire to marginalise the participatory democracy agenda; they see it as a threat to their position. Indeed it can be argued that the participation agenda has undermined processes that are widely regarded as providing elected councillors with democratic legitimacy, and which have also on many occasions had an important role in shaping local policy-making.

Evans reminds us (1997, p. 125) that despite all the new initiatives 'effective political participation is linked to educational attainment, political equality and most significantly, economic resources and political efficiency. Those who are disadvantaged under-participate [and] successful participation by elites remain the norm.' As we noted in Chapter 5, more participation is not the same thing as more democracy. The big challenge is not only maximising but also equalising participation.

Conclusion

'Modernisation' has been imposed upon local authorities by the Labour government. It is a reminder that the parameters of local authority activity are established by the centre. In its draft guidance on the 1999 Local Government Bill the government said that councils should make progress swiftly towards new patterns of political management. Executive leadership will become the norm in all but a number of small shire districts, although operating styles will continue to vary from authority to authority. The government's aim is for greater integration and strategic direction but it would be a mistake to underestimate the tenacity of the professional 'silos' that inhabit the world of local government. Professionalism is not about to leave the stage even if the structures within which it operates are set to change.

Executive leadership will undoubtedly change councillor roles. The government argues that these will incorporate enhanced scrutiny and representation elements; critics, many of them backbench councillors, see their role being marginalised as increased power resides with a small executive group. There is also a tension between the advent of executive government and the Labour government's desire to further develop public participation as part of its 'enhancing local democracy' agenda. For public participation to be meaningful, it has got to play a part in shaping local policy agendas. The proliferation of participatory initiatives, in itself, guarantees little. It is not more participation that enhances democracy but the equalisation of participation.

This chapter pointed to the different worlds of officers and councillors. It also warned against simplistic generalisations in what is a very complex arena. Theoretical models such as those outlined earlier help to frame material; for this reason they are useful. No single model, however, has a monopoly of the truth. Their relevance varies over time and from issue to issue. Running a local authority is a partnership between elected councillors and appointed officers; neither group is homogeneous. Context (e.g. local political culture, history, values, norms) is an essential ingredient of any study of power inside local authorities. Each local authority is distinctive in the way it operates. That is unlikely to alter even if structures change dramatically.

Further reading

A useful starting point is Wilson and Game (1998). Stewart (2000b) provides a wide-ranging analysis of the role of British local government, its methods of working and its historical and contemporary context. The best general overview of traditional patterns of management in local government is probably Leach *et al.* (1994). Several of the chapters in Horton and Farnham (1999b) provide a useful overview of NPM, the context out of which consumerism emerged. Two reports published by the DETR in 1998, *Enhancing Public Participation in Local Government* and *Guidance on Enhancing Public Participation* (Lowndes *et al.*, 1998a, 1998b), contain a wealth of material. They also contain descriptions of the various methods of public participation outlined in this chapter. Once again, the White Paper *Modern Local Government: In Touch with the People* (DETR, 1998a) is essential reading.

Chapter 7

Governance, partnerships and central control

Introduction

Although local authorities are elected and hence accountable to the local population this is, in practice, very difficult if central government controls are too constraining and if, as at present, a large number of local services are provided by non-elected bodies. Central/local relations are crucial to an understanding of the way local government works and to recognising its role within the world of local governance, a world which increasingly incorporates partnerships between a wide range of agencies. Unfortunately the relationships are far from simple, being characterised, according to Rhodes (1981, p. 28), by 'ambiguity, confusion and complexity'. Relationships vary over time, from authority to authority and from service to service.

The 1979–97 era, under a succession of Conservative governments, witnessed a clearly interventionist strategy in a wide range of areas (e.g. finance, compulsory competitive tendering, education, housing). Intervention became a reality even if control proved to be rather more elusive. The aim was to weaken and bypass elected local authorities and empower consumers.

The Labour Party's 1997 General Election manifesto, emphasised the need for better relations between central and local government: 'Local decision-making should be less constrained by central government, and also more accountable to local people ... [councils] should work in partnership with local people, local business and local voluntary organisations. They will have the powers to develop these partnerships.'

Soon after becoming Minister for Local Government, Hilary Armstrong (1997, p. 18) articulated her vision for the new pattern of relationships with local authorities. She emphasised that 'it is vital we lose the skills of battle and find the skills of organisation and partnership'. Yet despite such aspirations, regulatory powers have been retained – and, in some areas, increased – under Labour. There remains some distance between rhetoric and reality.

As we have already seen, local governance is now a central feature at community level, and in this context partnerships between elected local government and both the private and the voluntary sectors have flourished. The advent of Employment Zones, Health Action Zones and Education Action Zones has demonstrated the Labour government's commitment to working through a mixed economy of local provision. The establishment of an £800 million 'New Deal for Communities' programme for the regeneration of some of the country's poorest housing estates reflects the same thinking. This, of course, reflects the emphasis on 'joined-up' or holistic government which (as seen in Chapter 1) is a central feature of the White Paper *Modernising Government* (Prime Minister and Minister for the Cabinet Office, 1999). It has also become an integral part of the 'modernisation' process which the centre has set in train for local authorities.

As this chapter will demonstrate, councils responding positively to the modernisation agenda stand to be rewarded, but those dragging their heels or failing to deliver quality services will be penalised. This message was delivered loud and clear by Tony Blair (1998, p. 20):

Those authorities that persistently fail Best Value standards for any of their services will ultimately forfeit the right to be responsible for services they cannot manage effectively. The government will not hesitate to intervene directly to secure improvements where services fall below acceptable standards. And, if necessary, it will look to other authorities and agencies to take on duties where an authority is manifestly incapable of providing an effective service and unwilling to take action necessary to improve its performance.

The 'modernise or perish' message, so clearly articulated by the centre, means that tensions in central/local relations are unlikely to be dissipated quickly.

Governance, partnerships and networks

As we saw in Chapter 1, governance brings together governmental and non-governmental agencies in flexible partnerships to deal with different problems via a range of strategies. Local authorities now work with other agencies (e.g. health authorities, primary care groups, action zones), none of which is directly elected. It is paradoxical that although local authorities have lost many of their traditional service delivery tasks since about 1990 to bodies appointed directly or indirectly by ministers, they have begun to develop a broader leadership role in the community. As Stoker (1999a, p. 15) notes, economic development, urban regeneration, environmental protection, community safety and anti-crime measures, anti-poverty initiatives, preventive health care schemes and anti-domestic violence projects 'are among the areas where local authorities have sought to take forward the vision of community governance'. The White Paper *Modern Local Government: in Touch with the People* emphasised this community leadership role:

> The government intends to ensure that councils are truly at the centre of public service locally, and that they are able to take the lead in developing a clear sense of direction for their communities and building partnerships to ensure the best for local communities.
>
> (DETR, 1998a, para. 8.7)

The Local Government Act, 2000, has provided local authorities with a statutory basis for their community leadership role. Nevertheless, Jones and Stewart (2000, p. 16) argue that the legislation does not go far enough: 'The government has introduced neither the duty to promote well-being nor a requirement to develop community planning, only powers to do both.' Whereas 'duty' appeared in the 1998 White Paper, the word 'power' emerged in the Local Government Act, 2000.

Partnerships are at the heart of local governance. These can be relatively informal, taking the form of networks. Alternatively, they might be formalised contractual arrangements involving, for example, central government, local government and the voluntary and private sectors. Such partnerships help to overcome problems associated with the fragmentation of service delivery in localities; ideally, they integrate disparate services in the best interests of the consumer. Yet despite their advantages there are frequently problems of coordination. Inter-agency networks are also seen by some as a threat to formal political accountability, as appointed bodies gain influence at the expense of elected members. Others see networking as complementing formal democratic processes by providing opportunities for a wider range of stakeholders to influence local policy-making and service delivery.

Partnerships are sometimes the product of legislation. Two examples will suffice.

1   The Crime and Disorder Act, 1998, placed a duty on district councils to liaise with the relevant county council and police authority (a non-elected, single-purpose body) in order to prepare a strategy to reduce crime in the three-year period from 1 April 1999.

2   The Health Act, 1999, introduced a new duty of partnership between non-elected health authorities and elected local authorities, and provided for greater flexibility in joint budgeting and services. It emphasised the need to work in partnership in commissioning and delivering care as well as at the strategic planning level.

Partnerships such as these, imposed by statute, need to be accompanied by cultural change if they are to succeed. Given the different organisational and professional backgrounds of those involved and the differing patterns of accountability that frequently ensue, developing meaningful partnerships is a major challenge. Organisational frameworks are one thing; cultural change is quite another. The practical reality is that partnerships and networks require a considerable investment of time and effort if they are to actually deliver better-quality, more integrated, services. Despite the difficulties, partnerships remain at the cutting edge of the Labour government's vision for local government. To quote Tony Blair (1998, p. 13):

> It is in partnership with others – public agencies, private companies, community groups and voluntary organisations – that local government's future lies. Local authorities will still deliver some services but their distinctive leadership role will be to weave and knit together the contribution of the various local stakeholders.

The context of contemporary central/local relations

The last two decades have seen both the erosion of the powers of elected local authorities and the rise of a range of powerful unelected local quangos (see Chapter 8). Stoker (1999a, p. 1) provides a useful summary of the situation:

> What happened to British local government during the period of Conservative government from 1979 to 1997 was in many ways a brutal illustration of power politics. The funding system was reformed to provide central government with a considerable (and probably unprecedented) level of control over spending. Various functions and responsibilities were stripped away from local authorities or organised in a way that obliged local authorities to work in partnership with other public and private agencies in the carrying out of the functions.

The 1996 cross-party House of Lords Select Committee, chaired by Lord Hunt of Tanworth, produced a report entitled *Rebuilding Trust* which concluded, 'from the evidence we have received, the state of central–local relations is unsatisfactory' (House of Lords, 1996, p. 18). It called for a radical overhaul of central/local relations designed to ensure that local government 'does not wither away through sheer neglect'. The cross-party committee of peers warned:

> There is a risk of continued attrition of powers and responsibilities away from local government until nothing is left. We hope this report will help to alert the public to this danger, and lead to a more constructive partnership and the rebuilding of trust.

From 1979 to 1997, there were, in total, well over 200 Acts of Parliament passed by successive Conservative governments that impinged directly on local government. Most (though there certainly were exceptions) were designed to constrain the operation of local councils in some way. It was against this backdrop of increasingly hostile central/local relations that the Labour government was elected in 1997. The rhetoric of change was soon in evidence. In a speech in June 1997, Hilary Armstrong, the new government's first Minister for Local Government, told local authorities:

> We are not just a new Government, we are a new type of Government. Our decisions will not be handed down from on high . . . we do not have a monopoly of wisdom and ideas. We want to hear your ideas and we want you to tell us what you think of ours.

A few months later (November 1997) there was a positive step forward when Deputy Prime Minister John Prescott and Local Government Association (LGA) chairman Sir Jeremy Beecham signed a Concordat setting out the terms of the working relationship between central and local government. The framework document outlined six major principles, including a promise to give local government greater authority and financial freedom – within the constraints of national economic policy – and enshrined the commitment to 'best value' in service provision. The Concordat also recognised the 'independent democratic legitimacy of local government', but there were unmistakable signs in the accompanying schedule of the centre's determination to keep a firm hand on the tiller:

> Where the Government considers that a local authority (or a local authority service) is falling below an acceptable standard it will work with the authority to secure improvements. The Government reserves its powers under statute to intervene in cases of service failure.

The retention of such powers by central government – particularly the special improvement teams or 'hit squads' to address serious failings in education and social services standards – failed to inspire confidence at local level that relations with the centre really would change for the better under a Labour government.

Central/local relations: the formal framework

There are a number of formal elements shaping the relationship between central government departments and local authorities. Legislation is the most direct instrument of control. As we have already seen, local authorities can only perform those duties allowed by law. Therefore, in normal circumstances a government can use its majority in Parliament to pass legislation determing what local authorities can and cannot do, a power used with great frequency by central government. As already observed, there were well over 200 Acts of Parliament passed by Conservative governments between 1979 and 1997 that directly impinged upon local government. Nor did this slow down dramatically under the Labour government since as many as sixteen of the Bills announced in the November 1999 Queen's Speech were of direct concern to local government. (Their progress can be monitored on both the Government Information System web site at www.open.gov.uk and on the Houses of Parliament home page at www.parliament.uk.) In addition, government departments issue numerous *circulars* to local authorities containing 'advice' and 'guidance' on how they should exercise their various responsibilities.

Local authorities are also subject to the jurisdiction of the courts and the period 1979–97 saw a massive increase in the number of disputes between central government and local authorities being settled in the courts. In addition to constraints imposed by the doctrine of *ultra vires* (see Box 1.1) local authorities and other public bodies have to respect the principles of natural justice, and have been increasingly subject to judicial review (see Chapter 12). This reflects the deterioration of the old informal networks and indicates that the courts are increasingly being used to step in and regulate the relationship.

Default powers – central government intervention to take over 'failing' local services – have become increasingly topical, especially in the fields of education and social services. In 1995, the Education Secretary, Gillian Shepherd, appointed an 'Education Association' – or 'government hit squad', as the media labelled it – to run Hackney Downs Comprehensive School in east London following a critical report from the Office for Standards in Education (OFSTED). In a similar vein, the Blair government has repeatedly emphasised its 'zero tolerance' of poor standards. As Len Duvall, chair of the Improvement and Development Agency (IDeA), put it: 'death by inspection and hit squads lie in wait for authorities not up to scratch' (*Municipal Journal*, 30 July – 5 August 1999). In this context the potential for conflict with individual local authorities is clear (e.g. Hackney LBC over education in 1999). Following an adverse OFSTED report in March, the Secretary of State acted quickly and in July 1999 Nord Anglia Education plc assumed responsibility for a range of school support services in Hackney. This included the School Improvement Service and the Ethnic Minority Achievement Service, with effect from April 2000. This contract was the first in the DfEE's intervention initiative; the services in Hackney were so far below standard that contracting out was deemed a necessity. From April 2000 another private consulting firm, Cambridge Education Associates, took over school services at Islington LBC in what was the first wholesale privatisation of an education service. The contract runs for seven years. Islington is retaining a few services such as adult and early years education but the entire schools service is to be managed by Cambridge Education Associates.

Government-appointed *inspectorates*, like those of OFSTED referred to above, are a further means of central supervision and regulation of local authority services. Indeed, the Labour government has created new inspectorates such as the Best Value Inspectorate (incorporating a Housing Inspectorate) from 1 April 2000 under the auspices of the Audit Commission. This will sit alongside established inspectorates such as the Benefit Fraud Inspectorate, HM Fire Services Inspectorate, HM Inspectorate of Constabulary, the Social Services Inspectorate and OFSTED.

The new Best Value Inspectorate is designed to ensure that local authorities review their services in accordance with the legislation and that they have set 'challenging' and 'realistic' performance targets. In the year starting April 2000 it was estimated that there would be around 1,000 Best Value inspections – a substantial addition to the already extensive inspection regime. The government's commitment to developing and integrating the work of inspection agencies was emphasised in July 1999 when it established a coordinated Best Value Inspectorate Forum for England, the composition of which is presented in Box 7.1.

We saw in Chapter 5 that *finance* is a major vehicle through which central government is able to control local authorities. This is achieved firstly through influencing how much money local authorities receive, secondly by regulating the amount of money which can be spent locally, and thirdly by scrutinising the way in which money is actually spent. While the Labour government has pursued a modernisation programme for local government, there have been very few positive changes in the area of finance. Changes have been marginal and have certainly not provided local government with a new basis of accountability. While the 1999 Local Government Act abolished 'crude and universal capping', the minister has still retained reserve powers and finance still remains a major source of tension between central government and local authorities.

Of course, some of the above instruments can work in local government's favour. Legislation, for example, confers as well as removes power, and the courts can confirm as well as overturn a local authority's actions. Circulars, while often seen as vehicles for central direction, are in fact often the product of genuine negotiation with bodies such as the Local Government Association (an umbrella body representing local authorities) and contain useful practical advice for local councils. Inspectorates can identify and spread good practice. Even finance confers freedoms

---

Box 7.1 Best Value Inspectorate Forum

The Benefit Fraud Inspectorate

HM Fire Services Inspectorate

HM Inspectorate of Constabulary

The Social Services Inspectorate

The Office of Standards in Education (OFSTED)

The Best Value Inspectorate (incorporating a Housing Inspectorate)

---

on local government. Much of the money spent by local authorities is derived from central government, which allows considerable local discretion in how it is spent, whilst the council tax provides local councils with an independent source of locally raised taxation. The formal instruments of central 'control', in other words, can be something of a two-edged sword.

Central and local government have competing expectations and priorities. For central government greater autonomy and increased powers will only follow once local authorities have demonstrated their commitment to change, particularly in terms of renewing relationships with local communities. For its part, local government wants central government to grant it greater autonomy and new powers as an expression of a shared commitment to the principle of local self-government; in this context the increased promotional powers in relation to economic, social and environmental well-being contained in the Local Government Act, 2000, (see p. 103) represent a positive step forward.

Analytical models

This section examines some of the models that have been applied to the study and interpretation of central/local relations. Like all models they are deliberate simplifications of the real world but they do enable us to understand its complexities more readily. None has a monopoly of truth; all assist in providing helpful insights.

The agency model

This model sees local authorities as having a subordinate relationship to central government with little or no discretion in the task of implementing national policies. The increasing marginalisation of local authorities as direct service providers during the period 1979–97 made this an attractive model. Bogdanor (1988, p. 7) claimed that the 1979 Conservative government had 'been the most centralist since the Stuart monarchs of the 17th Century'. Particularly in the field of local finance this model seemed to have credibility. Yet this interpretation ignores the substantial diversity that still exists among British local authorities. Despite pressure from central government departments, local authorities still retain some policy discretion in a wide range of areas, which is why the agency model is not a completely satisfactory representation of central/local relationships. Local authorities are far more than simply the uncritical, unthinking agents of the centre.

Case studies also reveal evidence of local discretion in specific policy areas such as smoke control, comprehensive education and the sale of council houses. Dearlove (1973, p. 28) showed how the Royal Borough of Kensington and Chelsea frequently ignored or resisted central government 'advice and direction'. He concluded: 'The impact of central government upon day-to-day decisions of local authorities often depends on local responsiveness and the preparedness of local authorities to accept advice or guidance.' Distinctiveness, albeit within a framework established by the centre, still characterises local policy-making.

The partnership model

A second model, often regarded as the 'ideal' at the local level, sees authorities as more or less co-equal partners with central government in providing services. Traditional writers – noting the increased central constraints upon local government – often depicted a move from an earlier period of partnership to one where local government has become the agent of central government. In fact the partnership model, as Regan (1983, p. 46) put it, 'is so loose as to be almost vacuous'. He continued:

> Only in a formal constitutional sense are the government departments and the local authorities equal. In the sense of working together on common tasks partnership is a banal truism – of course both central and local government are involved in education, housing, transport, social services etc. but having said that there is little else one can say under the umbrella of partnership.

For Regan, then, the partnership model was too imprecise to be a useful analytical tool; hence the need for an alternative insight.

The power-dependence model

This is a sophisticated form of partnership model. Such models see central government and local authorities as more or less co-equal partners but they are imprecise – hence the development of the power-dependence model, a variant of the partnership model. The model suggests that both central departments and local authorities have resources – legal, financial, political, informational and so on – which each can use against the other as well as against other organisations. The model has a *bargaining* focus; it also argues that while there are likely to be inequalities in the distribution of resources, they are not necessarily cumulative. Rhodes (1979, pp. 29–31) observes:

> The fact that a local authority or a central department lacks one resource does not mean it lacks others. One resource could be substituted for another. For example, a central department lacking the constitutional/legal resources to prevent (or encourage) a specific local initiative can attempt to get its way by withholding (or supplying) financial resources. Conversely, a local authority which has been refused financial resources can attempt to reverse this state of affairs by embarrassing the central department. Press and television reports on the adverse consequences of the centre's decision may lead to the decision being reconsidered.

The power-dependence model is useful in emphasising that neither central nor local government should be seen as a monolithic bloc. It nonetheless probably underplays the power of central government and pays insufficient attention to the environment within which relationships take place. In a later reflection on his own model, Rhodes (1986, p. 28) moves away from a concern with interorganisational analysis to a focus upon policy communities. He argues that the very phrase 'central–local relationships' suggests a bias towards the analysis of institutional relationships. Such analysis, Rhodes maintains, 'does not always provide an adequate account of policy systems. . . . Intergovernmental theory with its emphasis on fragmentation, professionalism and policy network is more appropriate.' The power-dependence model contains sufficient insights to merit careful consideration.

The stewardship model

Dissatisfaction with the models outlined above led Chandler (1988, p. 185) to put forward what he called the stewardship model. He argues that Britain has not so much a system of local government as a system of local administration. He emphasises the ineffectiveness of agencies representing the world of local government in their dealings with central government. This would seem to point towards the agency model, but Chandler argues that the term 'agent' is not appropriate since the centre has always been prepared to allow local authorities a considerable measure of discretion. He maintains that 'stewardship' is a more appropriate metaphor, in the sense that the steward is delegated considerable authority by his master to order his estates. Chandler continues:

> The steward will, from time to time, consult with his employer on how best he should manage his estate and may often wish to suggest new policies or point out failures in existing strategies. A capable landlord will listen to the advice of his expert manager and may often be persuaded by his arguments. The master, nevertheless, will always retain the power either to accept or reject the advice. Should the steward fail to obey these orders he will be compelled to change his conduct or, like the councillors of Lambeth, Liverpool and Clay Cross, be removed from office.
>
> (ibid., p. 186)

Essentially, the stewardship model is a variation of the agency model. Other theoretical perspectives abound. For example, Cockburn (1977) provides a Marxist perspective in her study of Lambeth, arguing that local government is simply one arm of the capitalist state. Saunders (1981) attacks this as 'a surprisingly crass agency model' and comes up with what he calls the 'dual state thesis' as a further refinement. This itself has been criticised (see Cawson, 1977; King, 1983) not least for its pluralist characterisation of local politics. Models abound: utilisation of a variety of analytical perspectives is invariably helpful. No single model is able to provide a complete frame of reference for intergovernmental relations.

Best Value and Beacons

One example of the interplay of central/local relationships is the Labour government's pledge relating to Best Value and Beacon Councils. Under the Thatcher and Major governments a main thrust of policy was compulsory competitive tendering (CCT). Driven in part by New Right ideology, and minimalist concepts of 'enabling' (see p. 11), the effect was to require local authorities to put many services out to competition. A series of measures (notably, the Local Government, Planning and Land Act, 1980, and the Local Government Acts of 1988 and 1992) required specified services to be subjected to competition on terms and time-scales established by the centre. Local authorities could themselves compete, and as a result many underwent considerable internal reorganisation. In many councils client/contractor splits were created, which allowed Direct Service Organisations (DSOs) to prepare bids and, if these were the most competitive, to perform contracts. Although many DSO bids were successful, the effect was to transfer delivery of many local services to private contractors. In the mid-1990s private contractors were winning about 40 per cent of contracts, 25 per cent by value. (For further discussion see p. 217, also Greenwood and Wilson, 1994; Wilson and Game, 1998, Chapter 13.)

Best Value

In the context of the Labour government's modernisation agenda, the 1999 Local Government Act replaced the CCT regime with one that now requires the demonstration of efficiency and effectiveness for *all* services – known as Best Value (BV). Following a series of BV pilots involving forty councils, the full regime came into operation for all local authorities in England from 1 April 2000 and for those in Wales three months later. First details of the BV policy were provided in the '12 Principles of Best Practice', published in June 1997 (Box 7.2).

The thirty-seven BV pilot initiatives involved forty local authorities and two police forces in a two-year programme starting in April 1998. Table 7.1 indicates the extent of initiatives and the wide range of services covered. Essentially, BV places a duty on local authorities to run their services, balancing quality and cost, by the most effective and efficient means available but there is a continuing emphasis on competition. Indeed, it could be argued that the importance of competition has actually been strengthened under BV because it involves *all* services rather than the restrictive list covered by CCT legislation. Under BV, each authority is obliged to assess its priorities and draw up a programme of fundamental performance reviews. What have became known as the '4Cs' are central to such reviews, which will:

- *challenge* why and how a service is being provided;
- invite *comparison* with others' performance, across a range of relevant indicators, taking into account the views of both service users and potential suppliers;
- *consult* with local taxpayers, service users and the wider business community in the setting of new performance targets; and
- embrace fair *competition* as a means of securing efficient and effective services.

The BV regime is firmly rooted in the government's democratic renewal strategy since public consultation is an integral part of determining local priorities.

Under BV each authority must agree a prioritised programme of fundamental performance reviews, looking first at those areas where performance is worst, and

---

Box 7.2 The twelve principles of Best Value

1 Councils will owe a duty of Best Value to local people, both as taxpayers and service customers. Performance plans should support local accountability.
2 Best Value is about effectiveness and quality, not just economy and efficiency. Target-setting should underpin the new regime.
3 The Best Value duty should apply to a wider range of services than CCT.
4 There is no presumption that services must be privatised or delivered directly. What matters is what works.
5 Competition will continue as an important management tool but will not in itself demonstrate Best Value.
6 Central government will continue to set the basic framework for service provision.
7 Local targets should have regard to national targets and performance indicators to support competition between councils.
8 National and local targets should be built on performance information.
9 Auditors should confirm the integrity and comparability of performance information.
10 Auditors will report publicly on whether Best Value has been achieved and contribute to plans for remedial action.
11 There should be provision for DETR intervention, on Audit Commission advice, to tackle failing councils.
12 The form of intervention, including requirements to expose services to competition and accept external management support, should be appropriate to the nature of the failure.

Source: *Local Government Chronicle*, 6 June 1997

Table 7.1 Activities covered by Best Value pilots

Service/activity	Number of pilots
Regulatory services	2
Corporate processes	4
Transport	4
Central support functions	4
Leisure	8
Revenues and benefits	8
Education	8
Direct services	10
Social services	14
Housing	15

Source: Martin (1999, p. 59)

completing a full cycle of reviews over a four–five-year period. These reviews will be structured by the 4Cs, outlined above. New performance targets will flow from each review. These are brought together with other service targets in annual performance plans which constitute the principal means by which authorities are held to account for the quality and efficiency of their services. As we saw earlier in this chapter, there are regular inspections by the BV Inspectorate which will be the foundation upon which action will be taken should the authorities fail to act when performance falls short. Persistent performance failure will lead to intervention by the Secretary of State.

While broadly welcoming BV, and especially the accompanying abolition of CCT, there remain areas of concern for local authorities, notably the proposals for audit, inspection and intervention. The number of performance indicators (PIs) has also caused some concern. London boroughs, unitaries and metropolitan authorities have to set and publish targets and results against 192 PIs, counties against 151, and districts against 101. There are some inbuilt tensions associated with BV: on the one hand, the government wants to stress its commitment to local accountability; on the other, it has strengthened its rights to intervene at local level.

In Scotland all thirty-two unitary authorities (rather than selected 'pilots') were obliged to operate a BV regime earlier than local authorities in England or Wales. An important message from Scotland was that BV processes are only one influence on service standards. A more fundamental constraint on organisational performance was the level of financial resources, which 'remains unaddressed' in Scottish local government (see Midwinter and McGarvey, 1999, p. 99). It also remains unaddressed in England and Wales.

Boyne (1999, p. 14) reminds us that BV involves important political questions, the most important of which is 'best value for whom?' The local politics of BV includes struggles between a variety of interests: between those of local authority staff and residents; between service recipients and taxpayers; and between client groups for different services. The emphasis on consultation and involvement in BV might suggest that these issues could be resolved through greater public participation since this has the capacity to deliver services which are more locally sensitive. Yet, as we have seen, the list of possible triggers for central government intervention is far-reaching, embracing suspected failures of both process and substance. Determining the appropriate balance between safeguarding the national government's interests and enhancing local accountability remains a core tension within central/local relations.

Beacon Councils

To further stimulate modernisation, forty-two Beacon Councils were designated in December 1999. This pilot scheme aimed to (1) identify excellent performance in local government activities; and (2) provide opportunities for all local authorities to share this experience via feedback such as open days, conferences and seminars. Box 7.3 presents details of the forty-two authorities which were successful in the first round of Beacon pilots in December 1999. As Box 7.3 shows, seven service areas were selected for the first round. Camden LBC and Suffolk County Council each

---

Box 7.3 The first Beacon Councils

Community safety
*Preventing local shopping and town
  centre crime and disorder*
City of Bradford Metropolitan District
  Council (MDC)
Coventry City Council
Eastleigh Borough Council (BC)
Medway Council
Stevenage BC
Tameside Metropolitan Borough
  Council (MBC)

Education
*Helping to raise standards by tackling
  school failure*
Blackburn with Darwen BC
Camden London Borough Council (LBC)
Suffolk County Council (CC)
North Tyneside MBC

Housing
Improving housing maintenance
Carrick District Council (DC)
Kirklees Metropolitan Council
Leicester City Council
Manchester City Council
City of York Council

Modernising planning
*Streamlining the planning process for
  business*
Copeland BC
Halton BC

Modern service delivery
*Improving housing and council tax
  benefit administration*
Camden LBC
Exeter City Council
Harrow LBC
Leeds City Council
New Forest DC

Social services
Helping care leavers
Kensington and Chelsea LBC
Suffolk CC
Wakefield MDC
Westminster City Council

Sustainable development
Dealing with waste
Bath and NE Somerset Council
Bexley LBC
Hampshire CC with Basingstoke, East
  Hampshire, Fareham, Gosport, Hart,
  Havant, and New Forest DCs,
  Portsmouth City Council, Rushmoor
  DC, Southampton City Council and
  Test Valley DC, Winchester City
  Council
Hounslow LBC
St Edmundsbury BC
Stockport MBC
Wealden DC

Source: *Local Government Chronicle*, 7 January 2000

---

achieved Beacon status in two areas. New Forest District Council won one award for benefit services outright and another for dealing with waste as part of a joint bid by thirteen councils in Hampshire. Competition for the Beacon 'accolade of excellence' was intense, with 269 applications from 211 bidding councils.

Essentially, both BV and the Beacon process have the same objective – to raise performance. The Beacon process is also likely to help local authorities achieve Best

Value. There are, however, potential dangers associated with the Beacon Council idea, notably that councils classed in the lowest tier in terms of their performance measured against Beacon Council criteria could grow increasingly disenchanted with the scheme and pessimistic about their prospects of achieving Beacon status. The culture of lack of innovation and modernisation that persists in some councils could be further entrenched by the government's strong committment to driving up performance.

In March 2000 the government announced that up to fifty more councils would be awarded Beacon Council status in eleven selected service areas ranging from the use of sport and culture in recreation, to supporting independent living for older people, and tackling the wider causes of ill-health. Both the advent of BV and Beacon Councils are central to the Labour government's modernisation agenda, as is democratic renewal. The remainder of the chapter focuses on this topic.

Democratic renewal

The reform proposals for local governance associated with democratic renewal have a number of strands. The first element involves the adoption of new patterns of political leadership such as directly elected mayors/cabinets. The second involves new powers (contained in the Local Government Act, 2000) to promote the social, economic and environmental well-being of localities. These two strands have already been discussed. The third strand incorporates a set of measures designed to strengthen both representative and participatory democracy at community level. This strand will be evaluated in the remainder of this chapter. The tension between central directives and grassroots initiatives permeates the discussion.

What is the context of the call for democratic renewal? The White Paper *Modern Local Government: in Touch with the People* sets the scene:

> Modern councils should be in touch with the people, provide high quality services and give vision and leadership for local communities. Modern local government plays a vital role in improving the quality of people's lives. Change is needed so that councils everywhere can fulfil this potential. The old culture of paternalism and inwardness needs to be swept away. The framework in which councils operate needs to be renewed.
>
> (DETR, 1998a, p. 7)

The arrangements for local elections are confusing. Although all councillors are elected for four years, in metropolitan districts they are elected 'by thirds' (i.e. one-third of councillors stands for re-election each year with no election in the fourth year). Outside the metropolitan areas most councils (English and Welsh counties, London boroughs, Scottish and Welsh unitaries, and Northern Ireland districts) are now elected *en bloc* every four years. However, some councils (English unitaries and non-metropolitan districts) may choose either to have elections by thirds or 'all-out' elections every four years, but others are 'by thirds'. There is no single year in which all councillors (or all councils) are subject to elections. This confusion partly explains the low turnout in local elections. All-out elections at the same time throughout the

UK would help to give local government a higher profile. With the exception of Northern Ireland (where the single transferable vote system of proportional representation is used), local elections in the UK continue to be run on a 'first-past-the-post' system. There is further confusion, however, because some elections are to single member wards and others are to multi-member wards. There is now increased pressure to move towards some form of proportional representation, especially as the Scottish and Welsh devolved assemblies are elected by this method. So far, however, the government has resisted this pressure.

Nevertheless the Labour government has moved a little in the direction of the reform of representative democracy at local level. The 2000 Representation of the People Act allowed councils to experiment with new electoral arrangements such as voting on different days and electronic voting, and the government permitted thirty-two councils to pilot new schemes to make voting more accessible at the May 2000 local elections. For example, Doncaster Metropolitan Borough Council chose to experiment with an all-postal scheme where residents in a selected ward were sent voting slips in advance and then sent their ballot papers by return of post in a pre-paid envelope. Salford City Council experimented with electronic voting following months of pilot schemes in local supermarkets. Mobile polling stations also featured in some authorities. Feedback from the experiments indicated that while the public appreciated more convenient voting, only postal votes yielded significant results. For example, Gateshead Metropolitan Borough Council's all-postal voting in two wards had a marked impact: Wickham North's turnout rose from 30 per cent to 63 per cent and that in Bensham ward from 19 per cent to 46 per cent. Turnout in the rest of the borough was practically unchanged. Norwich City Council's experiment with all-postal ballots resulted in an 11.85 per cent average increase.

Improving the mechanics of representative democracy was spurred on by poor turnouts in local elections (see Chapter 5). While some of the technical changes outlined above are clearly beneficial, the government is also concerned to supplement representative democracy with participatory democracy. Engaging with the community is an integral part of the democratic renewal agenda. For example, Best Value includes a new *duty* on local authorities to consult service users, local taxpayers and the business community. The Blair government leaves nothing to chance, given the inherent conservatism of many local authorities: the top-down/bottom-up tension is still very much in evidence.

The Blair government sees public participation as vital in rebuilding the legitimacy of local authorities and as a precondition of the 'community leadership' role for local authorities. A major study of English local authorities for the DETR (Lowndes *et al.*, 1998a) revealed a wide diversity in methods used to engage with the public. In terms of 'old' forms of consultation, for example, some 85 per cent of English local authorities had organised public meetings or issued consultative documents during the previous year. Consumer-oriented schemes were also extensively used: during 1997 some 88 per cent of authorities had undertaken service satisfaction surveys. What is also clear is that more radical proposals for stimulating public participation are taking off. These include: (1) *seeking citizens' views* through citizens' juries, focus groups and deliberative opinion polls; and (2) *involving citizens directly* in decision-making through, for example, standing citizens' panels, community/user group fora and local referenda. The DETR survey revealed that during 1997 some 47 per cent of local authorities used focus groups, 18 per cent citizens' panels and 5 per cent citizens' juries. As seen in Chapter 6, the use of referenda has also increased at local level since 1997.

While central government is enthusiastic about enhancing public participation there remain a number of problems.

1   There is a deeply held view among many non-executive (backbench) councillors that local democracy means representative democracy – hence their desire to marginalise the participatory democracy agenda. It is seen as a threat to their position.

2   There is a potential tension between enhancing public participation on the one hand and developing small executive groups of senior councillors (or a directly elected mayor) to run local authorities on the other. To what extent are these two positions compatible?

3   There is a major tension between participation as a goal and the realities of public apathy. The public participation which currently exists is often partial and biased towards well-resourced interests. The socially excluded remain on the margins.

4   There is a potential tension between public participation and the economy, efficiency and effectiveness of the Best Value agenda. For example, the performance indicator league tables for planning applications focus on how many applications an authority can process in six weeks. Any authority taking this seriously would minimise consultation time. Public participation cuts across speed of response.

5   There is also a tension between central government claims about responding to local needs and preventing local authorities from acting through a lack of resources and other constraints.

As Pratchett (1999, pp. 16, 17) observes, at its best democratic renewal

> promises to change fundamentally the relationship between citizens, their communities and broader structure of government. It suggests a renewal of democracy not only within local government but also across a whole range of institutions by ushering in a new democratic polity which effectively combines elements of direct, deliberative and representative democracy.

Yet, as the same author notes, democratic renewal is 'plagued by contradictions, tensions and ambiguities'. The same government that is committed to the idea of local self-government also has a strong streak of centralism.

Conclusion

Throughout the modernisation debate the centre has kept a firm hand on the tiller. Tony Blair (1998, pp. 20, 22) set the tone: 'where councils show that they can embrace this agenda of change and show that they can adapt to play a part in modernising their locality then they will find their status and power enhanced'. At the same time, he emphasised, 'If you are unwilling or unable to work to the modern agenda then the government will have to look to other partners to take on your role.' The idea of 'centralist conditionality' (Game, 1998, p. 26) aptly sums up reality under the Blair government. Game argues that the government's approach is clear enough:

> Councils that enthusiastically 'modernise' along the lines of the Government's democratic renewal and best value proposals – and particularly any opting for the directly elected mayoral model of separate executive – can look forward to some selective concessions and rewards, even perhaps some modest relaxation of central financial control. Any councils that are judged by Ministers to be actively resistant or failing to 'perform well' enough, can expect equally selective retribution – surpassing in its Semtex-like severity anything contemplated by previous Conservative Governments.

Central/local relations are, according to Game, becoming characterised by a policy style of 'selective concessions' and 'selective retribution'. The best-performing authorities will be rewarded with new powers – primarily through the Beacon Council scheme but also through pilot projects and competitive funding regimes. At the same time, 'failing' and 'over-spending' councils will be subject to direct intervention, and ultimately to the removal of functions. Powers of intervention are to be held 'in reserve' and used selectively rather than applied across the board. As Lowndes (1999, p. 134) notes, 'The government's concerns with central/local dialogue, the use of pilots, and the potential role of local authorities as "community leaders" all serve to illustrate its preparedness to trust local councils, and to value their local expertise and democratic mandate.' The same author argues that local and central government are in the process of negotiating a new relationship of trust and that, ideally, this will grow out of ongoing interaction and learning. For Lowndes, democratic renewal, in its broadest sense, 'is contingent upon rebuilding trust in governance'.

Further reading

Probably the most useful text on governance is R.A.W. Rhodes's *Understanding Governance* (1997a). There is also an interesting piece by Stoker (1998). Tony Blair's pamphlet (1998) *Leading the Way: a New Vision for Local Government* is an essential read for anyone wanting to understand the modernisation agenda. Likewise, the White Paper *Modern Local Government: in Touch with the People* (DTER, 1998a) is a very useful source document. A special issue of the journal *Local Government Studies* (edited by Boyne) contains a number of excellent essays on Best Value (summer 1999). Likewise the winter 1999 volume of the same journal on renewing local democracy provides a very good overview of the modernisation agenda. Since this is a very fast-changing field of activity, the two weekly house journals, *Local Government Chronicle and Municipal Journal*, merit close scrutiny.

Quasi-government

Introduction

The term 'quasi-government' refers to both the government-created and semi-private organisations which both are distinct from, but usually relate to, either central departments or local authorities. As a field of study, quasi-government is both complex and confusing, being partly public and partly private, voluntary or commercial. So great are the number and variety of organisations included within it that generalisations, definitions and classifications are fraught with difficulty. Even terminology is a problem. The organisations comprising quasi-government are referred to by a variety of terms: 'fringe bodies', 'non-departmental public bodies', 'semi-autonomous authorities' and 'quangos', to name but a few. This latter term, 'quangos', has now become common parlance as an umbrella beneath which a wide variety of organisations shelter.

The term quangos (quasi-autonomous non-governmental organisations) was originally used to describe those bodies which were legally private but which performed statutory functions for government in a semi-independent way. Over the years, however, other organisations which were carrying out governmental functions but were deliberately set up at arm's length or semi-independently (e.g. the Equal Opportunities Commission) also became known as quangos.

Today the term quango is used 'generically to describe anything and everything that occupies the terrain between the public and private sectors' and thereby includes a wide range of bodies that 'have widely different powers, responsibilities and relationships with central government' (Dynes and Walker, 1996, p. 130). Quangos today play an important role in almost every area of public policy. The appointees to the boards of quangos exercise enormous influence in the British political system. This chapter will discuss the role played by quangos in the administrative state, focusing particularly on issues associated with accountability and control. First, however, numbers and types of quangos need to be delineated.

Numbers and types of quangos

The problem of discussing quasi-government is complicated, as Doig (1979, p. 311) notes, 'by the fact that there is no one characteristic, or lack of characteristic, that distinguishes quangos or non-departmental public bodies from other organisations in the structure of government'. Essentially, however, these organisations are characterised by carrying out their work at arm's length from central government departments or local authorities. While the rationale for the arm's length approach, as well as the length of the arm, varies widely from organisation to organisation, the desire to distance important areas of public administration from direct political control was a major factor in the twentieth-century growth of quasi-government. Of course, where politicians are denied control, they cannot normally be expected to assume accountability, which undermines the principle that public administration should be publicly accountable. As Sir Norman Chester (1979, p. 54) observed:

> The growth of fringe bodies is in retreat from the simple democratic principle evolved in the nineteenth century that those who perform a public duty should

be fully responsible to an electorate – by way either of a minister responsible to Parliament or of a locally elected council. The essence of the fringe body is that it is not so responsible for some or all of its actions.

A similar point is made by Skelcher (1998, p. 1) who argues that 'ideology and pragmatism have combined to reshape the British governmental system by including a class of organisations having considerable public significance yet remaining largely outside democratic political activity'. This issue of accountability is fundamental to any discussion about quangos and we return to it later in this chapter.

It is important to emphasise that while quangos have become high profile since 1970 (largely because they acquired a public image as disreputable, unaccountable and undemocratic), they are not new. Nor are they an exclusively British phenomenon. They have a long history in countries as diverse as the Netherlands, New Zealand, Denmark and Germany. In the British context, the Crown Agents originated in the mid-nineteenth century and the Horserace Totaliser Board (the Tote) began in 1928. During the period of urbanisation and industrialisation in the eighteenth and nineteenth centuries a proliferation of quangos emerged such as turnpike trusts, poor law boards and boards of improvement. There was a patchwork quilt of appointed bodies operating at local level.

Despite initially expressed reservations, the Conservatives in the 1980s were responsible for a significant increase in the number of quangos. One reason is that they were a convenient device with which to bypass increasingly hostile local authorities and they began to take over elected local authority functions. As Skelcher notes (1998, pp. 1, 2), there has been

a spectacular gr owth in this appointed sector of government since the 1980s. The creation of new types of public body and the transfer of activities from elected local government to appointed quangos has substantially increased both the number and range of policy areas in which they operate.

So while not new, they developed apace under successive Conservative governments and while the Blair government committed itself to reducing the number of quangos, in its first two years in office it created as many new quangos as it abolished, some of which, such as the Regional Development Agencies (RDAs), are of pivotal importance to government policy. Indeed, in their first full year of operation (1999–2000) the eight new RDAs spent around £900 million. As Flinders and Cole show (1999 p. 235), in the two-year period from May 1997 the government created thirty new non-departmental public bodies (NDPBs) and announced plans to create sixteen more. In the same period twenty-four NDPBs were abolished, and another thirty-seven given notice of their impending demise.

Cole (1998) emphasises Doig's point that there is no consensus among politicians, the media or academics about what constitutes a quango. Not surprisingly, therefore, there is disagreement about how many quangos exist. As Weir and Hall (1994, p. 6) observe, there is no satisfactory or universally agreed definition of a quango, with the result that 'the confusing variety of public agencies which now exist – and the unsystematic nature of Whitehall's ways of defining and categorising them – makes any reliable quango count impossible'.

Given the political imperative to keep the quango count as low as possible, successive governments have opted for a *narrow* definition of what they call non-departmental public bodies. An NDPB was defined in the Pliatzky Report (1980) as: 'A body which has a role in the processes of national government, but is not a government department or part of one, and accordingly operates to a greater or lesser extent at arm's length from ministers.' More simply, this means a national or regional body, operating independently of ministers, but for which ministers are ultimately responsible. NDPBs operating in devolved areas in Scotland, Wales and Northern Ireland are the responsibility of the Scottish Executive, the National Assembly for Wales and the Northern Ireland Assembly. This narrow official definition inevitably produces a relatively small number of quangos, as delineated in Table 8.1. Largely because of mergers, the number of NDPBs has declined from 2,167 in 1979 to 1,035 in 2000.

Table 8.1 Numbers and staffing of NDPBs, 1979–2000

	Executive NDPBs		Advisory NDPBs	Tribunal NDPBs	Boards of visitors	
	Number	Number of staff	Number	Number	Number	Total number of NDPBs
1979	492	217,000	1,485	70	120	2,167
1982	450	205,500	1,173	64	123	1,810
1983	431	196,700	1,074	65	121	1,691
1984	402	141,200	1,087	71	171	1,681
1985	399	138,300	1,069	65	121	1,654
1986	406	146,300	1,062	64	126	1,658
1987	396	148,700	1,057	64	126	1,643
1988	390	134,600	1,066	65	127	1,648
1989	395	118,300	969	64	127	1,555
1990	374	117,500	971	66	128	1,539
1991	375	116,400	874	64	131	1,444
1992	369	114,400	846	66	131	1,412
1993	358	111,300	829	68	134	1,389
1994	325	110,200	814	71	135	1,345
1995	320	109,000	699	73	135	1,227
1996	309	107,000	699	73	135	1,227
1997	305	106,400	610	75	138	1,128
1998	304	107,800	563	69	137	1,073
1999	306	108,400	544	69	138	1,057
2000	297	112,900	536	61	141	1,035

Source: Cabinet Office (2000c, Table 1.2)

There are four types of NDPBs:

- *executive bodies*, which carry out a wide range of administrative, regulatory, executive or commercial functions on behalf of the government, e.g. the Arts Council, the Police Complaints Authority and the Equal Opportunities Commission;
- *advisory committees*, which are set up to provide independent, expert advice to ministers and officials e.g. the National Disability Council, the Advisory Committee on Hazardous Substances and the Political Honours Scrutiny Committee;
- *tribunals*, which have jurisdiction in specialised fields of law, e.g. the Disability Appeals Tribunals and Employment Tribunals;
- *prison boards of visitors*, which are the independent watchdogs of the prison system.

In the 1999–2000 financial year, NDPB expenditure accounted for around £23 billion. The vast majority of this was programme expenditure, such as the giving of grants, legal aid, funding for higher and further education, etc. Some £18 billion of this was provided by the government, with the remainder being financed by a combination of fees, levies and charges. NDPBs are big business.

In contrast to the narrow official government definition of quangos, a *broad* definition is provided by others, most notably Weir and Hall (1994) who coined the term EGO (extra-governmental organisation). EGOs were defined as 'executive bodies of a semi-autonomous nature which effectively act as agencies for central government and carry out government policies'. This definition incorporated NDPBs as well as NHS Trusts and other health authorities. It also included what were termed 'non-recognised bodies' such as TECs, housing associations, and further/higher education corporations. Using this broad definition, some 6,424 EGOs were identified, compared with the 1,035 NDPBs (in 2000) using the government's narrow definition. The broad definition considers quangos to be 'any body that spends public money to fulfil a public task but with some degree of independence from elected representatives' (Flinders and Smith, 1999, p. 4). Unlike the 'official' definition this points to a proliferation of non-elected bodies. Table 8.2 provides a summary of the numbers of EGOs in the UK in 1996.

Interestingly, the presence of 'local public spending bodies' was accepted by the new Labour government, and *Public Bodies 1997* made reference to such bodies as a collective group and claimed that there were 4,651 local spending bodies in 1997 with 69,813 board members. By 2000 the figures were 3,232 and 42,682 respectively (see Cabinet Office, 2000c).

The bodies recognised by the government as 'local public spending bodies' in 2000 were (Cabinet Office, 2000c, Annex A):

Higher education institutions	166
Further education institutions	511
Training and enterprise councils	72
Local enterprise companies	22
Registered housing associations	295
Registered social landlords	2,166
Total	3,232

Table 8.2 Number of extra-governmental organisations in the UK, 1996

Executive NDBPs	309
NHS bodies	788
Advisory NDPBs	674
Non-recognised EGOs	4,653
Career service companies	*91*
Grant-maintained schools	*1,103*
City technology colleges	*15*
Further education corporations	*560*
Higher education corporations	*175*
Registered housing associations	*2,565*
Police authorities	*41*
Training and enterprise councils	*81*
Local enterprise companies	*22*
Total	6,424

Source: Hall and Weir (1996)

Nevertheless, despite admitting the presence of what it terms 'non-recognised bodies', the government is still not prepared to include them in its 'official' headcount of quangos, not least because it wants to avoid being accused of presiding over a massive expansion of the species.

Definitional anarchy is compounded because numbers in isolation from context can be very misleading. As Hood (1979, pp. 9–10) observes, 'the "heads" involved are of enormously differing size and importance – on a scale more like the difference between the head of an ant and an elephant than between one human head and another'. Quangos, in fact, are analogous to pressure groups: both include tiny, relatively insignificant groupings, as well as massive and extremely powerful organisations. Indeed, quangos are frequently the target of pressure group activity, and may at times behave like pressure groups exerting pressure in other parts of the government machine. This includes the world of local government.

The local scene: from elected to appointed government

The most dramatic increase in the number of quangos has come at local level, where, during the Thatcher and Major governments, there was a wholesale removal of functions from elected local authorities to appointed quangos. The list includes the following:

- *urban development corporations* – government-appointed agencies with powers to take over local councils' development control and planning responsibilities so as to promote market-led urban regeneration;
- *housing action trusts* (HATs) – government-appointed agencies with powers to take over temporary ownership of housing estates, refurbish them, then sell or transfer them to other landlords;
- *polytechnics and higher education colleges* – removed from local authority control and transferred to their own independent governing bodies;

- *further education and sixth-form colleges* – similarly transferred to their own independent governing bodies;
- *city technology colleges* – government- and private sector-funded schools, specialising in science, technology and maths, run by appointed governors;
- *grant-maintained schools* – government encouragement of secondary and primary schools to 'opt out' of their local authority's education service and be funded instead by direct central government grant;
- *training and enterprise councils* (TECs) – government-approved and private sector-dominated corporations, responsible for assessing and meeting skills and training requirements in their local areas;
- *careers service pathfinders* – partnership companies, set up to compete for and deliver careers services formerly run by councils;
- *police service* – transferred from local authorities to separate and more Home Office-influenced authorities.

In this context Stewart (1995) laments what he calls the rise of a 'new magistracy': non-elected, largely central government-appointed personnel controlling an increasing proportion of service provision at local level. Stewart's major concern is the inability of local people to hold such bodies to account. William Waldegrave, however (1993, pp. 10–11), adopted a very different perspective, arguing that the Conservative government (in which he was a cabinet minister) had 'broken crucial new ground in strengthening accountability'. Answering Stewart's 'new magistracy' claims, Waldegrave observed:

> The key point in this argument is not whether those who run our public services are elected, but whether they are producer-responsive or consumer-responsive. Services are not necessarily made to respond to the public simply by giving citizens a democratic voice . . . in their make-up.

The central point for Waldegrave was whether service consumers were more likely to encounter responsiveness and choice via local authority service provision or in a market-oriented appointed body. The task of what became known as the 'enabling authority' (see p. 11) was to find a range of other organisations (including quangos) to provide services. This has meant that today 'local quangos' outnumber Britain's elected local authorities by twelve to one, and their members – the more than 60,000 mainly ministerially appointed or self-appointed 'quangocrats' – outnumber elected councillors by almost three to one. There are few signs that significant changes are likely under Labour.

The Blair government's perspective

The Labour government's consultation paper *Opening up Quangos* (Cabinet Office, 1997) lamented inheriting large numbers of quangos 'whose lack of openness in appointments to their boards and in the business they were conducting attracted widespread criticism'. Criticisms of quangos abound, invariably focusing on issues relating to appointments and accountability, but *Opening up Quangos* also highlighted a number of positive features which are delineated below.

1   They are able to provide specialist expert advice to ministers on a wide range of topics. The Expert Advisory Group on Aids is one such example. Skelcher (1998, p. 3) reminds us that many advisory quangos

> play a central role in shaping government policy and legislation by virtue of the weight of authoritative opinion they contain and expert advice they offer [and are] of major significance to an understanding of the way in which government is informed and policy is shaped.

2   A number of government functions need to be carried out at arm's length from ministers (e.g. the Arts Council); quangos are an ideal vehicle for such policy areas.

3   Quangos can provide a quick and flexible response to matters of particular public concern. For example, the Nolan Committee on Standards in Public Life was set up to deal with concerns about sleaze. Weir and Beetham (1999, p. 196) go as far as describing quangos as the 'government's flexible friends', facilitating a speed of response that frequently suits the needs of central government.

4   Quangos can be a useful means of creating partnerships between government and other interests. For example, the boards of HATs include nominees from local authorities and nominees elected by residents of the trust's area.

5   Quangos carry out a range of commercial activities when board members need a degree of independence from government to make decisions, as in the case of the eight RDAs created by the Labour government and operational from April 1999.

6   Quangos provide opportunities to bring a large number of people into public life. As of March 2000 there were over 30,000 people serving on the boards of those public bodies listed in *Public Bodies 2000* (Cabinet Office, 2000c) (this includes 'local' public bodies). The downside, however, is that this remains very much a white, male-dominated sector, despite improvements in recent years. Between 1997 and 2000, for example, the proportion of women and members of ethnic minorities increased – from 32 per cent and 3.6 per cent respectively in 1997 to 33 per cent and 4.4 per cent in 2000. This reflects the Labour government's broader aim to increase the representation of under-represented groups in public life. The government-set target for NDPBs is to increase the proportion of women appointed to 38 per cent overall, and of women chairs appointed to 28 per cent, and to increase the number of people from ethnic minorities to 6.2 per cent by September 2001.

As seen in Chapter 4, since coming to power in 1997 the Labour government has massively expanded a new breed of quangos – taskforces – comprising people with relevant expertise to investigate specific issues. Taylor (2000, p. 69), in his study of a high-profile taskforce, the Social Exclusion Unit (SEU), argues that while at one level this development represented a shedding of functions by the core executive, at another level it represented an increased level of central control. This is not untypical of quangos as a species. (For details of three task forces operating in 2000 see Box 8.1. See also p.78 and Box 4.2.)

From a management standpoint there are also some positive attributes associated with quangos. For example, Flinders (1999, p. 34) argues that executive

---

Box 8.1 Examples of taskforces operating in 2000

- *Better Regulation Task Force.* Created to advise the government on action to improve the effectiveness and credibility of government regulation – by ensuring that it is necessary, fair, affordable, and simple to understand and administer, taking particular account of the needs of small business and ordinary people.

- *New Deal Task Force.* Created to ensure that the design of the New Deal meets the needs of client groups, to harness the commitment of all partners, and particularly the business community, to the success of the New Deal, and to monitor the New Deal on the ground and advise the government on its future development.

- *Disability Rights Task Force.* Created to consider how best to secure comprehensive, enforceable, civil rights for disabled people within the context of our wider society and to make recommendations on the role and functions of a Disability Rights Commission.

---

quangos have been important agents for the introduction of 'innovative new management practices', often imported from the private sector. Likewise, single-purpose agencies such as NHS Trusts have a specialised professional focus that would be less likely within a multifunctional organisation. Issues relating to efficient management are invariably in the forefront of discussions about the creation and development of quangos, as are concerns about accountability.

Accountability

With NDPBs, as Johnson (1982, p. 213) observes, 'accountability of Ministers' must remain 'attenuated', because 'otherwise there would be little point in having this form of administrative organisation'. Usually ministers are formally answerable to Parliament only for discharging their own responsibilities relating to sponsored bodies (such as terms of broad policy and general supervision), while responsibility for efficiency and day-to-day matters normally rests with the organisations' own management. In practice, however, as with Next Steps Agencies (see pp. 34–7), the precise boundaries of ministerial responsibility are often difficult to define. Not only is the borderline between ministers' policy and supervisory responsibilities and those of boards for efficiency and day-to-day administration often blurred, but in practice there is considerable variation in relationships between ministers and boards. For example, the Public Accounts Committee contrasted the Welsh Office's 'arm's length and detached' attitude to sponsorship of NDPBs with the Environment Department's 'involved, positive and disciplined' approach. In any event, the sheer volume and variety of bodies under departmental sponsorship often make ministerial responsibility something of a myth. In 2000 the Home Office alone sponsored some

160 NDPBs, many of them politically contentious, such as the Commission for Racial Equality, the Data Protection Register and the Police Complaints Authority.

Democratic accountability is central to contemporary debate about quasi-government. Direct accountability to the electorate via the ballot box is clearly missing but, arguably, other forms of accountability are not. As we saw earlier, the last Conservative government argued that the growth of quangos had produced a 'democratic gain' rather than the 'democratic deficit' so frequently claimed. Accountability, it maintained, was strengthened by making services more responsive to consumers, which was seen as more meaningful than giving citizens a distant and diffuse voice over the make-up of services to be provided. The Thatcher and Major governments argued that they provided increased opportunities to complain and secure redress, and hence enhanced accountability. The development of citizen's charters, grant-maintained schools, NHS Trusts, HATs and the like focused on the citizen as consumer. In such a context is the traditional form of direct account-ability most meaningful or can accountability emerge through other means such as contractual relationships and performance indicators? Contract or market account-ability cuts across many of the long-cherished forms of electoral accountability, but under the Conservatives this became an important strand of government policy.

Non-elected bodies are frequently summarily dismissed as being inherently anti-democratic and as undermining deeply held views about the nature of account-ability. Young (1994) counsels against such a knee-jerk reaction, arguing that the actual activities, priorities and motivations of non-elected bodies need to be examined before they are dismissed (simply because they are not directly elected) as inherently inferior to, or less desirable than, elected institutions: 'Being caught up as I am in public/private/voluntary/community partnerships in regeneration persuades me that accountability has not withered, nor is it in crisis. It has simply begun to develop along lines which complement the elective mechanisms.' Young emphasises that it is important to move debate on and to recognise the subtle complexity of accountability in the context of both elected and non-elected bodies: 'What we are presented with in many of the arguments about accountability is a false dichotomy. Accountability is not an "either/or" question; it is a "how much and in what ways?" question.'

It is important to set the accountability associated with elected local government against the accountability which characterises at least parts of the quango sector (such as the publication of accounts, scrutiny by the press and public). This strand of thinking was exemplified by Dr Brian Mawhinney who, as Conservative Junior Health Minister, provided the following Parliamentary answer:

> Every year each National Health Service Trust issues a summary business plan and an annual report, makes its accounts publicly available and holds a public meeting. In addition, the Trusts issue a strategic plan every three years. This is the minimum requirement that many Trusts exceed. It represents a high level of public accountability, which requires no improvement.

Following media criticism since 1990 quangos have become more conscious of the need to raise levels of accountability. A number now hold all their meetings in public; others publish summaries of the conclusions of meetings, while English Heritage undertook a massive consultation exercise with the public on one aspect of its policy.

In a similar vein the NHS Executive in England in 1998 issued over 250,000 copies of its code of practice on openness in the NHS. Simply because accountability is not via the ballot box does not necessarily mean that it is non-existent. Nevertheless, the fact remains that government by quangos means that many important areas of public policy are exempt from representative decision-making processes. As Skelcher (1998, p. 181) suggests, this 'represents a fundamental weakness in the ability of citizens to be involved in the structures by which society governs itself'.

Patronage

Considerable concern about quangos has focused on patronage, the number of appointments in the gift of ministers. As we have seen, in March 2000 the total number of appointments to the boards of NDPBs, nationalised industries and public corporations was over 30,000, of whom 33 per cent were women and only 4.4 per cent members of an ethnic minority. Parliamentary influence over appointments to chairs or boards of public bodies is minimal. In effect, the matter is almost entirely one of ministerial discretion and consequently party political factors have frequently been to the fore. Since 1996, however, appointments have been subject to a code supervised by the Committee for Public Appointments.

The catalyst for change was the publication in 1995 of the first report of the *Committee on Standards in Public Life* (Nolan Committee, 1995). This made a number of recommendations to the Major government designed to restore public confidence in the appointments process by ensuring greater openness and independent external scrutiny. The Blair government extended the provisions to encompass not only executive NDPBs but also advisory NDPBs and boards of visitors to penal establishments. An independent Commissioner for Public Appointments (Sir Leonard Peach) was appointed to regulate, monitor and report on the operation of the public appointments process. There is now much more openness, with regular advertisements in the national and local press and on the internet seeking nominees for NDPBs. Party political appointments, however, have not disappeared. The surprise, surely, would be if the placing of political supporters did *not* happen, given the dominance of central government and party politics in the contemporary political scene.

A long-standing concern about quangos is that their members are not representative of the population as a whole. As we have seen, both women and ethnic minorities are under-represented in the world of public appointments, although there is considerable variation between sponsoring departments. In 2000, for example, only 0.4 per cent of the 1,322 appointments made by the Ministry of Agriculture, Fisheries and Food were from the ethnic minorities. In the DfEE the percentage was 9.0. Each government department has drawn up plans covering the period 1998–2001 for increasing the representation of women and members of ethnic minorities on public bodies. It must be stressed, however, that the above proposal applies only to NDPBs and NHS bodies, and not to the vast majority of 'non-recognised' locally appointed bodies.

The unrepresentative nature of locally elected councillors was noted in Chapter 5. Although elected, local authority representatives do not even begin to mirror the whole of the community. In this context Stoker (1999c, p. 11) notes:

In private conversations ministers and their advisors make comparisons between the lively, ethnically diverse and gender-balanced representation on some local quangos and police authorities and the dull, middle-aged or elderly men that dominate the politics of many elected authorities. Indeed, they argue appointments to local quangos open up opportunities for involvement to a whole variety of people that would not stand in local elections.

Elected local government is far from ideal; as we have seen, in 1998 only 29 per cent of the electorate voted; in 1999, 32 per cent voted but by 2000 the figure was back down to 29 per cent. Those *elected* are frequently no more representative of local communities than those *appointed* to local quangos. Ironically, quangos have the potential to be a vehicle for broadening the basis of political participation at local level.

The greater transparency now accompanying appointments to quangos means that some of the earlier excesses of partisan behaviour are unlikely to be repeated on the same scale. For example, in 1993 one junior minister at the Department of Trade and Industry, Lady Denton, had responsibility for 804 public appointments. She was reported as saying: 'I can't remember knowingly appointing a Labour supporter' (*Independent on Sunday*, 23 March 1993). Again, in 1994, John Redwood, Secretary of State for Wales, was heavily criticised for appointing as chairman of the Welsh Development Agency a former Conservative Party fundraiser in Monte Carlo. Partisanship is, however, at the very core of British politics. Given the party system, it is unlikely to disappear. Every government is likely to want to have people sympathetic to their policies placed in organisations that are of central importance in terms of the delivery of policy.

Quangos and policy

In 1998 the Labour government published a consultation paper entitled *Quangos: Opening the Doors* (Cabinet Office, 1998c). This drew back from suggesting the abolition of quangos or advocating the wholesale transfer of functions back to either central or local government. Essentially, as we have seen, the proposals entailed refining the existing product rather than advocating radical change. The emphasis was upon greater openness, increased accountability, greater information, broadening the representative base of board appointees and (wherever possible) reducing quango numbers. Quangos are here to stay and are likely to continue to play a very important part in both formulating and implementing policy.

By creating quangos and by steering appointments, central government can shape the way specific issues are handled. From April 2001, for example, Learning and Skills Councils for England (LSCs) replaced TECs and the Further Education Funding Council (FEFC) in the planning and coordination of skills development and training for people over 16. These councils (forty-seven in total) have a budget of around £5 billion, saving some £50 million in the TEC/FEFC system. Business has a big role to play in the new LSCs. Some 40 per cent of members have substantial recent business or commercial experience, as do the national chairman and the majority of local chairmen. Direct accountability via the ballot box does not feature.

Johnson and Riley (1995, p. 109) argue that the creation of non-elected bodies has contributed to the centralisation of educational policy-making:

> The development of quangos as arm's-length agencies of government has created scope for indirect government intervention in key policy areas and has been part of a power realignment-strengthening central over local government. Within education, as many other areas of the public service, quangos are now major players. Through them, the tentacles of central government now reach into increasingly complex arenas.

In a similar vein, by creating urban development corporations and bypassing elected Labour-controlled local authorities in the 1980s, Conservative governments were able to usher in a more market- and private sector-oriented perspective to urban regeneration. HATs were used to bypass Labour-controlled local authorities with the aim of developing housing regeneration schemes in specific localities (e.g. Liverpool). Central policy can be driven at local level via government-appointed quangos.

As Hood (1981, pp. 120–1) argues, quangos are far too useful to be abolished too readily by politicians. There are, he maintains, at least four potential political uses which make them unlikely to disappear:

- government will always need bodies from which it can distance itself in sensitive areas;
- there is value in having temporary organisations outside the permanent government service that can be scrapped when chances permit;
- the use of such bodies as an administrative means of bypassing other public organisations, along with the patronage dimension, continues to attract politicians;
- they are useful as political 'window dressing'.

The above factors, along with those presented earlier from the Labour government's consultation paper *Opening up Quangos* (Cabinet Office, 1997) means that quangos are unlikely to become extinct.

Conclusion

Quangos cut across the Blair government's desire for 'joined-up' or holistic government. Through them, public policy and service management functions are parcelled out to separate single-purpose bodies. Given the separate organisational, professional and policy 'silos' which characterise the world of quasi-government, integration becomes problematic. The duplication and reduced efficiency which results from inadequate coordination can on occasion negate the benefits that accrue from the use of specialised, single-purpose bodies.

The role of quangos in the modern administrative state remains controversial. As Skelcher (1998, p. 5) observes, from one perspective quasi-government is the weighing of public values and the exercise of judgement – an essentially political activity – by a group of individuals appointed through a process of patronage (albeit one that is more transparent than a few years ago) and having no direct accountability or legitimacy with citizens. From another perspective, however, quangos can be seen as an effective and politically astute way of governing and managing public services by drawing on the skills and experience of experts who, by virtue of being insulated from public view and party competition, are able to reach the best decisions for a community. The fact that quango members are not directly elected nonetheless remains a cause of concern for many people.

Issues relating to accountability and appointments are being tackled; greater openness and transparency prevailed in 2000 than even five years earlier. Quangos have developed in an *ad hoc* manner and have become part of an increasingly complex, multilayered administrative state. They remain so incredibly diverse that there is little justification for derogatory generalisations. Without denying the accountability/control/patronage problems which accompany this form of governmental organisation, the survival of the species suggests that governments themselves see a continuing role for quangos, particularly when faced with politically hostile local authorities and bureaucratically organised government departments which are able to frustrate central government policy priorities. Flinders and Cole (1999, p. 238) argue that 'the quango state will probably grow more complex and the democratic deficit remain'. The demise of the quango does not appear to be imminent.

Further reading

Skelcher (1998) is an excellent discussion of the major themes and is probably the best place to start. The collection of essays edited by Flinders and Smith (1999) contains some perceptive analysis on a variety of quangos. Ridley and Wilson (1995) includes contributions from practitioners as well as academics and provides a wealth of empirical material relating to a wide range of sectors. A more theoretical perspective can be found in Weir and Beetham (1999). Taylor (2000) provides a very interesting article on the new breed of quangos, taskforces. The annual Cabinet Office publication, *Public Bodies*, contains a multitude of useful facts and figures. Likewise the excellent web site www.cabinet-office.gov.uk/quango is well worth a visit, especially if contemporary material is required.

Parliament

Introduction

Those seeking to fully understand the system of public administration in Britain cannot ignore Parliament. Lying at the very heart of the system, in strict constitutional terms, the Westminster Parliament consists of the directly elected House of Commons, the House of Lords (which has traditionally been unelected, but is subject to a process of reform that could lead to at least one of its elements being elected) and the monarch. Although there is a developing perception among some observers that legislatures are becoming increasingly marginal within modern systems of government and public administration, Philip Norton, one of the foremost analysts of the UK Parliament, has no doubts about this institution's significance. 'It is a multi-functional body. The consequences it has for the political system are several and significant' (Norton, 1993, pp. 202–3). From a slightly different perspective, Judge (1993, p. 2) has deplored the tendency on the part of some schools of political thought to downplay the significance of Parliament, or indeed to ignore it altogether. He argues that it is impossible to make proper sense of the British state, its system of politics and public administration, without giving this central feature of the polity proper attention: 'It is time to take parliament seriously.'

It is clear why we should take Parliament seriously. The executive arm of the state emerges from, and is accountable to, Westminster. The elected representatives of the people gather there to help formulate policy, process legislation and scrutinise the workings of the government machine. Nonetheless, Parliament's place in the system of government and public administration has undoubtedly been affected by shifts in power towards the European Union, devolved bodies within the UK, and a range of other national and sub-national bodies such as quangos. The Westminster Parliament continues to occupy a place of central importance in the UK polity, but, as the nature of the political system itself changes, so too does the body at its core.

Having encountered relatively little change in its basic role and functions for centuries, Parliament is now confronted with a series of challenges to its traditions and its place in the UK constitutional framework. Partly as a result of this, the House of Commons is being required to modernise its systems and procedures, while the composition and future role of the House of Lords are changing. The winds of change are blowing through Westminster, and as the entire edifice is adjusting to meet this series of new demands, it is attracting fresh interest from academics and politicians.

In this chapter we examine the roles and working practices of MPs, the key Westminster functions, and the issues of reform facing this central institution.

Honourable Members

The work of British Members of Parliament can be categorised in different ways. A simple classification of MPs' roles would encompass party political activities, constituency work, legislating, and scrutinising the executive. While performing these roles, MPs are considered to be performing as representatives rather than delegates. This distinction has some significance, at least in theory.

The original debate about representative and delegate functions in the context of the British Parliament took place from the late eighteenth century until the middle of the nineteenth century, when two schools of political philosophy were engaged in a dispute about the best means of safeguarding the people's interests. Jeremy Bentham argued that individual people were the best judges of their own interests, and the task of the elected representatives of the people was to follow the wishes of the electors. In other words, the people's representatives were really delegates, whose task was to discover the wishes of the electors, and then vote accordingly in Parliament. Contrary to this, Edmund Burke, Member of Parliament and political philosopher, and later John Stuart Mill, argued that the representatives of the people ought to be more than mere delegates. They should be accountable to the voters, but at the same time MPs should be allowed considerable discretion to exercise their own judgement on the issues coming before them in Parliament. This concept of the MP as a representative rather than a delegate bound by a restrictive mandate to vote in certain specified ways came to be accepted as the most appropriate description of the British Member of Parliament. However, we should not dismiss the debate which took place between these philosophers of the past as having no relevance to modern politics. The demands placed by political parties on twenty-first-century MPs lead some observers to argue that our elected representatives lack the freedom of true representatives. Party discipline, the whipping system, the need to abide by the mandate resulting from the election manifesto and the general pressure to conform to the requirements of leaders can combine to restrict the options available to our MPs as they go about their parliamentary work. This means that Members of Parliament occasionally have to strike an uneasy balance between being true to their consciences and being loyal to their parties.

The House of Commons is often characterised as a predominantly male, middle-class and white establishment. This remains fundamentally accurate although, as Norton (2001, pp. 345–8) points out, the demographic profile and characteristics of MPs are slightly more complex than this. The proportion of women MPs rose to 18 per cent after the 1997 General Election, largely due to the election of a record number (101) of female Labour MPs. At the same time, a record number (nine) of non-white MPs were elected, although this represented only 1 per cent of the total membership of the Commons. In terms of educational and social background, the House of Commons has become increasingly middle class in the period since 1945 as the proportions of public-school-educated, upper-class Conservatives, and Labour MPs from manual working-class backgrounds, have steadily fallen. Another related trend has been the growing numbers of career politicians: people whose pre-parliamentary and extra-parliamentary working experiences are limited (often to fields related to politics, such as party research). Viewed positively, this can be seen as enhancing the professionalism of our MPs. A more negative viewpoint would lament the loss of 'real-world' experience and capacity for broader perspectives among them.

Roles of MPs

Individual Members of Parliament might view their roles in different ways. Some will give greater emphasis to certain aspects of the job. Over time, a particular MP might change the emphasis given to different elements of the work. This is especially apparent when Members assume additional responsibilities, such as membership of committees, which can detract from the time available for the traditional role of constituency representation. The roles of MPs can be categorised in different ways. A simple approach would be to view the overall job of the Member of Parliament in terms of four basic roles: party politician, constituency representative, legislator and scrutineer.

The great majority of MPs have at least one role in common: that of the party politician. In 2000, only four out of the total of 659 Members did not have an official party affiliation. One was the Speaker (who traditionally renounces all party links). The other three were: Martin Bell, who had been elected as an Independent in the 1997 General Election, and Denis Canavan and Ken Livingstone, who were now designated simply as the Members of Parliament for Falkirk West and Brent East respectively, having been expelled from the Labour Party. For all other MPs, party affairs necessarily occupied some of their time.

Party work can take a number of different forms. The most obvious categories would be constituency-level party business, participation in the Parliamentary structures of the party (through the Parliamentary Labour Party, the Conservative 1922 Committee or any of their sub-elements, for example), or involvement in the national bodies of the party (including the various parts of a party's central organisation and bureaucracy).

The second role we have attributed to Members of Parliament, constituency representation, is conventionally viewed as the staple role of the MP. In fact, it might be argued that this is not merely one but a collection of roles. Each one of the 659 MPs in the House of Commons has a constituency. The interests of the constituency as a whole, and the needs of individual constituents, must be guarded assiduously by MPs. There are serious risks for any elected representative who neglects this aspect of the work. It is possible that a less than conscientious MP might be 'deselected' by the local party, and dropped as its candidate for the next election. For MPs in marginal constituencies, with no secure majority, there is the danger that the electorate will punish a Member who is deemed to have failed in this role by simply voting for the candidate of another party at the next General Election.

MPs can be seen to be performing this role most obviously when a major local issue arises, such as the threat of significant job losses, a hospital closure or a major emergency of some sort. In these circumstances, the diligent local MP will always want to be seen to be defending and supporting the needs of the constituency. On occasion, this might bring the MP into conflict with his or her party and lead to tension between two of the basic MP roles. It is not difficult to find illustrations of this. For example, during the construction of the Channel Tunnel rail link in the early 1990s, many Conservative MPs in Kent and the south-east of England stressed their role as guardians of the interests of their constituents (many of whom were concerned about the impact of this development on property prices) at the expense of their role as loyal party politicians supporting their own government's line on this project. Similarly, in 2000, Labour MPs in different parts of the country with airports and air traffic control services in their constituencies found themselves in conflict with their own government over the planned privatisation of the National Air Traffic Control System, which was opposed by those working in it.

Seeking out and securing redress of constituents' grievances is another key feature of the constituency representation role. The problems of individuals or groups can be brought to MPs through a variety of routes, most obviously at the regular constituency surgeries or by mail or email. Grievances can be handled in a number of different ways. Because many members of the public tend to see MPs as the first port of call for the resolution of virtually any type of problem, some cases must simply be redirected to a more appropriate source, such as a local authority or an NHS body. Where the grievance appears to fall within the legitimate sphere of the MP, it can be pursued via a range of mechanisms and devices. An informal approach to the government department or agency concerned might be sufficient to resolve the difficulty. Beyond this, in increasing order of importance, the MP might try to sort out the problem using a formal letter, a Parliamentary question, an Adjournment Debate or reference to a select committee for investigation. In Chapter 12 we examine in more detail the functioning and implications of these and other mechanisms of accountability and redress.

In constitutional terms, the third role of the MP has great significance. Members of Parliament are legislators in the sense that they vote on Bills passing through the House of Commons, participate in debates on these Bills, and, in standing committees, examine Bills in detail and amend them where necessary.

However, the growing power of the executive, the demands of the modern party system and the emergence of legislative forces (including the European Union and the Scottish Parliament) beyond Westminster have combined to dilute the significance of the MP as legislator. The business timetable of the House of Commons is controlled by the government. MPs have limited opportunities to legislate as individuals. Under the ten-minute rule MPs may propose Bills in brief speeches, but these are 'rarely serious attempts at legislation but . . . means to obtain some publicity on the need to change the law' (Garrett, 1992, p. 58). Some other avenues are open to MPs seeking to legislate in their own right, the most famous of which is the annual ballot for Private Members' Bills, which offers a rare chance to a very small number of MPs to introduce a Bill dealing with a specific topic. Even then, such a Bill stands little chance of success unless it is viewed sympathetically enough by the government of the day for it to allocate the measure some space within the crowded Parliamentary timetable and allow it to proceed.

Nonetheless, legislation sponsored by backbenchers should not be dismissed out of hand. Between 1979 and 1997, a total of 268 Acts of Parliament started off as Private Members' Bills (Silk and Walters, 1998, p. 113). Some of these addressed existing legislative anomalies, some introduced small-scale social reforms, including the Video Recordings Act of 1984, which regulated the sale of so-called 'video nasties', and the Knives Act of 1997, which banned the carrying of knives as offensive weapons.

However, the great majority of Bills which come before Parliament are part of the government's legislative programme, and this is strictly managed by the majority party's Whips. In order to ensure that the government's legislation is processed in good time, a range of devices are used to effectively limit the time and scope for MPs to delay or fundamentally change Bills. In extreme cases 'guillotine' motions can be introduced in order to place limits on the time available for debate, and 'kangaroo' motions can circumvent the need for a standing committee to examine every clause in a Bill (and allow the committee to 'jump over' whole sets of clauses at a time). More routinely, the whipping system is used to ensure that MPs 'toe the party line' and vote according to the wishes of the leadership when Bills come before them in committees or in the House at large.

Naturally, the use of these devices by governments does not guarantee success in every case. Backbench rebellions do occur, the wishes of the Whips are defied from time to time, and governments suffer defeats on some aspects of their legislative programmes. However, this is relatively rare, even when a government has a small majority. During the Major government's final session, 1996–7, it succeeded in getting all of its Bills passed, despite its precarious position in the Commons. Viewed in a negative light, this can be taken to mean that the power of the executive and the demands of party loyalty are such that MPs should be seen as mere 'lobby-fodder' whose role in legislation is simply to legitimate the wishes of the majority party. A more sympathetic interpretation would hold that MPs still retain significant powers to amend the details of government Bills, and even oblige the executive to drop legislative proposals before they reach Parliament (one example of the latter would include the Major government's decision not to proceed with a measure to introduce Post Office privatisation).

The fourth role of MPs is that of scrutineer. As a collection of agents of accountability, Members of Parliament are charged with the task of holding the government of the day to account for its policies and actions. As we noted above when examining the role of constituency representative, MPs have at their disposal an array of devices and mechanisms which can be used to probe the government machine. Chief among these are: informal contacts with ministers and senior civil servants, letters, debates, questions for oral or written answer, and work on the select committees which scrutinise the workings of government. Some further comments will be offered below on Parliamentary mechanisms of scrutiny.

These are the broad roles of Members of Parliament. Of course it must be remembered that for a significant number of MPs the basic backbench roles will be supplemented by the additional duties associated with frontbench posts. Government ministers and opposition party spokesmen and women (frontbenchers) will seek to carry out the roles we have examined above, while taking on the extra responsibilities of office. For ministers, this involves participating in the business of the Cabinet (in the case of the twenty or so most senior ministers), playing a part in the management of departments of state, leading debates for the government, steering legislation through its Commons stages, and defending the government under examination during Parliamentary questions and select committee hearings. The duties of opposition frontbenchers, although less onerous (they do not have to run departments), nonetheless add significantly to their basic workload.

Functions of Parliament

Parliament's key functions can be simply stated, and these are summarised in Box 9.1.

It is a representative forum for the airing of issues of national concern. Parliamentary traditionalists, including Enoch Powell, Michael Foot and Tony Benn, always attached considerable importance to this function, arguing that the will of the nation could be discerned (particularly at times of crisis) in the coming together of

---

Box 9.1 Parliament's functions

National representative forum
Produces executive
Provides Opposition
Legitimates government policy
Legislature
Scrutineer

---

the elected representatives of the people. This type of view is clearly linked to the ideas of representative democracy put forward by Burke and Mill, alluded to above.

If the concept of Parliament as the national representative forum can appear slightly abstract, our second key function is grounded in practical reality. Within the UK system of government and public administration there is no distinct separation of powers along the lines seen in, for example, the United States of America. In the UK, the executive arm of the state, the government, emerges out of the legislature rather than being totally distinct from it. In practice, this means that the government is formed by the leader of the party which can command a majority in the House of Commons, and the members of the Cabinet will be based in Parliament (primarily in the House of Commons) in order to ensure that they are accountable to the people via their elected representatives. Constitutional convention dictates that those government departments headed by a Cabinet minister from the House of Lords will normally have a second Cabinet minister based in the Commons. While prime ministers are free to choose members of their government from beyond Parliament, such appointments are relatively rare, and they are usually followed by moves to secure a Parliamentary base for the new minister. An illustration of this came in 1999, when Prime Minister Tony Blair appointed the media executive Gus Macdonald to a ministerial post, and a peerage was conferred on him in order to facilitate his accountability to Parliament.

Parliament not only produces the executive, it also provides the system with a formal, official opposition. The Speaker of the House of Commons has a statutory duty to designate the leader of the largest opposition party in the Commons as Leader of Her Majesty's Opposition. This has been a salaried post since 1937. Furthermore, since 1975 funds have been available ('Short Money', so called because it was introduced by the then Leader of the House of Commons Edward Short) to help the opposition parties pay for parliamentary support staff and research.

The next key function for Parliament to perform is the legitimisation of government policy. In formal terms, this refers to the requirement that any government must be able to carry a majority in Parliament with it, not only when securing passage of its legislation, but also when acting in national and international affairs. Therefore, the actions of the UK government are said to be legitimate in the specific sense that, if pushed to votes in Parliament, the government could secure a majority in favour of its measures. Parliament retains the power to check and control a government, and in certain circumstances to deny a government legitimacy. The mechanisms which might be used to accomplish this would include a formal vote of no confidence by Parliament, rejection of a Budget, failure to approve 'supply' (that is, a supply of funds from the Exchequer) or defeat of a key measure on which the government has staked its credibility. However significant this function might seem in theory, in practical terms it has limited usage. The fact that a government, by its very nature, will normally be able to command a Commons majority, coupled with the demands of the party system and the imposition of discipline through the Whips, means that the opportunities available to Parliament to withhold legitimacy are strictly limited. In modern times, only one government, that of James Callaghan in 1979, was forced to request a dissolution of Parliament and call a General Election as a direct consequence of losing a confidence motion in the House of Commons. The government of John Major came close to doing so on a number of occasions between 1992 and 1997, but managed to survive, despite some significant backbench rebellions, particularly on EU policy.

Parliament has a very specific and formal constitutional role to play in the public expenditure process. Government needs Parliamentary approval to secure 'supply' – access to a supply of public funds in order to give life to its policies and also to raise money with which to replenish the public accounts. Within the annual public expenditure cycle, Parliament plays a vital role at key stages, although it should be noted that the realities of the party system ensure that governments with majorities in the House of Commons can normally secure passage of all their key spending and revenue-raising proposals. The Chancellor of the Exchequer's Financial Statement (normally in November), which sets out the government's public expenditure proposals for the coming financial year and the medium term beyond, is subject to debate in the House of Commons. Supply of funds for public expenditure is secured through the passage of two Consolidated Fund Bills. The Budget statement and Financial Report by the Chancellor (in the spring) is also subject to debate, and the Finance Bill which emerges from the Budget (and sets out the government's plans for revenue raising through a combination of taxes, duties and borrowing) is scrutinised over a period of months in debates and standing committee.

We set out above some of the opportunities and limitations associated with the role of MPs as legislators. For Parliament as a whole, the business of law-making is a central activity. Procedures for the passage of legislation are well established and familiar (although, as we note below, some attempts are being made to modernise certain aspects of the process). The government's legislative proposals are announced each year in the Queen's Speech (written by ministers) at the start of the parlimentary session. Bills can be introduced in either the Commons or the Lords, and they move to the other chamber for consideration following successful passage in the House of origin. Even 'money Bills' (legislative measures containing significant financial elements and certified as money Bills by the Speaker of the House of Commons), over which the House of Lords has no powers of amendment, go through the formal process of passage in the upper chamber, although they cannot be introduced in the Lords. The principal stages through which legislation passes in each House are:

- first reading, which introduces the Bill formally;
- second reading, which involves a wide-ranging debate on the merits of the Bill;

- committee stage, where a Bill which has successfully passed its second reading is sent for detailed scrutiny. In the Commons this stage is normally held in a standing committee, but occasionally in a Committee of the Whole House. The House of Lords normally takes the committee stage on the floor of the House. Amendments are proposed at this stage;
- report stage (properly referred to as 'consideration stage'), where the Bill returns to the whole House in the amended form produced by the committee, and there are further opportunities for amendments to be proposed;
- third reading, which involves a short debate on the final version of the Bill followed by a vote. It is extremely rare for a Bill to be defeated at this stage, which is normally seen as a formality.

In cases where the second House makes amendments to a Bill, these must be referred back to the House where the legislation originated for approval before the Bill can be sent for Royal Assent. On some occasions, proposed amendments become the subject of protracted negotiations between the two chambers. Where no agreement is reached an entire Bill (for example, the legislation which attempted to nationalise the aircraft and shipbuilding industries in 1976) or a key element of a Bill (for example, the clause in the 2000 Local Government Bill which sought to repeal Section 28 – the law banning 'promotion' of homosexuality in schools) may be lost. However, the 1949 Parliament Act limits the capacity of the House of Lords to veto Bills to one Parliamentary session. Under the terms of the Parliament Act 1911 financial legislation has to be passed by the Lords within one month of its passage through the Commons.

An increasingly important aspect of Parliament's law-making function concerns delegated legislation (also known as secondary or subordinate legislation). Due to the need to complete the technical details of some Acts after they have been passed (for example, the 1991 Child Support Act) or to deal with emergencies, or simply to relieve the pressure on Parliamentary time, many statutes confer powers on ministers to issue rules or orders by means of statutory instruments, which have legislative force. Immigration rules, benefit levels and employment protection procedures, as well as government actions during emergencies, including the BSE ('mad cow disease') and foot and mouth outbreaks, are all determined by statutory instruments. While these effectively speed up the legislative process, they also escape the normal process of legislative scrutiny. In most but not all cases such instruments have to be laid before Parliament. The most important are subject to an affirmative resolution of the Commons (or in some cases both Houses); others become effective unless voted down. In practice, however, the vast majority of the nearly 3,000 statutory instruments passed each year are never debated. In effect, in many cases Parliament is simply informed about legal changes without being able to do much about them.

The Joint Committee on Statutory Instruments (composed of members of the Commons and the Lords) is the main mechanism of scrutiny. The Committee has seven members from each House of Parliament. It cannot comment on the merits of statutory instruments, its role being to consider and report on the technical implications of delegated legislation. For example, the Committee will examine the extent to which the legislation is properly drafted or uses the powers of the original, parent Act of Parliament in the expected way. The Committee does not have general powers to send for persons, papers and records, but it can require a government department to submit a memorandum or send a representative to appear before it. While it can refer an instrument to the House for consideration, there is no guarantee that a debate will occur (Craig, 1999, pp. 364–92).

In addition, since 1992 there has been a House of Lords Delegated Powers Scrutiny Committee concerned with the extent of legislative powers being delegated by Parliament to government ministers. It identifies the detailed provisions for delegated legislation within government bills, seeks explanations for the need for this type of approach, considers whether the grant of secondary power is appropriate, and examines the form of parliamentary control needed. The Delegated Powers Scrutiny Committee pays particular attention to the so-called 'Henry VIII' powers – provisions in Bills which allow primary legislation to be amended or repealed by subordinate legislation, sometimes without proper parliamentary scrutiny. This Committee has eight members, takes evidence in writing on each public Bill from the relevant department, and also occasionally takes oral evidence.

Finally, but arguably most importantly, Parliament is a scrutineer of government. The policies and actions of the executive, encompassing ministers and the civil service, must be subjected to proper supervision in the interests of a healthy, functioning democracy. Of course, the need for Parliament to check and influence the government can and does come into conflict with the desire of ministers and their officials to get on with the business of governing without distractions. The result is an ongoing power game in which the executive holds most of the trump cards and controls access to much vital information, while Parliamentarians attempt to deploy an array of mechanisms and devices designed to expose government to close examination.

As we noted above when discussing the roles of MPs, the mechanisms of Parliamentary scrutiny range from the relatively informal to the highly structured. In Chapter 12 we examine the mechanisms of Parliamentary scrutiny in the context of our analysis of the systems of public sector accountability. For the time being, however, we can briefly summarise the key weapons utilised by MPs seeking to scrutinise the workings of the government machine.

Some of the mechanisms have a fairly specific focus. For example, the standing committees, which deal with the committee stage of legislation, are clearly designed for the purpose of scrutinising Bills (although the extent to which they achieve adequate scrutiny is arguable, given the constraints under which they operate: for example, they function like the House of Commons in miniature, debating bills clause by clause, and are unable to call witnesses or commission research). Debates, on the other hand, may be focused on the task of legislative scrutiny (in the case of the second reading debate, for example) or on scrutiny of government policy and action (in the case of debates on adjournment or opposition motions). Debates also take place routinely on occasions such as the Queen's Speech (written by ministers) and on the adjournment of the House, although the government may also initiate debates on particular issues. In addition there are twenty days each year which are designated as 'Opposition Days'. On seventeen of these the leader of the opposition chooses the topic for debate, on the remaining three days the topic is chosen by the leader of the third largest party (the Liberal Democrats), though at least one day is usually given over to the minor parties. At the request of constituents, MPs may seek to scrutinise very specific failings, or alleged failings, on the part of government departments or agencies. The Parliamentary Commissioner for Administration (PCA or 'Ombudsman') is an officer appointed by Parliament for the purpose of investigation of allegations of maladministration. The part played by the PCA in securing redress of grievances and bringing government to account is discussed in Chapter 12.

Letters or informal approaches from MPs to ministers are important forms of scrutiny. As Norton (2001, p. 364) notes, the volume of MP–ministerial correspondence has increased significantly in recent years, to the point where 10,000 to 15,000 letters per month are sent, largely in order to pursue matters raised by constituents.

Parliamentary questions (PQs) will often be utilised by MPs who fail to achieve satisfaction through the informal and semi-formal approaches to ministers. All government ministers can be questioned, in a number of different ways, about virtually any aspect of their departmental responsibilities. Questions for oral answer are put to ministers on a rota basis, designed to bring about more frequent appearances at the dispatch box by the ministers from departments which attract most Parliamentary interest. These ministerial Question Times provide extensive opportunities for MPs to place members of the government under scrutiny, especially through the use of the unnotified supplementary questions. Additionally, MPs can put down PQs specifically for written answer. This is normally done when detailed factual information is required. Although limitations on time have resulted in reduced numbers of oral questions, there has been a remarkable growth in the number of PQs for written answer in modern times: over 50,000 of these were being tabled per year by the late 1990s (Franklin and Norton, 1993, p. 27; Norton, 2001, pp. 358–9). Clearly, this represents a significant volume of scrutiny.

The attraction of PQs as weapons of scrutiny must be set in the context of their relative weakness in certain respects. Oral Question Times all too often degenerate into exercises of party political point-scoring, certain topics (including the Royal Family and issues of national security) are not permissible for questions, ministers have the right to refuse to provide answers on the grounds that the information could only be gathered at 'unacceptable cost', and the advent of executive agencies in the 1980s meant that ministers would no longer personally answer PQs relating to significant areas of government work (see also Chapters 2 and 12).

Arguably, the most effective of the Parliamentary mechanisms of scrutiny are select committees. These committees of investigation and inquiry have existed in many different forms throughout Parliament's history, but the House of Commons select committees were systematised in the major reform of 1979 (see Drewry, 1985). This was designed to bring about more cohesive and coherent scrutiny of government departments by an array of committees composed of backbench MPs. By 2000, the Commons select committees could be categorised in the form set out in Box 9.2. The system of departmental select committees has evolved as the departmental pattern changed (see Chapter 2). The work of the 'housekeeping' committees related mainly to the internal functioning of the Commons. Among the 'others' there are some powerful committees of scrutiny, particularly the Public Accounts Committee (PAC). This powerful committee works in conjunction with the National Audit Office – an independent body headed by the Comptroller and Auditor General and charged with scrutinising the accounts of government departments and agencies and reporting on their legality and accuracy, as well as the extent to which value for money has been secured. Consisting of sixteen backbenchers, the PAC is chaired, by convention, by a member of the main opposition party. It receives detailed reports on all aspects of central government spending from the National Audit Office. The PAC is not concerned with the policies of government as such, but with the use of resources in pursuit of policies. It operates on a non-partisan basis, takes evidence from those charged with responsibility for managing public funds (primarily the permanent secretaries of departments and chief executives of agencies, who are normally designated as the Accounting Officers) and produces reports which carry considerable weight. The government responds to the reports of the PAC by means of Treasury Minutes, which set out the actions which will be taken to correct serious failings in financial management identified by the Committee. A good example of the type of detailed, highly critical work carried out by the PAC was its report into the mismanagement of the Home Office's computerisation programme which precipitated the collapse of the system for processing passport applications in 1999, causing massive inconvenience to thousands of people (Committee of Public Accounts, 2000).

The 'departmental' committees now include some which are subject-based (Science and Technology, and Public Administration) rather than focused specifically on the work of a government department. Although oriented towards scrutiny in the chamber itself rather than through committees, the House of Lords has its own select committees, chief among which is the European Union Committee. Select committees choose their own topics for investigation, take evidence in documentary and oral forms (some of this is generated in hearings during which ministers and civil servants will be questioned at length), and produce reports containing recommendations for action. However, there are restrictions on the information which civil servants can provide – for example, they cannot disclose advice given to ministers, nor information concerning interdepartmental exchanges about policy – and opportunities to debate their reports on the floor of the House are limited. There are also some important issues surrounding the limited resources available to committees (they have minimal support – normally one senior and one junior clerk, and a small number of expert advisers selected from an approved panel). Although the performance of select committees has been variable, and there have been reports of attempts by the party Whips to 'pack' the committees with 'trusted' backbenchers, these bodies still provide the potential for a form of detailed and sustained scrutiny of specific aspects of government policy and management which is difficult to achieve through other mechanisms. While they have no formal role in the legislative process, select committees do, however, have the potential to secure changes to government practices and procedures. Additionally, they can cause severe embarrassment and discomfort to government. An illustration of this came when the Foreign Affairs Committee produced a highly critical report on the conduct of ministers (including the Foreign Secretary, Robin Cook) and civil servants during the 'Sandline Affair', in which weapons were delivered by a British company to Sierra Leone, in contravention of a UK arms embargo, for use by that country's armed forces (Foreign Affairs Committee, 1999).

Box 9.2 Select committees of the House of Commons

Departmental
Agriculture
Culture, Media and Sport
Defence
Education and Employment
Environment, Transport and Regional Affairs
Foreign Affairs
Health
Home Affairs
International Development
Northern Ireland Affairs
Public Administration
Science and Technology
Scottish Affairs
Social Security
Trade and Industry
Treasury
Welsh Affairs

Housekeeping
Accommodation and Works
Information
Liaison
Modernisation
Joint Committee on Parliamentary Procedure
Standards and Privileges

Others
Deregulation
Environmental Audit
European Legislation
Public Accounts

House of Commons modernisation

On its election in 1997, the Labour government led by Tony Blair announced its commitment to a process of 'modernisation' which would aim to transform many of the structures and systems of British government and public administration. Parliament was not to be exempt from this, and the government began planning reform of the House of Lords (see below) and modernisation of the House of Commons. The first clear outcomes of the latter were changes to Prime Minister's Question Time (replacing the twice-weekly, fifteen-minute sessions with a more

Table 9.1 Reports from the Modernisation of the House of Commons Select Committee

Session 1997–8		
First Report	*The Legislative Process*	HC 190
Second Report	*Explanatory Material for Bills*	HC 389
Third Report	*Carry-Over of Public Bills*	HC 543
Fourth Report	*Conduct in the Chamber*	HC 600
Fifth Report	*Consultation paper on Voting Methods*	HC 699
Sixth Report	*Voting Methods*	HC 779
Seventh Report	*The Scrutiny of European Business*	HC 791
Session 1998–9		
First Report	*The Parliamentary Calendar: Initial Proposals*	HC 60
Second Report	*Sittings of the House in Westminster Hall*	HC 194
Third Report	*Thursday Sittings*	HC 719
Session 1999–2000		
First Report	*Facilities for the Media*	HC 408
Second Report	*Programming of Legislation and Timing of Votes*	HC 589

'efficient' single thirty-minute session on Wednesdays) and the appointment of a Modernisation of the House of Commons Select Committee, chaired by the Leader of the House (in turn, Ann Taylor and Margaret Beckett).

The subject of House of Commons modernisation has tended to produce three broad perspectives or schools of thought.

Radical reformers interpret modernisation in terms of fundamental change, designed to redress the balance of power between Parliament and the executive. Some of these reformers link Commons modernisation to programmes of thorough-going constitutional change, involving electoral reform for Westminster, rolling devolution through the English regions as well as Scotland, Wales and Northern Ireland, and bringing about much closer European integration. Through publications emanating from think tanks such as Demos and the Institute for Public Policy Research, significant internal House of Commons reforms and structural changes are generally seen as elements of sweeping programmes of political change.

In contrast, traditionalists oppose many or all aspects of Commons modernisation schemes, either because they believe in the basic right of a government with a legitimate mandate to get on with the job of governing without undue hindrance, or because they believe Parliament in general and the House of Commons in particular possess all the means necessary to achieve effective supervision, scrutiny and control of the executive. Additionally, those who are sceptical about the need for Commons modernisation, or oppose it outright, often express the fear that reforms will take MPs away from the chamber and reduce the quality of debates. This perspective was epitomised by the former Speaker of the House of Commons, Betty Boothroyd. It was perhaps significant that the Blair government sought to pursue modernisation through a select committee chaired by a minister, rather than in direct collaboration with the Speaker. On announcing her retirement, Boothroyd was openly critical of certain aspects of modernisation, specifically citing the danger that more 'family-friendly' working hours would conflict with the House's duty to deliver effective scrutiny of legislation (White, 2000).

The third perspective, and the one adopted by the Blair government, can be summarised as a belief in the need for some changes designed to update the processes and procedures of the House of Commons and enhance the effectiveness of its members, while avoiding the type of reforms which might seriously check the government's freedom of manoeuvre. This approach seemed to be broadly in line with the views of the majority of MPs elected in 1997 (see Norton, 2000b, p. 95). Thus, the reports produced by the Commons Modernisation Committee (see Table 9.1) have generally focused on worthy but (at least to those favouring more radical change) uninspiring reforms. Improvements to the legislative process have included the advent of arrangements for pre-legislative scrutiny, introducing greater balance to the legislative workload, allowing for the creation of special standing committees with powers to take evidence from witnesses, and strengthening the scrutiny of European legislation. Some of the more arcane aspects of conduct in the chamber were abolished, including the requirement that an MP seeking to raise a point of order during a division must wear an opera hat.

Cowley (2000, pp. 118–19) notes that with the exception of the idea that Westminster Hall should be used as a parallel debating chamber, few of the committee's recommendations have been particularly new or specially framed to enhance the Commons' scrutinising function, while 'others were designed for cosmetic or tidying-up purposes, or for the convenience of MPs'.

One aspect of modernisation, which was initiated in advance of the 1997 General Election, was the Commons' attempt to improve the policing of its own activities in the wake of a series of scandals which came to be described as 'sleaze'. During the early 1990s, the existing, fairly informal rules about consultancy work and the registration of members' outside interests had manifestly failed to prevent abuses by a small number of MPs who accepted 'cash for questions' or 'cash for amendments', or failed to declare interests when acting as 'advisers' to firms of lobbyists or PR consultants. As a result, the Commons approved a new Code of Conduct and appointed a Parliamentary Commissioner for Standards in order to ensure that the rules are adhered to.

Reform of the House of Lords

As we have seen, the House of Lords has an important role to play in the work of Parliament. All legislation – other than that imposed under the Parliament Acts – must have consent of both Houses, and the Lords, like the Commons, plays a full part in debating matters of general pubic concern, and holding the government to account. Indeed the non-elected nature of the House has traditionally led to less structured party discipline and a more consensual approach to the conduct of business. Its members, being free from constituency responsibilities, generally have more time than MPs to devote to legislation and debate; and in the case of life peer who have usually been appointed towards the end of distinguished careers in other walks of life, they collectively possess considerable expertise. Although at times serious clashes between the two Houses have occurred, the will of the House of Commons generally prevails and the Lords today plays an important role in the constructive revision of legislation. Indeed, the majority of the Lords' sitting hours are concerned with the revision of legislation, much of which has originated in the Commons. All main government departments contain ministers drawn from the Lords, whose roles include steering departmental legislation through the House, answering questions and participating in debates relating to departmental business.

In January 1999 the House of Lords consisted of 1,296 members, comprising 759 hereditary peers, 485 life peers, twenty-six 'law lords' (appointed to carry out the judicial functions of the House), twenty-four bishops and two archbishops. The Labour government elected in 1997, however, was strongly committed to reform the House of Lords. At earlier stages in the party's history it had favoured outright abolition of the upper house on the grounds that it was unrepresentative and contained an entrenched Conservative Party majority within the ranks of the hereditary peers. Limitations to the powers of the Lords (for example the 1949 Parliament Act's restrictions on the Lords' ability to delay legislation) and changes in the composition of the upper house (facilitated through the 1958 Life Peerages Act) blunted the edge of Labour's antipathy towards the Lords to some extent, although the party continued to flirt with the possibility of abolition after the failure of the Wilson government's attempt at reform in the late 1960s and the House of Lords' success in blocking some key legislation during the 1970s (Baldwin, 1995). Indeed, Labour fought the 1983 General Election with a renewed commitment to abolish the House of Lords. Neil Kinnock gradually dismantled this policy.

By 1992, Labour's policy was to introduce an elected second chamber. After he became party leader on the death of John Smith in 1994, Tony Blair quietly dropped this in favour of a vaguer commitment to reform. The revised policy was largely the creation of Blair himself, Lord Richard (Labour leader in the Lords) and Blair's mentor Derry Irvine, the future Lord Chancellor (Rentoul, 1996, pp. 465–7). The objective now was merely ending the voting rights of hereditary peers, with a promise to examine other options, and 'perhaps' introduce a directly elected 'element' (Mandelson and Liddle, 1996, p. 205).

At a very early stage in the life of the new government it became clear that devolution was to be the major priority and there would be no time in the first session of Parliament to implement the limited Lords reform pledged by the manifesto. At the party conference in October 1997 Blair succeeded in defusing criticism of this delay, and rallying his party, by warning the Lords not to 'try to wreck' the government's devolution proposals.

After this initial delay, the Blair government proceeded with a two-stage reform of the House of Lords (see Shell, 1998, pp. 25–9). Stage one involved the passage of the 1999 House of Lords Act, which ended the right of hereditary peers to sit in Parliament with effect from November of that year, with the exception of ninety-two hereditary Lords (from approximately 750) who, under a concession secured by the upper house during the Bill's passage, would be allowed to remain members of the house during the interim period until stage two of the reform process. By the start of session 1999–2000, therefore, the House of Lords had been transformed into a predominantly appointed House. The longer-term future of the Lords was the subject of stage two of the government's reform.

This was initiated by the publication of a White Paper in January 1999, which set out the options of a nominated, elected or mixed second chamber (Cabinet Office, 1999a), and the appointment of a Royal Commission of twelve members under the

---

Box 9.3 The Wakeham Report on reform of the House of Lords

Main recommendations:

- New second chamber (no name suggested) to comprise about 555 members.
- Majority of the members to be selected by an independent Appointments Commission of eight which will end the system of prime ministerial and party patronage of the second house.
- Remaining members (eighty-seven) to be elected from twelve regions across the UK, with one-third elected every five years and serving a fifteen-year term.
- Appointments Commission to review the composition of the new chamber regularly, and have powers to make adjustments in order to reflect political opinion (as recorded at the most recent General Election) and the UK's gender, faith and racial mix.
- No single party to have an overall majority, around 20 per cent of members to be independent cross benchers.
- Existing life peers to remain, if they wish.
- Future peerages not to confer membership of the new chamber.
- New chamber to retain the power to delay but not block Commons measures. Powers over statutory instruments and constitutional measures to be increased.

Source: Wakeham (2000)

---

chairmanship of the Conservative peer Lord Wakeham (a former Leader of both the Commons and the Lords) the following month. The Wakeham Commission took evidence throughout 1999 and reported in January 2000 (Wakeham, 2000). Box 9.3 sets out a summary of the Wakeham Report.

The Report was given a distinctly mixed reception, with many critics focusing on the fact that Wakeham's proposals would create a predominantly nominated second chamber, with the powers of nomination going to a quango, the Appointments Commission. The democratic element of the new House would be limited. The Wakeham Commission was divided on the precise number of new members who would be directly elected, but a majority favoured eighty-seven out of the total 550. *The Guardian* described the Report as 'a dog's dinner', and its scathing criticisms reflected the views of those who had argued for the early introduction of a directly elected chamber:

> To take one example from many, the report promises a new appointments commission, dispatching people to the chamber in order to reflect the regional, gender and ethnic make-up of the country and in accordance with the political complexion of the electorate expressed at the last general election – all the while keeping the total membership at the 550 mark. How does that add up? At present there are roughly that number of life peers around, and Wakeham elsewhere suggests these unelected folk should retain their seats in a reformed

chamber until the day they die. In other words, there will be no vacancies for the appointers to fill until the grim reaper has created them. It could take decades for the selection methods . . . to kick in.

(*The Guardian*, 2000)

It was clear that the government had no enthusiasm for a wholly or predominantly elected second chamber, since this could represent a significant challenge to the power of the Commons in future. The Wakeham proposals were therefore accepted, in principle, although both the Prime Minister and Baroness Jay, the Leader of the House of Lords, made it clear that there would be no rush to implement the Report. Instead, it would be given due consideration, with a view to introducing the second stage of House of Lords reform in the next Parliament.

Conclusion: Westminster's challenges

The future role of the Westminster Parliament within Britain's system of public administration is likely to depend, at least to some extent, on the way it faces up to a number of challenges. Three of these would seem to be worthy of specific comment.

The first pressing challenge for Westminster is to secure its status and adjust to new realities within the emerging parliamentary system in the United Kingdom. Judge (1993, Chapter 6) notes that Parliament, and the concept of Parliamentary sovereignty, historically played a vital role in reinforcing the centralist and unitary nature of the state in the UK. The central core of the constitution, Parliamentary sovereignty, referred to the fact that the central executive emerged from the sole law-making and legitimising body in the land. However, as centralism and the concept of the unitary state have come under pressure over recent years (see Chapter 10), so the place of the Westminster Parliament in the entire edifice has come to seem less stable. In particular, the EU institutions have effectively undermined the traditional concept of Parliamentary sovereignty from without, while, more recently, the advent of devolution within the UK has eroded the status of Westminster as the sole legislature within these shores. In place of the relative certainty of old, where the Westminster Parliament stood alone and unchallenged, we now have a developing system of parliaments and assemblies, in Strasbourg, Edinburgh, Cardiff and Belfast as well as in London. Each of these has its own executive and administrative apparatus, and each has added to the complexity of parliamentarianism in the UK. Chapter 10 provides a detailed discussion of the implications of this.

Some fairly practical implications have flowed, and are likely to continue to flow, from devolution. Norton (2000b, pp. 98–104) argues that the creation of the Scottish Parliament and the Welsh and Northern Ireland Assemblies has implications for the size, power, business and structures of the Westminster Parliament. For example, the House of Commons will not continue to have 659 members once the new bodies become fully established. The number of Westminster constituencies in Scotland and Wales (possibly also in Northern Ireland) will be reduced, leaving fewer MPs. Devolution conferred primary legislative power on the Scottish Parliament (though not on the two Assemblies) for all matters not specifically reserved to Westminster. The impact of this has been to further erode the constitutional power of Westminster and add to the dilution of Parliamentary sovereignty which started when the European Communities Act was passed in 1972. The business of Parliament has been affected too, with few bills devoted to Scotland, and less time needed for debates and PQs on Scottish, Welsh and Northern Irish matters. Structural changes gradually took place too, with less need for standing committees on Scottish Bills, although the Scottish and Welsh Grand Committees and the Scottish and Welsh Affairs Select Committees continued to function throughout the first post-devolution Parliament.

The second challenge is linked to the first, in one sense. The future image and status of Parliament will be affected by perceptions of the extent to which the modern-isation of the House of Commons and reform of the House of Lords are successful. Parliament's challenge is to complete these processes effectively. However, as the executive is largely leading these matters, Parliament itself does not have full control of the timing and scale of the changes. As we noted above, the pace of change on these fronts was initially rather slow, and there were doubts about the overall direction in which the reforms were moving.

The third challenge is for Parliament to assert itself in the face of apparently increasingly powerful executives. This is perhaps rather a tall order since the story of parliamentarianism the world over has been a tale of elected bodies steadily losing ground to governments. In the UK, there has perhaps been a tendency to hark back to a 'golden age' when Parliament was much more powerful and governments much more amenable to control. It is arguable whether things were ever as un-complicated as that, however, and even if they were, the demands of modern governance were such that power inevitably drifted increasingly towards the executive, and Parliament's time came to be increasingly at the disposal of ministers.

Nonetheless, it might be argued that real cause for concern was exemplified by the generally dismissive and occasionally contemptuous attitude adopted by the Thatcher governments towards Parliament. The Blair government has also seemed to have a certain propensity for riding roughshod over Parliament. For example, note the repeated criticisms from the Speaker of the House of Commons when important policy initiatives were launched in media 'events' before being presented to the House, the allegations that the votes of Labour backbenchers were regularly determined by paged instructions from the party Whips, and the arrogance shown by the Foreign Secretary Robin Cook during his dealings with the Foreign Affairs Select Committee over the 'arms to Sierra Leone' affair. It is perhaps no coincidence that both the Blair and Thatcher administrations enjoyed massive Commons majorities. Even if Parliament can no longer effectively control governments in normal circumstances, it can make the executive more accountable by utilising the full range of weapons at its disposal in a coordinated fashion and regularly demonstrating its independence from the restrictions of the party managers.

The part played by Parliament in the developing system of public administration in this country will depend in no small measure on the extent to which it is able to meet these challenges successfully.

Further reading

There is an extensive literature on Parliament. A sound, factual account of the processes, procedures and general functioning of the institution can be found in Silk and Walters (1998). Garrett (1992) provides a perspective from a friendly critic, who wants to see Parliament become a much more effective part of the system of public administration. The writings of Philip Norton (who now sits in Parliament as Lord Norton of Louth) can be depended upon to provide the reader with a blend of facts, commentary and analysis. Although his book, *Does Parliament Matter?* (1993) is now dated in some respects, it still merits attention. Norton's book chapters (see, for example, 2000b and 2001) and his numerous articles for journals such as *Politics Review* secure his place as the undisputed expert on Westminster. For those seeking a conceptual or theoretical approach, Judge (1993) is thought-provoking. Specialised studies of aspects of Parliamentary life include Drewry's (1985) edited collection on House of Commons select committees, Franklin and Norton (1993) on Parliamentary questions, and Shell (1992) on the pre-reform Lords.

Access can be gained to an array of official sources on Parliament, including the work of both houses, their committees and legislation, as well as research papers written by Parliamentary clerks and officers, via the website: www.parliament.uk.

Multi-level governance

Introduction

The time has long passed when it was possible to understand the workings of the UK system of public administration with reference only to Whitehall, Westminster and the world of local government. As we have seen in Chapter 8, the realm of quasi-government is now increasingly important. Beyond this, however, the workings of the European Union and the emerging systems of devolved and decentralised government are integral to the functioning of modern public administration. In this chapter we seek to examine some of the salient features of these elements of the system of government.

From the unitary state to multi-level governance

It would be wrong to say that there was a time when the single nation-state stood completely alone, and was able to determine its own fate. The impact of other states, as well as international, trans-national and multinational bodies and organisations, has always been of great importance. Nonetheless, it would be fair to argue that, until recent times, the key features of governance in the UK could be set out with some ease and clarity, with reference to the concept of the unitary state. Even allowing for the complex interdependencies between the UK and other states, and between the UK and international organisations including the Commonwealth, the United Nations and NATO, the existence of a unitary state based on the concept of Parliamentary sovereignty eased our understanding of the system.

Within a unitary state the source of governing power and authority is relatively centralised. In the UK, the Westminster Parliament produces the central executive, at the heart of which are the Cabinet and the Prime Minister. An array of central government departments and agencies administer the policies produced at the centre. The system of local government effectively exists as the creature of the centre, and, as we have seen in earlier chapters, the local authorities can be, and are, re-structured and in some cases merged or abolished, at the will of central government. Within this framework, allowance was made for some elements of sub-national and regional administration. In Scotland from the late nineteenth century, in Wales from the mid-1960s, and in Northern Ireland from the early 1970s, systems of devolved administration facilitated the implementation of central government policy with some distinctive features reflecting local traditions and requirements. Devolved administration entailed elements of decentralised policy-making and implementation, through the Scottish, Welsh and Northern Ireland Offices (departments of central government), but did not allow for decentralised legislative power (although we should note the abortive experiment with the Stormont Parliment in Northern Ireland between 1922 and 1972). Other types of regional administration could be seen in the sub-structures of certain central government departments and in the organisation of the National Health Service and the public utilities. Nonetheless, taken as a whole, the system of government was based upon the principle of the unitary state.

Within a relatively short period, matters have become much more complex. While the unitary state still exists, in important respects it now makes more sense to discuss government, public administration and management in the UK in terms of multi-level governance. In simple terms, this refers to the existence of numerous locations of power and authority – various layers of decision-making. While it is arguable whether we could ever really approach a proper understanding of government and public administration in the UK with reference only to the powers and jurisdictions of Whitehall and Westminster, it is certain that we can no longer do so. The relative clarity and certainty associated with the unitary state have been replaced by complexity, and we must now attempt to grapple with the implications of additional levels of governmental power, including the European Union and the devolved institutions in Scotland, Wales and Northern Ireland. Britain's accession to the then European Economic Community in 1973 heralded explicit recognition of the right of this supra-national organisation to create law and policy affecting the citizens of the UK. The Blair government's devolution programme saw the establishment of new governing institutions in Scotland, Wales and Northern Ireland in the late 1990s. These were granted powers which went far beyond the previous arrangements for devolved administration, to encompass a much fuller form of devolved policy-making, and, in the case of Scotland, devolved legislative power.

Within this chapter we will seek to set out some of the key features of the various levels of governance which impinge upon the functioning of the UK system of public administration. However, in the first instance, we can examine the basic theories and concepts which underpin the idea of multi-level governance.

Some initial thoughts on the concept of 'governance' were offered in Chapter 1. The use of the term 'governance' as opposed to 'government' is of significance: 'governance signifies a change in the meaning of government, referring to a *new* process of governing; or a *changed* condition of ordered rule; or the *new* method by which society is governed' (Rhodes, 1997a, p. 46). What is this new process, changed condition or new method? The key contributors to the debates about governance (see, for example, Rosenau, 1992; Kooiman, 1993; Rhodes, 1997a; Peters, 2000; Pierre, 2000) offer different perspectives on the concept. However, some common themes emerge. A combination of features characterise governance. Among these we can cite are those brought together by Rhodes (1997a, pp. 46–7) in his synthesis of the governance debates:

- a reduced role for government in some areas of public policy, with the *minimal state* witnessing attempts to cut the scale and scope of the public sector while generating greater use of the private sector for former state activities;
- increased attention paid to moral and ethical issues – in particular, attempts (not necessarily successful in all cases) to introduce improved standards of *corporate governance* in order to cope with rising concerns about 'sleaze';
- the introduction of a variety of initiatives under the banner of the *new public management*. These would include, for example, the transfer of a range of private sector management systems and techniques to the public sector, the advent of new structures for the delivery of public services, and the introduction of quasi- (or pseudo-?) markets, contractualism and consumerism;
- rolling programmes of *institutional and constitutional reform* encompassing policies, the political culture and the governing framework;
- creation and implementation of policy via increasingly complex *systems and*

networks of organisations drawn from the public, private and voluntary sectors. Increasingly, these networks, which can extend beyond national boundaries, become closely integrated, resistant to 'steering' by government, and capable of developing their own policy agendas.

The final point provides an obvious link with multi-level governance, since the latter places particular emphasis on the complex policy-making, implementation and accountability relationships between a variety of state and societal actors at the levels of supra-national activity (including the EU), central government, devolved government, local government and 'quasi-government'. Pierre and Stoker (2000, p. 30) encapsulate the core characteristics of multi-level governance:

> [it] emerges as a coordinating instrument in institutional systems where hier-archical command and control mechanisms have been relaxed or abolished. It draws on bargaining rather than submission and public–private mobilisation rather than public sector specificity. Most importantly, multi-level governance makes no pre-judgements about the hierarchical order of institutions: global patterns of governance can hook up with local institutions just as local or regional coalitions of actors can by-pass the nation-state level and pursue their interests in international arenas.

Pierre and Stoker (2000, pp. 44–5) go on to point out that multi-level governance is a fairly contentious concept in some respects, and they identify three different UK political responses to its future development. The first, epitomised by the Liberal Democrats, involves embracing the concept as a modern extension of federalism. The second approach, adopted by the Conservative Party, is sceptical, with a some-what reluctant acceptance of devolution in Scotland, Wales and Northern Ireland, and opposition to regional government for England and to any further extension of the powers of the European Union. The Conservatives (and indeed some people from quite different political perspectives) identify potential problems with the steady drift of power away from the unitary state, including the emergence of overlapping and contradictory spheres of responsibility and the loss of democratic legitimacy in some areas. The third approach, taken by the Labour government of Tony Blair, and mentioned in Chapter 1, involves recognising the opportunities presented by multi-level governance, while seeking to manage or control some of its implica-tions, partly through initiatives such as 'joined-up government' (which seeks to guide and coordinate the work of bodies and institutions involved in the creation and implementation of public policy – see p. 15).

So much for the theoretical and conceptual underpinnings of multi-level governance: now let us examine some of the practical implications.

The UK and the EU

The impact of the European Union on UK government should not be underestimated. On an administrative level, most senior British ministers and many senior civil servants spend many days each month commuting to Brussels for EU meetings.

Much of the rest of their time back in Westminster and Whitehall is spent tackling questions relating to the EU agenda. More significantly, on a policy level, British government is severely constrained by policy outputs from the EU system. The British government is still sovereign in deciding most of the main areas of public expenditure – such as social security, health care, transport and public housing. However, this is only one aspect of policy-making. In the area of regulation, over 80 per cent of rules governing the production, distribution and exchange of goods, services and capital in the British market are decided by the EU. In the area of macroeconomic policy, despite the fact that Britain is not a member of the single currency, decisions by the European Central Bank and the Council of Ministers have a direct impact on British monetary, fiscal and employment policies. In the area of foreign and defence policy, Britain is bound by its commitments under the EU's Common Foreign and Security Policy (Hix, 2000, p. 48).

Nugent (2000, pp. 194–5) argues that UK membership of the European Union has had four broad implications. EU issues demand detailed attention from the key decision-makers in UK government, are the focus of exchanges between the major political parties, serve to limit the power of the UK executive to make and implement its policies independently, and necessitate significant specific arrangements and facilities within the structures of government. In a book with a clear focus on public administration, it is the last category which is of special interest. Given the space limitations, we will not seek to cover the history of British involvement with the European Union, nor will we spend time describing the institutions of the EU (for details on each of these, see Cram *et al.*, 1999; Dinan, 1999; Hix, 1999; and Nugent, 1999). Instead, our focus will be on how UK public administration, especially at the level of central government, engages with the EU.

In broad terms, UK government ministers, Parliamentarians and civil servants must be both proactive and reactive towards the European Union. They seek to ensure that the national interest is properly represented within the decision-making processes and institutions of the European Union, and they secure effective implementation of EU law and policy within the UK. In order to achieve a closer understanding of how they do this, we can look at the basic EU roles and responsibilities of the UK executive (Prime Minister and Cabinet), key departments of state and civil service structures, and the Westminster Parliament.

The UK Prime Minister and Cabinet are involved in the workings of the European Union on a continuous basis. The PM will be a key figure in the European Council, which formally meets twice a year in order to allow the European Union heads of government to establish strategic policy for the EU as a whole, and settle any particularly intractable outstanding issues. Between these meetings, the PM will be in regular communication with the other heads of government, individually and collectively. Cabinet ministers participate continuously in the Council of Ministers which, in its varied forms, meets about ninety times a year (Nugent, 2000, p. 210). The Council of Ministers is really a series of councils, each of which covers a specific policy sphere and gives representation to the appropriate ministers from the member states – trade, health, foreign affairs, and so on. Here, consideration is given to proposals made by the EU Commission for new European laws, directives and policy initiatives. Depending on the nature of the proposal, the Council of Ministers will take decisions by unanimous agreement or simple-majority or qualified-majority voting (this gives weightings to the votes of the member states according to population sizes). The role of the Council of Ministers as a forum for important negotiations has been emphasised by James (1999, p. 9), who points out:

> the status of governmental decisions in EU matters is less definitive. Where once the British government took a decision and that was the end of the matter, its decisions on EU-related matters can only now be 'this is what our negotiating position must be' . . . as a consequence of this, some of the Cabinet's authority has to be devolved to the minister who carries out the negotiations, acting in consultation with the Prime Minister.

In order to cope with the implications of all of this high-level policy work, UK central government has gradually adapted its processes and procedures. Two key divisions within the Foreign Office deal with, respectively, internal and external EU issues (Nugent, 2000, p. 211). Subject to the overall authority of the Secretary of State, officials in these divisions report to a Foreign Office Minister of State (popularly known as the 'Minister for Europe'). Domestic departments of state also contain EU units and sections designed to provide a steady flow of policy advice to ministers and ensure that the component parts of the UK system of government and public administration are in a position to meet their EU obligations. These are particularly important in the departments which have a considerable volume of European business (including the Department of Trade and Industry, the Treasury and the Ministry of Agriculture, Fisheries and Food), although the pervasive nature of EU policy and administration in modern government is such that virtually every department and executive agency now has a 'European' dimension to its work.

Beyond this, central strategic and coordinating roles are played by the Cabinet committee on EU matters (the Ministerial Sub-Committee on European Issues, which is chaired by the Foreign Secretary) and the European Affairs Secretariat of the Cabinet Office (see Chapter 3). On a day-to-day basis, the interests of the UK government are represented in Brussels by the Permanent Representative, who is effectively an ambassador to the EU. The Permanent Representative participates in the Committee of Permanent Representatives (COREPER), which comprises 'ambassadors' from all the member states and carries out the detailed preparatory work required for meetings of the Council of Ministers. Additionally, the UK Permanent Representative heads a team of 120 seconded civil servants within UKREP (the UK Permanent Representation to the European Union) which liaises with the EU institutions on behalf of the UK government, advises all Whitehall negotiators coming to Brussels, and generally monitors all developments taking place within the EU institutions. Feedback is provided via a weekly meeting in London between the head of UKREP, the head of the Cabinet's European Secretariat and the senior officials responsible for European matters in the departments of state (Nugent, 2000, p. 212).

While the efficiency of the UK coordinating and negotiating machinery can be favourably compared with those of other member states (see James, 1999, p. 56), those who harbour suspicions about the embracing bureaucratic nature of the European Union, and its effect on those supposedly representing their own national interests, argue that it can be difficult for alternative policy views to be considered.

As a Trade Minister in the Conservative government during the 1980s, during a negotiating session in Brussels Alan Clark took a dim view of the way the UK's interests were handled, and recorded his impressions in his diary:

> soon closeted in the UKREP suite with officials. . . . Totally Europhile. Sole objective, as far as I could see, being to 'expedite business' – i.e. not make a fuss about anything, however monstrous. . . . Everything is decided, horse-traded off, by officials at COREPER. The Ministers arrive on the scene at the last minute, hot, tired, ill or drunk (sometimes all of these together), read out their piece, and depart . . . as always in politics everywhere, democratic or autocratic, it's the chaps on the spot who call the shot.
>
> (Clark, 1993, pp. 138–9)

Local, regional and sub-national units of the UK system of public administration also seek to ensure that their interests are sufficiently represented in Europe. This can be achieved through the use of consultants or agents, or more formally. For example, the Scottish Executive established an office in Brussels in 1999. Representation of this type is especially important, given the EU's adoption of the concept of 'subsidiarity', which stipulates that matters should be delegated to the lowest levels of government and administration commensurate with effective implementation. It is likely that the territorial aspects of EU policy-making and implementation will assume increasing significance in future (see Hogwood *et al.*, 2000b).

The European Parliament was (and, although its remit has been enhanced since the Maastricht Treaty, arguably still is) a relatively weak body, with limited powers to check the executive bodies of the EU. To make matters worse, because the institutions which came to be known as the European Union were originally created by governments, the parliaments of the member states were largely left out of the picture. The EU made no reference to the existence of national parliaments in its formal treaties, until the Maastricht Treaty in 1992. This contributed to a perceived 'democratic deficit', which continues to blight the image of the EU, despite some attempts (for example in the 1997 Amsterdam Treaty) to give national parliaments more time and opportunities to scrutinise EU legislative proposals. Like the other parliaments of the member states, Westminster faces the dual problem of trying to monitor an ever-increasing volume of EU executive activity with relatively few resources.

The formal powers of the Westminster Parliament in relation to European Union business are fairly limited (see Norton, 1993, pp. 114–28; Silk and Walters, 1998, pp. 228–37). Information about forthcoming business in the Council of Ministers is provided via a written statement in Hansard, or, in the case of particularly important matters, through a formal ministerial statement. Receiving information is one thing, however, and achieving effective scrutiny is something else. In practice, Parliament seeks to scrutinise the inputs of the UK government to the EU and the implications of European policy for this country by obliging ministers to participate in debates (two general debates are held each year before the meetings of the European Council) and subject themselves to scrutiny by select committees and Parliamentary questions. All too often, however, the latter mechanisms function retrospectively, with the result that Parliament fails to effectively influence the contributions made by government. Probably the most significant role is played by the House of Commons Select Committee on European Legislation. Although it has a broad watching brief on all policy, institutional and procedural developments in the EU, and will occasionally call ministers and civil servants as witnesses, this committee deals mainly with EU documents. Approximately 1,200 documents are handled by the committee each year (Nugent, 2000, p. 213) concerning proposed legislative and policy initiatives as well as reports from the EU institutions. The committee will refer about one-third of these documents to the two House of Commons European Standing Committees for further detailed scrutiny. In the House of Lords, the Select Committee on the European Communities (and its six sub-committees) produces around twenty reports each year on EU issues (see Box 10.1).

Box 10.1 Dealing with EU business in Whitehall and Westminster: the key bodies

Ministerial Sub-Committee on European Issues:
    Cabinet Committee (E)DOP

Foreign and Commonwealth Office:
    European Union Department (Internal)
    European Union Department (External)

Other departments of state:
    EU units and sections

Cabinet Office:
    European Affairs Secretariat

United Kingdom Permanent Representative to the EU and UKREP

House of Commons:
    Select Committee on European Legislation
    European Standing Committee A
    European Standing Committee B

House of Lords:
    Select Committee on the European Communities

Devolved governance: Scotland

In the late 1970s there was an abortive attempt by the Labour government to deliver devolution to Scotland and Wales. This culminated in the Wales Act being rejected outright in the post-legislative referendum in the spring of 1979, while the Scotland

Act was approved by a majority of those who voted in the referendum, but less than the 40 per cent of the total Scottish electorate required by legislation. There followed an extended period of Conservative government, during which there was no prospect of significant change to the unitary state. However, Labour's return to power in 1997 brought with it a certainty that a programme of constitutional change would be introduced, with devolution at its heart.

Based to a considerable extent upon the work of the unofficial Scottish Constitutional Convention (which provided a forum for discussion of Scotland's future governance and produced a series of papers between 1989 and 1995), after the 1997 General Election the devolution framework was set out in a White Paper (Scottish Office, 1997) published in July 1997. A pre-legislative referendum held in September confirmed in principle the support of the Scottish people for a Parliament with tax-varying powers (see Table 10.1), and the Scotland Bill was published before the end of the year. Both the White Paper and the Bill were couched in fairly general terms, and the detailed implications of devolution for Scotland were to be thrashed out by a Consultative Steering Group, headed by the Scottish Office Minister of State, Henry McLeish. The Scotland Act received Royal Assent in November 1998, and the report of the Consultative Steering Group was published two months later (Consultative Steering Group, 1999). The first elections to the Scottish Parliament took place on 6 May 1999, with Labour emerging as the largest party, but lacking an overall majority. The literature on the theory and practice of devolved governance in Scotland is developing apace (see, for example, Hassan, 1999; Hassan and Warhurst, 2000; McConnell, 2000; Mitchell, 2001). In the space available here, we can summarise the main features and emerging trends within the new arrangements.

Devolution did not alter the constitutional status of Scotland as a component part of the United Kingdom. The Westminster Parliament, which continues to contain

Table 10.1 Scotland votes

Devolution referendum, 11 September 1997

	Yes	No
Scottish Parliament	74.3%	25.7%
Tax-varying powers	63.5%	36.5%

Elections to Scottish Parliament, 6 May 1999

	Constituency MSPs	List MSPs	Total MSPs
Labour Party	53	3	56
SNP	7	28	35
Liberal Democrats	12	5	17
Conservative Party	0	18	18
Green Party	0	1	1
Scottish Socialist Party	0	1	1
Member for Falkirk West	1	0	1
			129

MPs representing Scottish constituencies, remains sovereign. Furthermore, a range of key policy spheres were designated as 'reserved matters', which would remain the province of Westminster and Whitehall. Most notably, these included constitutional matters, foreign policy, defence and national security, the economic and monetary system, transport safety and regulation, and employment and social security policy, legislation and administration. This still left a considerable range of policy matters to the new Scottish Parliament (sitting at Holyrood), including health, education, local government, social work, housing, economic development, inward investment, tourism, passenger and road transport, the criminal and civil law, criminal justice, prison and prosecution systems, police and fire services, agriculture and fisheries, the environment and the arts. Of course, in the past many of these had been subject to administrative devolution to the Scottish Office. The major difference now was that the Scottish Parliament would have primary legislative power over the devolved matters, and the Scottish Executive would have expanded capacity for strategic and detailed policy-making. The former Scottish Office was radically scaled down, becoming the Scotland Office. Although still led by a UK Cabinet minister charged with representing Scotland's interests at UK level (John Reid became Secretary of State for Scotland when Donald Dewar gave up the post to take office as First Minister in Edinburgh, and Reid was succeeded by Helen Liddell in January 2001), the Scotland Office's role was largely one of coordination and it was not the source of real political power – this had shifted to the new Executive.

It might be argued that the electoral system for the Scottish Parliament was specifically designed to produce a coalition Executive. The traditional dominance of the Labour Party in Scottish electoral politics meant there was a danger that one party would be able to secure long-term power in Edinburgh. The entire devolution experiment could have been compromised by the creation of an effective one-party state. In this light, the electoral arrangements combined the traditional plurality ('first-past-the-post') system with an additional member system based on party lists. Seventy-three MSPs were elected under the traditional system in the Westminster constituencies, while a further fifty-six members were elected in the eight European Parliamentary constituencies (seven MSPs per constituency). The Parliament was to operate on the basis of a four-year fixed term, and the number of MSPs would be reduced at the same time (as yet unspecified) as the number of Scottish MPs at Westminster is reduced (a change considered necessary to bring Scottish constituency populations more in line with those in England). During the remaining period of the Westminster Parliament elected in 1997, MSPs were to be allowed to hold a 'dual-mandate' (sitting for both Holyrood and Westminster constituencies), but thereafter politicians would have to decide whether to sit in Edinburgh or London.

While the combined system produced early tensions between some MSPs, with clashes over whether the 'constituency' or 'list' member was responsible for specific constituency matters, it served its basic function by producing a Parliament in which Labour was the largest single party, but a reasonably proportional outcome was secured (see Table 10.1).

Many members of the new Parliament were keen to see it demonstrate its distinctiveness from Westminster, and there was much talk of a 'new politics' which would be created by the mixed backgrounds of the MSPs (many of whom came from local government or beyond the traditional political breeding grounds) and would involve reduced partisanship and more cooperation across the parties (see Hassan and Warhurst, 2000). In practice, politics in Edinburgh came to resemble politics in other parts of the system, with party political squabbles very much in evidence, and the usual blend of effectiveness and incompetence. However, in some respects the Holyrood procedures were different from those at Westminster. The hours of business were more normal and the debating mode easier to understand. The most significant innovation, however, could be seen in the committee system. The sixteen committees have combined the functions of the Westminster select and standing committees, and added some more. This means that they have powers to conduct inquiries, scrutinise the legislation proposed by the Executive, and even initiate their own legislation (see Lynch, 2000).

Civil servants working in the former Scottish Office transferred to the new Scottish Executive (confusingly, this term was used to describe both the ministerial team and the devolved civil service). Devolution did not signal the creation of a distinct civil service for Scotland (or for Wales). Great emphasis was placed on the fact that officials working for the devolved bodies would remain part of the unified Home Civil Service, with no changes to their status or conditions of service (see Chapter 4 and also Pyper, 1999). A series of 'concordats' was produced, with the aim of establishing the ground rules for the relationships between the Cabinet Office, Whitehall departments and the new departments of the Scottish and Welsh administrations. Again, the focus here was on the need for official coordination and unity. However, it was clear that devolution would have a significant impact on the work of the civil service in Edinburgh, and there was a possibility that the structural, managerial and cultural implications would, over time, effectively create a distinctly Scottish branch of the civil service. The four areas of particular challenge facing the civil service in Scotland were:

1   Organisational and structural change. The former Scottish Office had to be reconfigured to reflect the changed public policy imperatives and develop working relationships with the new ministers and Parliament. Parry (2000) and Parry and Jones (2000) provide detailed analysis of this aspect of Scottish devolution.

2   Increase in volume of work. The need to cope with a full legislative programme plus the demands from the public, organised interests and the new MSPs for policy initiatives inevitably brought significant changes to the workload of the Edinburgh officials.

3   Changing nature of the work. The change from working with a Secretary of State and a small ministerial team to serving the First Minister and an array of Cabinet and sub-cabinet ministers meant that the senior officials in Edinburgh were required to assume roles akin to those occupied by civil servants in Downing Street and the Cabinet Office. A new Executive Secretariat was formed to coordinate the high-level policy work.

4   New accountability demands. Before devolution, Scottish Office civil servants were relatively remote from the imperatives of Parliamentary accountability. They helped ministers prepare for sporadic general and legislative debates and Parliamentary questions once each month, and faced only a remote prospect of appearing before the single select committee devoted to Scottish affairs. The

arrival of the Scottish Parliament brought with it the creation of sixteen committees of MSPs on the doorstep of the Edinburgh officials, and a weekly ministerial Question Time. In addition, increased volumes of correspondence, and a refocused external audit regime centred on Audit Scotland, served to create an enhanced system of accountability which placed fresh demands on civil servants.

The Executive formed by Donald Dewar was a Cabinet of eleven ministers, supported by a further eleven deputy ministers (see Pyper, 2000). Bitter enmity between Labour and the second and third largest parties in the Parliament, the SNP and the Conservatives, meant that the Liberal Democrats emerged as the coalition partners, with four ministerial posts overall (two in the Cabinet, including the Deputy First Minister, Jim Wallace).

The Cabinet met weekly, and operated on the basis of collective decision-making. The First Minister and the Executive were served by an Executive Secretariat within which was located the Cabinet Secretariat, the External Relations Division, the Constitutional Policy and Parliamentary Liaison Division and the Strategic Communications Branch. A series (initially eight) of ministerial committees and working groups was established to deal with issues spanning portfolios or requiring collective consideration.

Although the option of using its tax-varying power (to increase or decrease the rate of income tax in Scotland by up to 3 per cent) remained open in theory, the Labour/Liberal Democrat coalition committed itself not to use this power during the first Parliament. The basis for funding the devolved Executive therefore remained the same as before: the block grant system under which the Treasury allocates a budget to Edinburgh. The largest element of this is subject to the Barnett Formula, which links increases and decreases in Scottish public spending to changes in the equivalent English budgets, on a population basis. As the Scottish population is 10.66 per cent of the English population, this is the factor used to vary the budgetary changes in the key public services. However, the arrangement perpetuates a higher level of per capita expenditure in Scotland (and in Wales and Northern Ireland) than in the UK as a whole (for more on Barnett, see Mair and McCloud, 1999).

Genuine devolution creates the potential for policy divergence between the centre and the periphery, and examples of this started to mount. The Scottish Executive carved out distinct approaches to issues including aid to farmers (ending the ban on 'beef on the bone'), student fees, freedom of information (with Scotland becoming marginally more adventurous), teachers' salaries and funding care of the elderly. As distinct policies emerged, the role of the Scottish MPs at Westminster attracted renewed attention. These MPs are still able to vote on specifically English matters (whereas English MPs are not able to vote on Scottish matters within the jurisdiction of Holyrood), and this raises issues associated with the 'West Lothian Question' (actually a series of questions about the rights of Scottish MPs at Westminster after devolution, first tabled by Tam Dalyell, whose former constituency was West Lothian). Although it is likely that the number of Scottish seats at Westminster will be reduced in future, the voting rights of these MPs will probably remain unaffected. In the meantime, the Blair government attempted to strike a balance between allowing the spirit of genuine devolution to take its course, with all the possible implications for contradictory as well as complementary policies to emerge in the component parts of the UK, and maintaining some sense of co-ordination. The mechanism for coordination is the Joint Ministerial Council (JMC), which meets periodically as a forum for cooperation and problem-solving, comprising ministers from London, Edinburgh, Belfast and Cardiff (Macleod, 2000).

The early phase of the Executive's life was not entirely smooth. In fact, a series of minor crises and public relations disasters dogged the First Minister and his colleagues (see Pyper, 2000, pp. 81–2). There were some palpable tensions between ministers, policy advisers and senior civil servants and open resentment at the demands made upon ministers by the Parliamentary committees, in the wake of some embarrassments for members of the Executive during committee hearings. These matters would pale into insignificance in the summer of 2000, when the supposed jewel in the crown of Scottish public policy, the education system, degenerated into chaos as the Scottish Qualifications Authority (and executive) grossly mismanaged the secondary school examination procedures, resulting in the publication of thousands of erroneous results. Despite vigorous attacks in the Parliament, and detailed committee scrutiny, the Education Minister Sam Galbraith survived the scandal (although he was later moved to another post when Henry McLeish became First Minister).

However, the greatest blow sustained by the Scottish devolution settlement was undoubtedly the death of its architect Donald Dewar in October 2000. Despite the problems of the first year, Dewar's political weight and seniority seemed to offer reassurance that all would be well in due course. His sudden death, shortly after returning to work following heart surgery, led to the election of Henry McLeish as First Minister. Lacking many of Dewar's attributes (including a close working relationship with Blair), McLeish faced serious challenges as he attempted to bring stability and coherence to devolved governance north of the border.

It might be argued that the acid test for the devolution of governance to Scotland will come when the Scottish Executive and the Westminster government are led by different parties. Quite apart from anything else, this will place the civil service in Edinburgh under severe pressure, as it effectively has to serve two political masters. More broadly, if devolution is to function as a genuine support mechanism for the union (as its New Labour architects intended) there must be effective co-habitation between the London and Edinburgh administrations, regardless of the political hue of each government. However, if serious problems arise in those circumstances, devolution might come to be the stepping stone to independence, as desired by the Nationalists and predicted by many Conservatives.

Devolved governance: Wales

While there were some variations in the details of the devolution settlement in Wales (and at least two major differences in the powers of the National Assembly), the broad pattern resembled that put in place in Scotland. Certainly, the timetable of events in 1997 and 1998 was broadly similar. Soon after the 1997 General Election the government's proposals for Wales were published in a White Paper (Welsh Office, 1997), and a pre-legislative referendum was held in September. Wales had voted decisively against devolution in 1979, and came close to rejecting the concept once again. The result was an extremely narrow 'yes' vote (see Table 10.2). The Government of Wales Bill was introduced in the House of Commons in November 1997 and passed quickly, receiving Royal Assent in July 1998. Elections to the Welsh National Assembly were held on the same day as those for the Scottish Parliament in May 1999. Although the electoral system was the same as that used in Scotland (with forty members elected using first past the post in the Westminster constituencies and twenty elected using the additional member system of party lists in the five European Parliamentary constituencies) the Labour Party was expected to emerge with an overall majority. However, in a somewhat surprising result (see Table 10.2), Labour fell three seats short of this.

Table 10.2 Wales votes

Devolution referendum, 18 September 1997

	Yes	No
National Assembly for Wales	50.3%	49.7%

Elections to National Assembly for Wales, 6 May 1999

	Constituency AMs	List AMs	Total AMs
Labour Party	27	1	28
Plaid Cymru	9	8	17
Liberal Democrats	3	3	6
Conservative Party	1	8	9
			60

Under the terms of the Government of Wales Act, power was devolved to the National Assembly as a corporate body. In order to facilitate a cabinet style of executive (rather than, for example, a local government-style committee system), the Assembly delegated its decision-making functions to the First Secretary (elected by the whole Assembly), who was then in a position to make ministerial appointments. After a period during which Labour attempted to govern alone, they entered into a governing partnership with the Liberal Democrats. Until February 2000, the First Secretary was the former Secretary of State for Wales, Alun Michael, but a combination of factors, including his perceived proximity to Tony Blair and his dominant governing style, created a number of problems with his administration. Michael resigned rather than allow a 'no confidence' vote to take place in the Assembly, and he was replaced by Rhodri Morgan. Morgan heads a Cabinet of eight Assembly Secretaries (an additional five deputy ministers are outside the Cabinet) with policy portfolios covering a range of matters including inward investment, industrial policy, EU economic issues, education, Assembly business, tourism, the environment, transport, finance, local government, housing, health, social services, agriculture and fisheries, arts, culture and sport.

While the civil servants working in Wales would, like their colleagues in Edinburgh, remain part of the unified Home Civil Service, there was to be a subtle but important difference in their position. In formal terms, the officials would work for the National Assembly as a corporate body, and not just for the First Secretary and the Assembly Cabinet. As Osmond (1999) points out, this creates the potential, in the long term, for tensions and conflicts of loyalty to develop as these officials seek to serve three masters (the Assembly, the Cabinet and Whitehall). At the very least, civil servants in Wales had to adopt new modes of working, in order to cope with the demands placed upon them by individual AMs (Assembly Members), Assembly Committees, the First Minister and Assembly Secretaries.

The creation of the National Assembly did not change the position of Wales as a part of the United Kingdom. The new body inherited the policy responsibilities of the former Welsh Office, which was scaled down, given an essentially coordinating role, and restyled as the Wales Office under a new Secretary of State (who retained Cabinet rank), Paul Murphy, in 1999. However, unlike the Scottish Parliament, the Assembly was given secondary rather than primary legislative powers, which meant that it could pass only Assembly Orders to complete the details of Acts passed by the Westminster Parliament. A second significant difference from the Scottish model was that the Welsh Assembly had no tax-varying powers and would be entirely reliant upon the block grant from London (which continued to be shaped by the Welsh variant of the Barnett Formula).

The committee system in the Assembly is designed to facilitate policy-making as well as supervision and scrutiny. The Assembly Secretaries are members of the committees which cover their ministerial portfolios, although they are not permitted to chair the committees (Laffin and Thomas, 2000).

The emerging challenges for the Welsh National Assembly are quite significant. It lacks a clear mandate from the people of Wales, given that only a minority of the Welsh electorate voted in favour of devolution. In that light, the restrictions on its legislative powers would seem to be sensible. However, these restrictions themselves serve to complicate the process of strategic policy-making for the First Secretary and his ministers, who must engage in detailed negotiations with Whitehall and Westminster as well as the members of their own Assembly. They are denied the relative freedom of manoeuvre of their Scottish counterparts. Policy-making and implementation are further complicated due to the design of the Assembly as a corporate body, combining legislative (albeit secondary), executive, scrutiny and administration functions.

Devolved governance: Northern Ireland

The perennial problem in Northern Ireland relates to the need to reconcile the hopes and aspirations of the various strands of Unionism, which aspire to as much self-government as can be obtained while maintaining the union, with those of the numerous nationalist and republican factions, which seek the creation of a united Ireland. The problem is exacerbated by the readiness of extremists on both sides to resort to terrorism in order to achieve their objectives.

Northern Ireland experienced devolution within the UK between 1922 and 1972, but the record of the Unionist-dominated Stormont Parliament was distinctly mixed, and the eruption of violence during the late 1960s led inexorably to the introduction of 'direct rule'. A department of central government, the Northern Ireland Office, was charged with responsibility for the myriad problems facing the province. The Sunningdale Agreement of 1973 led to the resumption of limited devolution in the form of a power-sharing experiment which guaranteed some representation on the executive to nationalist politicians. However, this was brought down by hard-line Unionists in 1974. Thereafter, the violence continued, the Northern Ireland Office remained the focus of government in the province, and further attempts to restore devolution (most significantly, the 'rolling devolution' project of Secretary of State James Prior in 1982) came to nothing.

However, a series of events (see Box 10.2) starting with the Anglo-Irish Agreement in 1985 eventually succeeded in bringing about a settlement, encapsulated in the 'Good Friday' or Belfast Agreement of 1998 (see Hopkins, 1999; Meehan, 1999; McConnell, 2000). This established a framework for the resumption of devolved government in Northern Ireland. Together with a North–South ministerial council and a British–Irish council (see Box 10.2), the centrepiece of the new devolved government is an elected Northern Ireland Assembly.

Box 10.2 Key stages in the return of devolution to Northern Ireland

Stormont Parliament, 1922–72

'The Troubles' begin, 1969

Suspension of Stormont and introduction of Direct Rule via the Northern Ireland Office, 1972

Sunningdale Agreement, 1973

Abortive power-sharing, 1973–4

Abortive New Assembly and 'rolling devolution', 1982

Anglo-Irish Agreement, 1985
UK and Irish Governments agree that:

*   the consent of a majority in Northern Ireland is required for constitutional change;
*   a North–South intergovernmental conference will meet regularly;
*   devolution should be introduced in the long term, in a form acceptable to the whole community.

Downing Street Declaration, 1993
UK and Irish governments announce:

*   the UK has no long-term objection to the prospect of a united Ireland;
*   the consent of the majority in Northern Ireland will be needed for any constitutional change.

Framework documents, February 1995
These cover proposals for a new Northern Ireland Assembly and future Anglo-Irish relations.

Provisional IRA cease-fire, August 1995

Mitchell Commission 1995–6
US Senator Mitchell chairs inquiry into decommissioning of illegal arms. He recommends commitment to six principles of democracy and non-violence and all-party negotiations on devolution *while* decommissioning takes place.

Provisional IRA cease-fire ends, January 1996
Provisionals bomb London Docklands in protest at the UK government's insistence that decommissioning of weapons *precedes* devolution talks.

Forum elections, May 1996
Parties committed to peace have 110 representatives elected to the Forum, which is to discuss the constitutional path to devolution.

Provisional IRA cease-fire, July 1997
The Provisionals' political wing, Sinn Fein, is allowed to enter the talks.

Belfast 'Good Friday' Agreement, April 1998
Agreement between UK and Irish governments, and most of the political parties in Northern Ireland (including Sinn Fein):

- all signatories committed to complete disarmament of paramilitaries;
- an accelerated programme of release for paramilitary prisoners under a new review process;
- Northern Ireland to remain part of the UK, its long-term future a matter for the majority in the province; the people of Ireland as a whole have the right to self-determination; a referendum to be held in the Irish Republic on amending its constitution to renounce its claim on Northern Ireland;
- Northern Ireland Assembly to be elected by single transferable vote (using Westminster constituencies), the 108 members to have primary legislative power over policy areas currently in the Northern Ireland Office, and an executive to be formed which guarantees a share of power to representatives of all parts of the community;
- North–South Ministerial Council to provide a forum for ministers from Belfast and Dublin to develop all-Ireland policies in appropriate spheres (including aspects of health, education and social security);
- British–Irish Council ('Council of the Isles') to give representatives of UK, Irish, Northern Irish, Scottish and Welsh administrations opportunities to exchange information and develop collaboration on matters of mutual concern;
- the Agreement to be put to the people in Northern Ireland in a referendum.

Referenda, May 1998
Northern Ireland: 71.1 per cent for the 'Good Friday' Agreement;
Irish Republic: 56.3 per cent for constitutional change.

Elections to Northern Ireland Assembly, June 1998

Given the historical background, it is not surprising that the reintroduction of devolution was not entirely smooth. The process was characterised by a 'stop–start' approach in the early stages. Under the terms of the 'Good Friday' Agreement, 108 members were elected to the Northern Ireland Assembly in June 1998, by the single transferable vote version of proportional representation, with six members elected from each of the eighteen Westminster constituencies. The pro-Agreement parties (including the Ulster Unionists, the SDLP and Sinn Fein) won eighty seats, while the anti-Agreement parties (Democratic Unionists, UK Unionist Party and Independent Unionists) took twenty-eight seats. The Assembly was to assume full legislative and executive authority over matters previously within the remit of six Northern Ireland Office departments: agriculture, economic development, education, the environment, finance and personnel, and health and social services. Certain policy spheres, including defence and foreign affairs, were reserved for Westminster in perpetuity, but other areas, such as law and order, might be devolved in future, provided there is clear evidence of cross-community support for this.

When it met in July 1998, the Assembly elected the Ulster Unionist leader David Trimble as First Minister and the SDLP's Seamus Mallon as Deputy First Minister. However, no agreement could be reached on the nomination of ministers to the Executive Committee (representation was required for all political viewpoints, but the Unionists wanted to see progress with arms decommissioning before allowing Sinn Fein to have ministers). The Assembly was then suspended by Mo Mowlam, the Secretary of State for Northern Ireland. Following a review of the process conducted by US Senator George Mitchell, the new Northern Ireland Secretary, Peter Mandelson, reconvened the Assembly in November 1999, and this time the ministerial team was nominated. Devolution was suspended again between February and May 2000, due to continuing disputes between the Ulster Unionists and Sinn Fein over progress with arms decommissioning.

The Executive Committee contains twelve ministers, including the First Minister and his Deputy. Sinn Fein initially had two ministerial posts, including the education portfolio. Within the Assembly, business is conducted in debates and within sixteen standing and departmental committees, as well as a number of *ad hoc* committees. The departmental committees have both scrutiny and policy-making roles. They approve secondary legislation and deal with the committee stage of primary legislation. In all of the committees, as in the Executive, there are built-in requirements that the representatives and aspirations of all sections of the community are given sufficient weight.

The long-term development of the devolution settlement in Northern Ireland clearly hinges upon a range of complex factors which go far beyond those relevant to the cases of Scotland and Wales.

English regional governance: a summary of issues and themes

Holliday (2000, p. 100) has noted that: 'The UK's is an instance of asymmetric devolution, similar to Spain's region-building process of the late 1970s and early 1980s, in the sense that distinct regions are being given different sets of powers at variable times and speeds.'

The regions of England can certainly be seen as the slow starters and late developers in this process. Lacking the sense of a cohesive identity, geographical coherence and background in 'nationhood' to be seen in Scotland and Wales, and without the political saliency of Northern Ireland, the English regions still occupy a rather minor role in the developing story of multi-level governance.

Despite the Labour Party's election commitment to introduce, in time, 'legislation to allow the people, region by region, to decide in a referendum whether they want directly elected regional government' (Labour Party, 1997, p. 35), progress has been rather slow. Only in the rather special case of London was there a move to direct elections. In the spring of 2000, elections resulted in Ken Livingstone becoming Mayor, with budgetary and policy responsibility for the Greater London Authority (which has functional roles in transport, development, policing, and fire and emergency planning). The Mayor has a four-year term, and is required to devise strategies and action plans to tackle London-wide issues. A twenty-five-member London Assembly was also elected with a four-year term, to scrutinise the activities of the Mayor, and share some of his powers of appointment to the Greater London Authority (for details on the London Mayor and Assembly, see www.london.gov.uk).

For other parts of England, between 1997 and 2001, the Department of the Environment, Transport and the Regions attempted to supplement the role of the regional government offices of Whitehall (see Chapter 2) by overseeing the creation of a series of Regional Development Agencies, designed to aid economic growth (see Box 10.3).

In conjunction with these quangos, regional chambers have been set up to give representation to the relevant local authorities and other interested parties. It is possible that these chambers could evolve into fully fledged elected regional assemblies at some future stage, although there is no clear timetable for this. Simon Lee (2000) argues that Whitehall departments have failed to cede control over important areas of policy to the RDAs, and criticises the prevailing centralism of the Blair government in this sphere. If Scotland and Wales appear to be reaping significant economic benefits from the process of devolution, the case for English devolution might come to be heard more clearly, especially in those regions such as the north-east, where geographical proximity to a strong devolution settlement will generate detailed comparisons of relative economic well-being.

The NHS: an aspect of regional administration

The National Health Service stands as a further illustration of regional administration in the UK (for general background, see Baggott, 1998). This key area of public policy and administration is subject to the overall control of central (and now devolved) government, but is largely managed at local levels, with distinct structures for the component parts of the United Kingdom.

Since its inception in 1948, the structure, management and organisation of the NHS have been subjected to almost continuous change. Four major restructuring exercises had taken place by the late 1990s, and the Blair government was embarking upon another series of reforms as this book was being written (see below). The details of each of these structural changes need not concern us here. However, it is important to note that the main motivations behind the structural changes were similar to those

---

Box 10.3 English Regional Development Agencies and Regional Chambers

RDAs:
> One North East
> North West Development Agency
> Yorkshire Forward
> Advantage West Midlands
> East Midlands Development Agency
> East of England Development Agency
> South West of England Regional Development Agency
> South East England Development Agency

The RDAs are:
- non-departmental public bodies (quangos);
- with a remit to further economic development and regeneration, business efficiency, employment, inward investment;
- accountable to ministers and Parliament;
- bound to consult with Chambers on strategy.

Regional Chambers:
> North East Regional Chamber
> North West Regional Chamber
> Yorkshire and the Humber Regional Chamber
> West Midlands Regional Chamber
> East Midlands Regional Chamber
> East of England Regional Chamber
> South West Regional Chamber
> South East England Regional Assembly

The Regional Chambers are:
- voluntary groupings of local government councillors and other representatives of a region's economy, society and environment;
- intended to scrutinise and advise the RDAs;
- developing a role in regional planning processes.

---

which drove the changes to local government structures over this period: political expediency, managerial fashions and a desire on the part of the centre to exert greater control. While the rhetoric might speak of the importance of delegation, regionalism and localism, the reality was increasing central control. As structures changed, there was a distinct move away from the elective principle in certain areas of service provision, epitomised by the dilution of local authority rights of representation on Health Boards.

Klein (1995, p. 144) notes as a recurring theme in the history of the NHS 'the cycle of experiments with delegation quickly followed by reversion to centralisation'. A similar trend is identified by Ranade (1997, p. 2):

[the NHS] tries to reconcile central funding and government accountability for national standards of service with the need for local autonomy to meet local need. The result has been a policy see-saw, with governments alternating between periods of centralisation . . . followed by a decentralising reaction against the rigidities which are caused as a consequence.

Between 1982 and 1990 the NHS in England and Wales was essentially based on a three-tier administrative structure designed to allow delegation to the district level. This consisted of the Department of Health; Regional Health Authorities (which had strategic responsibilities); and District Health Authorities responsible for coordination and management at the district level. In addition Family Practitioner Committees administered local services provided by general practitioners, opticians, pharmacists and dentists, while a network of Community Health Councils represented consumer interests. Although local authority nominees and representatives of voluntary bodies and the professions sat on some of these bodies, the membership was appointed, not elected. The 1980s, however, also saw a move towards greater 'managerialisation' within the NHS, which resulted in the creation of a Health Services Supervisory Board and a full-time NHS Management Board and subsequently an NHS Executive that significantly strengthened central planning and oversight (see Greenwood and Wilson, 1989, pp. 260–71).

In 1989 significant structural changes were proposed in the White Paper *Working for Patients* (Department of Health, 1989). These were implemented under the terms of the 1990 National Health Service and Community Care Act. As Bruce (1997, pp. 184–5) points out, this reform was the product of a number of factors, including a funding crisis, growing public and professional concern about apparently falling standards of patient care, and 'an ideological dimension' within which proposals for the introduction of competitive markets were especially significant. Consequently, the existing structure of health care, in which District Health Authorities (and their Scottish equivalents, Area Health Boards) managed hospitals directly, was replaced by a rolling programme of reform which led to the creation of a 'purchaser–provider split'. This involved allocating a new, more focused role to the Health Authorities' resident populations.

With the separation of responsibility for purchasing health care from that of provision, the role of the major purchasers of services, in the form of DHAs and AHBs, underwent a process of change. Alleviated of responsibility for providing services directly to their resident populations, purchasers . . . [were] forced to confront the realities of expressing locally defined need in terms of contractual agreements with providers.

(Bruce and Jonsson, 1996, 79)

In effect, this meant that the Authorities and Boards became purchasers (later styled 'commissioners') of health care (utilising central government funding), while the providers (individual hospitals and community health services) assumed a new status as NHS Trusts whose income would be generated mainly through the negotiation of contracts with Health Authorities and Boards, the new breed of general practitioner (GP) fundholders, and perhaps also the private sector of health care. GP practices were openly encouraged by the government to apply for fundholding status, which brought with it the allocation of a budget from the centre (via the District Health Authorities and Area Health Boards), as opposed to the traditional system whereby financial management was the preserve of the Authorities and Boards. Non-GP fundholders remained secure in the knowledge that they would not 'run out' of funds for certain courses of treatment before the end of the financial year, but they lacked the new flexibility which fundholding conveyed upon practices regarding the 'purchase' of specialist hospital treatment for their patients. By the late 1990s, a variety of forms of GP fundholding could be seen within the NHS in England and Wales, although it was notable that GPs in Scotland were relatively less enthusiastic about fundholding, and the majority of practices there continued to operate within the traditional system of centralised financial management.

As a direct consequence of the 1989 White Paper, the Family Practitioner Committees were firstly refashioned as smaller management bodies, and then recast as Family Health Service Authorities (FHSAs) in 1990. A review of functions and manpower resulted in FHSAs being formally merged with the District Health Authorities to form unitary Health Authorities in 1996. At the same time, the Regional Health Authorities in England were abolished, and replaced by regional offices of the Department of Health, in an attempt to exert much greater control over the regional tier (see Dopson *et al.*, 1999).

One of the other creations of the 1989 White Paper was the NHS Trusts. By 1998 there were 450 of these in England and Wales, operating within a framework of 100 Health Authorities, while in Scotland there were forty-seven Trusts and fifteen Health Boards. These were managed by boards containing executive and non-executive directors, the appointment of whom ultimately lay in the hands of central government ministers. A new wave of quangos had been created, and ministerial patronage extended.

The general impact of the 1990s restructuring exercises was to produce a multiplicity of bodies concerned, in one way or another, with the system of health care. The organisational structure of the NHS became significantly more complex, to the point of fragmentation. However, beyond the rhetoric about 'decentralisation' and 'delegated management', the reality was that this area of regional administration was being subjected to increased central control: 'paradoxically, the new structure has also facilitated centralisation and the NHS is now more politically directed and controlled than at any time in its history' (Kendall *et al.*, 1996, p. 211)

Klein (1995, p. 214) contrasts the 'rhetoric of devolving decision-making' with 'the reality [of] hyper-activity by the NHS Management Executive driving, directing and dominating the agenda of the service as it implemented the policies of Ministers'. The ministerial appointees within the Management Executive (and its Scottish equivalent) came from a mixture of backgrounds (about one-third were from the world of business and commerce), were led by a Chief Executive and were charged with responsibility for overseeing the implementation of the minister's strategy.

The bewilderingly complex NHS structure was to be subject to at least a partial rationalisation following the election of the Blair government. Reflecting the government's commitment to devolution, health White Papers were produced for each part of the UK (Department of Health, 1997; Scottish Office Department of Health, 1997; Welsh Office, 1998; Department of Health and Social Services

Northern Ireland, 1999). These plans had a common theme: abolition of the previous Conservative governments' internal market (including the abolition of GP fund-holding), retaining a distinction between those commissioning health services and those providing them, a primary care-led NHS (placing the commissioning of services in the hands of professionals closest to the patient, such as GPs and community nurses), more lay representation and greater openness (via more public meetings of NHS Boards and Trusts), and closer working relationships with local government (which has retained responsibilities for social care, social services and environmental health).

In England these reforms led to the creation in 1999 of Primary Care Groups (PCGs), which gained responsibility for planning and commissioning most of the health care for their local populations. The PCGs covered around 100,000 people, based on an aggregation of the practice lists of GPs which together form the PCG (plus non-registered patients within the geographical boundaries of the PCG). They were to be managed by a board consisting of a majority of GPs (usually with one of them as Chair), community nurses, members of the health authority, lay members and social services representatives, and a chief executive. These bodies would initially be constituted as committees of the Health Authority. It was envisaged that they would, in time, become free-standing Primary Care Trusts (PCTs) which could combine commissioning with the provision of community health services. The first wave of PCTs was created in 2000, and it is anticipated that all PCGs will become PCTs by 2004. In Wales, similar arrangements were set out, with Local Health Groups based on local authority areas assuming the role of the PCGs in England. There were no plans to create the equivalent of PCTs in Wales.

In Scotland, there were to be no Primary Care Groups. Instead, PCTs, funded by the Health Boards, were created, with GPs forming local health cooperatives under their auspices. The NHS in Scotland also declared that it would end the division between commissioning and provision, with service development being based instead on collaboration between Trusts and Health Boards.

As these new arrangements were being introduced, a crisis during the winter of 1999–2000 triggered off yet another review, and the formulation of a National Plan for investment and reform in the NHS (see Department of Health, 2000). The focus here was on issues such as management processes, lay involvement, quality of service and professional regulation, although some structural reform was also proposed. This included the creation of a Modernisation Agency at national level (with boards at regional and local levels) to steer the process of investment and reform. In another development, the formal division of responsibilities between the NHS and the Department of Health, established in the later 1980s, was ended, with the posts of Chief Executive of the NHS and permanent secretary of the department being combined. At the launch of the NHS Modernisation Agency in the spring of 2001, the Health Secretary announced new plans to cut the number of Health Authorities in England from ninety-nine to thirty, and abolish the ten regional offices. This signalled a shift of financial power towards the Primary Care Trusts (see Wintour and Carvel, 2001).

The National Plan foresaw much closer working relations between the NHS and local government. Local authorities would have an enhanced role in scrutinising health services and they would be given much more say on major service changes, including hospital closures. The National Plan stated that there would be greater cooperation at regional level between the NHS and regional government in England (with the creation of single public health groups spanning NHS regional offices and the government's offices of the regions). The NHS will be expected to play a full part in the government's National Strategy for Neighbourhood Renewal, and to help develop local strategic partnerships to tackle deprivation in conjunction with local authorities and the voluntary sector. The NHS Plan took this a stage further by proposing the creation of Care Trusts, which would be able to commission and deliver primary and community health care and social care for groups such as elderly people and those suffering from mental illness. All of these proposals built upon an earlier commitment (set out in the Health Act of 1999) to give Health Authorities and Trusts a duty to cooperate with each other and with local authorities, in an effort to improve health. In addition, it should be noted that this legislation enabled NHS and local authorities to pool budgets, transfer commissioning roles among themselves, and cooperate in integrated services in an attempt to create a more coherent system.

Another major theme of the Blair government's strategy for the NHS was increased user empowerment. The NHS Plan outlined a range of new fora involving patients, carers and the public, to advise health authorities and trusts on policy and services. Patients' representatives were allocated seats on key bodies such as the Modernisation Board (which advises the Health Secretary on the implementation of the NHS Plan). A new Patient Advisory and Liaison Service was also proposed to help deal with patients' concerns and complaints at a local level. Interestingly, the government's plans did not envisage a future for the Community Health Councils (CHCs) in England. At the time of writing, the future of CHCs looks uncertain amid plans to create a new network of patients' bodies to take on the CHCs' 'watchdog' role and coordinate patient advocacy at the local level.

The story of structural change in this sphere of regional administration goes on, and can best be followed on the relevant web sites mentioned in the Further reading section.

Conclusion

The challenges of multi-level governance would appear to be here to stay. The United Kingdom is likely to remain a part of the developing European Union, and the process of constitutional change which resulted in devolution for Scotland, Wales and Northern Ireland is unlikely to be reversed. It is possible, though by no means certain, that further moves towards the introduction of regional government within England could take place. However, even if regional government, as such, remains relatively underdeveloped in England, the form of regional administration upon which the NHS is based will probably remain in place, albeit in its characteristically ever-changing shape and structure. The interactions, negotiations and accommodations between these levels of public administration will command the interest of those seeking to understand the details of our governing order, and the theories and concepts of multi-level governance will play their part in aiding our understanding of an increasingly complex system. Public administration in a multi-level polity is likely to be unpredictable, even a little bit messy, but it will require close attention.

Further reading

The sources for the topics covered within this chapter are many and varied, as one might expect. Pierre and Stoker (2000) offer a good basic grounding on some of the important ideas surrounding multi-level governance. Nugent (1999, 2000) provides invaluable coverage of the EU dimension of UK governance, while the web site of the European Commission in the UK www.cec.org.uk offers guidance on a range of EU information sources. The literature on Scottish and Welsh devolution is just starting to develop, and students would be advised to keep up to date with developments in these areas by reading the regular short articles in *Talking Politics* and *Politics Review*, as well as the sources cited above. A useful introductory account of public administration in devolved Scotland can be found in Lynch (2001). In additon, the key web sites provide a wealth of useful information: the Scottish Parliament on www.scottish.parliament.uk and the National Assembly for Wales on www.wales.gov.uk.

Useful background to the issues of governance in Northern Ireland can be found in Boyce (1996) and Loughlin (1998), while detailed information on the current functioning of the devolution settlement in the province can be accessed through the Northern Ireland Assembly web site: www.ni-assembly.gov.uk. Again the politics magazines are also of use. Up-to-date information about the London Mayor and Assembly can be found at www.london.gov.uk, while details of the English Regional Development Agencies and Chambers are contained within the Department of the Environment, Transport and the Regions web site: www.local-regions.detr.gov.uk. Data on the ever-changing NHS can be found at the Department of Health web site www.doh.gov.uk and in the relevant parts of the devolved government sites.

Chapter 11

Privatisation and the regulatory state

Introduction

On the surface at least, it might seem rather odd to discuss the management and operation of private sector bodies in a book on public administration. However, students of government and public administration must come to terms with the implications of the policy which resulted in the transfer of large parts of the former public sector into private hands during the 1980s and 1990s. The public sector was itself restructured as a result of the process of privatisation. The central government departments which had acted as 'sponsors' of particular nationalised industries (for example, the Department of Transport in the case of the nationalised rail network) lost key functions. In the case of the Department of Energy, the privatisation of the gas and electricity supply industries effectively made the sponsoring department redundant, with the result that its remaining functions and its staff were transferred elsewhere and the department was abolished. As we shall see, privatisation also had important consequences for public finance, reducing and then eliminating the role of the Treasury as a source of subsidy for nationalised industries, while generating cash surpluses via the sale of assets. However, while it undoubtedly had the effect of reducing the role of the state in many respects, privatisation also gave increased emphasis to the state's function as a regulator, or a guardian of the public interest. This meant that the transfer of many key services from the public to the private sector was accompanied by the creation of new regulatory frameworks, within which government would play a major role.

For these reasons, privatisation could never simply result in the removal of large areas of government activity from the domain of 'public administration'. The process of privatisation, and its aftermath, highlighted the state's roles as facilitator or enabler, and as regulator. For this reason, the causes, effects and continuing consequences of privatisation remain matters of legitimate concern for students of government, public administration and management.

Why privatise?

Public ownership has traditionally assumed a number of different forms (Greenwood and Wilson, 1989, pp. 226–32). In a simple sense, all government undertakings and facilities, including schools, hospitals and libraries, come into the category of public ownership. However, in Britain the concept usually applied in a more specific sense to governmental involvement in commercial and industrial undertakings, including the nationalised industries and the public corporations. In fact, there was some overlap between these categorisations, and the logic behind the use of the terms was often confused. Nonetheless, in simple terms, most of the major nationalised industries were created by the Labour governments of 1945–51, and included the coal and steel industries as well as the rail network, while the public corporations encompassed non-industrial bodies such as the BBC.

Privatisation, formerly described as 'de-nationalisation', was the process which resulted in the replacement of public ownership with one of the many forms of private sector ownership. This happened in most spheres, although it should be noted that some important areas of public administration, including the provision of water and sewerage service in Scotland, the London transport system and the state broadcasting network (the BBC), continue to be managed using variations of the public ownership model. As we note below, privatisation can take a number of different shapes, including the total or partial conversion of a public corporation or nationalised industry into a limited company, government disposal of all or some of the shares it holds in specific bodies, breaking the monopoly held by a state concern, or simply injecting elements of private provision into public services. However, common to all forms of privatisation is the introduction of a significant role for private companies in spheres where previously state bodies enjoyed a dominant, leading role (for details of the literature, see Marsh, 1991).

The traditional, if rather superficial, view of British party politics categorised the Conservatives as the party of privatisation, and Labour as the party of state ownership. According to this perspective, any analysis of the reasons for, and importance of, privatisation should hinge upon the fact that the Conservative Party enjoyed eighteen years in power between 1979 and 1997, during which time the post-war consensus about the proper balance between the role of the state and the role of the private sector was discarded. However, this rather begs the question: why did the 'party of privatisation' fail to pursue this policy to any great extent during its periods in power before 1979? In fact, despite the rhetoric associated with the party (particularly during General Elections and party conferences), Conservative governments of 1951–64 and 1970–4 rarely attempted to privatise (or 'de-nationalise', to use the jargon of the time). Although the iron and steel industry was returned to the private sector under the Conservatives, they largely accepted the public/private 'mixed economy' created by the post-Second World War Labour government, and even increased state control in some spheres (most notably through the nationalisation of Rolls Royce in 1971). All of this suggests that the commitment to privatisation shown by the Conservatives in power after 1979 was only partly attributable to the revival of the Tory Right under Margaret Thatcher, and the consequent emphasis this gave to the party's traditional stance as the representative of free enterprise.

Privatisation became a key feature of government policy in the UK during the 1980s and 1990s, not simply because the Conservatives were in power (although this was clearly a major factor), but because the policy, in all its distinct forms, offered solutions to a number of contemporary problems. This helps to explain why Labour, traditionally the party of state ownership, did not set about dismantling the privatisation policy when it returned to power in 1997. On the contrary, as we shall see, the Blair government continued to expand the role of the private sector in areas which had previously been regarded as preserves of the state. Put simply, just as nationalisation seemed to fit the circumstances and challenges of the immediate post-war period, so privatisation appeared to address some of the prevailing concerns of government in the latter part of the twentieth century.

The rationale for privatisation can be analysed in a number of different ways. However, we can simplify matters by establishing the three broad reasons why the policy was introduced and pursued with such vigour.

The first reason was managerial. The nationalised industries and public corporations had come to be seen (with some justice in at least certain cases) as inefficient, uncompetitive organisations which delivered a poor quality of service to consumers. Critics of state ownership argued that low standards of management would prevail for as long as these bodies could avoid the harsh realities of the open market and rely upon subsidies from the Treasury. It was further argued that the management structures of the nationalised industries, with boards of ministerial appointees often subject to unofficial and unacknowledged political interference, were not conducive to sound strategic decision-making (Greenwood and Wilson, 1989, pp. 230–45).

The second reason was economic. Almost at a stroke, privatisation could achieve three economic objectives. The public sector wage bill would be cut by transferring large numbers of workers from the public to the private sector. The strain on the Public Sector Borrowing Requirement would be further relieved by the reduction which would take place in Treasury lending. Finally, the policy would also provide a flow of funds into the Exchequer (which could then be used for other purposes, including tax cuts) through the sale of assets. Privatisation therefore offered the opportunity for government to shed responsibility for the costs of significant parts of the former public sector, while at the same time generating income through the sales.

The third reason was ideological. In her retirement, Margaret Thatcher reflected on the attractions of privatisation. '[It] . . . was fundamental to improving Britain's economic performance. But for me it was also far more than that: it was one of the central means of reversing the corrosive and corrupting effects of socialism' (Thatcher, 1993, p. 676). This ideological imperative became increasingly important as the privatisation policy moved into top gear during the second and third Thatcher administrations. Privatisation fitted neatly into the New Right's crusade against socialism and the culture of the post-war consensus. This political perspective drew upon some of the theories and concepts which had emerged from the work of the critics of 'big government' and the proponents of individualism and 'public choice'. Margaret Thatcher was personally influenced by the vigorous attack on the state contained within the ideas of von Hayek (1944), which found a new and more receptive audience some thirty years after their original publication. Meanwhile, Niskanen's (1973) arguments about the tendency of bureaucracies to generate their own agendas and squeeze out the interests of the public fitted neatly into the developing Conservative enthusiasm for large-scale privatisation of government functions. In practical terms, transferring industries and services from the public to the private sector addressed three of the prevailing concerns of Thatcherite Conservatism. These were: the desire to encourage economic 'freedom' by allowing market forces to take their course, the need to break the 'dependency culture' and create a 'property- and share-owning democracy', and finally, the mission to cut the scale and power of the state bureaucracy (see Chapter 1).

The ideological motivation behind privatisation was the subject of particular criticism. Some critics, including the Labour Party during the 1980s and early 1990s, opposed ideologically driven privatisation on political grounds (Labour Research, 1993). It was pointed out that in some cases (including the gas, water and telecommunications sell-offs) the immediate effect of privatisation was merely to replace a public monopoly with a private monopoly. In addition, the social costs of the policy (including the loss of jobs consequential upon new private sector ownership and the dilution of the service principle which had governed, *inter alia*, the provision of rural bus routes) were identified, and the apparent loss of public accountability was criticised, also the relatively cheap sell-off of national assets ('selling the family silver' in the immortal phrase of Lord Stockton, the former Conservative Prime Minister Harold Macmillan). Other critics, including Osborne and Gaebler, the fashionable proponents of managerial change in US public administration, were distinctly sceptical about the value of privatisation when it was introduced for dogmatic reasons. In their key work, *Reinventing Government*, which rapidly came to assume the status of a Biblical text for politicians and officials at all levels of the American system of government and beyond, Osborne and Gaebler (1992, p. 45) argued that privatisation was *'one* answer, not *the* answer' to some of the challenges of public administration and management. They cautioned against accepting the arguments of the ideological proponents of this policy, likening the latter to 'snake oil salesmen'.

Although this ideological imperative was a very significant factor in the privatisation agenda of the Thatcher governments, the decline in the influence of the ideologues within the Major administration from November 1990, and the election of a Labour government in 1997, did not signal an end to privatisation. As we note below, even Labour, largely for pragmatic rather than ideological reasons, retained forms of privatisation as policy options.

To summarise, we can say that the combination of these managerial, economic and ideological factors produced, and then drove on, the policy of privatisation.

Types of privatisation

Privatisation is a rather loosely defined concept. In its purest and most extreme form, it involves the complete conversion of a publicly owned entity into a private company. However, 'privatisation' is often used to describe a range of trends and practices which fall short of this. In its various guises, the policy of privatisation has affected public services at all levels of the system of government and public administration. In local authorities, the National Health Service, central government, and the parts of the system which did not fall neatly into one or other of these spheres (in the world of quangos for example), assets and services moved from the public to the private sector throughout the 1980s and 1990s. Although it is possible to categorise the usages of this concept in a number of different ways, we have identified six key types:

1   Partial conversion to a limited company. Here, an element of a public corporation or nationalised industry is floated off into the private sector, normally through a share issue. Normally, this would be a precursor to full privatisation – effectively, a two-stage process.
2   Total conversion to a limited company. In this case, an entire state-owned body is sold off in one major transaction. Examples of this were the privatisations of British Telecom in 1984 and British Gas in 1986.
3   Piecemeal or fragmentary privatisation. Here, a state-run enterprise is broken up into discrete components which are sold off to different private companies. The prime illustration of this was to be seen in the treatment of British Rail, which was disaggregated into train services and the railway and station infrastructure. These were sold to a multiplicity of train-operating companies, including Virgin, GNER, Scotrail and Connex, and a single track, station and general infrastructure company, Railtrack.

4   Disposal of government shareholdings. In these instances, some or all of the shares the state has acquired in private companies are sold off, as with the disposal of the government's shares in Cable and Wireless between 1981 and 1985 and Amersham International in 1982.

5   Breaking of a state monopoly. Privatisation is also used, rather loosely, to describe the process whereby a field of activity, previously reserved for government, is opened up to competition. In some cases, as with the deregulation of bus routes during the 1980s, private companies were ready and able to participate in the new market. In others, as with the ending of the state monopoly in the generation of electricity brought about by the 1983 Energy Act, it would take some time for effective private sector competitors to emerge.

6   Injection of elements of private provision within a public service framework. Again, the word privatisation is used rather more loosely here, since the result might fall short of an outright transfer of assets from the public to the private sector. The main examples in this category are the introduction of competitive tendering or market testing (see Chapter 2), the increased use of fees and charges for formerly free public services and the use of the Private Finance Initiative (PFI) for major public sector capital projects.

In some cases, ownership restrictions were attached to privatised undertakings. For example, the articles of association could place limits on individual shareholdings (typically 15 per cent of the total shares) or restrict foreign shareholdings (this applied in the cases of British Aerospace and British Airways). Another form of residual government control, particularly obvious during the early phase of the policy's development, was the use of a 'golden share' which allowed the government to outvote all other shareholders on certain strategic matters such as asset sales and takeovers (although there is no evidence of these shares being used, and they were viewed by one of the architects of the Thatcher government's privatisation policy, Nicholas Ridley, as little more than window dressing).

The Labour Party's return to power in 1997 did not bring an end to the use of privatisation as a policy tool. In fact, the Blair government adopted a similar approach to that of its immediate predecessor. Privatisation, in its various forms, was viewed pragmatically, as a set of devices which offered possible solutions to some public management problems. In comparison with the Thatcher period, a more partial and selective use of the privatisation option was the order of the day. Under New Labour, major share flotations and the introduction of private ownership were not ruled out in certain circumstances. For example, after only six months in office, the government announced its intention to sell off 60 per cent of the Commonwealth Development Corporation, and, more dramatically, in June 1998 the Chancellor of the Exchequer set out a planned sale of public assets worth £4 billion a year for the next three years (Elliot and MacAskill, 1998). As time passed, the government sold off part of HMSO, the official publishing house, as The Stationery Office, and announced plans to sell 51 per cent of the shares in the National Air Traffic Control Service as well as introducing private ownership in some of London Underground's busiest lines. Nonetheless, in spite of all this, the Blair administration tended to place more emphasis on the types of privatisation set out in category 6, above. In particular, New Labour continued to use competitive tendering (albeit under a new guise) and the Private Finance Initiative. Let us offer some further comments on these in turn.

Competitive tendering had emerged, in its compulsory form (CCT), during the 1980s, when the Thatcher government drove the policy through local government and the National Health Service. The compulsory competitive tendering regime specified that certain activities such as catering, cleaning and refuse collection were to be put out to tender, with the contract for providing the service being awarded to the most competitive bid. As a result, in some cases the service was contracted-out, with private companies winning the contracts. In local government, approximately 25 per cent of the contracts were won by the in-house teams, which meant that the public body still managed the service, albeit on a contractual basis. At the level of central government, the civil service was initially affected by these developments only marginally. Central government services and functions were not subject to compulsory competitive tendering. However, the result of the essentially voluntary nature of the process at that level was that only a relatively small number of quite low-grade manual and clerical tasks were exposed to competitive tendering. The White Paper *Competing for Quality* (HM Treasury, 1991) announced the expansion of CCT throughout the public sector, this time including the civil service, where the process was to be styled 'market testing'. This new wave of competition was to involve professional 'white-collar' activities including accountancy, information and legal services, as well as the more traditional targets for tendering (see Chapter 2).

The proponents of CCT in its varied forms argued that even where services ultimately remained 'in-house', with the existing local authority, NHS or civil service providers, the tendering process would have the effect of sharpening up management and enhancing efficiency. In fact, the results were mixed. The government's deadlines and targets for CCT and market testing were repeatedly revised and shifted, debates raged about the cost of the process – including 'additional' costs involved in contract specification and monitoring – and the extent of the savings generated. The trade unions and the opposition parties attacked the CCT and market-testing processes on the grounds that they spawned their own bureaucracies, cost millions of pounds in management consultancy fees, led to job cuts, often resulted in no discernible difference in the quality of service provided, adversely affected morale and threatened the principle of public service provision in some spheres.

The Labour Party's opposition to the dogmatic elements of market testing led to a new approach following the 1997 election. The new government's stated objective was to ensure that all departments reviewed the full range of their services and functions over a five-year period starting in 1999. The aim was to identify the 'best supplier' of each service and function, while improving quality and value for money across government. Under this initiative, styled Better Quality Services (BQS) for central government, and Best Value for local authorities (see Chapter 5), plans were put in place for the programme of reviews starting in October 1999.

The focus of BQS and Best Value is on end results and service standards with the best quality and value for money for the taxpayer. The 'best supplier' of a service is identified through considering the possibility of competition, but in a major change from the market testing and CCT programme, there is no compulsion to set up a tendering process. If quality can be improved through internal restructuring or managerial 'reprocessing', no competition is necessary. However, these internal reviews must be seen to be 'robust', and they are subject to oversight by the Cabinet Office, the Treasury and a key Cabinet Committee (PSX).

The Private Finance Initiative had been introduced in 1992 as a device which would allow government departments, and public authorities more generally, to minimise their capital investment outlays. From the perspective of central government, an attractive outcome of this would be the opportunity to keep public expenditure under control. Under the PFI, private sector expertise would be exploited, while maintenance costs for the facility were transferred. What this meant in effect was that government would buy maintained highways instead of building roads, purchase custodial or healthcare services instead of building prisons and hospitals, and pay for managed IT services instead of buying computers and software. When a contract ends, in, say, thirty years' time, the facility is handed back to the public sector body which made the original deal. The private sector contractors provide the initial capital, as well as assuming the risks associated with construction, in return for operating licences for the resulting facility, which enable them to recoup their costs. As the PFI was implemented, it became clear that projects tend to take two forms, financially free-standing projects and joint ventures, as set out in Box 11.1.

Under the Major government, the PFI started fairly slowly, and it failed to have the expected impact on public expenditure plans. All public sector capital projects were to be tested for PFI potential, but the initiative became associated with high tendering costs and bureaucratic bidding procedures (Terry, 1996). Nonetheless, the PFI developed in significance as time passed, and it came to underpin some major infrastructure projects, including the Channel Tunnel, the high-speed rail link to the Tunnel, toll bridges including the Skye road bridge, prisons, hospitals and a range of other facilities.

Following its election in 1997, the Labour government immediately ended the requirement that all public sector capital projects should be PFI tested, but ministers remained fully committed to a revised and refocused version of the initiative. During the first two years of the Labour government, some £4.7 billion worth of PFI deals were signed (making a total of £13 billion since the launch of PFI), with another £11 billion worth projected for the period 1999–2002. In the NHS alone, PFI deals would underpin the building of thirteen new hospitals.

The administrative and managerial problems associated with PFI were to be addressed by the government's acceptance of recommendations contained in a report by Sir Malcolm Bates, Chairman of Pearl, and the establishment of a new taskforce based in the Treasury and headed by Adrian Montague, a former city banker. In July 1999 the government responded to a second Bates report by announcing that the taskforce would be replaced in 2000 by Partnerships UK, a permanent body which would improve the central coordination of the initiative by acting as the overall project manager for PFI deals. Greater standardisation of the bidding and contractual process would follow. The new body would be set up as a plc, and it would symbolise the public/private partnership ethos. The private sector would take a majority share in Partnerships UK, which would provide public sector organisations with expert advice on PFI matters. It was hoped that this would prevent any repetition of the disastrous problems associated with the large PFI computer contracts, epitomised by the Passport Agency's misconceived deal with the electronics corporation Siemens, which produced massive backlogs in the passport application system in

Box 11.1 The Private Finance Initiative

Types of Project:

1 Financially free-standing projects. Here, the private sector supplier designs, builds, finances and then operates the asset. Costs are recovered through charges on the users of the facility. Examples are the Second Severn Bridge and the Dartford River Crossing.

2 Joint ventures. In these, the costs of the project are not met fully through charges, but are partly subsidised from public funds because there are wider social benefits involved, such as reduced congestion or local economic regeneration. Examples are business park developments, city-centre regeneration schemes, Manchester's Metrolink and the Docklands Light Railway Extension.

A joint venture PFI project: the Docklands Light Railway Extension
A joint venture between: the Department of the Environment, Transport and the Regions *and* City Greenwich Lewisham (CGL) Rail Link plc.

The project: A 24.5-year concession (from September 1996) to design, build, finance and maintain a 4.2 km extension to the DLR. The line will run under the Thames and add five new stations south of the river to create direct access between the City and Docklands, and south-east London and Kent. Opened to passengers in 2000, the line provided improved public transport access to Greenwich for the Millennium Exhibition events.

Cost: £200 million.

Private sector £165 million raised through bond issue.
funding:

Public sector £35 million in contributions from central government, Deptford
funding: City Challenge and the London Boroughs of Lewisham and Greenwich.

CGL Rail The company receives fees for use of the extension. The risks
opportunities include franchising; cost and time overruns; levels of passenger
and risks: usage; construction; installation of automatic train control system; integrating the extension with the existing rail system.

Source: HM Treasury

1999. Companies considering bidding for PFI deals would also be able to use Partnerships UK on a voluntary basis. Although it would not function as a bank, the new body would provide development funds to get PFI deals off the ground, perhaps by bundling together a number of projects which, individually, would be too small to attract private sector bidders.

Clearly committed to the long-term development of the PFI, the Labour government's confidence in its management of this controversial scheme was emphasised in September 1999, when ministers welcomed a new independent inquiry into the entire initiative, to be conducted by the Institute for Public Policy Research (Atkinson, 1999).

Nonetheless, the PFI remained controversial, and some critics were totally unconvinced by the claims made for this particular brand of privatisation. One observer described the PFI as a 'wheeze' which would allow public projects to be built or modernised without the capital spending being recorded in the national accounts: 'PFI is what poor people used to call the "never-never": you get something bright and shiny now but end up paying a lot more than its present cost over the long run' (Walker, 1999).

A former senior Treasury and Cabinet Office civil servant, Sir Peter Kemp (1999), argued that the case for the PFI type of public/private partnership was 'pretty thin' and he raised serious questions about the 'hidden spending' and unconventional 'value for money' studies surrounding PFI projects. It seems clear that there will be a high long-term price to pay in return for quick access to new assets. For example, it was calculated that the new infirmary in Edinburgh would have cost £180 million if paid for from taxation or government borrowing. A PFI deal allowed a private consortium to design, own and service the hospital, and then rent it to the public for £30 million a year over thirty years – making a total cost of £900 million (Cohen, 1999).

The state steps back: from provider to regulator

Privatisation, in its myriad forms, posed some specific accountability challenges. In particular, announcements of plans to transfer major public utilities to the private sector resulted in serious questions being raised about the possible dilution of public accountability which might result.

Partly in an effort to address this issue, in the sphere of the public utilities privatisation was accompanied by the creation of regulatory agencies which would issue licences to the commercial participants in the developing markets (or 'quasi-markets' where privatisation had not brought immediate competition), negotiate and then enforce the pricing formulas, obtain and publish information helpful to the service users, and oversee the systems for resolving consumer complaints. Box 11.2 sets out the powers and jurisdiction of a typical regulatory agency.

Some critics (see, for example, Ayres and Braithwaite, 1994, and Prosser, 1994) argued that the regulatory framework established in the UK was too limited and lacking in coherence. At the heart of the framework lay the price-capping formula devised by Professor Stephen Littlechild (who went on the become the first Director General of the Office of Electricity Regulation (OFFER)). When the Thatcher government was devising the ground rules for regulation of the utilities at the time

Box 11.2 Portrait of a regulator: OFTEL

Background
The Office of Telecommunications was set up under the Telecommunications Act, 1984, and headed by the Director General of Telecommunications, normally appointed for five years. David Edmonds was appointed director general in 1998. The director general has extensive powers under the Act to enforce and modify the licence conditions of telecommunications operators, to require that information is supplied to him by operators, and to set the terms for interconnections between networks. The goal of OFTEL is to get the best possible deal for telecommunications customers in terms of quality, choice and value for money.

Functions and powers:
- to ensure that licensees, including BT, local cable companies and mobile network operators, comply with their licence conditions;
- to initiate the modification of licence conditions;
- to advise the Secretary of State for Trade and Industry on telecommunications matters and the granting of new licences;
- to obtain information and arrange for publication where this would help users;
- to consider complaints and inquiries made about telecommunications services or apparatus;
- to maintain a register of approved telecommunications apparatus;
- to administer the telephone numbering scheme.

Additionally, the Director General has a duty to:
- ensure that telecommunications services are provided in the UK in order to meet all reasonable demands for them; this includes emergency services, public call boxes, directory information services and services in rural areas;
- ensure that those providing the services are able to finance them;
- promote the interests of customers;
- maintain and promote effective competition;
- ensure that those providing services are doing so efficiently;
- promote research and development;
- encourage major users of telecommunications services outside the UK to establish businesses here;
- enable UK-based telecommunications companies to compete effectively overseas;
- submit an Annual Report to the Secretary of State, which will be laid before Parliament.

Management
OFTEL is a non-ministerial government department, independent of ministerial control and headed by a director general. Funding is provided by Parliament, but the licence fees paid by telecommunications operators offset the cost almost entirely. OFTEL's 160 staff, all based in London, come from backgrounds in the civil service, consumer affairs, business and industry.

Source: Extracted from the OFTEL website, at www.oftel.gov.uk

of British Telecom's privatisation, it accepted Littlechild's recommendation that Britain should eschew the type of regulation favoured in the United States, which involved limiting profits, in favour of a price-cap mechanism (Jackson and Price, 1994, p. 12). The Littlechild formula was RPI–X. This meant that the maximum price increase in the utilities would be determined by the annual changes in the Retail Price Index (RPI) minus an amount (X) set by the regulator, usually for a four- or five-year period, after which it would be reviewed. The critics pointed out that the focus on prices alone could expose the regulators to public anger about excessive profits in the utilities, and they identified the lack of a procedural code for the agencies as a failing which would leave them susceptible to influence by a range of external and internal factors. As we note below, these criticisms turned out to have some validity.

The new regulatory regimes emerged in parts of the public sector which had previously been badly served by rather diffuse, weak and distinctly problematic forms of accountability. This could be seen most clearly in the public utilities, charged with the provision of gas, water and electricity supplies and telecommunications facilities, where the Offices of Gas Supply (OFGAS), Electricity Regulation (OFFER), Water Services (OFWAT) and Telecommunications (OFTEL) were established (Pyper, 1996, Chapter 5). Under the terms of the Utilities Act, 2000, OFGAS and OFFER were merged into a single energy regulator, the Office of Gas and Electricity Markets (OFGEM). The regulatory agency model was, however, extended beyond these spheres, eventually encompassing rail services and a myriad public services and organisations.

Therefore, the disengagement of government from ownership of the former public utilities was accompanied by the assumption of a new role: that of regulator (see Jackson and Price, 1994). The divestment of a service function by government, and the concomitant restructuring of the public sector, were coupled with the establishment of new organs of public administration. In broad terms, privatisation was accompanied by the retention of a form of public accountability, and the emergence of a new set of scrutineers. This was to have both negative and positive effects.

On the negative side of the equation, the focus of public accountability shifted away from Parliament, and the records of the regulators were variable. The style and effectiveness of each regulatory agency were affected by a number of external and internal factors. The former included matters over which the agencies themselves had little or no control, including the legal powers conveyed upon them, the type of person appointed as director general, the scale of the utility to be regulated, the prevailing style of its board of directors, and the extent to which real competition could be introduced in its sphere of operation. The internal factors included the quality, expertise and deployment of staff, and the relative importance attached by the director general to the regulatory agency's diverse responsibilities. As Prosser (1994, p. 259) notes, the style and approach of the director general could be a key factor in determining the effectiveness of a regulatory agency.

The importance of these external and internal factors stemmed in no small measure from the fact that the new regulatory framework contained inherent tensions and contradictions. The legislative setting within which the agencies operated was curiously imprecise in relation to their fundamental roles and responsibilities. In particular, there was a basic tension between two possible agency functions: as overseers and guarantors of competitive markets (or 'quasi-markets' where full competition in service provision was not yet in place) and as scrutineers, or agents of public accountability and control. It might be argued that these fundamental roles, of securing effective competition and ensuring full public accountability, were not necessarily contradictory, but the fact that the relative importance attached to each role was never made entirely clear served to produce a tension at the heart of the regulatory regime. In practice, some directors general of the regulatory agencies positioned themselves primarily as guarantors of competition, while others saw their main role as 'watchdogs', securing the accountability of the utility to its consumers. For example, Ian Byatt, the first Director General of OFWAT, argued that his fundamental duty was 'to achieve through regulation the same balance as would otherwise have been achieved by competitive markets' (cited by Maloney and Richardson, 1992, p. 15). On the other hand, Sir James McKinnon, the first Director General of OFTEL, established his reputation (and incurred the enduring enmity of BT) by vigorously championing the interests of the customers.

The accountability issue raised further, associated, questions. There were different perspectives on the sources to which the privatised utilities should be deemed accountable. Since they remained providers of public services, even after privatisation, the concept of accountability to service users or customers was very important. In that light, the main role of the regulatory agencies would seem to be as consumer 'watchdogs' focused on the task of enforcing the accountability of the utilities. However, there was a possible contradiction between this concept and the more conventional private sector approach to corporate governance, within which prime importance is attached to accountability to shareholders. While the shareholders will be delighted by announcements of increased profits, the customers might well ask (as did those of the water utilities during the early 1990s) why prices are increasing and service standards declining.

While in some spheres the existence of these dedicated and specialised agencies successfully addressed most of the concerns about the impact of privatisation on public accountability, serious problems arose in others. Public concerns about the excessive profits being generated by some of the newly privatised utilities during the 1990s led OFTEL, OFWAT and OFGAS to tighten their price-cap formulas. Even more seriously, in the rail utility, generally poor service standards and the fatal train crashes at Southall in 1997, Paddington in 1999 and Hatfield in 2000 raised major doubts about the effectiveness of the regulatory regime. Following rail privatisation, regulatory functions had been dispersed and a confusing array of 'regulators' emerged:

- ministers: set the regulatory framework;
- Office of the Rail Regulator: issues licences to train-operating companies and enforces licence conditions relating to safety;
- Chief Inspector of Railways: leads the Rail Inspectorate, which is part of the Health and Safety Executive; approves and monitors safety systems;
- Strategic Rail Authority: sets and monitors service standards for the twenty-five train-operating companies;
- Railtrack: owns and manages track, stations, tunnels, level crossings, viaducts and bridges; set and policed safety standards until this role was restricted following the Paddington rail disaster in October 1999.

However, when allowance is made for the weaknesses and negative features of the new regulatory regimes, in some areas at least it could be argued that the move away from traditional accountability frameworks, and into the new regime of regulation, also brought some positive outcomes. These can be seen if we examine the pre- and post-privatisation regimes of accountability in the utilities. While in the public sector, the water, gas, electricity and telecommunications utilities had been subjected to different regimes of accountability.

In the case of water, the Scottish water and sewerage authorities were integrated with local government, with the result that the services were delivered through conventional local authority departments. In terms of accountability, this meant that internal lines ran from officers to members, and the latter were then accountable externally to the electorate and central government via the array of mechanisms designed to bring about local government accountability (including elections, the local ombudsman and the Accounts Commission). The water utility was not privatised in Scotland, although it was restructured in 1996, when three regionally based authorities were set up. These quangos were made accountable to central government (the Scottish Office, then, from 1999, the Scottish Executive). Arguably, this led to a dilution of accountability overall, with the outright replacement of one strand by another, overtly based on centralisation.

In all the other utilities, however, it could be argued, with some justification, that the post-privatisation regimes of accountability represented an improvement on the former system.

In England and Wales, before privatisation, the Regional Water Authorities were composed of local authority nominees plus ministerial appointees, thus producing a hybrid form of accountability, with lines running both to the world of local government and to central government ministers. In the gas, electricity and telecommunication utilities, the public corporation model of accountability applied. This meant that government ministers were accountable to Parliament for the work of their departments, and if a minister's department happened to be the 'sponsoring department' for a public corporation (for example, the Department of Energy for the gas and electricity utilities) this accountability encompassed the work of the corporation. Under this model ministers were largely responsible for policy and the boards of the public corporations for 'day-to-day management'. In reality, however, as ministers appointed boards and were largely responsible for approving major capital investment and borrowing, there was generally scope for considerable ministerial interference in managerial and commercial decisions. In practice, moreover, Parliament had at its disposal relatively few mechanisms for scrutinising the public corporations (see Greenwood and Wilson, 1989, pp. 238–40). Until 1979 there was only one dedicated select committee for this purpose, and its powers were dispersed among a range of other committees as a consequence of the reform to the select committee system which took place that year. Only sporadic Parliamentary debates took place on the working of the utilities, and the Public Accounts Committee of the House of Commons was denied access to much financial information on grounds of 'commercial sensitivity'. Government ministers became skilled at refusing to provide Parliament with information on these grounds and repeatedly referred difficult questions to the boards on the grounds that day-to-day managerial issues were no business of ministers. On the other hand, Members of Parliament encountered extreme difficulty in securing the accountability of board members, who were only too eager to argue that ministers were ultimately in charge. This mirrored the division of responsibility, and the concomitant accountability issues, which would later be integral to the management of Next Steps executive agencies (see Chapter 2). In summary, Parliamentary questions, debates and the Public Accounts Committee proved inadequate for the task of securing the accountability of ministers for the work of these bodies, while the Select Committee on the Nationalised Industries and its successors were overstretched and unable to cope with the task of providing detailed scrutiny of all the public corporations. Serious accountability gaps were the order of the day.

Given these problems, it is difficult to argue with the conclusion that the accountability arrangements which accompanied the privatisation of these utilities, though not flawless, represented something of an improvement on the old order. At the point of privatisation, the establishment of regulatory agencies shifted the locus of accountability away from Parliament. However, in general, the existence of these dedicated and specialised agencies in the sphere of each utility marked a clear improvement in the quantity and quality of accountability. Furthermore, as one observer noted, transparency, one of the vital prerequisites for a properly functioning system of accountability, was secured by the regulatory agencies:

> the creation of the regulators has resulted in considerably greater openness than was the case under nationalisation, through imposing a form of external supervision which . . . did not exist previously . . . individual regulators have been, by the standards of British public bodies, exceptionally open in reaching some of their decisions.
>
> (Prosser, 1994, p. 255)

Conclusion

In this chapter we have set out the basic rationale for, and the major forms of, privatisation. Despite its association with the Thatcher era, and its attractions for the New Right, privatisation continued to be used pragmatically, rather than ideologically, as a policy tool by the New Labour government headed by Tony Blair.

The consequences and effects of privatisation are of interest to students of public administration for a number of reasons. Most obviously, because some forms of the policy do not necessarily lead to an outright transfer of functions from the public to the private sector, but to types of public/private partnership, there remains a clear and legitimate area of study for those concerned with public policy, management and administration. Even where the policy results in the wholesale transfer of assets and services from the public to the private sector, as in the case of the former public utilities, the continuing public interest in securing proper accountability, via the regulatory agencies, means this remains a sub-sphere of public administration.

Further reading

The regulatory agencies produce annual reports, containing much useful data about the major issues confronting those regulating the activities of the former public utilities. In addition, the agencies' web sites are sources of valuable information (see, for example, www.ofgem.gov.uk and www.oftel.gov.uk). Jackson and Price (1994) offer an excellent collection of contributions which analyse the key issues and debates surrounding privatisation and regulation. Prosser's work is also well worth reading. In addition to Prosser (1994) see also his contribution, 'Regulation of Privatised Enterprises', in M. Moran and P. Hancher (eds) *Capitalism, Culture and Regulation* (London: Routledge, 1988), and (with Cosmo Graham) *Privatising Public Enterprises* (Oxford: Oxford University Press, 1991).

Chapter 12

Accountability and redress

Citizens, clients and customers

Introduction

Good systems of government and public administration are properly accountable to the people. Open, transparent and effective processes of accountability are benchmarks against which governing orders can be judged. Systems of government and public administration, which are deemed to be unaccountable or deficient in accountability, are invariably viewed as problematic. In simple terms, in modern democratic states we expect those who exercise power to be held accountable.

Within the British system of public administration an array of mechanisms and devices exists in order to facilitate the operation of accountable government. In due course, we shall examine the functioning of these mechanisms and devices. However, to begin with, we need to establish a secure understanding of accountability, and the connection between this concept and redress of grievances.

Approaches to understanding accountability

Before we attempt to map out some of the conceptual approaches to understanding accountability, some comments should be made about the twin conventions of individual and collective ministerial responsibility, which establish the basic framework of accountability at the top levels of central government, and to some extent influence the modes of accountability in other parts of the British system of public administration.

Collective responsibility implies that in public ministers will support the agreed policies of the government, regardless of their personal reservations, and will respect the confidentiality of discussions which take place within departments, the Cabinet or Cabinet committees. In modern government, this encompasses all ministers, not only those in the Cabinet. Ministers who are unable or unwilling to abide by the terms of this convention should, in theory at least, resign, or run the risk of being dismissed by the Prime Minister. The convention of collective responsibility has been officially suspended on only three occasions:

- 1932 – when the National Government (a coalition) led by Ramsay MacDonald agreed to differ on the issue of import duties;
- 1975 – when the Labour government led by Harold Wilson divided during the referendum on Britain's continued membership of the European Community;
- 1977 – when the Labour government led by James Callaghan divided on the issue of which electoral system should be used in Britain for elections to the European Parliament.

However, the convention has been breached over the years. The publication of ministerial diaries and memoirs breaks the 'confidentiality' element of the convention. Beyond this, ministers have, on occasion, effectively broken the convention by overtly or covertly distancing themselves from aspects of their own government's policy while continuing to sit in the Cabinet. Tony Benn repeatedly made known his disenchantment with the economic policy of both the Wilson and Callaghan governments, Peter Walker and James Prior did the same during the Thatcher administrations, and a group of 'Euro-sceptic' ministers led by John Redwood and Peter Lilley were clearly detached from the Major government's policy towards the European Union.

The key factors which determine whether ministers are likely to be dismissed when they break or strain the convention of collective responsibility include the particular issue at stake, the political weight and standing of the minister concerned, and the attitude and strength of the Prime Minister at any given time.

Individual ministerial responsibility is the second strand of this constitutional convention (for full discussions of this, see Pyper, 1994, 1996). In simple terms, this starts with the fact that ministers have a collection of matters for which they might be said to be responsible. Some of these are associated with the role of being a minister (including policy leadership, management of a government department, piloting legislation through its various Parliamentary stages, and representing the department's interests in Cabinet and with pressure groups and departmental clients), and some are more personal (including the need for ministers to obey the law in their private lives, abide by Parliamentary and governmental rules of conduct, and act in accordance with the uncodified moral expectations of their peers). Ministers are accountable for these 'role' and 'personal' responsibilities to a range of sources, including Parliament (see Chapter 10 for a discussion of the Parliamentary mechanisms used to call ministers to account), their party (at Westminster and in the country) and the government as a whole. The most important line of accountability, of course, is to the Prime Minister, who has the ultimate power to dismiss a minister who has failed in an aspect of his or her role or personal responsibilities. Ministerial resignations (forced and unforced) occasionally stem from this aspect of the convention. However, resignations due to failures in the realm of 'role' responsibilities tend to be less frequent than those caused by weaknesses in the 'personal' sphere. This is perhaps due to the fact that it is usually easier for prime ministers to minimise the embarrassment to their governments by shielding (and later quietly reshuffling) colleagues who are failing to do their jobs properly than it is to escape the consequences of spectacular failings in the private conduct of ministers (for example the 'error of judgement' on Clapham Common which led to the resignation of the Welsh Secretary Ron Davies in October 1998 and the revelations two months later about the financing of a home loan which precipitated the departure of Peter Mandelson and Geoffrey Robinson from their posts as, respectively, Trade and Industry Secretary and Paymaster General).

Now let us move to consider the broader meaning and implications of accountability in government and public administration. This, as we saw in Chapter 1 (Box 1.1), is a key concept in public administration and students have adopted a range of different approaches in an attempt to come to terms with the concept. Some analysts see close links between accountability and the idea of stewardship. According to this perspective, accountability involves a liability to 'present an account of, and answer for, the execution of responsibilities to those entrusting those responsibilities. Thus accountability is intrinsically linked to *stewardship*. . . . Stewardship is established when one party trusts another party with resources and/or responsibilities' (Gray and Jenkins, 1985, p. 138). The 'resources' and 'responsibilities' to which Gray and Jenkins refer can be defined in different ways. At their broadest, they could encompass 'the public interest' (Oliver, 1991, p. 23), or more specifically refer to the duties and expected standards of conduct associated with post-holders or office-holders in public administration ('role' and 'personal' responsibilities, as discussed above, and in Pyper, 1996, pp. 3–5).

However, some other approaches to understanding accountability place less emphasis on the matters *for which* politicians and officials are said to be accountable, and instead stress the importance of the sources *to which*, and the mechanisms *through which*, accountability can be achieved. In a basic sense, this might involve producing catalogues of simple information, as shown in the illustrative example set out in Box 12.1.

Box 12.1 Accountability of government ministers

Accountable for: a broad set of 'role' and 'personal' responsibilities

Accountable to: ministerial colleagues in general, PM in particular; party; Parliament

Accountable via: a range of parliamentary and extra-parliamentary mechanisms including: questions, debates, select committees, standing committees, 'ombudsmen', National Audit Office, courts, inquiries, party fora

---

Catalogues of this type could be used to chart the accountability of central government ministers, civil servants, local government officers and members, NHS managers and executives, and, indeed, any office-holder of any description in the sphere of public administration. Nonetheless, although information of this kind can be useful in a limited way, it is fundamentally descriptive and tends to beg further questions. As a result, attempts are often made to move beyond the compilation of this type of simple catalogue. One move in this direction is normally to seek to identify twin, external and internal lines of accountability, each with associated mechanisms.

External accountability is said to function when politicians or officials are obliged to account for their work to individuals or bodies beyond their own organisations or institutions. An example of this would be the accountability of ministers to Parliament for their departmental responsibilities. This takes place through a range of mechanisms including questions, debates and select committees. Accountability for finance in local government and the National Health Service is secured externally through the work of the Audit Commission and Audit Scotland. Such mechanisms of external accountability might primarily be concerned with the work of politicians, while indirectly touching upon officials (as with the Parliamentary mechanisms cited above) or they might focus on the ultimate accountability of elected office-holders while bringing close scrutiny to bear on the work of officials. Examples here would include the Parliamentary, health service and local government ombudsmen, as well as the agencies of external financial audit, the Audit Commission and Audit Scotland, and the regulatory agencies monitoring the work of public utilities.

On the other hand, internal accountability operates, as one would expect, within organisations or institutions. In central government, this can be seen in relation to a civil servant's accountability to departmental or agency line managers, up to the permanent secretary and/or the agency chief executive, and beyond to ministers. The mechanisms which exist to secure internal accountability vary considerably but include systems of performance appraisal and review which identify key indicators against which the work of officials can be judged. In addition, some mechanisms of internal accountability are specifically designed to meet the requirements of financial management, and these would include delegated budget and resource allocation systems which apply reporting and control procedures to cost centres which have been given decentralised financial powers.

Beyond all of this, some analysts seek to take our understanding of accountability further by discarding either simple catalogues or broad classifications of internal and external accountability, in favour of models and concepts. One example of this would be Elcock's directional model, within which accountability is said to flow upwards, outwards and downwards. Officials may be 'simultaneously accountable *upwards*, ultimately to politicians, *outwards* to professional colleagues and *downwards* to citizens' (Elcock, 1991, p. 162). Although superficially straightforward and attractive, Elcock's model has certain limitations. By leaving politicians out of the analysis (he makes it clear that he intends the model to apply primarily to officials) he avoids some potentially difficult problems, but perhaps sacrifices clarity as a consequence. For example, how should the accountability of ministers to Parliament properly be characterised: as *upward*, *outward* or *downward*? Even in the area of official accountability, the usefulness of this type of directional model would seem to be limited. To say that officials are accountable '*downwards* to citizens' is misleading because constitutional theory in the United Kingdom prescribes precisely the opposite. The conditions of service which govern the work of civil servants specifically preclude the concept of accountability to the people, or even to Parliament (except in limited circumstances).

Arguably a more typical approach to analysing and modelling accountability can be seen in the work of Lawton and Rose who put forward five types of accountability: political, managerial, legal, consumer and professional (1991, p. 23). For them, political accountability can be seen in terms of the traditional concept of Parliamentary accountability, which embraces both brands of ministerial responsibility (individual and collective). Again, there are some attractions in this approach, but also a few problems. Attempts to classify and categorise accountability in this manner tend to suffer from two main disadvantages. Firstly, typologies of accountability tend to minimise elements of conflict and overlap between types. For example, it is entirely possible that a local government officer could experience the conflicting pull of accountability to customers and clients for the effective delivery of a service, and to senior managers for effective budgetary control. Viewing two of the Lawton and Rose types of accountability ('consumer' and 'managerial') in isolation would lead to this kind of potential conflict being ignored. Similar criticisms could be levelled at almost any other configuration of the Lawton and Rose typology. The second main disadvantage with this approach is the sheer inevitability of omission. It is always possible to identify other types of accountability, which have been ignored. For example, the Lawton and Rose typology makes no mention of popular accountability

---

Box 12.2 Some approaches to understanding accountability

'Stewardship' models – e.g. Gray and Jenkins

'Catalogues' – e.g. UK government ministers, example in Box 12.1

'Internal/external' differentiation

'Directional' models – e.g. Elcock: *upwards, outwards, downwards*

'Typologies' – e.g. Lawton and Rose: *political, managerial, legal, consumer* and *professional*

(for more on this, see McConnell, 1996) and the omission of an explicitly ethical or moral dimension has been noted by other commentators (Hinton and Wilson, 1993, p. 129).

Redressing grievances: a component of accountability

It is already clear that the term 'accountability' can be used in different ways. A limited form of accountability, probably best termed 'answerability' or 'explanatory accountability' (see Butler, 1973; Marshall, 1986), involves a commitment, on the part of office-holders (political or official), to provide answers to questions, and nothing more. This rather weak, diluted form of accountability conveys no liability for matters which may have gone wrong. Ministers in British government have come to place great stress on this distinction between explanatory accountability/ answerability and accountability proper. This can be seen, for example, in their preparedness to answer questions about the failures of executive agencies (including the Prison Service Agency until 1997 when ministers again accepted the implications of full accountability, and the Child Support Agency – see Chapter 2) while showing a marked reluctance to see themselves as accountable. In these cases, the agency chief executives are required to 'carry the can'.

A fuller version of accountability, on the other hand, goes beyond a mere commitment to provide answers to questions. Full accountability encompasses explanatory accountability or answerability, but it involves much more besides. Three additional features are present in the full, proper form of accountability.

1   The possibility of sanctions – negative consequences for the office-holder. This might involve displacement, demotion, dismissal in the case of ministers; formal reprimands, financial penalties, demotion or dismissal in the case of civil servants or other public officials.
2   Amendatory accountability – correcting or amending the systems, procedures or behaviour which have contributed to the problem.

3   Redress of grievances – ensuring that those who have suffered as a result of the faulty policy or administrative practice are offered restitution. Depending on the circumstances, and the powers of the adjudicatory body, redress might involve one of a whole range of initiatives, from an apology for inconvenience caused, to financial compensation.

To summarise, we can say that accountability has several components, the first and weakest of which is answerability, or explanatory accountability. The stronger and more complete version of accountability adds to answerability the components of sanctions, amendatory accountability and redress of grievances.

What are the sources of grievances for which citizens might seek redress? Since the 1980s we have been living in an era of the 'shrinking state', with a significant dilution of 'big', assertive government. Nonetheless, government, in its many shapes and forms, still affects the lives of ordinary citizens in ways which would have been inconceivable less than a century ago. In fact, it could be argued that the state has not really 'shrunk' to the extent that we once believed. Reduced numbers of civil servants and public sector workers indicate diminution of some kind, but in other respects it seems that the state has changed shape rather than simply 'shrunk'. Concepts such as the 'hollowing out' of the state (see Chapter 1) show the effects of privatisation, alternative policy delivery systems, Europeanisation and the new public management to have been the transfer of power within the state, as opposed to shrinkage pure and simple.

In this light, it can be seen that the possible institutional and organisational sources of potential grievances are quite varied. It is not only central government departments which have an impact on the lives of ordinary citizens. Indeed, it might be argued that mainstream departments of state touch their lives less now than in the recent past. Of more significance are the Next Steps executive agencies (see Chapter 2). Thus, the Department of Social Security now matters less in terms of direct impact upon citizens than the executive agencies of the DSS, especially the Benefits Agency and the Child Support Agency. Beyond the centre, local authorities and the National Health Service impinge upon people's lives virtually continuously (despite the relative decline in the policy-making autonomy of local government). As we saw in Chapter 11, the former public utilities such as the electricity, gas and water supply industries, and the telecommunications industry, though privatised (with the exception of the Scottish water supply industry), operate within a legal and regulatory framework established by the state, and some of them affect most, if not all, citizens. In addition to all this, as Chapter 8 showed, there is the burgeoning 'quangocracy', the myriad public bodies staffed by ministerial appointees and charged with a range of functions, many of which will have an impact on people's lives.

These are the territories of public administration within which grievances might be generated. The grievances themselves could stem from matters of policy, from the mode of delivery or execution of policy, or from a combination of the two. What channels and mechanisms are available to people seeking redress?

Channels and mechanisms for redress

For the average UK citizen seeking redress for a grievance, the problem is not a lack of channels and mechanisms through which to pursue the matter, but rather the confusing array of options available. With this range of options for securing the redress of grievances, what factors govern the citizen's choice? Of considerable importance will be the nature of the grievance, the source/cause of the grievance, the complainant's knowledge of the system, the quality of advice received by the complainant, and, in some cases, the availability of funds to pursue the grievance using certain mechanisms or channels. In this diverse and complex system some channels and mechanisms are more accessible and stronger than others. Students of the system should be wary of sweeping generalisations which refer indiscriminately to an 'inaccessible and weak system' or to 'watchdogs which bark but do not bite'. The sheer variety and diversity of the system must be given some recognition.

Elected representatives

The most traditional and conventional route for citizens seeking redress of grievances is through their elected representatives at national and local level. Despite the emergence of complementary and alternative channels and mechanisms, there is no evidence to suggest that MPs and councillors are used less frequently or by fewer people than in the past. Indeed, the contrary is true.

Members of Parliament (also Members of the Scottish Parliament, the Welsh Assembly and the Northern Ireland Assembly) and local councillors may be able to secure satisfaction for the complainant by pursuing the matter directly with the relevant authority, or they may guide the complainant to another appropriate channel or mechanism. Elected representatives have a range of options open to them as they pursue constituents' complaints. For example, at central government level, an MP may choose to speak directly with, or write a letter to, the appropriate departmental minister or civil servant. Beyond, this, a Parliamentary question (in either oral or written form) may be asked. MPs' questions relating to the work of executive agencies are answered in writing by the chief executives, and published in Hansard. If these initiatives fail to have matters dealt with satisfactorily, and if the issue is important enough, the MP might then seek to initiate a debate, normally using one of the daily half-hour Adjournment debates at the end of the sitting for this purpose.

The Crichel Down affair, which culminated in 1954, saw the legitimate rights of a group of citizens repeatedly ignored over an extended period by a succession of officials, and illustrated the weakness of an over-reliance on traditional avenues for seeking redress (Nicolson, 1986; Griffith, 1987; Jones, 1993). Nonetheless, seeking redress through elected representatives was a hallmark of the British system, partly because government in this country developed without a distinct system of administrative law and administrative courts, designed to facilitate challenges against the power of the state and secure redress of citizens' grievances. However, the courts have played a part, and an increasingly important part, in the system of redress. Over the past forty years an array of legal and quasi-legal and administrative channels and mechanisms have opened up new opportunities for citizens who need to go beyond their local councillors and MPs in the attempt to secure redress.

UK courts

Although it is much more common for appeals to be directed to tribunals, there are some limited circumstances in which the courts may be used to appeal against the merits of certain types of administrative decision. Judicial remedies include injunctions, declarations and three prerogative orders: *certiorari* (which removes decisions of administrative bodies to the High Court for review); *prohibition* (which requires a public body to desist or refrain from unlawful – *ultra vires* – actions); and *mandamus* (which compels public bodies to perform their statutory duties according to law). Indeed, the courts have become increasingly active in recent years in the realm of judicial review, which is concerned not with the merits or demerits of a decision taken by an administrative authority but with the process by which the decision was reached. In practice, however, this can be a narrow distinction, since the main grounds for seeking judicial review relate to the 'illegality', 'procedural impropriety' or 'unreasonableness or irrationality' of a decision. A court exercising judicial review cannot substitute its own decision for that of the administrative authority, but it can grant certain remedies, including setting aside the original decision.

Cases of judicial review were numbered in tens in the 1960s, in hundreds in the 1970s and 1980s, and in thousands by the 1990s (Butler and Butler, 1994; James, 1996). While most cases (approximately 75 per cent) are directed against local government, and of those directed against central government the great majority (again, approximately 75 per cent) are against the Home Office, the landmark cases which attract most public attention have concerned other parts of the government machine. Two examples are the Laker Airways case and the Pergau Dam case.

In 1977 Sir Freddie Laker sought judicial review of a decision by the Secretary of State for Trade to revoke Laker Airways' licence to operate a service between London and New York. The court ruled that the minister had acted *ultra vires* (beyond his powers) in attempting to give British Airways a monopoly on long-distance flights from the UK, and Laker's licence was restored.

In 1994, a pressure group, the World Development Movement, sought judicial review of the Foreign Secretary's decision to spend money from the overseas development budget on the Pergau Dam project in Malaysia. British support for this project had been linked to arms sales to that country. The High Court ruled that £34 million had been spent illegally, and the Foreign Secretary was obliged to reallocate a further £65.5 million which had been earmarked for similar projects back to the aid budget.

For ordinary citizens, the judicial review route to redress of grievances is fraught with difficulties. Access to the system is difficult due to the limited availability of legal aid and the relatively small number of solicitors with the necessary knowledge and experience to pursue cases. Beyond this, actions for judicial review have a poor 'survival' rate, with only a third allowed by judges to proceed to a final hearing (in some policy areas such as immigration, the figure is even lower, 11 per cent). There are huge variations in the attitude of judges towards judicial review, with some granting over 80 per cent of applicants leave to apply, and others only 20 per cent. Finally, only one in six of the cases which proceed to a final hearing result in a ruling against the administrative authority (O'Donnell, 1996, p. 113).

Administrative tribunals

In some cases, there may be grievances for which there are no judicial remedies; or else leave to seek judicial review has been denied, or, for one reason or another, it is not possible for the complainant to gain access to the courts. In these instances, it may be possible for the grievance to be pursued through an administrative tribunal.

These exist in a wide variety of different forms. Some adjudicate in disputes between individuals or between individuals and private organisations (for example, rent tribunals and industrial tribunals), but most deal with disputes between individuals and public authorities.

The Council on Tribunals, which supervises this sub-system, has responsibility for over 100 different types of tribunal. One type alone, the Social Security Appeal Tribunals, accounts for over 160 bodies. Other types include Income Tax, Disability, National Insurance, Immigration, NHS and Child Support Tribunals. These bodies vary considerably in their composition and modes of operation, but they share the guiding principles which were set out by the 1958 Franks Report, 'openness, fairness and impartiality'. They establish the facts of a case, and apply the relevant rules. It is possible in some cases to appeal against the decision of a tribunal to a superior tribunal, court or the minister (although no appeal is possible in the case of NHS, Social Security and Immigration Tribunals).

The merits of the system for the aggrieved citizen are its relative simplicity, accessibility, informality and cheapness compared with the courts. Additionally, the tribunals offer a degree of detailed expertise in the particular sphere of administrative policy which concerns the complainant. Under the terms of the 1992 Tribunals and Inquiries Act, tribunals are obliged, on request, to provide reasons for their decisions (Turpin, 1995, p. 526).

However, critics point to the increasing tendency on the part of some government departments to substitute the right to an internal departmental review for the right to take complaints to a tribunal. Where tribunals exist, the right of appeal against their decisions is not universal, and they are only required to give reasons for their decisions if requested. There can be considerable delays before cases are heard: Social Security Appeals Tribunals can take over twenty weeks to process cases. The outcome of cases is influenced to some extent by the quality of advice received by the complainant: those who secure legal advice tend to fare better. Furthermore, the relatively informal nature of tribunal hearings compared with the courts should not disguise the fact that the atmosphere still tends to be adversarial. Finally, some critics point to inconsistencies in the decisions reached by tribunals: they place less reliance on precedent than the courts (O'Donnell, 1996, pp. 96–9).

The Lord Chancellor, Lord Irvine, announced a wide-ranging review of the tribunal system in England and Wales in May 2000. In a speech to the Council on Tribunals, he pointed out that the system had grown in a haphazard fashion since the last review, by Franks in 1957, to the point where its diversity had become confusing:

the largest tribunal hears over 300,000 cases a year; some rarely sit. Some are based on a presidential structure, some are regional. Some panels are legally qualified. Some are not. Some are very formal, with legal representation common. Many are not.

(Irvine, 2000)

The Lord Chancellor appointed Sir Andrew Leggatt, a retired appeal court judge, to head the review, and report by March 2001, although no report had been published by the summer of that year.

Inquiries

Public inquiries are held for two broad purposes: to gather information and canvass views about a possible development such as the building of a power station or a new road, or to investigate and report on a past event involving a policy controversy, such as the 'arms for Iraq' affair or prison escapes. The redress of grievance function tends to be associated with the first type of inquiry, although an inquiry into events which involve loss of life, such as the rail crash at Paddington, will also, in part, seek to address (if not redress) the grievances of the relatives of those who died.

Environmental matters feature prominently in the first type of inquiry. The basic format is for an inspector (usually a civil servant or a judge), appointed by the minister, to take evidence from the promoters and objectors, use an expert assessor to evaluate technical issues, and report to the minister, who makes the final decision.

Arguably the most significant environmental public inquiry of modern times was the 1985 inquiry into the building of the Sizewell-B nuclear reactor, which lasted 340 days. In the wake of Sizewell, the government tended to limit the terms of reference of inquiries, or insert special clauses in legislation to take the proposal beyond the scope of an inquiry, or deem legislation to be 'hybrid' (that is, partly public, partly private – as with the Channel Tunnel project), again with the effect of avoiding lengthy public inquiries.

The European Court of Human Rights

Established in 1950, the European Court of Human Rights (ECHR) was charged with the responsibility for protecting certain basic rights, including freedom of speech, assembly and religion, and the right to due process of criminal law. In 1951 Britain ratified the Convention under which the court was set up but it did not incorporate the Convention into UK law until the Blair government secured passage of the Human Rights Act, which came into force in 2000 (a Scots Law equivalent was activated by the Scottish Parliament at the same time).

Even before the Convention's legal incorporation, British citizens had, since 1966, the right to take cases to the European Commission on Human Rights, provided they had first tried and failed to find redress in the British courts. Between 1966 and 2000, the Commission received about 800 cases annually from British citizens, and declared a small number of these 'admissible' to be referred to the Court. By 2000, a

---

Box 12.3 Some British cases at the European Court of Human Rights

1976: *The Little Red School Book*. In the case of *Handyside* v. *the United Kingdom* the Court found that the government was justified in banning this sex education book on the grounds that it was 'an obscene publication'.

1979: *Thalidomide*. The law on contempt of court had to be amended when the Court ruled that an injunction preventing publication of a *Sunday Times* article on birth defects caused by the drug thalidomide violated freedom of expression.

1981: *Closed shops*. Although the right to join a trade union is protected under the Convention, in the case of *Young, James and Webster* v. *the United Kingdom*, the Court held that a closed-shop agreement which forced people to join a union in order to keep their jobs was a violation of the Convention.

1982: *Corporal punishment*. Corporal punishment was abolished in UK state schools as a result of the Court's ruling in *Campbell and Cosans* v. *the United Kingdom* that beating children infringed parents' rights to have their children educated according to their philosophical convictions.

1995: *Death on the Rock*. In *McCann and others* v. *the United Kingdom* the Court ruled that SAS soldiers used unreasonable force and unjustifiably took lives when shooting three suspected IRA terrorists in Gibraltar, and ordered that the British government pay over £38,000 towards the legal fees of the families who had brought the case.

---

total of 133 British cases had been referred to the Court for full hearings (Travis, 1997; Burton, 2000). Box 12.3 provides details of some key British cases referred to the ECHR.

Until the point where the Convention was incorporated into law in the UK, the European Court of Human Rights had formed a fairly remote part of the system for redressing grievances. It dealt with small numbers of cases, and played a part only after all domestic legal avenues had been exhausted; no legal aid was available for those using this mechanism (the process cost on average £30,000 per case), and it took an average of five years for a case to make its way through the system. However, with legal incorporation of the Convention comes the prospect of direct access to the ECHR, and this seems certain to result in significantly increased numbers of British cases being referred.

Ombudsmen

Since 1967, a largely uncoordinated 'system' of ombudsmen has developed in the UK. In general terms, these individuals and their supporting staffs receive complaints about alleged maladministration leading to injustice, investigate where appropriate, reach decisions, and where appropriate recommend redress of proven grievances. The current array of public sector ombudsmen is set out in Box 12.4.

Box 12.4 Who are the ombudsmen?

Parliamentary Commissioner for Administration
Established 1967, investigates complaints against central government departments and agencies. Accessible via MPs.

Scottish Parliamentary Commissioner for Administration
Established 1999, investigates complaints against the Scottish Executive and other bodies responsible for devolved policy matters in Scotland. Accessible via MSPs. Post held by PCA.

Welsh Administration Ombudsman
Established 1999, investigates complaints against the National Assembly for Wales and other bodies responsible for devolved policy matters in Wales. Directly accessible by members of the public. Post held by PCA.

Health Service Ombudsman
Established 1974, investigates complaints relating to administrative matters in the NHS. Also, since 1996, complaints about hospital care and treatment, and complaints about GPs, dentists, pharmacists or opticians providing NHS services. Directly accessible by members of the public. Post (technically three posts, covering NHS in England, Scotland and Wales) held by the PCA.

Commissioners for Local Administration
Established by 1972 and 1973 Local Government Acts. Three CLAs for England, one for Wales, one for Scotland, investigate complaints against local authorities. Since 1988, directly accessible by members of the public.

Parliamentary Commissioner for Northern Ireland and Northern Ireland Commissioner for Complaints
Established 1969, investigate complaints against, respectively, the Northern Ireland Executive and local authorities in Northern Ireland. Since 1972 both posts have been held by one person.

Housing Association Tenants Ombudsman
Established 1993, investigates complaints from the increasing numbers of tenants living in Housing Association accommodation. Directly accessible.

Prison Service Ombudsman and Scottish Prison Complaints Commission
Established 1994, investigate complaints from prisoners. Directly accessible.

The Parliamentary Commissioner for Administration (PCA) was the forerunner of, and the model for, all of the UK ombudsmen (see Gregory and Hutchesson, 1975; Gregory and Pearson, 1992; Seneviratne, 1994), and the comments below on the PCA can be taken as a general guide to the functioning of the ombudsmen collectively.

The PCA receives complaints (through MPs) from members of the public who allege they have sustained injustice through maladministration by central government departments, agencies and associated bodies. The concept of maladministration is rather vague. It was inadequately defined in the 1967 Act and covered in only broad terms by the so-called 'Crossman Catalogue' ('bias, neglect, inattention, delay, incompetence, inaptitude, perversity, turpitude, arbitrariness and so on') enunciated by the Leader of the Commons who steered the legislation through. However, in practice successive Commissioners have exercised discretion when interpreting the term. The PCA also has responsibility for overseeing 'open government' initiatives, and can receive complaints about the unavailability of certain types of information.

If satisfied that the complaint falls within the appropriate jurisdiction, and is related to an appropriate department or agency, and that there is no alternative avenue of redress open to the complainant, the PCA launches an investigation. This might involve questioning civil servants and ministers, and examining all relevant documents (with the exception of Cabinet papers which are covered by the 'Thirty Year Rule' which governs the release of certain state papers). As with all ombudsmen, the PCA will seek to achieve a 'local settlement' if at all possible, although the Commissioners for Local Administration seem to be flexible in this respect. If an investigation is carried through to a conclusion, without a prior settlement, a report will be filed which will generally reach one of four conclusions:

- no maladministration;
- no maladministration, but some need for faulty administrative arrangements to be amended;
- maladministration, but no significant harm or injustice to the complainant;
- maladministration involving harm or injustice – in which case appropriate redress will be recommended.

The case trends in relation to the PCA are set out in Box 12.5. The significant increase in cases received since 1993 can largely be attributed to the impact of the Child Support Agency, a new executive agency which generated high numbers of complaints, coupled with the cumulative impact of civil service staff cuts, which have reduced the quality of service delivered to the public.

Most of the cases handled by the PCA concern matters of relatively low-level managerial or administrative failure (or alleged failure). However, in the years since 1967 a number of very high-profile cases have raised significant political issues. Of these, three can be mentioned briefly:

- the Sachsenhausen Case, 1967, in which the Foreign Office had repeatedly denied payment to a group of former British prisoners of war who claimed that they came within the terms of the government's compensation scheme for inmates of Nazi concentration camps;

Box 12.5 The Parliamentary Commissioner for Administration: case trends

- Since 1967, the trend has been for steadily increasing numbers of complaints to be received. However, only 10–15 per cent of complaints were upheld in the early years.
- Large numbers of cases are screened out before investigations begin, and a small number of investigations are started, then discontinued.
- Most cases relate to the executive agencies of the Department of Social Security, and the Inland Revenue.
- In 1999–2000, out of 313 cases fully investigated, 291 complaints (93 per cent) were found to be 'justified' or 'partly justified'.

Cases received

1990:	704
1991:	801
1992:	945
1993:	986
1994:	1,332
1995:	1,706
1996:	1,933
1997–8:	1,459
1998–9:	1,506
1999–2000:	1,612

Sources: Gregory and Pearson, 1992; Parliamentary Commissioner for Administration, 1999

- the Barlow Clowes Case, 1989, in which the collapse of a financial investment company which had been issued with a licence by the Department of Trade and Industry brought financial ruin to thousands of investors;
- the Channel Tunnel Rail Link Case, 1995, in which the Department of Transport had refused to consider offering financial compensation to property owners suffering exceptional hardship due to the blight on property prices caused by the rail link.

In each of these cases, the government explicitly rejected the PCA's conclusions, but in the first two it reluctantly agreed to respect his findings and redress was delivered through compensation payments to the complainants. From the perspective of the citizen seeking redress, the Parliamentary Commissioner for Administration, and indeed, the broad system of ombudsmen, is attractive in many respects, although there are also some potential drawbacks. The advantages and disadvantages are summarised in Box 12.6.

Box 12.6 Ombudsmen: advantages and disadvantages

Advantages

THEY COVER A VERY WIDE RANGE OF PUBLIC BODIES
They reach parts of the system other mechanisms (courts/tribunals) cannot reach.

CHEAP TO USE
The service is free.

NO NEED FOR LEGAL ADVICE

PROCESS IS CONCILIATORY, NOT ADVERSARIAL
There is no need for potentially intimidating public appearances by complainants.
Those called to give evidence are guaranteed anonymity.

RECOMMENDATIONS ARE ADHERED TO (LARGELY)

'RIPPLE' EFFECT
The finding in one case may affect many other people with similar cases.

Disadvantages

POORLY PUBLICISED
Although some ombudsmen make greater efforts than others, in general the system is
not well publicised.

PASSIVE NATURE
Ombudsmen must await complaints – they cannot initiate inquiries themselves.

JURISDICTIONAL LIMITATIONS
Some important spheres of government activity, including contractual and commercial
transactions, are excluded, as are matters which may be pursued through the courts
or tribunals.

PROBLEMS OF ACCESS
While most ombudsmen are directly accessible via letters or even telephone calls from
complainants, the Parliamentary Commissioner still functions thorough the 'MP filter'.

NO LEGAL POWERS OF ENFORCEMENT
Only in Northern Ireland can complainants take public authorities to court to enforce
an ombudsman's decision.

NATURE OF THE POST-HOLDERS
They tend to come from the world they are investigating (former civil servants or local
government officers). While this might be an advantage in terms of their knowledge
and expertise, it could mean they have a natural tendency to sympathise with
officialdom.

DELAYS IN REACHING DECISIONS
In the case of the Parliamentary Commissioner, the average time taken to conclude an
investigation is over seventy weeks.

Miscellaneous channels and mechanisms

Beyond the channels and mechanisms already surveyed, there is a collection of miscellaneous bodies such as the consumers' councils and regulatory agencies which oversee the work of the former public utilities. For example, in the sphere of the gas and electricity supply industries, the Office of Gas and Electricity Markets (OFGEM) enforces the pricing formulae and ensures that the regionally based Gas and Electricity Consumer Councils settle customers' complaints and secure redress of grievances wherever possible. The consumer councils generally lack enforcement powers, however, and are perceived to be rather weak watchdogs, while the more powerful regulatory agencies are mainly concerned with pricing issues.

Mention should also be made of internal complaints systems, of the kind exemplified by the Police Complaints Authority, which supervises the internal police investigations of serious complaints. Again, the criticism is that this is a rather weak mechanism, since those who are the subject of a complaint are responsible for organising what is at best a semi-independent investigation (that is, investigation by officers from another police force) under the auspices of a body (the Police Complaints Authority) which lacks serious enforcement powers.

Charters and *Service First*

The *Citizen's Charter* was launched in 1991, as a means of improving aspects of public service delivery. The *Charter* spawned numerous spin-offs, including the Chartermark scheme, which was designed to acknowledge high standards of service provision in the public sector by rewarding individuals and organisations annually. The entire Charter project was relaunched and refocused by the Blair government as *Service First* in June 1998 (Cabinet Office, 1998d). This is not a channel or mechanism for redressing grievances as such. It does not establish new systems for securing redress, and it provides no machinery for overturning decisions, but instead seeks to facilitate the improved functioning of, and shed fresh light upon, existing mechanisms and channels, including internal complaints systems. The Charter set out six 'Principles of Public Service', which were later expanded and developed under *Service First* (see Box 12.7).

One of the Principles is 'putting things right', and refers to the need for public authorities to provide apologies, explanations and swift remedies when things go wrong. Additionally, well-publicised and accessible complaints procedures must be put in place, and independent review systems organised wherever possible. In 1993, a Complaints Task Force composed of 'outsiders' began providing advice to public sector organisations regarding the establishment and improvement of their internal complaints systems.

This entire initiative is coordinated by the Service First Unit, based within the Cabinet Office, and the framework of ideas contained in the original Charter has been disseminated by the Unit. All public sector organisations produce their own Charters, setting out the rights of their service-users, together with quality of service and performance standards. There is now a plethora of these documents, and many of the Charters have regional variations. The Charters cover all public service-users,

243

Box 12.7 *Service First* principles of public service delivery

(These built upon and expanded the existing *Citizen's Charter* principles)

- SET STANDARDS OF SERVICE
- BE OPEN AND PROVIDE FULL INFORMATION
- CONSULT AND INVOLVE
- ENCOURAGE ACCESS AND THE PROMOTION OF CHOICE
- TREAT ALL FAIRLY
- PUT THINGS RIGHT WHEN THEY GO WRONG
- USE RESOURCES EFFECTIVELY
- INNOVATE AND IMPROVE
- WORK WITH OTHER PROVIDERS

Redressing citizens' grievances by 'putting things right':

'If things go wrong, an apology, a full explanation and a swift and effective remedy. Well publicized and easy-to-use complaints procedures, with independent review wherever possible.'

---

from taxpayers to rail-users, Child Support Agency clients to jobseekers, council tenants to NHS patients, London Underground users to college and university students, and so on.

Although a government review in 1996 praised the Charter's achievements (Prime Minister, 1996), some observers viewed Charterism as a triumph of style over substance, pointing to the initiative's limited definition of citizenship (citizens as mere consumers), the fact that service standards are set by the service providers themselves and are not legally enforceable, the failure to create genuinely new mechanisms of accountability and redress, and the elements of farce such as the abortive telephone helpline Charterline and the widely mocked Cones Hotline (see Falconer and Ross, 1999, for a summary of the main political and academic arguments surrounding the Charter). The opposition parties supported the idea of improved answerability and better service delivery and Labour even argued that the Major government had 'stolen' the Charter concept from the customer contract initiatives within some Labour-controlled local authorities. Once in power, Labour's approach was to replace the 'top-down' system it had inherited from the Conservatives with a 'bottom-up' approach. In simple terms, this meant the existing Charters were seen as having been the property of the service providers, drawn up with little or no consultation with those who use the services. New charters would be drawn up in consultation with the public, and the vague statements and easily achievable targets of old would be replaced with clear information about the 'outcomes' service-users should expect, together with meaningful indicators of service quality (Cabinet Office, 1998d). Under the *Service First* programme, new principles of public service delivery were published, building upon the existing charter principles (see Box 12.7). All existing Charters would be reviewed, and replaced with new versions. A new audit team would continually monitor the quality of Charters, while the Charter Mark scheme would be made more rigorous. The first indication of progress on this front came when the Passport Agency, which had held a Charter Mark since 1992, was stripped of the award in the summer of 1999 following weeks of chaos in its operations and a backlog of around 500,000 passport applications. Although some organisations had voluntarily given up their Charter Marks in the past, or failed to have them renewed after the initial three-year period, this was the first instance of an award being removed.

Despite the criticisms, it can be argued that the impact of Charterism has been generally positive. It has obliged the providers of public services 'to engage directly with the question of service standard and service quality' (Falconer, 1996, p. 197) and created a system wherein public service managers are obliged to answer to service-users (a form of accountability) for the performance of their organisations and for the use they have made of public resources.

Conclusion: emerging themes in the modernisation of accountability

If we stand aside from the details of particular accountability mechanisms and devices, it is possible to discern some broad themes and issues surrounding the functioning of accountability in British public administration. As with the institutions of government, the processes of accountability have been subjected to a certain degree of modernisation, although it would be wrong to argue that there has been a coherent plan for this. Instead, modernisation in the realm of accountability has been driven by other, wider changes in British governance: in particular, by the increasing application of managerial approaches to public administration.

Proponents of the new public management (see Chapter 1) tended to denigrate what they described as 'traditional' systems of accountability. In fact, when examining accountability, these critics normally failed to look beyond the conventions of ministerial responsibility, and ignored the complexities of the various devices, mechanisms and processes functioning at all levels of the system. The subtleties of accountability, even within the so-called 'traditional' systems of government and public administration, were played down. A negative conclusion was usually reached without too much difficulty, and 'the perceived failure of the system of accountability under the traditional model of public administration' was identified as 'a major reason for the adoption of managerialism' (Hughes, 1998, p. 234). According to this perspective, accountability was 'a major factor' in the managerial reforms introduced by the Thatcher governments.

Impartial observers would encounter two basic problems with this type of argument, quite apart from the crudely oversimplified version of 'traditional' accountability which it adopts. Firstly, the founding ideas and concepts of the new public management paid relatively little attention to issues of accountability, but placed significant emphasis on the achievement of 'value for money', 'quality' improvements to services and the adoption of micro-management techniques and processes derived from private sector practice. A quick glance at the Thatcherite managerial reforms, typified by the Next Steps initiative which, as we saw in Chapter 2, brought about a basic restructuring of the civil service, reveals an absence of detailed thought about accountability. Indeed, as we note below, the relegation of accountability issues to a relatively minor place in the scheme of things produced some serious problems as the Next Steps programme was implemented. Secondly, the types and forms of accountability which were of interest to the proponents of the new public management were fairly narrowly focused. While the improvement of accountability in any form should not be dismissed as an insignificant objective, it should be noted that the new public management had a tendency to emphasise particular strains of accountability, such as internal managerial and external 'consumerist' accountability at the expense of other, potentially more powerful forms.

There were both advantages and disadvantages associated with the importance attached to these 'modern' forms of accountability.

Four positive developments can be noted:

1   The improvement of internal lines of accountability, particularly in relation to financial matters, to senior managers and ultimately to politicians. This was achieved in central government through a range of schemes under the umbrella of the Financial Management Initiative, including devolved budgeting (see Chapter 2). The emergence of resource accounting and budgeting represented a further development of this type of internal accountability, which led to the emergence of much clearer and more open relationships of accountability between middle managers on the one hand, and senior officials and ministers on the other. Further emphasis was given to these matters within central government under the Next Steps initiative, as seen in Chapter 2. The executive agencies which emerged from this operated within a context set out in Framework Documents, which contained specific statements about the lines of internal accountability which would prevail within the agencies and between the agencies and parent departments.

2   The enhancement of official accountability to Parliament through a series of changes which led to the creation of a broader and, arguably, more meaningful concept of ministerial responsibility. It has been argued (see, for example, Pyper, 1996, Chapter 2) that the 'new regime' of parliamentary accountability which developed in the period from the mid-1960s owed its origins to a combination of key contributory factors. In simple terms, this 'new regime' saw the traditional mechanisms of parliamentary scrutiny (informal contacts, Parliamentary questions, debates, standing committees, the Public Accounts Committee and the array of uncoordinated and rather disjointed select committees) supplemented by the modern, more systematic select committees (from 1966 onwards, but especially following the major reform of 1979) and the Parliamentary Commissioner for Administration (from 1967). As they developed, these mechanisms came to offer a much wider range of Parliamentary scrutiny over the executive than had ever existed before (Drewry, 1988; Gregory and Pearson, 1992). In most cases, the introduction of the Next Steps executive agencies also served to clarify the respective roles, responsibilities and parliamentary lines of accountability of ministers and civil servants (although problems arose in specific cases, as noted below).

3   The increasing emphasis given to grassroots accountability to 'clients', 'customers' or 'consumers'. To a considerable extent, this was epitomised by the emergence of Charterism, and the *Service First* programme, discussed above. As a supplement to more remote and distant forms of accountability, this was a positive development, although, as we noted, there were some concerns about the specific strengths and weaknesses of the accountability systems produced by Charters, and the apparent strains and contradictions produced by the new emphasis on direct official accountability to service users.

4   The creation of modern regulatory regimes in parts of the public sector which had previously been badly served by rather diffuse, weak and distinctly problematic forms of accountability. This could be seen most clearly in the public utilities (see Chapter 11).

These positive points were balanced to some extent by the negative consequences of some of the more 'modern' approaches to accountability.

1   There was a marked tendency to promote certain types of accountability at the expense of others. Thus, while less importance was attached to traditional forms of popular accountability, increasing emphasis was given to account-ability upwards to central government and to particular, and quite narrow, strains of accountability to 'consumers'. One example of this was in the water and sewerage service in Scotland. This was removed from the ambit of local authorities and reconfigured as a service delivered by quangos accountable to central government. Effectively, a more remote form of accountability was substituted for a localised one. Although there were some sensible managerial reasons for this reorganisation, it undoubtedly diluted a specific form of accountability.

2   Problems arose from the attempts to differentiate between forms and types of accountability, in order to give particular emphasis to such concepts as managerial and consumer accountability. In part, this resulted from the belief that public sector functions and operations could be clearly divided into matters of 'policy' and 'management', a division which confronts the policy/administration dichotomy (see Chapter 1). However, the attempt to make the concept of accountability divisible, through giving emphasis to supposedly distinct strands of political, managerial, consumer and other brands of account-ability, is inherently flawed and runs the risk of creating accountability gaps and vacuums. Clear illustrations of the problems this can cause came in some of the executive agencies established under the Next Steps initiative (see Chapter 2). The accountability problems arising in these cases were explicitly recognised when the Labour Party returned to power in 1997. The Child Support Agency was subjected to much closer ministerial oversight through a medium- to long-term process of review, while the Home Secretary announced that the accountability arrangements for the Prison Service were to be changed, with ministers assuming full responsibility for accounting to Parliament for this area of public policy and management.

3   Even in areas where modern approaches to accountability have had broadly positive outcomes, including the moves towards enhanced accountability to

customers, clients and service-users within the Charterist and consumerist initiatives, some caution is required. Charterism and *Service First* offer service-users opportunities to have much more information about the types and quality of service they should expect from public sector organisations. They also promote the development of clear, easy-to-use complaints systems. In these respects, the modern approaches certainly promote answerability or explanatory accountability. The principle of 'putting things right' is embedded in the Charters, and this signifies a commitment to redressing grievances and taking amendatory actions to ensure there is no repetition of the same failing. However, the forms of redress available vary quite considerably, and at their weakest the Charters fail to recognise the need for financial compensation. Charter commitments are not enforceable by law, which means that service-users who are still unhappy about the redress offered after successfully pursuing a complaint, have no further recourse available. Furthermore, the extent to which amendatory actions are taken in order to avoid any future recurrence of the same failing also varies, and there is no force compelling such actions. In general, therefore, while undoubtedly enhancing the weaker forms of accountability, including answerability and the milder forms of redress, the Charters are relatively weak in terms of the stronger forms of accountability, including sanctions.

4   Other elements of the modern, 'consumerist' approach to public service delivery, especially the concept of 'contractualism', raised accountability problems. The general implication of such initiatives as compulsory competitive tendering, market testing, Best Value, internal markets, purchaser/provider splits, and the Private Finance Initiative for accountability was a muddying of the waters. The most obvious effect of 'contractualism' has been to insert additional organisations, in the form of the contractors directly delivering the service or facility, into the accountability relationships. Therefore, as well as the service-users and the public sector provider, there are issues surrounding the accountability of the direct deliverer of the service, for example the company holding the contract for refuse collection within a local authority area, the firm responsible for the cleaning service within an NHS Trust, or the in-house team which has secured the catering contract for schools and colleges. The result has been the creation of situations wherein the bodies responsible for direct delivery of services are formally accountable not to the service-users but to the contracting authorities. Service-users seeking redress for an inadequate level of service provision have to take their case to the contracting authority, which then seeks redress from the contractor. Whatever else might be said about such arrangements, they are not designed primarily to promote the full openness, transparency and speed of redress which are the hallmarks of all effective systems of accountability.

On the whole, therefore, the effect of more modern approaches to account-ability, with their increased stress on the importance of customers, clients and consumers, has been mixed. In some respects, there would seem to have been a definite weakening of systems of accountability, largely caused by the creation of new imperatives (including the separation of policy and management and matters of financial management) which have come to override the importance of accountability. However, in other respects matters are not quite so clear, and the general impact would seem to have been an improved functioning of systems of accountability. This is especially obvious in the new and improved regimes of accountability in the realm of the former public utilities and the strengthening of civil service accountability (in some respects at least) brought about by the executive agencies and associated developments.

Further reading

The theoretical and conceptual aspects of accountability and redress are discussed in Marshall (1986), Lawton and Rose (1991), Oliver (1991) and Pyper (1996). The specific mechanisms and channels of redress have their own extensive range of sources. Of particular use is Seneviratne (1994) on the ombudsmen. Original documents, as well as general factual information, are now easily accessible via a range of web sites, including www.echr.coe.int for the European Court of Human rights, www.parliament.ombudsman.org.uk for the Parliamentary Commissioner for Administration, and www.cabinet-office.gov.uk/servicefirst for charters and *Service First*.

Bibliography

Alderman, R.K. (1995) 'A Defence of Frequent Ministerial Turnover', *Public Administration*, 73, 4: 497–512.

Armstrong, H. (1997) 'Five Sides to a New Leaf', *Municipal Journal*, 4 July: 18–19.

Armstrong, H. (1999) 'Key Themes of Democratic Renewal', *Local Government Studies* 25, 4: 19–25.

Armstrong Memorandum (1985) Sir R. Armstrong, 'A Note of Guidance on the Duties and Responsibilities of Civil Servants in Relation to Ministers' (reproduced in P. Barberis (1996) *The Whitehall Reader*, Buckingham: Open University Press).

Atkinson, M. (1999) 'Inquiry to Look at PFI', *Guardian*, 20 September.

Audit Commission (1984) *Improving Economy, Efficiency and Effectiveness in Local Government in England and Wales*, London: HMSO.

Ayres, I. and Braithwaite, J. (1994) *Responsive Regulation*, Oxford: Oxford University Press.

Bagehot, W. [1867] (1963) *The English Constitution*, London: Fontana.

Baggott, R. (1998) *Health and Health Care in Britain* (second edn), London: Macmillan.

Bains Committee (1972) *The New Local Authorities: Management and Structure*, London: HMSO.

Baldwin, Nicholas D.J. (1995) 'The House of Lords and the Labour Government 1974–79', *Journal of Legislative Studies* 1, 2.

Barberis, P. (1996a) *The Elite of the Elite: Permanent Secretaries in the British Higher Civil Service*, Aldershot: Dartmouth.

Barberis, P. (1996b) *The Whitehall Reader*, Buckingham: Open University Press.

Barberis, P. (1997) *The Civil Service in an Era of Change*, Aldershot: Dartmouth.

Barberis, P. (2000) 'Prime Minister and Cabinet', in R. Pyper and L. Robins (eds) *United Kingdom Governance*, London: Macmillan: 14–38.

Barker, A. (1998) 'Political Responsibility for UK Prison Security – Ministers Escape Again', *Public Administration* 76, 1: 1–23.

Barker, A. (2000) 'Invite to the Party', in A. Barker with I. Byrne and A. Veall, *Ruling by Task Force; Politico's Guide to Labour's New Elite*, London: Politico's Publishing.

Barker, A. with Byrne, I. and Veall, A. (2000) *Ruling by Task Force; Politico's Guide to Labour's New Elite*, London: Politico's Publishing.

Beetham, D. (1996), 'Theorising Democracy and Local Government', in D. King and G. Stoker (eds) *Rethinking Local Democracy*, London: Macmillan: 28–49.

Bellamy, C. (1999) 'Exploiting Information and Communications Technologies', in S. Horton and D. Farnham (eds) *Public Management in Britain*, London: Macmillan: 128–41.

Benn, T. (1982) *Arguments for Democracy,* Harmondsworth: Penguin.

Benson, L., Bruce, A. and Forbes, T. (2000) 'Reforming the National Health Service: Comparing Developments in England and Scotland', *Faculty of Business Working Paper No. 27,* Glasgow: Glasgow Caledonian University.

Berrill, Sir K. (1985) 'Strength at the Centre: the Case for a Prime Minister's Department', in A. King (ed.) *The British Prime Minister* (second edn), London: Macmillan: 242–57.

Bishop, J. and Hoggett, P. (1986) *Organising around Enthusiasms: Mutual Aid in Leisure,* London: Comedia.

Blair, T. (1998) *Leading the Way: a New Vision for Local Government*, London: Institute for Public Policy.

Bloch, A. (1992) *The Turnover of Local Councillors*, York: Joseph Rowntree Foundation.

Bogdanor, V. (1988) *Against the Overmighty State: a Future for Local Government in Britain,* London: Federal Trust for Education and Research.

Boyce, D.G. (1996) *The Irish Question and British Politics 1868–1996*, Harlow: Longman.

Boyne, G. (1999) 'Introduction: Processes, Performance and Best Value in Local Government', *Local Government Studies* 25, 2: 1–15.

Brazier, R. (1991) *Constitutional Reform: Reshaping the British Political System*, Oxford: Oxford University Press.

Brown, G. (1972) *In My Way,* Harmondsworth: Penguin.

Bruce, A. (1997) 'Competitive Markets in the National Health Service', *Talking Politics*, 9, 3: 184–8.

Bruce, A. and Jonsson, E. (1996) *Competition in the Provision of Health Care. The Experience of the US, Sweden and Britain*, Aldershot: Arena.

Budge, I. and McKay, D. (1993) *The Developing British Political System: the 1990s*, Harlow: Longman.

Bulpitt, J. (1993) Review in *Public Administration* 71, 4: 621–3.

Burch, M. and Holliday, I. (1996) *The British Cabinet System*, Hemel Hempstead: Harvester Wheatsheaf.

Burch, M. and Holliday, I. (1999) 'The Prime Minister's and Cabinet Offices: an Executive Office in All But Name', *Parliamentary Affairs*, 52, 1: 33–45.

Burnham, J. and Jones, G. (2000) 'The Evolving Prime Minister's Office: 1868–1997', in R.A.W. Rhodes (ed.) *Transforming British Government*, vol. 1: *Changing Institutions,* London: Macmillan: 176–91.

Burton, C. (2000) 'Human Rights Coming Home at Last', *New Statesman,* 25 September: 18–19.

Butcher, T. (1998) 'The Blair Government and the Civil Service: Continuity and Change', *Teaching Public Administration*, XVIII, 1: 1–14.

Butcher, T. (2000), 'The Civil Service Structure and Management', in R. Pyper and L. Robins (eds) *United Kingdom Governance*, London: Macmillan: 61–81.

Butler, D. (1973) 'Ministerial Responsibility in Australia and Britain', *Parliamentary Affairs*, 26, 4.

Butler, D. and Butler, G. (1994) *British Political Facts 1900–1994*, London: Macmillan.

Cabinet Office (1992) *Questions of Procedure for Ministers,* London: Cabinet Office.

Cabinet Office (1996) *Government Direct*, Cm 3438, London: HMSO.

Cabinet Office (1997) *Opening up Quangos*, London: Cabinet Office.

Cabinet Office (March 1997) *Next Steps Briefing Note March 1997*, London: Cabinet Office.

Cabinet Office (July 1997) *Ministerial Code: a Code of Conduct and Guidance on Procedures for Ministers,* London: Cabinet Office.

Cabinet Office (October 1997) *Next Steps Briefing Note October 1997*, London: Cabinet Office.

Cabinet Office (1998a) *The 1997 Next Steps Report,* Cm 3889, London: The Stationery Office.

Cabinet Office (1998b) *Public Bodies 1998*, London: The Stationery Office.

Cabinet Office (1998c) *Quangos: Opening the Doors*, London: Cabinet Office.

Cabinet Office (1998d) *Service First: the New Charter Programme*, London: Cabinet Office.

Cabinet Office (September 1998) *Next Steps Briefing Note September 1998*, London: Cabinet Office.

Cabinet Office (1999a) *Modernising Parliament: Reforming the House of Lords,* Cm 4183, London: The Stationery Office.

Cabinet Office (1999b) *Public Bodies 1999*, London: The Stationery Office.

Cabinet Office (November 1999) *List of Ministerial Responsibilities Including Agencies*, London: Cabinet Office (also available at www.cabinet-office.gov.uk/central/2000/minister.htm).

Cabinet Office (2000a) *Civil Service Statistics 1999*, London: Cabinet Office.

Cabinet Office (2000b) *Fast Stream Recruitment Report 1999–2000*, London: Cabinet Office.

Cabinet Office (2000c) *Public Bodies 2000*, London: Cabinet Office.

Cabinet Office (November 2000) 'Civil Service Staff in Post – Summary Table at 1 April 2000' (at www.cabinet-office.gov.uk/civilservice/statistics/qsr/qsr.htm).

Callaghan, Lord (1996) 'Whitehall under One Party Rule', in P. Barberis *The Whitehall Reader*, Buckingham: Open University Press: 75–8.

Carter, N. (1994), 'Performance Indicators: "Backseat Driving" or "Hands off" Control?' in D. McKevitt and A. Lawton, *Public Sector Management*, London Sage: 208–19.

Castle, B. (1980) *The Castle Diaries 1974–76*, London: Weidenfeld & Nicolson.

Catterall, P. and Brady, C. (2000) 'The Development and Role of Cabinet Committees in Britain', in R.A.W. Rhodes (ed.) *Transforming British Government*, vol. 1: *Changing Institutions*, London: Macmillan:156–75.

Cawson, A. (1977) 'Environmental Planning and the Politics of Corporatism', Working Papers in Urban and Regional Studies, No. 7, University of Sussex.

Chandler, J.A. (1988) *Public Policy-Making for Local Government,* London: Croom Helm.

Chapman, R.A. (1988) *Ethics in the British Civil Service,* London: Routledge.

Chapman, R.A. (1992) 'The End of the Civil Service?', *Teaching Public Administration*, XII, 2: 1–5.

Chapman, R. A. (1997)'The End of the British Civil Service', in P. Barberis (ed.) *The Civil Service in an Era of Change*, Aldershot: Dartmouth: 23–37.

Chapman, R.A. (1999) 'The Importance of "Modernising Government"', *Teaching Public Administration,* XIX, 1: 1–18.

Chapman, R.A. (2000) 'Recruitment to the Civil Service Fast Stream Development Programme', *Public Policy and Administration*, 15, 1: 3–14.

Chester, Sir Norman (1979) 'Fringe Bodies, Quangos and All That', *Public Administration,* 57, 1: 51–4.

Clark, A. (1993) *Diaries*, London: Weidenfeld & Nicolson.

Clarke, M. and Stewart, J. (1988) *The Enabling Council*, Luton: LGTB.

Clarke, Sir R. (1975) 'The Machinery of Government', in W. Thornhill (ed.) *The Modernisation of British Government*, London: Pitman: 63–95.

Clegg, S. (1990) *Modern Organizations: Organization Studies in the Postmodern World*, London: Routledge.

Clifford, C., McMillan, A. and McLean, I. (1997) *The Organisation of Central Government Departments: a History 1964–92*, Oxford: Nuffield College, 3 vols in 5 parts.

Cochrane, A. (1993) *Whatever Happened to Local Government?,* Buckingham: Open University Press.

Cockburn, C. (1977) *The Local State*, London: Pluto.

Cockerell, M., Hennessy, P. and Walker, D. (1984) *Sources Close to the Prime Minister,* London: Macmillan.

Cohen, N. (1999) 'How Britain Mortgaged the Future', *New Statesman,* 18 October: 25–7.

COI (1997) *Our Information Age: the Government's Vision,* London: Central Office of Information.

Cole, M. (1998) 'Quasi-government in Britain: the Origins, Persistence and Implications of the Term "Quango"', *Public Policy and Administration,* 13, 1: 65–78.

Committee of Public Accounts (2000) 24th Report 1999–2000, *The Passport Delays of Summer 1999,* HC 208, London: The Stationery Office.

Consultative Steering Group (1999) *Shaping Scotland's Parliament,.* Edinburgh: The Stationery Office.

Cowley, P. (2000) 'Legislatures and Assemblies', in P. Dunleavy, A. Gamble, I. Holliday and G. Peele (eds) *Developments in British Politics 6,* London: Macmillan: 109–26.

Craig, P. (1999) *Administrative Law* (fourth edn), London: Sweet and Maxwell.

Cram, L., Dinan, D. and Nugent, N. (1999) *Developments in the European Union,* London: Macmillan.

Crossman, R.H.S. (1963) 'Introduction', in W. Bagehot, *The English Constitution,* London: Fontana.

Crossman, R. H. S. (1975) *The Diaries of a Cabinet Minister,* vol. I, London: Hamilton and Cape.

Davies, M.R. (2000) 'Concluding Thoughts: Perspectives on Training and Education for the Public Service', in Davies, M.R. *et al.* (eds) *Serving the State: Global Public Administration, Education and Training,* vol. 2: *Diversity and Change,* Aldershot: Ashgate: 185–94.

Davies, M.R., Greenwood, J.R., Robins, L. and Walkely, N. (eds) (1998) *Serving the State: Global Public Administration Education and Training,* vol. 1: *The Anglo-American Tradition,* Aldershot: Ashgate.

Davies, M.R., Greenwood, J.R., Robins, L. and Walkely, N. (eds) (2000) *Serving the State: Global Public Administration Education and Training,* vol. 2: *Diversity and Change,* Aldershot: Ashgate.

Davis, G. (1997) 'Executive Co-ordinating Mechanisms', in P. Weller, H. Bakvis and R.A.W Rhodes (eds) *The Hollow Crown: Countervailing Trends in Core Executives,* London: Macmillan: 126–47.

Day, P. and Klein, R. (1987) *Accountabilities; Five Public Services,* London: Tavistock.

Dearlove, J. (1973) *The Politics of Policy in Local Government,* Cambridge: Cambridge University Press.

Denham, A. and Garnett, M. (1999) 'Influence Without Responsibility? Think-Tanks in Britain', *Parliamentary Affairs,* 52, 1: 46–57.

Department of Health (1989) *Working for Patients,* Cm 555, London: HMSO.

Department of Health (1997) *The New NHS: Modern, Dependable,* Cm 3807, London: The Stationery Office.

Department of Health (1998) *Departmental Report, April 1998*: the Government's Expenditure Plans 1998–99, Cm 3912, London: The Stationery Office.

Department of Health (2000) *The NHS Plan – a Plan for Investment. A Plan for Reform,* Cm 4818, London: The Stationery Office.

Department of Health and Social Services Northern Ireland (1999) *Fit for the Future: A New Approach,* Belfast: DHSSNI.

DETR (1998a) *Modern Local Government: in Touch with the People,* London: Department of the Environment, Transport and the Regions.

DETR (1998b) *Modernising Local Government: Local Democracy and Community Leadership,* Consultation Paper, London: DETR.

DETR (1999a) *Local Government Finance Key Facts: England,* London: Department of the Environment, Transport and the Regions.

DETR (1999b) *Local Leadership: Local Choice*, Cm 4298, London: The Stationery Office.

DETR (2000) *Local Government Employment Digest*, January.

DETR (March 2000) *Local Government Statistics Key Facts: England*, London: DETR.

Dinan, D. (1999) *Ever Closer Union. An Introduction to European Integration* (second edn), London: Macmillan.

Doig, A. (1979) 'The Machinery of Government and the Growth of Governmental Bodies', *Public Administration,* 59, 3: 309–31.

Dopson, S., Locock, L. and Stewart, R. (1999) Regional Offices in the New NHS: an Analysis of the Effects and Significance of Recent Changes', *Public Administration*, 77, 1: 91–110.

Draper, P. (1977) *Creation of the DOE*, London: HMSO.

Drewry, G. (ed.) (1985) *The New Select Committees. A Study of the 1979 Reforms*, Oxford: Clarendon.

Drewry, G. (ed.) (1988) *The New Select Committees. A Study of the 1979 Reforms* (second edn), Oxford: Clarendon.

Drewry, G. and Butcher, T. (1991) *The Civil Service Today* (second edn), London: Blackwell.

du Gay, P. (2000) *In Praise of Bureaucracy*, London: Sage.

Duggett, M. (1996) 'Training Civil Servants for Change', *Teaching Public Administration*, XVI, 1: 54–64.

Dunleavy, P. (1982) 'Is There a Radical Approach to Public Administration?', *Public Administration,* 60, 2: 215–25.

Dunleavy, P. (1989) 'The Architecture of the British Central State, Part 1: Framework for Analysis', *Public Administration,* 67, 3: 249–75.

Dunleavy, P. (1995) 'Estimating the Distribution of Positional Influence in Cabinet Committees under Major' in R.A.W. Rhodes and P. Dunleavy (eds) *Prime Minister, Cabinet and Core Executive*, London: Macmillan: 298–321.

Dunsire, A. (1956) 'Accountability in Local Government', *Administration,* 4:80–8.

Dunsire, A. (1973) *Public Administration: the Word and the Science*, London: Martin Robertson.

Dynes, M. and Walker, D. (1995) *The New British State*, London: Times Books.

Dynes, M. and Walker, D. (1996) *The Times Guide to the New British State*, London: Times Books.

Eckstein, H. (1960) *Pressure Group Politics*, London: Allen & Unwin.

Efficiency and Effectiveness in the Civil Service, Government Observations on the Third Report from the Treasury and Civil Service Select Committee, HC 236 (1982), Cmnd 8616, London: HMSO.

Efficiency Unit (1988) *Improving Management in Government: the Next Steps*, London: HMSO.

Elcock, H. (1991) *Change and Decay? Public Administration in the 1990s*, Harlow: Longman.

Elliot, L. and MacAskill, E. (1998) 'Brown's £12 Billion Sale', *Guardian*, 12 June.

Evans, M. (1997) 'Political Participation', in P. Dunleavy *et al.*, *Developments in British Politics 5*, London: Macmillan: 110–25.

Expenditure Committee (1977) *The Civil Service, Eleventh Report, and Volumes of Evidence*, 1977, vols 1–111, HC 535, London: HMSO.

Falconer, P. (1996) 'Charterism and Consumerism', in R. Pyper (ed.) *Aspects of Accountability in the British System of Government*, Eastham: Tudor.

Falconer, P.K. and Ross, K. (1999) 'Citizen's Charters and Public Service Provision: Lesson from the UK Experience', *International Review of Administrative Sciences* 65, 3: 339–52.

Farnham, D. and Horton, S. (1999) 'Managing Public and Private Organisations', in S. Horton and D. Farnham (eds) *Public Management in Britain*, London: Macmillan: 26–45.

Financial Management in Government Departments (1983) Cmnd 9058, London: HMSO.

Fletcher, P. (1967) 'Public Administration', in H.V. Wiseman (ed.) *Political Science*, London Routledge & Kegan Paul: 51–77.

Flinders, M. (1999) 'Quangos: Why Do Governments Love Them?', in M. Flinders and M. Smith (eds) *Quangos, Accountability and Reform*, London: Macmillan.

Flinders, M. and Cole, M. (1999) 'Opening Pandora's Box? New Labour and the Quango State', *Talking Politics*, 12, 1: 234–9.

Flinders, M. and Smith, M. (eds) (1999) *Quangos, Accountability and Reform*, London: Macmillan.

Flynn, N. (1997) *Public Sector Management*, Hemel Hempstead: Prentice Hall/Harvester Wheatsheaf.

Foley, M. (1993) *The Rise of the British Presidency*, Manchester: Manchester University Press.

Foreign Affairs Committee (1999) *2nd Report 1998–99: Sierra Leone*, HC116, London: The Stationery Office.

Foster, Sir Christopher and Plowden, F. (1996) *The State Under Stress*, Buckingham: Open University Press.

Foster, C.D. (1997) *A Stronger Centre of Government*, London: Constitutional Unit.

Franklin, M. and Norton, P. (1993) *Parliamentary Questions*, Oxford: Clarendon.

Fry, G.K. (1984) 'The Development of the Thatcher Government's "Grand Strategy" for the Civil Service: a Public Policy Perspective', *Public Administration*, 2, 3: 322–35.

Fulton Report (1968) *The Civil Service*, Vol. I: *Report of the Committee*, Cmnd 3638, London: HMSO.

Game, C. (1998) 'Carrots and Semtex: New Labour's Modernisation Agenda for British Local Government', paper presented to the Annual Conference of the International Association of Schools and Institutes of Administration, Paris.

Garrett, J. (1992) *Westminster. Does Parliament Work?*, London: Victor Gollancz.

Goodsell, C. (1994) *The Case for Bureaucracy: a Public Administration Polemic*, Chatham, NJ: Chatham House.

Gordon Walker, P. (1972) *The Cabinet*, London: Fontana.

Gray, A. and Jenkins, W.I. (1985) *Administrative Politics in British Government*, Brighton: Wheatsheaf.

Gray, A. and Jenkins, W.I. (1986) 'Accountable Management in British Government: Some Reflections on the Financial Management Initiative', *Financial Accountability and Management*, 2, 3: 171–8.

Gray, A. and Jenkins, B. (1999) 'Democratic Renewal in Local Government: Continuity and Change', *Local Government Studies*, 25, 4: 26–45.

Gray, C. (2000) 'A Hollow State?', in R. Pyper and L. Robins (eds) *United Kingdom Governance*, London: Macmillan: 283–300.

Greenwood, J.R. (1988) 'Mrs. Thatcher's Whitehall Revolution: Public Administration or Public Management?', *Teaching Politics*, 17, 2: 208–29.

Greenwood, J.R. (2000) 'Should the Civil Service Become Fully Politicised?', in L. Robins and B. Jones (eds) *Debates in British Politics Today*, Manchester: Manchester University Press: 63–77.

Greenwood, J.R. and Eggins, H. (1995) 'Shifting Sands: Teaching Public Administration in a Climate of Change', *Public Administration*, 73: 143–64.

Greenwood, J.R. and Robins, L.(1998a) 'Searching for Identity, Defining Skills and Competencies: Public Administration Education and Training in the United Kingdom', in Davies, M.R. *et al. Serving the State: Global Public Administration, Education and Training*, vol. 2: *Diversity and Change*, Aldershot: Ashgate: 183–206.

Greenwood, J.R. and Robins, L. (1998b) 'Public Administration Curriculum Development in Britain: Outsider or Insider Influence?', *International Review of Administrative Sciences*, 64, 3: 409–21.

Greenwood, J.R. and Wilson, D.J. (1989) *Public Administration in Britain Today*, London: Unwin Hyman.

Greenwood, J.R. and Wilson, D.J. (1994) 'Towards the Contract State: CCT in Local Government', *Parliamentary Affairs*, 47, 3: 405–19.

Greer, P. (1994) *Transforming Central Government: the Next Steps Initiative*, Buckingham: Open University Press.

Gregory, R. and Hutchesson, P. (1975) *The Parliamentary Ombudsman*, London: Allen & Unwin.

Gregory, R. and Pearson, J. (1992) 'The Parliamentary Ombudsman After Twenty Five Years', *Public Administration*, 70, 4.

Gretton, J., Harrison, A. and Beeton, D. (1987) 'How Far Have the Frontiers of the State Been Rolled Back Between 1979 and 1987?', *Public Money*, 7, 3: 17–25.

Griffith, J. (1987) 'Crichel Down: the Most Famous Farm in British Constitutional History', *Contemporary Record*, 1, 1.

Guardian (2000) 'Who Doesn't Dare, Loses. The Wakeham Report Oozes Complacency', Editorial, 21 January.

Gulick, L. (1937) 'Notes on the Theory of Organization', in L. Gulick and L. Urwick (eds), *Papers on the Science of Administration*, New York: Institute of Public Administration, Columbia University Press.

Gunn, L. (1988) 'Public Management: a Third Approach', *Public Money and Management*, 8, 1 and 2: 21–6.

Haldane Report (1918) *Report of the Machinery of Government Committee*, Cd 9230, London: HMSO.

Hall, W. and Weir, S. (1996) *The Untouchables: Power and Accountability in the Quango State*, Democratic Audit Paper No. 8, University of Essex: The Scarman Trust and Human Rights Centre.

Hassan, G. (1999) *A Guide to the Scottish Parliament. The Shape of Things to Come*, Edinburgh: The Stationery Office.

Hassan, G. and Warhurst, C. (eds) (2000) *The New Scottish Politics. The First Year of the Scottish Parliament and Beyond*, Edinburgh: The Stationery Office.

Heclo, H., and Wildavsky, A. (1981) *The Private Government of Public Money*, London: Macmillan.

Held, D., McGrew, A., Goldblatt, D. and Perraton, J. (1999) *Global Transformations – Politics, Economics and Culture*, Cambridge: Polity Press.

Hennessy, P. (1986a) *Cabinet*, London: Blackwell.

Hennessy, P. (1986b) 'Helicopter Crashes into Cabinet: Prime Minister and Constitution Hurt', *Journal of Law and Society*, 13, 3: 423–32.

Hennessy, P. (1990) *Whitehall*, London: Fontana.

Hennessy, P. (1995) *The Hidden Wiring: Unearthing the British Constitution*, London: Victor Gollancz.

Hennessy, P. (2000) *The Prime Minister: The Office and its Holders since 1945*, London: Allen Lane.

Hennessy, P., Hughes, P. and Seaton, J. (1997) *Ready, Steady, Go! New Labour and Whitehall*, London: Fabian Society.

Hill, D.M. (2000) *Urban Policy and Politics in Britain*, London: Macmillan.

Hinton, P. and Wilson, E. (1993) 'Accountability', in J. Wilson and P. Hinton (eds) *Public Services and the 1990s*, Sevenoaks: Tudor: 123–42 .

Hix, S. (1999) *The Political System of the European Union*, London and Basingstoke: Macmillan.

Hix, S. (2000) 'Britain, the EU and the Euro', in P. Dunleavy, A. Gamble, I. Holliday and G. Peele (eds) *Developments in British Politics 6*, London: Macmillan: 47–68.

HM Treasury (1986) *Output and Performance Measurement in Central Government Departments: Progress in Departments*, ed. S. Lewis, Treasury Working Paper No. 38, London: HM Treasury.

HM Treasury (1991) *Competing for Quality: Buying Better Public Services*, Cm 1730, London: HMSO.

HM Treasury (1998) *Modern Public Services for Britain: Comprehensive Spending Review: 1999–2002*, Cm 4011, London: The Stationery Office.

Hoggett, P. (1987) 'A Farewell to Mass Production? Decentralization as an Emergent Private Sector Paradigm', in P. Hoggett and R. Hambleton (eds) *Decentralization and Democracy*, Occasional Paper 28, School of Advanced Urban Studies, University of Bristol.

Hogwood, B. (1992) *Trends in British Public Policy*, Buckingham: Open University Press.

Hogwood, B. (1995), 'Whitehall Families: Core Departments and Agency Forms', *International Review of Administrative Sciences*, 61: 511–30.

Hogwood, B., Judge, D. and McVicar, M. (2000a) 'Agencies and Accountability', in R.A.W. Rhodes (ed.) *Transforming British Government*, vol. 1: *Changing Institutions*, London: Macmillan: 195–222.

Hogwood, P., Carter, C., Bulmer, S., Burch, M. and Scott, A. (2000b) 'Devolution and EU Policy Making: the Territorial Challenge', *Public Policy and Administration*, 15, 2: 81–95.

Holliday, I. (2000) 'Executives and Administrations', in P. Dunleavy, A. Gamble, I. Holliday and G. Peele (eds) *Developments in British Politics 6*, London: Macmillan: 88–107.

Hollis, P. (1987) *Ladies Elect: Women in English Local Government, 1865–1914*, Oxford: Oxford University Press.

Hood, C. (1979) 'The World of Quasi-government', paper presented to PSA Annual Conference.

Hood, C. (1981) 'Axeperson Spare that Quango', in C. Hood, and M. Wright (eds) *Big Government in Hard Times*, Oxford: Martin Robertson: 100–22.

Hood, C. and Dunsire, A. (1981) *Bureaumetrics*, Farnborough: Gower.

Hopkins, S. (1999) 'The Good Friday Agreement in Northern Ireland', *Politics Review*, 8, 3: 2–6.

Horton, S. (1999) 'The Civil Service', in S. Horton and D. Farnham (eds) *Public Management in Britain*, London: Macmillan: 145–61.

Horton, S. and Farnham, D. (1999a) 'The Politics of Public Sector Change', in S. Horton and D. Farnham (eds) *Public Management in Britain*, London: Macmillan: 3–25.

Horton, S. and Farnham, D. (eds) (1999b) *Public Management in Britain*, London: Macmillan.

Hoskyns, Sir J. (1983) 'Whitehall and Westminster: an Outsider's View', *Parliamentary Affairs*, 36, 2: 137–47.

House of Lords (1996) *Rebuilding Trust*, vol. 1, *Report*, Select Committee on Relations Between Central and Local Government, London: HMSO.

Hughes, O. (1998) *Public Management and Administration: an Introduction* (second edn), London: Macmillan.

Irvine, Lord (2000) *Speech to the Council of Tribunals Conference* (www.tribunals-review.org.uk).

Isaac-Henry, K. (1993) 'Development and Change in the Public Sector', in K. Isaac-Henry, C. Painter and C. Barnes (eds) *Management in the Public Sector*, London: Chapman and Hall: 1–20.

Isaac-Henry, K. (1997) 'Development and Change in the Public Sector', in K. Isaac-Henry, C. Painter and C. Barnes (eds) *Management in the Public Sector: Challenge and Change* (second edn), London: International Thomson Business Press.

Isaac-Henry, K., Painter, C. and Barnes, C. (eds) (1993) *Management in the Public Sector,* London: Chapman and Hall.

Jackson, Peter M. and Price, Catherine M. (eds) (1994) *Privatisation and Regulation: a Review of the Issues*, Harlow: Longman.

James, S. (1996) 'The Political and Administrative Consequences of Judicial Review', *Public Administration*, 74, 4.

James, S. (1997) *British Government: a Reader in Policy Making*, London: Routledge.

James, S. (1999) *British Cabinet Government* (second edn), London: Routledge.

John, P. (1997) 'Local Governance', in P. Dunleavy, A. Gamble, I. Holliday and G. Peele (eds) *Developments in British Politics 5*, London: Macmillan: 253–76.

Johnson, H. and Riley, K. (1995) 'The Impact of Quangos and New Government Agencies on Education', in F.F. Ridley and D. Wilson (eds) *The Quango Debate*, Oxford: Oxford University Press: 106–18.

Johnson, N. (1982) 'Accountability, Control and Complexity: Moving Beyond Ministerial Responsibility', in A. Barker (ed.) *Quangos in Britain*, London: Macmillan: 206–18.

Jones, A. (1993) 'Crichel Down: a Case of Ministerial Responsibility?', *Talking Politics*, 5, 3: 161–5.

Jones, G. and Stewart, J. (2000) 'Survival Tactics', *Local Government Chronicle,* 17 March: 16.

Jones, G.W. (1985) 'The Prime Minister's Powers', in A. King (ed.) *The British Prime Minister* (second edn), London: Macmillan: 72–95.

Jordan, G. (1994) *The British Administrative System: Principles and Practice*, London: Routledge.

Jordan, G. and Richardson, J. (1987), *British Politics and the Policy Process*, London: Allen & Unwin.

Judge, D. (1993) *The Parliamentary State*, London: Sage.

Kavanagh, D. (1990) *Thatcherism and British Politics: the End of Consensus* (second edn), Oxford: Oxford University Press.

Kavanagh, D. and Seldon, A. (2000) 'The Power Behind the Prime Minister: the Hidden Influence of No. 10', in R.A.W. Rhodes (ed.) *Transforming British Government*, vol. 2: *Changing Roles and Relationships*, London: Macmillan: 63–78.

Kemp, Sir Peter (1999) 'Please Stop Fiddling the Books', *New Statesman*, 18 October: 28–9.

Kendall, I., Moon, G., North, N. and Horton, S. (1996) 'The National Health Service', in D. Farnham and S. Horton (eds) *Managing the New Public Services* (second edn), London: Macmillan: 200–18.

King, D. (1996) 'Conclusion', in D. King and G. Stoker (eds) *Rethinking Local Democracy*, London: Macmillan: 214–23.

King, D. and Stoker, G. (eds) (1996) *Rethinking Local Democracy,* London: Macmillan.

King, R. (1983) 'The Political Practice of Local Capitalist Associations', in R. King (ed.) *Capital and Politics*, London: Routledge and Kegan Paul: 101–31.

Klein, R. (1995) *The New Politics of the NHS* (third edn), London: Longman.

Kooiman, J. (1993) 'Social-Political Governance: Introduction', in J. Kooiman, (ed.) *Modern Governance*, London: Sage.

Labour Party (1997) *New Labour – Because Britain Deserves Better*, London: Labour Party Publications.

Labour Research (1993) *Privatising the Government,* London: Labour Research.

Laffin, M. and Thomas, A. (2000) 'Designing the National Assembly for Wales', *Parliamentary Affairs*, 53, 3.

Lawton, A. and Rose, A. (1991) *Organisation and Management in the Public Sector*, London: Pitman.

Layfield Committee (1976) *Report of the Committee of Enquiry into Local Government Finance,* Cmnd 6543, London: HMSO.

Leach, S. (1995) 'The Strange Case of the Local Government Review', in J. Stewart and G. Stoker (eds) *Local Government in the 1990s*, London: Macmillan: 49–68.

Leach, S. and Collinge, C. (1998) *Strategic Planning and Management in Local Government,* London: Pitman.

Leach, S. and Pratchett, L. (1996) *The Management of Balanced Authorities*, Luton: Local Government Management Board.

Leach, S. and Stewart, M. (1992) *Local Government: Its Role and Function*, York: Joseph Rowntree Foundation.

Leach, S. and Wilson, D. (1998) 'Voluntary Groups and Local Authorities: Rethinking the Relationship', *Local Government Studies*, 24, 2: 1–18.

Leach, S. and Wilson, D. (2000) *Local Political Leadership*, Bristol: Policy Press.

Leach, S., Stewart, J. and Walsh, K. (1994) *The Changing Organisation and Management of Local Government*, London: Macmillan.

Learmont, J. (1995) *Review of the Prison Service in England and Wales and the Escape from Parkhurst Prison on 3.1.95*, Cm 3020, London: HMSO.

Lee, J.M., Jones, G.W. and Burnham, J. (1998*) At the Centre of Whitehall: Advising the Prime Minister and Cabinet*, London: Macmillan.

Lee, S. (2000) 'New Labour, New Centralism: the Centralisation of Policy and the Devolution of Administration in England and its Regions', *Public Policy and Administration*, 15, 2.

LGMB (1998) *Census of Councillors, 1998*, Luton: Local Government Management Board.

Liverpool Democracy Commission (1999) *Future: the Leading of Liverpool*, Liverpool: New Local Government Network for the Liverpool Democracy Commission.

Loughlin, J. (1998) *The Ulster Question Since 1945*, London: Macmillan.

Loughlin, M. (1996) 'The Constitutional Status of Local Government', in L. Pratchett and D. Wilson (eds) *Local Democracy and Local Government*, London: Macmillan: 38–61.

Lowndes, V. (1999) 'Rebuilding Trust in Central/Local Relations: Policy or Passion?', *Local Government Studies*, 25, 4: 116–36.

Lowndes, V., Stoker, G., Pratchett, L., Leach, S., Wingfield, M. and Wilson, D. (1998a) *Enhancing Public Participation in Local Government*, London: DETR.

Lowndes, V., Stoker, G., Pratchett, L., Leach, S., Wingfield, M. and Wilson, D. (1998b) *Guidance on Enhancing Public Participation*, London: DETR.

Lynch, P. (2000) 'The Committee System of the Scottish Parliament', in G. Hassan and C. Warhurst (eds) *The New Scottish Politics. The First Year of the Scottish Parliament and Beyond*, Edinburgh: The Stationery Office: 66–74.

Lynch, P. (2001) *Scottish Government and Politics*, Edinburgh: Edinburgh University Press.

Macleod, C. (2000) 'Relations with Westminster', in G. Hassan, and C. Warhurst (eds) *The New Scottish Politics. The First Year of the Scottish Parliament and Beyond,* Edinburgh: The Stationery Office: 117–23.

Mair, C. and McCloud, B. (1999) 'Financial Arrangements', in G. Hassan, *A Guide to the Scottish Parliament. The Shape of Things to Come*, Edinburgh: The Stationery Office: 73–80.

Maloney, W., Smith, G. and Stoker, G. (2000) 'Social Capital and Urban Governance: Adding a More Contextualised "Top-Down" Perspective', *Political Studies,* 48, 4: 802–20.

Maloney, W.A. and Richardson, J.J. (1992) 'Post-Privatisation Regulation in Britain', *Politics* 12, 2: 14–20.

Mandelson, P. and Liddle, R. (1996) *The Blair Revolution. Can New Labour Deliver?*, London: Faber and Faber.

Marsh, D. (1991) 'Privatisation Under Mrs. Thatcher: a Review of the Literature', *Public Administration* 69, 4: 459–80.

Marsh, D. and Rhodes, R.A.W. (1992) *Policy Networks in British Government,* Oxford: Clarendon Press.

Marsh, D., Richards, D. and Smith, M.J. (2000) 'Re-Assessing the Role of Departmental Cabinet Ministers', *Public Administration*, 78, 2: 305–26.

Marshall, G. (1986) *Constitutional Conventions. The Rules and Forms of Political Accountability*, Oxford: Clarendon.

Martin, S. (1999) 'Picking Winners or Piloting Best Value? An Analysis of English Best Value Bids', *Local Government Studies*, 25, 2.

Massey, A. (1999) *The State of Britain: a Guide to the UK Public Sector,* London: Public Policy and Management Association.

Maud Report (1967) *Committee on the Management of Local Government*, London: HMSO.

Mawson, J. (1998) 'The New Territorial Politics and Administration, and the Issues and Challenges for Local Government', *Local Governance,* 24, 3: 195–204.

Mawson, J. and Spencer, K. (1997) 'The Government Offices for the English Regions: Towards Regional Governance?', *Policy and Politics*, 25, 1: 71–84.

McConnell, A. (1996) 'Popular Accountability' in R. Pyper (ed.) *Aspects of Accountability in the British System of Government*, Eastham: Tudor: 13–44.

McConnell, A. (1999) *The Politics and Policy of Local Taxation Britain*, London: Tudor Press.

McConnell, A. (2000) 'Governance in Scotland, Wales and Northern Ireland', in R. Pyper and L. Robins (eds) *United Kingdom Governance*, London: Macmillan: 219–55.

McLean, I., Clifford, C. and McMillan, A. (2000) 'The Organisation of Central Government Departments: a History, 1964–92', in R.A.W. Rhodes (ed.) *Transforming British Government*, London: Macmillan: 135–55.

Meehan, E. (1999) 'The Belfast Agreement: Distinctiveness and Cross-Fertilisation in the UK's Devolution Programme', *Parliamentary Affairs*, 52, 1: 19–31.

Midwinter, A. (1995) *Local Government in Scotland: Reform or Decline?*, London: Macmillan.

Midwinter, A. and McGarvey, W. (1999) 'Developing Best Value in Scotland: Concepts and Contradictions', *Local Government Studies,* 25, 2: 87–101.

Miller, B. and Dickson, M. (2000) 'Local Governance: the Assessments of Councillors, Quango Members and the Public', in G. Stoker (ed.) *The New Politics of British Local Governance*, London: Macmillan: 130–49.

Mitchell, J. (2001) *Governing Scotland. The British State and Scottish Politics*, London: Macmillan.

Modern Public Services for Britain: Investing in Reform, Cm 4011, London: The Stationery Office.

Moran, M. (1995) 'Reshaping the British State', *Talking Politics*, 7, 3: 174–7.

Mueller, D.C. (1989) *Public Choice II: a Revised Edition*, Cambridge: Cambridge University Press.

National Audit Office (1986) *The Financial Management Initiative*, HC 588, London: HMSO.

Newton, K. (1976) *Second City Politics*, Oxford: Oxford University Press.

Nicolson, I.F. (1986) *The Mystery of Crichel Down*, Oxford: Clarendon.

Nigro, F.A. and Nigro, L.G. (1973) *Modern Public Administration*, New York: Harper & Row.

Niskanen, W.A. (1971) *Bureaucracy and Representative Government*, Chicago: Aldine-Atherton.

Niskanen, W. A.(1973) *Bureaucracy: Servant or Master?,* London: Institute of Economic Affairs.

Nolan Committee (1995) *Committee on Standards in Public Life*, vol. 1: *Report*, Cmnd 2850–1, London: HMSO.

Nolan Committee (1996) *Committee on Standards in Public Life. Local Public Spending Bodies,* vol. 1: *Report*, Cm 3270–1, London: HMSO.

Northcote, S. and Trevelyan, C. (1854) *Report on the Organisation of the Permanent Civil Service*, Parliamentary Paper 1713.

Norton, P. (1982) *The Constitution in Flux*, Oxford: Martin Robertson.

Norton, P. (1993) *Does Parliament Matter?*, Hemel Hempstead: Harvester Wheatsheaf.

Norton, P. (2000a) 'Barons in a Shrinking Kingdom: Senior Ministers in British Government', in R.A.W. Rhodes (ed.) *Transforming British Government*, vol. 2: *Changing Roles and Relationships*, London: Macmillan: 101–24.

Norton, P. (2000b) 'Parliament in Transition', in R. Pyper and L. Robins (eds) *United Kingdom Governance*, London: Macmillan: 82–106.

Norton, P. (2001) 'The House of Commons', in B. Jones, D. Kavanagh, M. Moran and P. Norton (eds) *Politics UK*, Harlow: Pearson Education: 339–76.

Nugent, N. (1999) *The Government and Politics of the European Union* (fourth edn), London: Macmillan.

Nugent, N. (2000) 'The European Union and UK Governance', in R. Pyper and L. Robins (eds) *United Kingdom Governance*, London: Macmillan: 194–218.

O'Donnell, A. (1996) 'Legal and Quasi-Legal Accountability', in R. Pyper (ed.) *Aspects of Accountability in the British System of Government*, Eastham: Tudor: 82–118.

Office of National Statistics (June 2000) *Economic Trends* No. 559, London: The Stationery Office.

Oliver, D. (1991) *Government in the United Kingdom. The Search for Accountability, Effectiveness and Citizenship*, Buckingham: Open University Press.

Osborne, D. and Gaebler, T. (1992) *Reinventing Government: How the Entrepreneurial Spirit is Transforming the Public Sector*, Reading, MA: Addison-Wesley.

Osmond, J. (ed.) (1998) *The National Assembly Agenda*, Cardiff: The Institute of Welsh Affairs.

Osmond, J. (1999) *The Civil Service and the National Assembly*, Cardiff: The Institute of Welsh Affairs.

O'Toole, B. (1995) 'Accountability', in J.Wilson (ed.) *Managing Public Services: Dealing with Dogma*, London: Tudor: 58–70.

O'Toole, B. and Chapman, R. (1995) 'Parliamentary Accountability', in B.J. O'Toole and G. Jordan (eds) *Next Steps: Improving Management in Government?*, Aldershot: Dartmouth: 37–52.

O'Toole, B.J. and Jordan, G. (eds) (1995) *Next Steps: Improving Management in Government?*, Aldershot: Dartmouth.

Painter, M.J. (1980) 'Policy Co-ordination in the Department of the Environment, 1970–1976', *Public Administration*, 58, 2: 135–54.

Parkinson, M. (1985) *Liverpool on the Brink,* Bristol: Policy Journals.

Parliamentary Commissioner for Administration (1999) *Sixth Report, Session 1999–00, Annual Report 1999–00,* HC 593, London: The Stationery Office.

Parris, H. (1969) *Constitutional Bureaucracy*, London: Allen & Unwin.

Parry, R. (2000) 'The Civil Service and the Scottish Executive's Structure and Style', in G. Hassan and C. Warhurst (eds) *The New Scottish Politics. The First Year of the Scottish Parliament and Beyond*, Edinburgh: The Stationery Office: 85–9.

Parry, G. and Moyser, G. (1990) 'A Map of Political Participation in Britain', *Government and Opposition,* 25, 2: 147–69.

Parry, G., Moyser, G. and Day, N. (1992) *Political Participation and Democracy in Britain,* Cambridge: Cambridge University Press.

Parry, R. and Jones, A. (2000) 'The Transition from the Scottish Office to the Scottish Executive', *Public Policy and Administration* 15, 2: 53–66.

Pateman, C. (1970) *Participation and Democratic Theory*, Cambridge: Cambridge University Press.

Paterson Report (1973*) The New Scottish Local Authorities: Organisation and Management Structures*, Edinburgh: Scottish Development Department.

Peden, G.C. (1983) 'The Treasury as the Central Department of Government 1919–1939', *Public Administration*, 61, 4: 371–85.

Pendlebury, M.W. (ed.) (1989) *Management Accounting in the Public Sector*, Oxford: Heinemann.

Perry, J.L. and Kramer, K.L. (eds) (1983) *Public Management: Public and Private Perspectives*, Palo Alto, CA: Mayfield.

Peters, B.G. (2000) 'Governance and Comparative Politics', in J. Pierre (ed.) *Debating Governance*, Oxford: Oxford University Press.

Peters, G.B. and Waterman, R. (1982) *In Search of Excellence*, New York: Harper & Row.

Pierre, J. (2000) *Debating Governance*, Oxford: Oxford University Press.

Pierre, J. and Stoker, G. (2000) 'Towards Multi-Level Governance', in P. Dunleavy, A. Gamble,

I. Holliday and G. Peele (eds) *Developments in British Politics 6*, London: Macmillan: 29–46.

Pilkington, C. (1999) *The Civil Service in Britain Today*, Manchester: Manchester University Press.

Pitt, D. and Smith, B. (1981) *Government Departments*, London: Routledge & Kegan Paul.

Pliatzky Report (1980) *Report on Non-Departmental Public Bodies*, Cmnd 7197, London: HMSO.

Plowden, W. (1994) *Ministers and Mandarins*, London: Institute for Public Policy Research.

Pollitt, C. and Harrison, S. (eds) (1992) *Handbook of Public Services Management,* Oxford: Blackwell.

Ponting, C. (1986) *Whitehall: Tragedy and Farce*, London: Hamish Hamilton.

Pratchett, L. (1999) 'Introduction: Defining Democratic Renewal', *Local Government Studies,* 25, 4: 1–18.

Pratchett, L. and Wilson, D. (eds) (1996) *Local Democracy and Local Government*, London: Macmillan.

Prime Minister (1994) *The Civil Service: Continuity and Change,* Cm 2627, London: HMSO.

Prime Minister (1995) *The Civil Service: Taking Forward Continuity and Change*, Cm 2748, London: HMSO.

Prime Minister (1996) *The Citizen's Charter – Five Years On*, Cm 3370 Session 1995–96.

Prime Minister's Office (1991) *The Citizen's Charter*, Cm 1599, London: HMSO.

Prime Minister and Minister for the Cabinet Office (1999) *Modernising Government*, Cm 4310, London: The Stationery Office.

Prime Minister and Minister for the Civil Service (1970) *Reorganisation of Central Government*, White Paper, Cmnd 4506, London: HMSO.

Progress in Financial Management in Government Departments (1984) Cmnd 9297, London: HMSO.

Prosser, T. (1994) 'Regulation, Markets and Legitimacy', in J. Jowell and D. Oliver (eds) *The Changing Constitution,* Oxford: Clarendon: 237–60.

Public Accounts Committee (1986–7) 'Thirteenth Report', *The Financial Management Initiative*, HC 61, London: HMSO.

Pyper, R. (1994) 'Individual Ministerial Responsibility: Dissecting the Doctrine', *Politics Review*, 4, 1: 12–16.

Pyper, R. (ed.) (1996) *Aspects of Accountability in the British System of Government,* Eastham: Tudor.

Pyper, R. (1999) 'The Civil Service: a Neglected Dimension of Devolution', *Public Money and Management,* 19, 2: 45–9.

Pyper, R. (2000) 'The First Minister and the Scottish Executive', in G. Hassan and C. Warhurst (eds) *The New Scottish Politics. The First Year of the Scottish Parliament and Beyond*, Edinburgh: The Stationery Office: 77–83.

Pyper, R. and Robins, L. (eds) (2000) *United Kingdom Governance*, London: Macmillan.

Ranade, W. (1997) *A Future for the NHS? Health Care for the Millennium* (second edn), Harlow: Longman.

Ranson, S. and Stewart, J. (1994) *Management for the Public Domain: Enabling the Learning Society*, London: Macmillan.

Rao, N. (1994) *The Making and Unmaking of Local Self-Government*, Aldershot: Dartmouth.

Rao, N. and Young, K. (1999) 'Revitalising Local Democracy', in R. Jowell, J. Curtice, A. Park and K. Thomson (eds) *British Social Attitudes: the 6ᵗʰ Report – Who Shares New Labour Values?*, Aldershot: Ashgate: 45–63.

Rathbone, M. (2000) 'The Wilson Report and the Future of the Civil Service', *Talking Politics*, 13, 1: 26–30.

Regan, D.E. (1983) 'Central–Local Relationships in Britain: Applying the Power-dependence Model', *Teaching Politics,* 12, 1: 44–53.

Rentoul, J. (1996) *Tony Blair*, London: Warner Books.

Rhodes, R.A.W. (1979) 'Research into Central–Local Relations in Britain: a Framework for Analysis', unpublished paper, Department of Government, University of Essex.

Rhodes, R.A.W. (1981) *Control and Power in Central–Local Government Relations*, Farnborough: Gower.

Rhodes, R.A.W. (1986) *The National World of Local Government*, London: Allen & Unwin.

Rhodes, R.A.W. (1991) 'Theory and Methods in British Public Administration; the View from Political Science', *Political Studies,* 34, 3: 533–54.

Rhodes, R.A.W. (1992) *Policy Networks in British Government*, Oxford: Clarendon Press.

Rhodes, R.A.W. (1994) 'The Hollowing out of the State: the Changing Nature of the Public Service in Britain', *Political Quarterly,* 65, 2: 138–51.

Rhodes, R.A.W. (1995) 'From Prime Ministerial Power to Core Executive', in R.A.W. Rhodes and P. Dunleavy (eds) *Prime Minister, Cabinet and Core Executive*, London: Macmillan: 11–37.

Rhodes, R.A.W. (1996) 'The New Governance: Governing without Government', *Political Studies,* 44: 652–67.

Rhodes, R.A.W. (1997a) *Understanding Governance: Policy Networks, Governance, Reflexivity and Accountability,* Buckingham: Open University Press.

Rhodes, R.A.W. (1997b) 'Diplomacy in Government', *Politics Today,* 7,3: 24–7.

Rhodes, R.A.W. (1999) 'Foreword: Governance and Networks', in G. Stoker (ed.) *The New Management of British Local Governance*, London: Macmillan: xxi–xxvi.

Rhodes, R.A.W. (ed.) (2000a) *Transforming British Government*, vol. 1.: *Changing Institutions*, London: Macmillan.

Rhodes, R.A.W. (ed.) (2000b) *Transforming British Government*, vol. 2: *Changing Roles and Relationships*, London: Macmillan.

Rhodes, R.A.W. (2000c) 'New Labour's Civil Service: Summing-up Joining-up', *Political Quarterly,* 71, 2: 151–66.

Rhodes, R.A.W. (2000d) *The Governance Narrative: Key Findings and Lessons from the ESRC's Whitehall Programme*, London: Public Policy and Management Association.

Rhodes, R.A.W. (2000e) 'Introduction; the ESRC Whitehall Programme: a Guide to Institutional Change', in R.A.W. Rhodes (ed.) *Transforming British Government*, vol. 1: *Changing Institutions*, London: Macmillan: 1–22.

Rhodes, R.A.W. and Dunleavy, P. (eds) (1995) *Prime Minister, Cabinet and Core Executive*, London: Macmillan.

Richards, D. (1997) *The Civil Service under the Conservatives, 1979–1997; Whitehall's Political Poodles?*, Brighton: Sussex Academic Press.

Richards, S. (1987) 'The Financial Management Initiative', in A. Harrison and J. Gretton (eds) *Reshaping Central Government*, Hermitage: Policy Journals: 22–41.

Richardson, J.J. and Jordan, A.G. (1979) *Governing Under Pressure*, Oxford: Martin Robertson.

Ridley, F.F. (1986) 'Political Neutrality in the Civil Service', *Social Studies Review,* 1, 4: 23–8.

Ridley, F.F. and Wilson, D. (eds) (1995) *The Quango Debate*, Oxford: Oxford University Press.

Ridley, N. (1988) *The Local Right*, London: Centre for Policy Studies.

Robins, L.J. and Robins, V. (2000) 'Should Citizenship Education Be Compulsory?', in L. Robins and B. Jones (eds) *Debates in British Politics Today,* Manchester: Manchester University Press: 130–40.

Rose, R. (1987) *Ministers and Ministries: a Functional Analysis*, Oxford: Clarendon.

Rose, R. (1991) 'The Political Economy of Cabinet Change', in S. Haseler *et al., Britain's Constitutional Futures,* London: Institute of Economic Affairs: 45–61.

Rosenau, J.N. (1992) 'Governance, Order and Change in World Politics', in J.N. Rosenau and E.-O. Czempiel (eds) *Governance Without Government: Order and Change in World Politics*, Cambridge: Cambridge University Press.

Rouse, J. (1997) 'Resource and Performance Management in Public Sector Organizations', in K. Isaac-Henry, C. Painter and C. Barnes (eds) *Management in the Public Sector*, London: Chapman and Hall: 73–104.

Rouse, J. (1999) 'Performance Management, Quality Management and Contracts', in S. Horton and D. Farnham (eds) *Public Management in Britain*, London: Macmillan: 76–93.

Royal Institute of Public Administration (1987) *Top Jobs in Whitehall: Appointments and Promotions in the Senior Civil Service*, London: RIPA.

Salmon, T. (1995) 'The European Union Dimension', in Robert Pyper and Lynton Robins (eds) *Governing the UK in the 1990s*, London: Macmillan; 177–99.

Samuels, M. (1998) *Towards Best Practice: an Evaluation of the First Two Years of the Public Sector Benchmarking Project 1996–98*, London: Cabinet Office.

Saunders, P. (1981) 'The Crisis of Central–Local Relations in Britain', unpublished paper presented to the Issues in Contemporary Planning Senior, University of Melbourne.

Scott Report (1996) *Report of the Inquiry into the Export of Defence Equipment and Dual-Use Goods to Iraq and Related Prosecutions*, HC 115, 1995–6, vols 1–5, London: HMSO.

Scottish Office (1997) *Scotland's Parliament*, Cm 3658, London: The Stationery Office.

Scottish Office Department of Health (1997) *Designed to Care: Renewing the National Health Service in Scotland*, Cm 3811, Edinburgh: The Stationery Office.

Seldon, A. (1995) 'The Cabinet Office and Coordination, 1979–87', in R.A.W. Rhodes and P. Dunleavy (eds) *Prime Minister, Cabinet and Core Executive*, London: Macmillan: 125–48.

Seneviratne, M. (1994) *Ombudsmen in the Public Sector*, Buckingham: Open University Press.

Seymour-Ure, C. (1984) 'British War Cabinets in Limited Wars: Korea, Suez and the Falklands', *Public Administration*, 62, 2: 181–200.

Shell, D.R. (1992) *The House of Lords* (second edn), London: Harvester Wheatsheaf.

Shell, D.R. (1998) 'The Second Chamber Question', *The Journal of Legislative Studies*, 4, 2.

Silk, P. and Walters, R. (1998) *How Parliament Works* (fourth edn), Harlow: Longman.

Skelcher, C. (1998) *The Appointed State*, Buckingham: Open University Press.

Smith, M.J. (1999) *The Core Executive in Britain*, London: Macmillan.

Smith, M.J. (2000) 'Prime Ministers, Ministers and Civil Servants in the Core Executive', in R.A.W. Rhodes (ed.) *Transforming British Government*, vol. 1: *Changing Institutions*, London: Macmillan: 25–45.

Smith, M.J., Marsh, D. and Richards, D. (1995), 'Central Government Departments and the Policy Process', in R.A.W. Rhodes and P. Dunleavy (eds) *Prime Minister, Cabinet and Core Executive*, London: Macmillan: 38–60.

Smith, M.J., Richards, D. and Marsh, D. (2000) 'The Changing Role of Central Government Departments', in R.A.W. Rhodes (ed.) *Transforming British Government*, vol. 2: *Changing Roles and Relationships*, London: Macmillan: 146–63.

Spencer, K. and Mawson, J. (1998) 'Government Offices and Policy Co-ordination in the English Regions', *Local Governance*, 24, 2: 101–9.

Spencer, K. and Mawson, J. (2000) 'Transforming Regional Government Offices in England', in R.A.W. Rhodes (ed.) *Transforming British Government*, vol. 2: *Changing Roles and Relationships*, London: Macmillan: 223–36.

Stanyer, J. and Smith, B. (1976) *Administering Britain*, London: Fontana/Collins.

Stationery Office (2000) *The 35th Civil Service Year Book*, London: The Stationery Office.

Stewart, J. (1995) 'Appointed Boards and Local Government', in F.F. Ridley and D. Wilson (eds) *The Quango Debate*, Oxford: Oxford University Press: 48–63.

Stewart, J. (2000a) 'A Dogma of our Times – Separation of Policy-making and Implementation', *Public Money and Management*, 16, 3: 33–40.

Stewart, J. (2000b) *The Nature of British Local Government*, London: Macmillan.

Stoker, G. (1991) *The Politics of Local Government* (second edn), London: Macmillan.

Stoker, G. (1996) 'Introduction: Normative Theories of Local Government and Democracy', in D. King and G. Stoker (eds) *Rethinking Local Democracy*, London: Macmillan: 1–27.

Stoker, G. (1998) 'Governance as Theory: Five Propositions', *International Social Science Journal*, 50: 17–28 .

Stoker, G. (ed.) (1999a) *The New Management of British Local Governance*, London: Macmillan.

Stoker, G. (1999b) 'Introduction: the Unintended Costs and Benefits of New Management Reform for British Local Government', in G. Stoker (ed.) *The New Management of British Local Governance*, London: Macmillan: 1–21.

Stoker, G. (1999c) 'Remaking Local Democracy: Lessons from New Labour's Reform Strategy', paper presented at University of Manchester's Department of Government's Golden Anniversary, 10 September.

Stoker, G. (ed.) (2000) *The New Politics of British Local Governance*, London: Macmillan.

Stoker, G. and Brindley, T. (1985) 'Asian Politics and Housing Renewal', *Policy and Politics*, 13, 3: 281–303.

Stoker, G. and Wilson, D. (1986) 'Intra-Organizational Politics in Local Authorities', *Public Administration*, 64, 3: 285–302.

Stoker, G. and Wilson, D. (1991) 'The Lost World of British Local Pressure Groups', *Public Policy and Administration*, 6, 2: 20–34.

Stoker, G. and Mossberger, K. (1995) 'The Post-Fordist Local State; the Dynamics of its Development', in J. Stewart and G. Stoker (eds) (1995) *Local Government in the 1990s*, London: Macmillan: 210–27.

Strauss, A., Schatzman, L., Ehrlich, D., Bucher, R. and Sabshin, M. (1971) 'The Hospital and its Negotiated Order', reprinted in F.G. Castles, D.J. Murray and D.C. Potter, *Decisions, Organisations and Society*, Harmondsworth: Penguin in association with Open University Press: 103–23.

Taylor, A. (2000) 'Hollowing out or Filling in? Taskforces and the Management of Cross-cutting Issues in British government', *The British Journal of Politics and International Relations*, 2, 1: 46–71.

Taylor, J. and Williams, H. (1991) 'Public Administration and the Information Polity', *Public Administration*, 69, 2: 170–90.

Terry, F. (1996) 'The Private Finance Initiative – Overdue Reform or Policy Breakthrough?', *Public Money and Management*, 16, 1: 9–16.

Thain, C. and Wright, M. (1995) *The Treasury and Whitehall*, Oxford: Clarendon.

Thatcher, M. (1993) *The Downing Street Years,* London: Harper Collins.

Theakston, K. (1991–2) 'Ministers and Mandarins', *Talking Politics*, 4,. 2: 92–5.

Theakston, K. (1995) *The Civil Service since 1945*, Oxford: Blackwell.

Theakston, K. (2000a) 'Ministers and Civil Servants', in R. Pyper and L. Robins (eds) *United Kingdom Governance*, London: Macmillan: 39–60.

Theakston, K. (2000b) 'Permanent Secretaries: Comparative Biography and Leadership in Whitehall', in R.A.W. Rhodes (ed.) *Transforming British Government*, vol. 2: *Changing Roles and Relationships*, London: Macmillan: 125–45.

Thomas, G.P. (1998) *Prime Minister and Cabinet Today*, Manchester: Manchester University Press.

Times Books (1995) *Times Guide to the British State,* London: Times Books.

Travis, A. (1997) 'Rights Given Legal Status', *Guardian*, 25 October.

Treasury and Civil Service Select Committee (1982) *Third Report: Efficiency and Effectiveness in the Civil Service*, HC 236, I, II, III, London: HMSO.

Treasury and Civil Service Select Committee (1990–1) *The Next Steps Initiative*, HC 496, London: HMSO.

Treasury and Civil Service Select Committee (1992–3) *The Role of the Civil Service*, Interim Report, HC 390–I, xi, London: HMSO.

Treasury and Civil Service Committee (TCSC) (1993–4) *Fifth Report: The Role of the Civil Service,* HC 27–1, London: HMSO.

Turpin, C. (1995) *British Government and the Constitution. Text, Cases and Materials,* London: Butterworth.

von Hayek, Friedrich A. (1944) *The Road to Serfdom,* London: Routledge and Kegan Paul.

Wakeham, Lord (2000) *A House for the Future,* Royal Commission on the Reform of the House of Lords, Cm 4534, London: Stationery Office.

Waldegrave, W. (1993) 'The Reality of Reform and Accountability in Today's Public Service', Public Finance Foundation/BDO Consulting, Public Services Lecture, July.

Waldo, D. (1955) *The Study of Public Administration,* Garden City: Doubleday.

Walker, D. (1999) 'Malignant Growth', *Guardian,* 5 July.

Weir, S. and Beetham, D. (1999) *Political Power and Democratic Control in Britain,* London: Routledge.

Weir, S. and Hall, W. (eds) (1994) *EGO Trip,* London: The Charter 88 Trust for Democratic Audit.

Welsh Office (1997) *A Voice for Wales,* Cm 3718, London: The Stationery Office.

Welsh Office (1998) *Putting Patients First,* London: The Stationery Office.

White, M. (2000) 'Speaker Warns of Cynicism in Farewell to MPs', *Guardian,* 27 July.

Widdicombe Report (1986) *The Conduct of Local Authority Business: Report of the Committee of Inquiry into the Conduct of Local Authority Business,* Cmnd 9797, London: HMSO.

Wilson, D. (1995) 'Quangos in the Skeletal State', in F.F. Ridley and D. Wilson (eds) *The Quango Debate,* Oxford: Oxford University Press: 3–13.

Wilson, D. (1999) 'Exploring the Limits of Public Participation in Local Government, *Parliamentary Affairs* 52, 2: 246–59.

Wilson, D. and Game, C. (1998) *Local Government in the United Kingdom,* London: Macmillan.

Wilson, G. (1993) 'Changing Networks; the Bureaucratic Setting for Government Action', in I. Budge and D. McKay (eds) *The Developing British Political System; the 1990s,* Harlow, Longman: 30–51.

Wilson Report (1999) *Report to the Prime Minister from Sir Richard Wilson, Head of the Home Civil Service* (www.Cabinet office.gov.uk /civil service-reform/index.htm).

Wintour, P. and Carvel, J. (2001) 'Labour's NHS Power Shift', *Guardian,* 25 April.

Wood, S. (1998) 'Regional Government in England', House of Commons Research Paper, 13, January, London: House of Commons.

Wright, T. (ed.) (2000) *The British Political Process: an Introduction,* London: Routledge.

Young, H. and Sloman, A. (1982) *No, Minister,* London: BBC Publications.

Young, K. (1994) 'Rethinking Accountability', QMC Public Policy Seminar, April.

Index